VELO
press

VELOPRESS • BOULDER, COLORADO • USA

the TRIATHLETE'S
TRAINING BIBLE

A complete training guide for the competitive multisport athlete

BY JOE FRIEL

The Triathlete's Training Bible

Before embarking on any strenuous exercise program, including the training described in this book, everyone, particularly anyone with a known heart or blood-pressure problem, should be examined by a physician.

Library of Congress Cataloguing-in-Publication data applied for.

Printed in the U.S.A.

VELO
press

VeloPress
1830 N 55th Street
Boulder, Colorado 80301-2700
303/440-0601 • fax 303/444-6788 • e-mail: velopress@7dogs.com

To purchase additional copies of this book or other VeloPress products, call 800/234-8356 or visit us on the Web at www.velocatalogue.com

Cover photograph by Robert Oliver
Photographs on pages xviii, 54, 88 and 138 by Robert Oliver
Photographs on pages 18 and 170 by Nate Cox
Design by Erin Johnson
Illustrations by Todd Telander

To Team Friel
Joyce, Kim and Dirk

CONTENTS

PREFACE

It is with some trepidation that I offer this book on how to train for what is one of the most intricate of all athletic endeavors. Triathletes and duathletes are well-read and serious about their sport. I know you will study and dissect what I have to say with some degree of skepticism, which is as it should be. Any book that claims the lofty title of "Bible" must be suspect until it proves itself. I hope it lives up to the high standards that the many who have written before me have set, but most of all, that it helps you become a better triathlete or duathlete.

Writing a definitive book on the complexities of training reminds me of the story of the college student taking a physics exam. There was but one question: "How could one determine the height of a tall building by using a barometer?" The ingenious student answered, "Offer to give the barometer to the building superintendent if he will tell you how tall the building is." You can imagine his professor's reaction, and the grade the student received regardless of his providing a plausible solution for the problem.

Sometimes otherwise intelligent athletes and coaches insist that there is only one way — theirs — to train for multisport when there are actually many perfectly effective and even simple ways for racing faster. In fact, it's quite obvious that there is more than one way since successful triathletes and duathletes don't all do exactly the same things in training.

The bottom line is that multisport, due in part to its complexity, is very individualized with as many unique methods of training as there are participants. It is also a relatively new sport with a rapidly growing body of expertise. Multisport is just now moving into its second generation of evolution as those who were its original competitors are aging and becoming coaches, lecturers and writers. Their wisdom will give a more definitive shape to multisport for years to come.

The purpose of this book is to hasten that process by describing not only what successful athletes have in common when it comes to training, but also what the latest scientific research has to say on the subject. My hope is that this book will help triathletes and duathletes of all abilities increase their training savvy and become more methodical in their approach. Too many in the sport train spontaneously with little forethought or purpose.

What is described on these pages is a system of training based on accepted scientific principles that have a track record in the real world of athletics. I don't propose that mine is the only system possible. Just as the story about the physics student demonstrated, there are other methodical systems for multisport training. It really isn't important which system you use, so long as you stick with one that fits your style. The problem is that athletes grab at random training ideas in monthly magazines as if a new workout is the answer. Effective training is so much more than a collection of workouts. An effective training system — one that produces results in the form of better race performances — has many interrelated facets. But although intricate, such a system doesn't have to be complicated.

The training system described in this book developed over two decades. In the late 1970s I began to apply my recently acquired knowledge from a masters-degree program in exercise science to my own running. I experienced moderate success as a runner, but it was clear I was not destined to join the elite ranks at any time soon. Undaunted, I came to enjoy the sport so much that I bought a running store in 1980. By 1983 I had taken up the new sport of triathlon and soon transformed the business into a triathlon store, one of the first in the world, with a full range of bikes and a bicycle service department in addition to running and swimming gear. As I sold equipment to customers, I'd offer tips on how to train. Soon I was developing training programs for local athletes and discovered I enjoyed coaching more than retail sales. In 1987 I sold the business and began to coach more seriously along with other pursuits. By 1991, freelance coaching became my full-time occupation.

Throughout these years, my constant desire was to find the best way to train. That quest kept me in contact with successful athletes and coaches who were sometimes reluctant to reveal their training "secrets," but I was persistent. I also read everything I could find on the subject of training, especially the scientific literature. What I learned, I tried on myself and the athletes I coached, many of whom were now elite amateur and professional triathletes, duathletes, road cyclists and mountain bikers. Out of this passion and experimentation grew the system of training described on the following pages.

You'll find that the training system I describe here is quite methodical, meaning that it proceeds in a regular and systematic order. I hope that you don't feel as some do that a structured and purposeful approach to training detracts from the fun of swimming, cycling and running. I don't think it does since training is always more fun when racing success results.

The Triathlete's Training Bible is divided into five parts. Part I offers a philosophical basis for methodical training. In Part II the scientific foundation of training is added. These subjects are brought together in Part III in which a system of purposeful training is described. The "heart" of the book is found in Part IV. In these three chapters you will design your own training plan for one season right down to the types of workouts you will do each week. This is the section you will come back to in subsequent years as you plan for another new racing season. Part V takes you through the many details of preparing to race, and recovering from such all-out efforts. In Part VI I describe other supplemental aspects of comprehensive training that contribute to peak fitness.

Along the way, several terms are used, some of which may not be familiar. The Glossary at the end of the book is offered for that purpose. Before starting, it may help to define certain terms used to describe race distances. As the sport has changed over the years, the nomenclature that defines the common race distances has also changed. That evolution is likely to continue. For the purposes of this book, a "sprint" race includes the shortest distances, such as a half-mile swim, 5- to 15-mile bike leg, and a 1- to 3-mile run. "International" distance means races with swim legs of approximately one mile, 18- to 25-mile bike portions, and runs of five to seven miles. "Half Ironman" refers to a race with a swim of 1 to 1.5 miles, a 30- to 60-mile bike leg, and a 10- to 15-mile run. "Ironman" includes races with 2- to 2.5-mile swims, 80- to 112-mile bike portions, and 18- to 26.2-mile runs. These distances, minus the swim legs, also include duathlons. All of these distances are approximate, and there are some that fall between the "cracks."

This book was written specifically for the serious, self-coached athlete who wants to know more about how to better train and race. Effectively coaching yourself is more difficult than it sounds, especially if you have very high aspirations. Those who aim high are usually better off with a professional coach as another person's point of view is more objective, especially if that person has extensive experience. But there are many who simply enjoy the challenge of self-coaching. Others are unable to afford a coach. And there are some who simply don't trust their training to anyone else. Whatever the reason for self-coaching, I have tried to make this book not only useful, but also understandable for those who don't have degrees in exercise physiology. I hope I have been successful and that your enjoyment of the sport increases as a result.

Joe Friel
Fort Collins, Colorado
February 1998

ACKNOWLEDGMENTS

I am indebted to the many athletes who worked in my retail store, Foot of the Rockies, in the early 1980s, especially Greg Haase and Ross Brownson. Our many discussions about athletic training during those years helped shape the philosophy that is the foundation of the system described here. The studied works of Dr. Tudor Bompa, notably The Theory and Methodology of Training, gave shape to this philosophy. The combining of philosophy and method would not have been possible without the feedback of the many athletes I trained in the last two decades.

I particularly want to thank my colleague, Gale Bernhardt, who tirelessly read every word, offered excellent suggestions and asked good questions. The many concepts discussed herein are more understandable for her dedication to clarity.

I also gratefully acknowledge the many people who contributed: Dave Scott for details of his 1994 Ironman and thoughts on career longevity; Paula Newby-Fraser for insights on extending the careers of elite athletes; Bill Cofer, Marc Evans, Terry Laughlin, Rick Niles, Nicholas Romanov and Cyle Sage for their assistance with Chapter 12; Dr. Loren Cordain for reviewing Chapter 16 and for enduring my many questions on nutrition; and Chad Matteson for keeping my business running while I wrote.

Finally, I want to thank my family — Joyce, Kim and Dirk — for supporting me while I pursue my dreams.

FOREWARD

I have been racing triathlons for more than half of my life. One would think that after so many years of training and racing, I would have learned how to train, race, and understand all of the elements it takes to be consistently at my peak in the sport of triathlon. But the trials and tribulations of triathlon continue for me to this day.

Joe Friel's *The Triathlete's Training Bible* contains all of the information a triathlete needs, whether he or she is a novice, a budding junior, at the top of their age group, or competing at the elite level. Unlike the single disciplines of swimming, biking and running, the combination of all three strengthens almost all of the muscles in your body. Feeling healthy and fit enhances all aspects of your life.

The Triathlete's Training Bible is the most comprehensive triathlon book I have read. It is formatted in a way that you can find detailed information on any question of immediate concern. What should you do the week before the race? Find the answer in Chapter 10. What types of foods are best for all of the demands you put on your body? Turn to Chapter 16. What distance are you planning to race? See Chapter 9. A key chapter for me is Chapter 4 on training intensity and fighting fatigue. Joe leaves no rock unturned. His twenty years of racing, coaching and analyzing every tidbit of pertinent information on fitness is compacted into this one book.

Only a handful of people can claim to swim, bike *and* run, whether it is a one-hour, sprint-distance triathlon or a twelve-hour Ironman. Training for three sports is more time consuming than just preparing for a 10-kilometer running race. We juggle work, family and numerous other affairs in our busy lives, so triathletes need to use their time to train wisely. *The Triathlete's Training Bible* is your coach. It will maximize the limited training time you have in order to prepare you to race at an optimal level.

For those of you who are constantly striving to improve your performance, this book will lead you in the right direction.

Keep Tri-ing,
Wesley Hobson

1997-98 USA Triathlon national team member • 1992 U.S. Olympic Center male triathlete of the year • 1997 U.S. national sprint champion • 1992-93 world championship bronze medalist • Ranked in the top 10 in the world every year since 1992

The SELF-TRAINED TRIATHLETE

Multisport is a huge challenge, one that is greatly simplified by hiring a coach. While training under the watchful eye of a good coach often makes for effective use of limited workout time, it's not an option that everyone wants or can afford. Self-training is far more common, and often just as effective. After all, no one knows you as well as you do. There are, however, many pitfalls to self-training. The obvious one has to do with knowledge of the scientific principles of training. Less obvious, but no less important, is the wisdom of training: having a systematic approach, developing a philosophy of training, fully understanding and accepting the importance of consistency, creating a determined and purposeful attitude, and committing to a well-defined mission. Before the physical training begins, these mental attributes need exploration. The successful self-trained athlete is first and foremost wise.

SMART
TRAINING

*"Many dedicated endurance athletes don't need to be
told what to do — they need to be told what not to do."*

— SCOTT TINLEY, PROFESSIONAL TRIATHLETE

Multisport is both amazingly simple and incredibly complex. It's simplicity is apparent to anyone who has ever swam, ridden a bike or run. All are easily accomplished by children, and even performed at advanced levels by many with only a little practice. And finishing a short-course triathlon or duathlon is achievable by almost anyone who dabbles in the sport. Multisport's complexity is apparent as soon as the novice decides to improve performance, leading to such questions as, Should I do all three sports each day? How long should I workout? Why am I tired all the time? and What should I eat?

The experienced multisport competitor also has questions, but these are born of a higher level of understanding of the intricacies of the sport. Seasoned athletes ask, How can I predict a fitness peak? What's the best way to blend workouts for maximum fitness gains without overtraining? and Is there a way to speed recovery so I can train hard more frequently? In fact, it appears that the more experienced an athlete is, the more complex the training issues become.

While it's the purpose of this book to answer such questions, understand that there is not one and only one answer for each. Due to individual differences, there are as many ways to train for multisport as there are triathletes and duathletes. Yet there is much that athletes — regardless of experience, age, gender and natural ability — have in common. All rely on the same fuel sources, all have the same number of bones and muscles that are put together in the same manner, and the nervous systems of all athletes operate in the same way.

Athlete similarities

When it comes to the specifics of training, however, each athlete is unique. There are individual motivations for racing, genetic capabilities differ, time constraints vary and particular outcomes are sought. Since the spectrum of such possibilities is wide, the key to success in multisport does not come from following a one-size-fits-all training regimen. If it was so, this book could cover the topic in a few pages.

Success in multisport racing results from understanding two aspects of training: the commonly accepted principles of training and your own exceptional needs. What this means is that training is both science and art. The promising athlete is one who understands both training aspects and blends this knowledge into a systematic training program.

SYSTEMATIC TRAINING

Multisport training is much like putting a jigsaw puzzle together. To the novice in either endeavor, the many pieces of the puzzle are overwhelming. What comes first? It's like the old saying: You can't see the forest for the trees. If the details of jigsaw-puzzle solving, just like multisport training, get in the way of seeing the big picture, wasted effort and time are a certainty. It will take far longer to get to the end result of a completed puzzle. There is a great possibility that you'll give up early in the process.

The way to solve the puzzle, any puzzle, is to have a system, which is nothing more than a set of guidelines to get you organized. An elaborate or complex system isn't needed; a simple one will work just as well. Almost any system will do, but some are better than others. The less time you have available to waste in putting the puzzle together, the more critical the system becomes. Staying with the analogy of solving a jigsaw puzzle, here is a system, a set of guidelines, that simplifies the task and makes efficient use of time. Spread the pieces out on the table so all are seen.

• Put pieces of similar colors together in groups.
• Start by putting the edge pieces together.
• Work only one section at a time.
• Position completed sections relative to the finished product.
• Try to connect the finished sections.
• Protect the finished sections so they aren't broken up by the wind or the family cat.

The most important aspect of a jigsaw-puzzle system is keeping the picture of the finished puzzle on the box lid where it is visible. A clear picture is always needed of what the finished product is supposed to look like. Without the picture the task is an immense one that takes far longer to accomplish and continually raises doubts about progress.

Anyone who has ever worked on a complex jigsaw puzzle knows that it takes a long time. Working straight through to completion is often an all-night ordeal, and puzzle burnout is likely. By the time you get done with it, you don't want to see it again or even think about doing another one for a long, long time. To keep this from happening, frequent breaks are needed. While most are short, it's best that some of these breaks are quite long. That way, every time you come back to the puzzle you start with renewed enthusiasm and heightened creativity.

What this system does is add some science to the puzzle-solving project. Although the thought of science scares some, as seen in this example it's really nothing more than a methodical way of acting. Without using such a scientific method, the task of putting a puzzle together, or training for a multisport, is a random activity based largely on luck.

Scientific method is necessary.

So that's the science, but where does the art of a training system come in? Art is the aspect of training in which you learn to better understand yourself as an individual. Using the puzzle analogy one last time, art, or the ability to make creative decisions based on intuition and experience, plays a role because:

Art is the individualization of training.

• Not everyone's puzzle is the same — some have big puzzles, and others have small ones.

• The picture may, and probably will, change several times while working on it.

• Certain areas of the picture are fuzzy.

• Some pieces of the puzzle are more important than others.

• Pieces get lost or broken along the way and need replacing.

• Some people have precious little time to work on their puzzle.

• The current puzzle is part of a bigger puzzle that also needs solving.

• Others tell you what a bad job of puzzle solving you are doing.

• The puzzle isn't turning out exactly as you had hoped, so it needs reworking.

This book will help you devise a personal training system employing both science and art. The science part is easy to describe; the art of training *can* be described, but is only learned from doing. The system you devise will differ from those of your training partners. It won't duplicate the system used by the pro athlete you most admire. It will work only for you. For any system to work you must have confidence in it, confidence derived from understanding the "whys" and "hows." But you must also remain open-minded as no system is foolproof and no one has all the answers.

PHILOSOPHY OF TRAINING

Because it is critical to success in multisport, the art of training needs a firm foundation.

A philosophy guides training decisions.

The way to establish that foundation is with a personal training philosophy. While you have probably never thought about it, you already have one. Each athlete has one since training decisions must be made every day, and the answers spring from an underlying personal philosophy. For example, the following questions may need answering at some point during your training.

What should I do when I…

Everyday training questions.

- feel tired, but have a hard workout planned?
- can't decide which workout to do?
- am afraid I will lose my fitness while taking time off?
- know my competition is doing more than me?
- dread doing a certain workout?
- feel like my training partners are going too fast?
- know my weaknesses, but prefer working on my strengths?
- sense there is only one interval left in me?
- think I could do more, but I'm not sure?
- have a bad race?
- seem to have lost fitness?

If your philosophy is "More is better — always train as hard as I can," you will answer these questions in a certain way. In fact, this philosophy of training is quite common in multisport and is the leading cause of breakdown from illness, injury, burnout and overtraining. By adopting a philosophy that is more moderate, such problems are avoided and racing performance improves.

Suggested philosophy.

Consider how a person with the following philosophy would answer the same questions listed above: *Do the least amount of the most specific training that causes gradual improvement at the right times.*

What does this mean? Let's examine the key parts to better understand it.

"Least amount" of training.

Least amount implies that less is better. How can that be? Most successful athletes support the notion that small fitness gains made over a long time are better than quick fitness changes over a short time. We all know that "too much, too soon" leads to breakdown, yet we keep doing it.

"Most specific" training.

Most specific has to do with how daily workouts benefit triathlon- and duathlon-specific fitness, which is the ultimate goal of training. Each and every workout should have a purpose, either to improve fitness, maintain fitness or recover. Getting the balance of these three right is the key to success.

Gradual improvement has to do with taking a long-term approach to training.

Gradual workout changes from week to week produce fitness that stays with you longer and ultimately reaches a higher level than when big changes are made. Your body is prepared to handle changes of a bit more than 10 percent. Doing more than what you are physically capable of absorbing is worse than simply wasting effort as it often leads to breakdown.

Right times refers to the progression of workouts. There is a sequence to training that most athletes have found to work for developing fitness. It starts with aerobic endurance, then adds lactate threshold training, progresses to aerobic capacity, and culminates with speed and power. All of this is sequentially accomplished over several weeks.

The idea of placing limits on training is a scary thought for some. Many athletes are so used to existing on the edge of overtraining that it seems a natural state. Such athletes are no less addicted than drug users. And just as with drug abuse, those who abuse training are not getting any better, but they can't bring themselves to change. That is the way addictions are. Changing your philosophy means taking a risk by trying something new and different, but the potential rewards are great.

"Gradual improvement."

"Right times."

Changing training philosophy is difficult.

CONSISTENT TRAINING

So far, there have been several references to training breakdowns caused by illness, injury, burnout and overtraining. Extended or frequent downtime from such problems inevitably results in a loss of fitness and the need to rebuild by returning to previous levels of training. Multisport athletes who experience these problems with some regularity seldom achieve their potential in the sport.

Consistent training, not extreme training, is the way to attain the highest possible fitness, so it must serve as the ultimate standard in all training decisions. Consistency results from following a philosophy such as the one described above, and from striving for moderation in training while resting at regular intervals.

Consistent training brings great fitness.

MODERATION AND CONSISTENCY

Your body has limits when it comes to endurance, strength and speed, and you should seldom test them. By usually staying within those limits, and infrequently stretching them just a little, breakdowns are avoided and consistent training results. Aim to finish workouts feeling as though you could have done more. For example, when there is only one interval left in you, and digging deep is the only way to complete it, stop. Don't do it.

The time to abandon a workout is when it is perceived as very hard, your speed has decreased noticeably or your technique has changed. For athletes with a strong

Excess is harmful.

work ethic, this is difficult to do. For this reason many successful athletes have coaches; training under the watchful eye of an objective person whose emotions are not linked to the workout helps avoid breakdowns. Self-coaching requires you to think objectively and nonemotionally. While this is possible, it is difficult for many of us to do. There are many times when you are unsure whether to continue or stop. Doubt is a good reason to discontinue the session. When in doubt — leave it out.

When to stop a workout.

Hard workouts progress through a discomfort-hurt-agony sequence. Be assured that when "agony" is reached, nothing physiologically advantageous happens beyond the benefits achieved at the "hurt" level, but the risk of injury and overtraining rises dramatically. There is no scientific evidence to support the need for supreme effort in training, but there is a great deal that supports the notion of moderate stress as beneficial.

The hardest workouts should occur infrequently throughout the year and used judiciously only in the few weeks immediately preceding a major race as ceiling levels of the extreme components of fitness are achieved in a relatively short time. As you will see in a later chapter, a season should only include three or four of these major events. Training at the highest intensities year-round is ultimately detrimental to performance.

Do intense workouts infrequently.

During the times of the year when you are not doing intense, race-specific training, workouts are best devoted to building or maintaining endurance and strength, recovering or refining skills.

REST AND CONSISTENCY

Rest is the most abused aspect of training by the serious multisport athlete. Few fully appreciate the physiological benefits that accrue during rest, especially while asleep. While sleeping the body releases growth hormone to repair damage from the day's training stress and to shore up any of the systems weakened by training. Without adequate sleep, fitness is lost regardless of how intense or long workouts are. As the intensity and duration of training increase, rest must also increase to maintain balance in the body. Besides sleep, rest includes regular easy training days, days off from training altogether, frequent recovery weeks, and extended interruptions from training at the end of a race season.

Growth hormone released during sleep.

Intellectually, multisport athletes know they should rest, but emotionally they fear that taking an appropriately timed break for even a couple of days will lead to a loss of fitness. There is no scientific evidence to support this. There is, however, a mountain of research that shows frequent rest as beneficial to fitness.

Regular rest improves fitness.

A well-rested athlete looks forward to workouts, enjoys doing them, feels sharp and in control during training sessions and grows stronger afterward. The chronically

Losin'? May need more snoozin'...

Most triathletes and duathletes are busy people. It's difficult for them to find time for all the activities in their lives — family, work, hobbies, community involvement and workouts.

Going to bed later or getting up earlier is the solution many choose for this problem. As the responsibilities accumulate, sleep is cut back even more. Eventually they are snoozing only five to six hours a night. This pattern of sleep deprivation eventually leads to a drop in performance, feelings of depression and frustration with training and life in general.

If this describes you, accept the fact that sleep is not an expendable commodity. Cutting it short frequently will eventually undermine all of your training, for it's during sleep that the body restores energy levels, and releases growth hormone to repair damage and grow stronger. Fewer Z's may mean more quantity of life, but it also means less quality.

The average person seems to need seven or more hours of sleep each day. As the intensity and volume of training increase, sleep requirements also rise. Professional athletes typically sleep 10 to 12 hours a day. They usually break this down into eight- to 10-hour nights with the rest in one or two daily naps. Now you probably aren't a professional athlete and don't have time for naps, but the more volume and intensity of training you do, the more rest you need, regardless of ability and available time.

You also aren't Superman or Wonder Woman. If too many daily activities are cutting into sleep, either something has to go or you must resign yourself to mediocre athletic performance. You can't cram 28 hours of activity into a 24-hour day and expect your body to keep going as if nothing was wrong.

Quality of sleep is another concern. Difficulty going to sleep and awakening frequently cuts into the benefits derived from it. Here are some tips from a 1982 study that may help improve the quality of your sleep.

- Go to bed at a regular time every day including weekends and the night before races.
- As bed time approaches unwind slowly by reading, going for a short walk or engaging in light conversation.
- Sleep in a darkened room that is 60-64 degrees and well ventilated.
- Use a comfortable bed and pillow.
- Take a warm bath before retiring.
- Drink warm milk, if you're not lactose intolerant, or herbal tea to promote relaxation.
- Try to sleep only when feeling tired.
- Progressively contract and relax muscles to induce total body relaxation.

Also, avoid stimulants such as coffee, tea and cola in the last few hours before going to bed. Salt and refined sugar may even cause sleep problems for some. Although alcohol is a depressant that may help you fall asleep, it can also interfere with sleep patterns causing you to awake early.

Besides milk and herbal tea, other foods that may help induce sleep are tuna fish and cottage cheese since they're high in sleep-inducing L-tryptophan. Avoid eating a large meal right before going to bed, but don't go to bed hungry, either.

Happy dreams.

❖

tired triathlete is dragged through workouts only by the force of extreme willpower, performs sluggishly, recovers poorly and derives little benefit. You will not improve without adequate rest.

REFERENCES

Bunt, J.C., et al. 1986. Sex and training differences in human growth hormone levels during prolonged exercise. *Journal of Applied physiology* 61: 1796.

Farrell, P.A., et al. 1987. Enkephalins, catecholamines, and psychological mood alterations: Effects of prolonged exercise. *Medicine and Science in Sports and Exercise* 19: 347.

Heath, G.W., et al. 1991. Exercise and the incidence of upper respiratory tract infections. *Medicine and Science in Sports and Exercise* 23:152.

Houmard, J.A., et al. 1990. Testosterone, cortisol, and creatine kinase levels in male distance runners during reduced training. *International Journal of Sports Medicine* 11: 41.

MacIntyre, J.G. 1987. Growth hormone and athletes. *Sports Medicine* 4: 129.

Weltman, A., et al. 1992. Endurance training amplifies the pulsatile release of growth hormone: Effects of training intensity. *Journal of Applied physiology* 72: 2188.

ATTITUDE

*"I saw the Ironman for the first time on television in 1982, when Julie
Moss fell and crawled across the finish line. Everyone in the room was all
choked up. People were crying and cheering. I thought, 'This is incredible.'"*

— MARK ALLEN, PROFESSIONAL TRIATHLETE

In February 1982, ABC's "Wide World of Sports" program covered the fifth Hawaii
Ironman and, unintentionally, established mainstream recognition for the fledg-
ling sport of triathlon, and also the attitude of an entire generation of triathletes.

That summer, repeated broadcasts of the dramatic finish riveted sports-hungry
Americans to their television sets. A freckle-faced, red-haired former waitress from
Carlsbad, California, named Julie Moss had a big lead going into the run. Moss, a
strong swimmer and cyclist, soon found herself losing ground to a quickly closing
Kathleen McCartney. Near the end of the marathon, Moss was reduced to walking, and
with the finish line in sight she began to wobble. Then, she fell and struggled to her
feet while refusing assistance that would have disqualified her. Finally she crawled on
hands and knees to "stay low where no one could bother me," she later said. Just short
of the finish line McCartney passed Moss to win. Twenty-nine seconds later Julie Moss
broke the finish line to take second.

Moss's dramatic finish, played out repeatedly on the American sports program,
brought an explosion of interest in the Ironman. That year, a second race was held in
October — and continues as the month of the great race to this day — which allowed
those from the northern states to train in the summer instead of winter. The second
1982 race swelled to more than 900 entrants from the 580 who competed only eight
months earlier. In 1983, there were thousands of applicants causing Ironman officials
to set a limit of 1500 and establish the lottery system for entry.

The television coverage of Moss's finish did more than promote the growth of
the Ironman — it also established a stereotype of the triathlete as a mix of crazy,

1982 Ironman TV coverage.

macho and heroic. And it gave the impression that triathlons are "gruelathons." These initial images attracted people to the sport who favored the extremes of training — either massive swim, bike and run volumes, or minimal training to enhance the mental tenacity required to deal with extreme suffering.

Stereotype of triathlete established.

The first triathletes really weren't crazy; they actually had a lot going for themselves mentally, if not scientifically. Their greatest mental attribute was a "can-do" attitude. Show them a challenge, no matter how big, and they knew it was not only doable, but they could excel at it. Most came to triathlon with a strong background in one or two of the three disciplines and soon became passingly proficient in the others due to their mental tenacity.

Today, many people, especially juniors, come to the sport as multisport athletes first and foremost. Their attitudes differ from those of their predecessors in the sport. For one thing, the new triathletes and duathletes are more willing to listen to science and pay attention to the needs of their bodies. What they lack, however, is the swashbuckling, never-say-quit attitude of the original multisport athletes. While that may be an advantage for long-term success, some degree of relentless motivation is required to conquer big challenges like the triathlon and duathlon. The trick is to balance a determined attitude with a purposeful approach.

Determination and purpose are needed.

BUMBLEBEES AND RACE HORSES

A few years ago, the story goes, scientists at the National Aeronautics and Space Administration (NASA) developed an interest in the bumblebee. The lab folks reckoned that the little insect held some secrets of flight that may provide answers to questions about operating in space. After all, they asked, how could such small wings produce efficient lift for a relatively large and hairy torso? And how could a round body and flight position that violated many principles of aerodynamics move so effectively through the air? Indeed, there was much to learn from the little hummer.

So the scientists set about studying the bumblebee to discover its flying secrets. As scientists always do, they hypothesized about, scrutinized, examined, dissected, measured, timed, filmed, observed, compared, quantified, thought about and debated the bumblebee. After weeks of study they came to one conclusion: Bumblebees are not capable of flight.

Bumblebees "can't fly."

Fortunately, no one told the bumblebee. The silly insects go right on believing that flight is normal for them despite what the best minds in the scientific world know as fact.

We can learn a lot from the bumblebee. The single most critical piece of the multisport puzzle is believing in yourself and your capacity to succeed. "If you think you can or think you can't," automobile manufacturer Henry Ford said, "you're probably right." The bumblebee thinks it can fly. Actually, the thought of anything else never even crosses its tiny mind. It just keeps on flying.

Then there's the race horse. Have you ever been to the Kentucky Derby or other big horse race? The physiology of the equine athlete is similar to the human athlete's, and they are trained in much the same manner as a runner. They use heart-rate monitors, train with intervals and endurance, follow a periodization plan and eat a diet designed to enhance performance.

Race horses and triathletes are similar.

Psychologically, race horses differ a great deal from multisport athletes. They never question their training preparation. When it comes time for a workout designed by their trainer, they do it without wondering if it's enough. They don't go out in the morning and put in a few extra junk miles for "insurance." They don't worry and fret after a poor performance. Stable life goes on as usual.

On Derby day, race horses are nervous just as human athletes are; they know what is about to happen, but they don't magnify the tension by comparing themselves with the other horses ("Look at the legs on that stud!"). Instead, they are very purposeful in their approach to training and racing. There is but one reason for every day existence — to get faster. If the horse is physically strong and the trainer is smart, this happens.

If you are to succeed in multisport, the first thing you must do is believe in yourself just as the bumblebee does. Without this, all of the science in the world won't do any good. Also, if this book is to help, you must have a purposeful, race-horse trust in your training. Continually second-guessing and changing training direction after every race is a sure way to fail. Think like a bumblebee; train like a horse.

Think like a bumblebee; train like a horse.

MISSION

In 1994, Dave "The Man" Scott had a bumblebee and race horse year. On turning 40 years old, he decided to come out of retirement and take on the Hawaii Ironman following a five-year absence. This was going to be a daunting challenge.

Dave Scott's 1994 Hawaii Ironman.

Many triathlon and aging experts said his presence wouldn't be an issue; Scott was too old to compete head-to-head with men 10 to 15 years his junior. And besides, they pontificated, the Ironman had become more competitive since his swan song as a runner-up to Mark Allen in 1989. This was not an old-man's race. Better to stay comfortably in retirement than to risk losing badly and damaging his reputation as a six-time winner of the Hawaii Ironman and the undisputed King of Kona, they explained.

Like the bumblebee, Scott didn't listen to all the reasons why he didn't seem to have a chance. Instead, he did what the race horse does — eat, sleep and live in order to become faster. He went off to train alone for several weeks leading up to the race. He prepared for this greatest challenge of a long and storied career by staying away, both physically and emotionally, from the naysayers and those who would try to convince him he "couldn't fly."

On race day, Scott came out of the water near the front, moved up on the bike, and was strongly in second place late in the run. By 19 miles into the marathon, he had closed the gap to within 11 seconds of race leader Greg Welch. But run as hard as he could, Scott couldn't narrow the lead any further. He crossed the finish line on Ali'i Drive in second place. Later he proclaimed it his "best race, ever."

Dave Scott's best race, ever.

That a 40-year-old "has-been" triathlete could come out of retirement and beat the best in the world, minus one, at the greatest challenge in the sport is nothing short of remarkable. Had Scott listened to the experts he would never have even attempted the comeback. But he didn't listen. He was on a mission.

Unlike Dave Scott, you may never have experts telling you that it can't be done. Maybe that's because you have surrounded yourself with supportive people and a positive atmosphere. If so, you are a wise and fortunate person. Most are not so blessed. Not having anyone to pollute your mind with negative attitudes, however, also results from never taking on a big challenge that threatens others' well-established notions about you. Which is it?

Are you challenged?

What is it you want to achieve in multisport? Do you know? Can you put it in a few words? Can you write it down in such a way that it motivates and gives direction to training? Are you convinced it is possible? If so, you are a rare athlete. Unfortunately, most have only a vague idea of what they are doing in the sport and why they train a certain way. Often there is a nebulous notion of "getting faster." Seldom is there anything done to define and give direction to such wishes.

Most of us go through life never coming close to our limits and living only on wishes. But wishes are important; they're the start of great feats. Wishes grow into dreams when mentally "seeing" yourself accomplish the wish is possible. Dreams turn into goals when a plan for attaining them is defined. Goals become a mission when unwavering self-belief and purposeful zeal are realized. Big challenges require mission status. The difference between a goal and a mission is attitude. Missions are evident by an accompanying passionate commitment. With the proper attitude, almost anything is possible. What you believe, you will achieve.

Wishes, dreams, goals and mission.

Entering Ironman

There is no bigger challenge in triathlon than the Hawaii Ironman. Just getting *in* is perhaps the more formidable task. Attaining one of the coveted 1350 spots by qualifying at a selected event provides many triathletes with a quest that may last for years.

An alternative is to enter through the lottery system. There are 150 lottery spots available each year. Considering there are typically about 5000 applications for those entries, the chances are slim, but there is a chance. Here's how the lottery works:

1. You must be a U.S. citizen to apply. To request an application, call the Ironman office, in Florida, at 813/942-4767, or in Hawaii, at 808/329-0063. As of this writing there were plans to put the application on the Ironman Web site, which is http://www.Ironman.sportsline.com.

2. Of the 150 lottery slots, 100 are awarded to Ironman Passport Club members. So, joining increases your chances considerably. And club membership brings other benefits such as a quarterly newsletter, discounts on merchandise purchases and free gifts.

3. Return your application to the Ironman office by the end of March along with the entry fee and a processing fee. If you are not one of the lucky few, the entry fee is refunded.

4. In mid-April, a computer at the Ironman organization picks the winners, and on May 1, the local newspapers and television stations of those selected are notified.

5. If you are one of the fortunate, all that remains is to complete one of the designated triathlons in the coming summer to establish your preparedness.

Good luck!   ❖

COMMITMENT

Talk is cheap. It's easy to have big dreams and set high goals before the race season starts. The true test of commitment to better racing results is not in the talking, but in the doing. Commitment doesn't start with the first race of the season; it's all the things you do today to get stronger, faster and more enduring. Real commitment means 365 days a year and 24 hours a day.

Talk to the best athletes you know. Ask them about commitment. Once you probe past all of the "aw, shucks" stuff you'll discover how big a role multisport plays in their lives. The better they are, the more you'll hear about life revolving around the sport. The most likely remark you will hear is that each day is arranged around training. It's a rare champion who fits in workouts randomly.

Multisport success requires passionate commitment.

Racing to your potential can't be an on-again, off-again endeavor. It's a full-time commitment — a passion. Achieving the pinnacle of excellence requires living, breathing, eating and sleeping triathlon every day. Literally.

Growth hormone stimulated by exercise and sleep.

The greater the commitment, the more life pivots around the basic three factors of training: eating, sleeping and working out. Eating fuels the body for training and speeds recovery by replacing depleted energy and nutrient stores and providing the building blocks for a stronger body. Sleeping and working out have a synergistic effect on fitness. Each can cause the release of growth hormone from the pituitary gland. Growth hormone speeds recovery, rebuilds muscles and breaks down body fat. By training twice daily and taking a nap, the dedicated athlete gets four hits of growth hormone daily resulting in higher levels of fitness sooner.

In the final analysis, greater fitness is what we are all after. It's the product of three ingredients: stress, rest and fuel. Figure 2.1 — Suggested Daily Routines — shows how training, sleeping and eating can be built into your day. This is not the final word on daily routines, but only intended to offer suggested ways of fitting training into your day along with the many other activities. Notice that there are no three-a-day routines. Few, if any, amateur multisport athletes should train more than twice a day. Even two is too many for most.

Reality check necessary.

This level of commitment may not be for you. In fact, there comes a point at which each of us has to check our "want to" against our "have to." You can't forsake jobs, families and other responsibilities for multisport. Even the pros must consider other aspects of life. Realistically, there are limits to passion, otherwise we'd soon alienate everyone who wasn't equally zealous and be reduced to slobbering zombies.

Small changes bring big results over time.

What can you do to improve fitness and race performances given the obvious constraints placed on training? Small changes in lifestyle are certainly possible, and go a long way in improving fitness. Balancing training and other responsibilities is hard to achieve, but remolding daily activities by 10 percent in the direction of better fitness doesn't take much and brings noticeable improvement. How about committing to hitting the sack 30 minutes earlier each night so that you are more rested? Another small, daily change that can bring better results is healthier eating. Can you cut out 10 percent of the junk food you eat by replacing it with wholesome foods? What you put in your mouth is the stuff the body uses to completely rebuild and replace each muscle cell every six months. Do you want muscles made from potato chips, Twinkies and pop? Or from fruits, vegetables and lean meat? What can you change?

REFERENCES

Evans, M. 1997. *Endurance Athlete's Edge*. Champaign, IL: Human Kinetics.

Friel, J. 1996. *The Cyclist's Training Bible*. Boulder, CO: VeloPress.

Inside Triathlon. February, 1997. "Ironman Lottery."

FIGURE 2.1

Suggested Daily Routines

	Two Workouts Daily		One Workout Daily	
	Work day	No-work day	Work day	No-work day
6:00 am	Awake	Awake	Awake	Awake
:30	Workout 1	Eat	Workout	Eat
7:00	|	Stretch	|	Stretch
:30	|	Personal	|	Personal
8:00	Eat	|	Eat	|
:30	Shower	Workout 1	Shower	Workout
9:00	Work	|	Work	|
:30	|	|	|	|
10:00	|	|	|	|
:30	|	Eat	|	|
11:00	|	Shower	|	|
:30	Eat	Nap	|	Eat
12:00 pm	Nap	Stretch	Eat	Shower
:30	Work	Personal	Nap	Nap
1:00	|	Eat	Work	Personal
:30	|	Personal	|	|
2:00	|	|	|	|
:30	|	Workout 2	|	|
3:00	Eat	|	|	|
:30	|	|	Eat	Eat
4:00	|	|	|	Personal
:30	|	Eat	|	|
5:00	End work	Shower	End work	|
:30	Workout 2	Nap	Personal	|
6:00	|	Stretch	|	|
:30	Eat	Personal	Eat	Eat
7:00	Shower	|	Personal	Personal
:30	Personal	Eat	|	|
8:00	|	Personal	|	|
:30	Eat	|	|	|
9:00	To bed	To bed	To bed	To bed

part two

FROM LAB TO REAL WORLD

The availability of training information is greater now than at any time in the history of sport. Scientific journals, scholarly periodicals, popular magazines, newspaper reports, training books, clinics by professional athletes and coaches, Internet newsgroups and discussions, and television programs widely disseminate this cornucopia of physiological information. There is so much data that one of the greatest challenges facing the self-coached multisport athlete is sifting through all of it, and then deciding how to blend the various bits of information worth keeping into a comprehensive training program.

The purpose of Part II is to simplify and "demystify" the scientific aspects of training by describing how and why a training program is organized, and especially the role of intensity in training. Intensity is probably the least understood component of preparation for multisport racing.

For the reader who has little interest in science or theory, this part of the The Triathlete's Training Bible *may present a challenge. But a base of understanding of why and how to organize training will help in the development of an effective personal training program and greater race fitness.*

THE SCIENCE OF TRAINING

"It is not a matter of how much you train, but of how you train."

— RICK NILES, TRIATHLON COACH

The multisport athlete's body is made up of structures and systems that may be measured and quantified. Science knows quite a bit about the workings of such tissues as the muscles, bones and internal organs. The chemistry and mechanics of the cardiovascular, respiratory, immune and other systems have also yielded to scientific inquiry. The rate at which this knowledge grows is staggering. In the decade of the 1980s, science learned more about the human athlete than in the previous eight decades combined.

Few question the notion that science provides tremendous insight into how to physically and psychologically improve multisport performance. So it appears that science holds all of the answers for better racing, right? Well, actually it doesn't. The best scientists in the world can take a group of the most fit athletes into a state-of-the-art lab, test, poke, prod, measure, analyze and predict how they will do in a race — and fail miserably. Labs are just not the real world of racing where many individual variables, beyond the ken of the scientist, escape quantification.

There are limitations on science.

For all of our technology, exactly how the athlete's body performs under race conditions remains largely a mystery. Unfortunately, when it comes to contributing anything really extraordinary to the training and techniques of athletes, science has a poor record. It works best in observing the performances of elite athletes who have made a breakthrough and then explaining why they were successful. Take the high jump, for example. For decades, most high jumpers used a rolling technique in which the arm and leg on one side of the body went over the bar first followed by the other arm and leg with the belly facing down. Then in the late 1960s a college jumper named Dick Fosbury revolutionized the event by clearing the bar head first with his belly pointing up. Soon other jumpers adopted this technique and quickly pushed the world record up. Later, the "Fosbury Flop" as it was called, was painstakingly analyzed by scientists who explained that the Flop worked better because the center of gravity went under the bar instead of over it as in the older technique thus requiring less vertical lift.

Sport science is best at explaining, not discovering.

The world of sport is replete with such stories of science later explaining what athletes previously discovered, such as Bjorn Borg's two-handed backhand in tennis, Jan Boklov's "V" style in ski jumping, the "skate" technique of cross-country skiing popularized by Jim Koch, Frank Shorter's altitude training, and the bicycle aero' bars developed by Boone Lennon.

Science is seldom on the leading edge, and is far from perfect. Research studies all too often have design flaws, and even the biases of those doing the investigation may shade the conclusions. That's just the way life is: Nothing is 100-percent guaranteed. Science is not perfect, but until something better comes along, it's the best thing we have going for us.

Science is not perfect.

Remember the first year you did triathlons or duathlons? All you had to do was train more and you chopped several minutes off of your time. The second year, the same strategy worked, but the gains weren't quite as great. By the third year you were probably scratching your head and looking for answers. The more you learned, the more you discovered that you didn't know. One answer led to a half dozen new questions. So you turned to the experts — the scientists, coaches and elite athletes. On big-picture issues, you probably found there was some general agreement, although there were dissenters. The more complex your questions became, the more confusing the answers were. Scientist X says this, while coach Y says that, and athlete Z says something altogether different. What do you do?

Unfortunately, there is no sure-fire solution to this quandary. That's why training is both a science *and* an art. Every athlete is an experiment of one or the other. You have to find what works best for you. Each source of training information can help with this quest, but don't expect easy answers. While science is only one source, it is probably the most likely to discover solutions that fit a broad range of athletes.

A personal training program is needed.

Always keep the limitations of science in mind. It cannot provide us with answers to big questions such as how to train. Science is best at finding solutions to small questions, such as those having to do with recovery, hydration, overtraining and illness. A six- to twelve-week research project must, of necessity, allow little time for adaptation. What would have happened had the study continued for a year, or a decade? Research also stifles individual uniqueness in order to find out what works for most people most of the

time. Perhaps you don't fit the mold. Science can help you improve as an athlete, but be   **Skepticism needed.**
skeptical. Remember the bumblebee.

Coaches and elite athletes are also helpful sources. A little skepticism is healthy here,
also. Observe them, listen to what they have to say, compare them with each other and
with science, ask questions, experiment and then decide for yourself.

TRAINING STRESS

In order to bring positive changes, physical stress to the body is necessary. That is why we
train. Stress can be changed by manipulating three elements of training: workout frequency, workout duration and workout intensity.

FREQUENCY

How often you work out is the most basic element of training. Novice multisport athletes
typically work out five or six times each week. Such a frequency is appropriate for their
level, and improvement will occur rapidly, probably in the range of 10 to 15 percent after
a few weeks. An Olympic hopeful might work out 12 to 18 times in a week. That's also
appropriate, but may only result in a 1- or 2-percent gain.

Studies have found that training three to five times a week brings the greatest benefit for the time invested, and that additional workouts have diminishing returns. In other
words, a few weekly workouts will produce the bulk of your fitness, and anything beyond
about five weekly sessions is "icing on the cake." This is an example of the "80-20 rule"   **Frequency increases as goals get higher.**
working: 80 percent of the desired results come from 20 percent of the work required to
realize 100-percent gain. If you are an elite triathlete or duathlete trying to realize your
racing potential, however, that last 20 percent of the potential gains are worth it since
competition is quite close at the top and rewards are few.

Frequency varies throughout the season. Early in the training year, it increases in
order to add stress. Just prior to, and during the race season, it decreases to allow more
time for recovery.

DURATION

Swimming, cycling and running workouts are often referred to in terms of the distance
covered in miles, kilometers, yards or meters. Another method of referring to duration,
and the one generally used in this book, is the elapsed time of the workout including warm
up, cool down and the recovery periods within an interval workout.

Workout length varies dramatically from day to day. Some workouts are long to build greater endurance, while others are short to allow more emphasis on higher intensities, or to promote recovery.

A general rule of thumb is that the longest workouts are about the same duration as, or slightly longer than, the longest race you will compete in. There are obvious exceptions at both ends of the race-duration spectrum. For example, it's not wise when training for an Ironman to go the full race distance in a workout, but training at twice sprint-distance duration can be beneficial.

Early in the season the higher-intensity workouts are done on low-duration days, but as the most important races approach, long duration and high intensity are occasionally combined. This prepares the body for the specific stresses of racing.

INTENSITY

Since frequency and duration are easy to measure, we often refer to them in describing our training regimen. Workout intensity is somewhat more difficult to quantify, but in many ways better defines our training.

High intensity training is powerful medicine. Too much, too frequently and you wind up sick, injured, burned out or overtrained, and on the sidelines watching. Too little intensity in training and you are off the back in races and unlikely to achieve high goals. Chapter 4 explains how to measure intensity, determine your individual intensity zones and use it wisely in training. Pay close attention to the intensity of training. If you get this part wrong, it doesn't matter what else you may be doing right.

VOLUME

The terms volume and duration are often confused; they aren't interchangeable. While duration refers to the time or distance of a given workout, volume is the combination of duration and frequency. In other words, volume is the total of all durations for a given period, such as a week. So if an athlete runs three times in a week for an hour each time (duration), the running volume for that week is three hours.

WORK LOAD

The combination of all the three stress elements — frequency, duration and intensity — is referred to as "work load." An athlete who trains frequently with long durations and high intensity is training at a high work load. Infrequent, short duration workouts done at a low intensity produce a low work load. By manipulating the three elements, work loads may be designed to fit every athlete's needs. It's important to understand that there are individual differences in what is an appropriate work load. Generally, several years of experience, a high level of fitness and youth favor high work loads, but there are exceptional individuals. The art of training is the ability to determine what is the appropriate work load for you. Experience and cautious trial and error are the basis for work-load decisions.

Work load = duration x frequency x intensity.

PRINCIPLES OF TRAINING

Although science has not produced any detailed, guaranteed training plans for multisport, or any other sport, it has developed a set of guidelines from which direction in the quest for peak performance is found. The following training principles are generally accepted throughout the world of athletics, but exceptions have also been noted. Understanding and applying these concepts will make you a better self-coach.

PROGRESSIVE OVERLOAD

Greek mythology describes how Milon of Croton became the strongest man in ancient Greece, allowing him to win the Olympic wrestling contest five times. Everyday, Milon would hoist a calf above his head and carry it around the stable. As the calf grew, so did his strength until he could eventually carry the full-grown cow. The training principle Milon was using — progressive overload — is still the basis of athletic training today.

Overloading the body with progressively increasing stress appears simple: Lift more, run farther, swim faster, ride harder and your fitness will improve. Unfortunately, it's not quite that simple. The confounding element is that the body's cells are sensitive. They do indeed respond and grow stronger, but only when the proper amount of stress is applied. Theoretically, there is a threshold, or level of stress that is appropriate for the improvement of every cell. Too much stress applied too soon and the cell is considerably weakened and struggles for days, perhaps weeks, merely to recover.

Cells are sensitive.

Training builds up fitness by first tearing it down. Following a stressful workout, one in which the work load was high, you are in worse shape than before starting. If the work load was appropriate and rest follows, the body will respond in a few hours or a couple of days and you'll be slightly more fit. This is called "overcompensation" and is illustrated in figure 3.1.

Repeated overcompensation leading to increased fitness results from applying the correct overloads at the right times. The more fit an athlete is, the more difficult it is to apply just the right load of stress since the highly fit athlete has a narrowed overload threshold. Being close to one's fitness potential means there is little room for error. For the novice triathlete or duathlete, almost any low-level stress provides an overload.

High fitness means narrow tolerance for overloads.

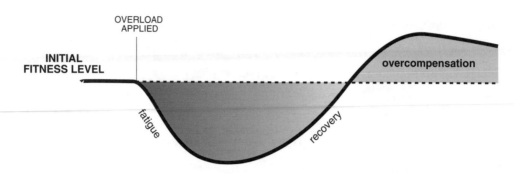

FIGURE 3.1
*Overcompensation
resulting from a
training overload.*

**Overcompensation rate
varies with the system.**

Each physiological system responds to an overload at a unique rate. For example, muscle strength improves quickly when compared with aerobic endurance. Even within a given system there are varying speeds of adaptation since the cells don't all respond at the same rate. In the cardiovascular system, for example, blood plasma increases significantly with a week of high work load, but the capillaries that carry the blood to the muscles take years of training to fully develop.

Knowing what the optimal work load is, and when to apply it, is one aspect of the art of training discussed earlier. Science can point the way, but you must determine through trial and error what is appropriate for you. Erring on the side of too little rather than too much is the key to consistency.

SPECIFICITY

Fitness is specific to training. In other words, you won't reach peak triathlon or duathlon fitness by jumping rope, doing aerobics or rock climbing. High levels of triathlon fitness require swimming, cycling and running. Some crossover may result from other endurance activities, primarily in the heart and lungs and their related structures, but this is minimal considering all that is necessary for multisport fitness.

**Guidelines for
specific training.**

For the best results, the training stress must follow two maxims. First, it should have a pattern of joint and muscle coordination that is specific to the sport. Second, the exercise must place specific duration and intensity stresses on specific muscles. An example may help explain these maxims. Running and cross-country skiing appear quite similar since many of the same muscles are used in almost the same manner. Yet scientific studies have shown that there is no relationship between the aerobic capacities of running and cross-country skiing. Aerobic capacity is one measure of endurance fitness. Someone trained for skiing who never runs is likely to have a high aerobic capacity when skiing, but not when running. To achieve peak fitness for running, you must run.

Does this mean you should never do anything except swim, bike and run? No. There are good reasons to include other activities, especially during a period of preparation many weeks or months before the racing begins. These reasons may include mental breaks from the exercise routine, bad weather, injury avoidance, recovery and the development of the most basic fitness elements. But consider all such exercise a supplement to, and not a substitute for, multisport training.

Non-specific training has benefits, too.

REVERSIBILITY

Fitness is always changing and is never stagnant. Right now your race-specific physiology is either improving or deteriorating depending on what you have done recently. Don't take this to mean that you must train hard every day, since it's during rest that fitness improves. Even during periods of extended rest, as when building to a peak, physical conditioning improves if the right amount of stress is applied at the right times.

Fitness is never constant.

The problem comes when a pattern of consistent, fitness-producing training is interrupted by an unscheduled event that prevents stresses of adequate magnitude to produce an overload. Training interruptions typically result from illness, injury, burnout and overtraining, but also from job, family and other obligations. When consistency is broken by one of these, the body's systems begin to slip back to previous conditioning levels. For the

Inconsistent training reverses fitness gains.

TABLE 3.1

Changes resulting from three weeks of not training

(Adapted from Wilber, R.L. and R.J. Moffatt. 1994. Physiological and biochemical consequences of detraining in aerobically trained individuals. Journal of Strength Conditioning Research 8: 110.)

Measure of Fitness	Change
Aerobic capacity (VO$_2$ max)	-8 %
Heart stroke volume (blood pumped per beat)	-10 %
Submaximum heart rate (beats/minute)	+4 %
Blood plasma volume	-12 %
Muscle capillary density	-7 %
Oxidative enzymes	-29 %
Blood insulin at rest	+17-120 %
Blood lactate during exercise	+88 %
Lactate threshold	-7 %
Use of fat for fuel during exercise	-52 %
Time to fatigue (minutes)	-10 %

endurance athlete, noticeable losses of fitness are evident within two weeks of the cessation of workouts. By three weeks many of the elements crucial to race performance erode. Each system has its own rate of decline. For example, aerobic fitness declines faster than anaerobic conditioning. Strength, however, remains relatively constant for about four weeks although power declines by up to 14 percent in the same time, according to one study. Interestingly, highly conditioned athletes lose their fitness at a faster rate than the less well-conditioned. Table 3.1 lists changes that commonly occur during a period of detraining.

Retraining takes longer than detraining.

So it appears that two to three weeks of inactivity result in significant losses of fitness, especially of the critical endurance components necessary for success in multisport. The time required to regain previous levels depends on how intensive and extensive the down time was. From experience, it appears that a very fit athlete can count on the return to competitive form taking about twice as long as the break lasted.

INDIVIDUALITY

From the training principles discussed so far, it appears that science has everything neatly measured and packaged. It isn't so. The problem is that research results are based on averages within given groups of subjects. What the reported conclusions don't usually tell us is that some subjects responded quite well, but others failed to improve much at all. One study, for example, looked at the response of aerobic capacity to a standard exercise protocol. The average improvement was 14 percent, but one subject only boosted his aerobic capacity by 4 percent while another saw a whopping 40-percent increase.

Individuality is the most important principle.

The most important principle to remember is that we're all individuals when it comes to training. Some of us are slow responders, what the body builders call "hard gainers," and others are fast responders. Given the same workouts, the same number of weeks of training, and the exact same starting fitness levels, it's unlikely that two athletes will achieve the same degree of performance. This difference is more than likely a result of genetics.

Training must meet the exact needs of the athlete.

This is why triathletes and duathletes cannot simply duplicate the training programs of others. No matter how good the program is, it can't meet everyone's needs to the same extent. Not only will the physiological responses to a shared program vary, but since each athlete has unique strengths and weaknesses, what one person really needs to work on the most, the other may already have in abundance.

Keep in mind, however, that the various fitness parameters of all multisport athletes theoretically may be represented by a bell-shaped curve. In the middle of the curve are those who are "average" for any specific performance measure. To the left of center are those who are low in the quality; those to the right end are high in it. Chances are

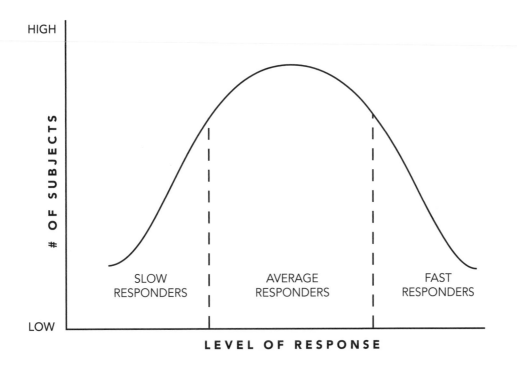

Figure 3.2
*Theoretical bell-shaped curve
indicating level of response to
a given training stimulus.*

good that you fall into the average group in any particular area of physiology. But don't count on it. Knowing yourself is an important tenet of training. Figure 3.2 illustrates the bell-shaped curve.

PEAKING

Coming to a fitness peak at just the right times in the season is the ultimate reason for training. Creating that moment when racing seems effortless makes months of hard work and sweat worth it. Yet few athletes ever experience such a fitness high. Even fewer know how to create it.

Most multisport athletes believe that peaking is as simple as reducing the work load for a few days before a big race. There's more to it than that. In fact, such a "taper" will not produce a true fitness peak: The athlete is unlikely to be rested, let alone at the apex of his or her potential.

When a true peak comes about, you will experience several physical changes that combine to create a performance that borders on astonishing. These changes include increased leg power, reduced lactic acid production, increased blood volume, a greater red blood cell concentration and increased fuel storage. Top these physical transformations with sharper mental skills such as concentration, confidence and motivation, and you are truly in top race form. All of this and no illegal drugs are needed.

Brief interludes of peak performance can be mapped out weeks in advance if you are willing to train in a highly structured manner and then cut back on training for sev-

**Peaking produces
greater fitness.**

Peak periods can be predicted.

eral days. The problem is that few serious multisport triathletes are willing to reduce their training for that long for fear of losing fitness. Many have become so familiar with the feeling of chronic fatigue that even a small reduction in training feels like a lot.

In the last fifteen years there have been numerous scientific studies of the peaking process. The following concepts have emerged from this research and are applicable to peaking for a triathlon or duathlon.

TAPER 10-17 DAYS

Taper length varies.

The exact length of the taper depends on two elements: how fit you are coming into it, and the nature of the race for which you're peaking. If you have a great base of fitness — meaning endurance, strength and speed are at high levels — taper longer than if your fitness level is low. The more unfit you are, the more important it is to continue training and creating higher levels of fitness until perhaps as little as ten days before the big race. Since it takes about ten days to realize the full benefits of a given workout, training with a high work load beyond the tenth day prior to the event will produce no additional fitness.

Deciding how fit you are is a subjective call. If you err, make it on the side of allowing too much taper time.

The longer the race is for which you are tapering, the longer the taper should be. An Ironman-distance race needs a longer taper than a sprint-distance event. This, in part, is to allow time for accumulated fatigue and possible muscle damage to completely improve.

REDUCE VOLUME

Big cutbacks necessary.

If you're tapering for seventeen days, reduce each week's volume by about 20 percent of the previous week. A two-week taper involves cutting back on volume by about 30 percent each week. For a ten-day taper, cut volume by 50 percent for the entire period.

MAINTAIN FREQUENCY

Maintain frequency to maintain "feel."

In reducing volume, you are better off to cut back on the number of hours you train each day rather than the number of weekly workouts. Reducing how often you swim, ride or run can cause a loss of "feel." You may not seem as smooth and comfortable in the movements of the sport as you normally do. It's probably best to keep a minimum of two or three workouts in each sport weekly during the taper period.

MAINTAIN INTENSITY

High intensity training is the most potent stimulus for both improving and maintaining fitness. Two race-intensity workouts weekly is all the stimulus needed at this point in the season to peak your fitness. One of these could be a tune-up race on the weekend or a combined swim-bike-run workout that simulates a portion of the race. The other should focus on your greatest weakness for the target race. For example, if climbing is what you are most worried about, do a hill workout at mid-week. The intensity of these key workouts should closely simulate the effort you expect in the race.

Simulate race effort.

OTHERWISE, TRAIN EASILY

All other workouts should be easy enough to allow for recovery. Work on swim skills, ride in the small chainring and run slowly. By taking it easy you will come into the two race-effort weekly workouts fully rested. Rest is the key to greater fitness at this time both because it allows the body to absorb the stress you have been placing on it, and because it results in more intense workouts when the time is right.

All other workouts are low intensity.

Such a peaking process should only be done two or three times in a season. Each of these peaks could last four to six weeks by doing a race or simulation and an intense workout each week. Eventually there will be an erosion of aerobic fitness necessitating a return to more endurance training. At that point the build up to the next peak begins.

Peak two or three times a year at most.

PERIODIZATION

Scientific conclusions and concepts are the easy part; putting it all together into an effective training plan that brings you into peak form for the most important races is where the rubber meets the road. Multisport success, or lack of it, is determined by how the stresses of frequency, duration and intensity are blended into a comprehensive plan while also taking into consideration the training principles of progressive overload, specificity, reversibility and individuality. Exactly how you should do this is beyond the ability of science to determine as there are many variables. Consequently, at this point we begin to move away from hard-core science and into the realm of opinion.

TRAINING SYSTEMS

Whether or not they even think about it, all athletes follow a training system of some type just by the mere fact that their workouts progress from day to day. The three most common training programs used by athletes are random, mixed and periodization.

In random training the athlete does whatever he or she feels like every day. Little or no forethought goes into the decision, and the weather and training partners frequently dictate the workout. This method is common for the strictly recreational athlete who has no concern with performance beyond simply participating and finishing. Beyond resting for a couple of days before, peaking for races is nonexistent, workouts are frequently too hard and high levels of fitness are seldom achieved. Random training is common among novices and is appropriate at this level as the new multisport athlete explores the world of training. But if growth is to occur, this method must be abandoned after the first year.

Random training is unpredictable.

Mixed training represents an improvement over random training as the athlete generally gives more thought as to what to do on a daily basis. Training this way means doing all types of workouts, such as endurance, intervals, hills and steady state, every week throughout the year. Rest breaks may or may not be planned. If they aren't routinely included, the mixed trainer is a candidate for overtraining. Even if rest is inserted, following such a program often leads to a belief that fitness must progress linearly throughout the season with the workouts becoming progressively harder every week often resulting in a severe case of overtraining. Boredom, low motivation and burnout are also common with this type of training as each week becomes a reflection of the previous one. Although peaking is difficult with mixed training, many athletes perform well when training this way.

Overtraining is common with mixed training.

Periodization is a training concept in which the year is divided into periods with each having a specific aspect of fitness to improve while maintaining the gains made in previous periods. It has become such a standard among serious athletes in all sports that it is often mistakenly referred to as a *principle* of training. Even though it is quite effective in producing fitness peaks at the right times while avoiding overtraining and burnout, it is not the only path to excellence. Training by following the concepts of periodization is, however, the most likely way to achieve athletic success.

Periodization is used by most successful athletes.

PERIODIZATION THEORY

In the late 1940s Soviet sports scientists discovered that athletic performance was improved by varying the training stresses throughout the year rather than maintaining a constant training focus as in mixed training. This led to dividing the year into multiweek periods with the stresses changing in some way with each new period. The East Germans and Romanians further developed this concept by establishing goals for the various periods and the system of "periodization" was born.

Periodization discovered by Soviets.

In the 1960s, Tudor Bompa, on the faculty of the Romanian Institute of Sport, so refined the concept of that he became known as the "father of periodization." This system was so effective that Eastern Bloc countries dominated world competition for three decades by using it. Dr. Bompa's seminal work, *Theory and Methodology of Training* (Kendall/Hunt, 1983), introduced Western athletes to this training system in the early

1980s. A decade earlier, however, a handful of European and American athletes studied the training methods of their Eastern Bloc competitors, adopted periodization, and challenged the superiority of Soviet, East German and Romanian athletes.

Tudor Bompa's contribution to periodization.

Periodization means more than simply dividing the year into periods. It carefully employs the training principles discussed earlier. The basic premise of all periodization programs is that training should progress from general to specific (principle of specificity), and always emphasize the unique needs of the athlete (principle of individuality). For example, early in the season an athlete needing greater cycling strength may work with weights to develop general fitness. Later in the season, as the first important races approach, more time is spent riding in the hills while simulating race intensities, and less time is devoted to weights. Figure 3.3 illustrates this concept.

Principles of specificity and individuality applied.

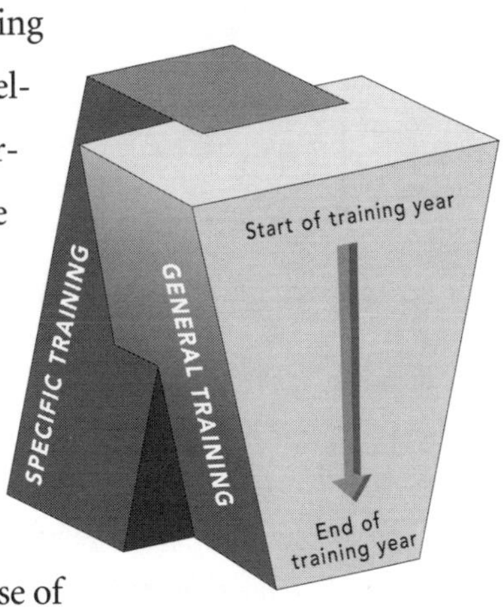

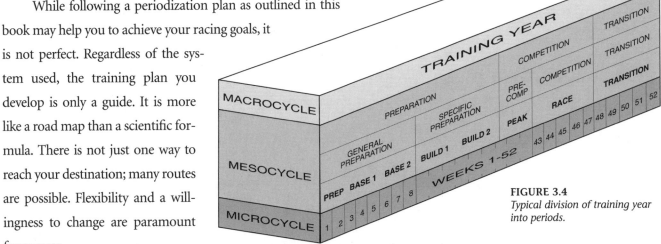

FIGURE 3.3
General to specific training emphasis throughout the training year.

Of course, periodization also goes well beyond simply training more specifically throughout the year. It also involves arranging the workouts in such a way that elements of fitness achieved in an earlier phase of training are maintained (principle of reversibility) while new ones are addressed and gradually improved (principle of progressive overload). Small changes are introduced into workouts typically during three- to eight-week periods. The targeted physiological system gradually becomes more fit with such a pattern of change and is then maintained as a new system is targeted.

Principles of reversibility and progressive overload applied.

Figure 3.4 shows how the training year is divided into periods and Figure 3.5 represents a theoretical development of fitness as a result.

While following a periodization plan as outlined in this book may help you to achieve your racing goals, it is not perfect. Regardless of the system used, the training plan you develop is only a guide. It is more like a road map than a scientific formula. There is not just one way to reach your destination; many routes are possible. Flexibility and a willingness to change are paramount for success.

FIGURE 3.4
Typical division of training year into periods.

FIGURE 3.5
A simple periodization plan to produce a fitness peak by varying volume and intensity

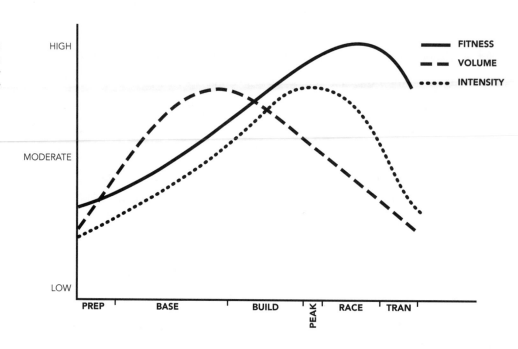

REFERENCES

Bompa, T. 1988. Physiological intensity values employed to plan endurance training. *New Studies in Athletics* 3 (4): 37-52.

Bompa, T. 1983. *Theory and Methodology of Training*. Dubuque, IA: Kendall/Hunt.

Brynteson, P. and W.E. Sinning. 1973. The effects of training frequencies on the retention of cardiovascular fitness. *Medicine and Science in Sports and Exercise* 5: 29-33.

Costill, D.L., et al. 1985. Effects of reduced training on muscular power in swimmers. *Physician and Sports Medicine* 13 (2) : 94-101.

Costill, D.L., et al. 1991. Adaptations to swimming training: Influence of training volume. *Medicine and Science in Sports and Exercise* 23: 371-377.

Coyle, E.F., et al. 1984. Time course of loss of adaptations after stopping prolonged intense endurance training. *Journal of Applied Physiology* 57: 1857.

Daniels, J. 1989. Training distance runners — A primer. *Sports Science Exchange* 1 (11) : 1-4.

Fitts, R.H., et al. 1989. Effect of swim-exercise training on human muscle fiber function. *Journal of Applied Physiology* 66: 465-475.

Kearney, J.T. 1996. Training the Olympic Athlete. *The Scientific American*, June: 52-63.

Hickson, R.C., et al. 1985. Reduced training intensities and loss of aerobic power, endurance, and cardiac growth. *Journal of Applied Physiology* 58:492-499.

Houmard, J.A., et al. 1990. Reduced training maintains performance in distance runners. *International Journal of Sports Medicine* 11: 46-51.

Houmard, J.A., et al. 1994. The effects of taper on performance in distance runners.

Medicine and Science in Sports and Exercise 26 (5): 624-631.

Matveyev, L. 1977. *Fundamentals of Sports Training.* Moscow: Progress Publishers.

Neufer, P.D., et al. 1987. Effects of reduced training on muscular strength and endurance in competitive swimmers. *Medicine and Science in Sports and Exercise* 19: 486-490.

Velikorodnih, Y., et al. 1986. The marathon (precompetitive preparation). *Soviet Sport Review* 22 (3): 125-128.

Wenger, H.A. and G.J. Bell. 1986. The interactions of intensity, frequency, and duration of exercise training in altering cardiorespiratory fitness. *Sports Medicine* 3 (5): 346-356.

Wilber, R.L. and R.J. Moffatt. 1994. Physiological and biochemical consequences of detraining in aerobically trained individuals. *Journal of Strength Conditioning Research* 8: 110.

Wilmore, J.H. and D.L. Costill. 1988. *Training for Sport and Activity: The Physiological Basis of the Conditioning Process.* Champaign, IL: Human Kinetics.

INTENSITY

*"Simply put, the most profound training
responses will occur when you train faster."*

— RICK NILES

Multisport athletes often place high emphasis on volume and pay scant attention to intensity. That's too bad since it's intensity, rather than volume, that has the potential to lift fitness to the highest levels. For example, in a study of runners done in Germany in 1995, four weeks of increased intensity — while volume held constant — produced significant performance gains, but four weeks of increasing volume as intensity remained unchanged led to performance stagnation. In this study, fitness was measured as time to exhaustion in a steady treadmill run, and speed at approximate 15 kilometers and marathon paces. All three measures significantly improved after four weeks of high intensity, but high volume improved only the marathon pace — and by a slight margin at that.

It isn't the miles; it's what you do with the miles.

This is not to say that training volume is unimportant and that low mileage is the way to achieve peak performance. For each athlete there is a correct blend of volume and intensity that must be discovered, largely through trial and error. This is the principle of individualization described in the previous chapter. Later chapters will help you determine what is an appropriate volume and how much intensity to include in training. For now, however, our purpose is to better understand high-intensity training.

Volume and intensity are individual matters.

FIGHTING FATIGUE

The word "fitness" has frequently appeared on these pages, but until now there's been no attempt to define it. Before going any further, it may be a good idea to do so. Fitness is best defined in terms of the activity for which one is preparing. For example, a body builder may be just as fit as a marathon runner, only in a different way. When it comes to endurance events such as triathlon and duathlon, fitness is the ability to resist or delay fatigue at a desired speed. Reduced fatigue means faster race times at the same effort. So for the purposes of this book, we'll define fitness in terms of limiting fatigue.

Fitness is the ability to resist fatigue.

The reason we train, then, is to reduce the effects of fatigue that accompany maximal effort. That sounds simple enough, but there are at least three physiological causes of fatigue that slow the endurance athlete:

- the accumulation of lactic acid in the muscles and blood,

The causes of fatigue.

- the depletion of carbohydrate-based fuel stored in the muscles (glycogen) and blood (glucose), and

- failure of the muscles' contractile mechanisms.

A scientifically based training program improves fitness by stressing the systems associated with these causes of fatigue. The following is a brief summary of how training improves resistance to each of these fatigue causes.

BUILD UP OF LACTIC ACID

To produce energy for movement, the muscles primarily use fat and carbohydrate for fuel. When carbohydrate — which is the sugar-based fuel source — breaks down, lactic acid is produced in the muscles. As it seeps out of the muscle cell and into the blood, hydrogen ions are released and the resulting salt is called "lactate." As the intensity of exercise increases, the amount of lactate also increases. At low levels of production, the body efficiently removes and recycles lactate. Even while you are reading this page, lactate is appearing in the blood, but is rapidly removed.

Lactic acid results from the breakdown of carbohydrate.

The level of exertion at which the body shifts from aerobic (light breathing) to anaerobic (labored breathing) is marked by such rapid lactate production that the body can't keep up with its removal, and lactate begins to accumulate in the blood interfering with energy production and muscular contractions thus causing fatigue. This type of fatigue occurs in very short, high-intensity races such as sprint triathlons, and then only during near-maximal efforts such as a finishing kick or a short hill climb.

This is not a major cause of fatigue in most multisport races. If, however, you compete primarily in short events, it may be a limiter for you. The way to improve both the body's ability to remove lactate and your tolerance of it is with short, high-intensity efforts followed by long recoveries. The specifics of this type of training will be discussed in later chapters.

DEPLETION OF FUEL

Fat is the primary source of fuel at low levels of effort such as a long, slow bike ride. As the intensity of exercise increases, the body increasingly turns to carbohydrate for fuel, and fat usage diminishes (see Figure 4.1). Carbohydrate is stored in the muscles and liver as glycogen and is available in the blood as glucose. A well-nourished athlete will sock away between 1500 and 2000 calories of combined glycogen and glucose, depending on body size and fitness level, with about 75 percent of this in the muscles. While competing in an international-distance race (1500 meter swim, 40km bike, 10km run) a triathlete may burn 1000 calories per hour with about 650 of them coming from carbohydrate. At this rate, without using a sports drink, it is easy to see that glucose and glycogen may be challenged before the finish resulting in a "DNF" (did not finish).

The body has limited stores of carbohydrate.

This is a critical cause of fatigue for the multisport athlete that must be addressed in training. Moderately hard workouts done up to the highest level of aerobic intensity without going deeply anaerobic are quite effective

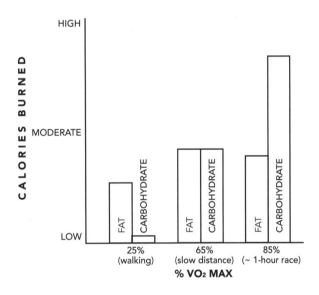

FIGURE 4.1
Relative contribution of fat and carbohydrate (glycogen and glucose) to exercise fuel at three levels of aerobic capacity (VO_2 max).

for teaching the body to conserve glycogen and glucose while becoming more proficient at using fat for fuel. In addition, training at paces similar to what is expected in races teaches the muscles to work more economically, thus sparing precious carbohydrate. Diet may also have an effect on the ratio of fat and carbohydrate used. This is further discussed in Chapter 16.

This type of fatigue is central to training.

FAILURE OF MUSCLES

The exact mechanism that results in the failure of muscles to continue contractions is unknown, but it is probably related to either chemical failure at the point where the nervous system connects with the muscles, or to a protective mechanism in the central nervous system meant to prevent muscular damage.

Exercising at high intensities may fortify the body against muscle failure by training the nervous system to call on more of its muscles for endurance activities. At higher

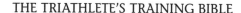

levels of intensity, as in intervals, more fast-twitch muscles are recruited than when exercising at low intensity, as in long, slow workouts. Fast-twitch muscles contract quickly and need a long time to recover. They are best for sprinting, but by training at moderately high effort, some of these muscles take on the characteristics of slow-twitch, or endurance, muscles allowing the athlete to continue exercising longer.

Fast-twitch muscles take on slow-twitch characteristics.

UNDERSTANDING INTENSITY

To understand how to intelligently use intensity in your training, it's important to grasp the concept of lactate threshold. A few paragraphs back you learned that lactic acid is produced from the breakdown of carbohydrate and becomes lactate that builds up in the blood interfering with muscle contraction. The level of intensity at which accumulation of lactate begins is called the "lactate threshold." This is a critical event. An analogy may help to understand this important concept.

Imagine slowly pouring water into a paper cup that has a hole in the bottom allowing the water to run out as fast as it goes in. This is what happens to lactate in the blood at low levels of exertion. By pouring faster, there comes a rate at which the water goes in faster than it goes out, and so the cup begins to fill. This is similar to what happens with lactate in your blood stream during exercise of increasing intensity. The point at which the water first began to accumulate is analogous to the lactate threshold (LT). You may have also seen the term "anaerobic threshold" used to describe this concept.

Lactate threshold is the point at which lactate accumulates.

By swimming, cycling or running at near the LT, muscular-endurance training improves the body's ability to process lactate while also teaching the muscles to conserve precious glycogen and glucose fuel sources. In addition, the muscles' contractile mechanisms become more resistant to fatigue. The result of this type of training is an increase in your speed at and near LT. Later on you will learn the details of how to do these workouts.

Another significant use of lactate threshold is as an intensity "landmark." Exercising below LT, working aerobically, is relatively easy and may be continued for hours, depending on fitness. But the duration of the workout or race is greatly reduced when exercising above LT, or exercising anaerobically. LT is such a critical point that we can easily describe how intense the workout is in relation to it just as we did by using the terms aerobic and anaerobic. The next section offers a system for categorizing intensity into zones based on LT. The following chapter will describe how you can find your lactate threshold.

While all of this may sound simple and straight forward, your LT remains, at best, an estimate even when it's determined in a lab by scientists using state-of-the-art equipment and procedures. One reason for this inability to tightly define LT is that it's a moving target. It drifts down during workouts due to weariness and increasing body temperature. It can even vary on a daily basis due to fatigue, an altered diet and changing environmental conditions. This is yet another reason why training is as much art as science.

INTENSITY ZONES

Energy production from fat and carbohydrate, and the efficient conservation of fuel is at the heart of training for multisport. Each workout you do during the year contributes to, or detracts from, this purpose. By varying the three stresses of frequency, duration and, especially, intensity, certain benefits accrue. The following are the six workout intensity zones used in this book regardless of the measuring technique, a summary of what each involves and their benefits. All zone 5 intensities are anaerobic; zones 1 through 4 are aerobic.

> **The six workout intensity zones.**

• **Recovery (Zone 1)** As the name implies, these are the easiest workouts, and the ones that help fit and experienced athletes rejuvenate the body following hard workouts, or periods of difficult training. Intensity is quite low, well below the lactate threshold. Inexperienced athletes, or those with low fitness levels, generally recover sooner by not training, rather than exercising easily. This is the intensity most often used during the recovery periods in an interval workout.

> **Recovery training depends on the individual.**

• **Extensive endurance (Zone 2)** Long, endurance workouts are common at this intensity. Aerobic endurance is built and eventually maintained by exercising at this "conversational" effort. Lactate production is low enough to allow extensive, although comfortable, training sessions to the limits of the athlete's aerobic endurance and slightly beyond. Slow twitch, endurance muscles become stronger, more capable of using oxygen to produce energy while learning to conserve glycogen and glucose. Extensive endurance is the most commonly used intensity by the multisport athlete.

> **Extensive endurance is the most commonly used.**

• **Intensive endurance (Zone 3)** At this slightly higher intensity, lactate production rises above the previous levels as more fast-twitch muscles are called on to support the work of the slow-twitch muscles. Training in this zone is employed primarily in the early preparation or base period, and after that is avoided in favor of the next intensity.

> **Intensive endurance is limited to certain times of the season.**

• **Threshold (Zones 4 and 5a)** Other than extensive endurance, threshold intensity is perhaps the most important training zone for the multisport athlete. This effort brings the athlete to just below or slightly above the lactate threshold, so long durations at this intensity are measured in minutes, not hours. Since work is now maximally aerobic, the slow-twitch muscles and energy production systems are highly stressed. A significant

> **The threshold zone is critical for the multisport athlete.**

portion of the work is now occurring anaerobically, and so improvements also accrue in the areas of lactate tolerance and removal, and fast-twitch muscle conversion to slow-twitch characteristics. Two zone designations are used here to separate above and below LT efforts.

Anaerobic endurance training is a leading cause of overtraining.

• **Anaerobic endurance (Zone 5b)** Intensity now exceeds the lactate threshold and so intervals are common with this type of training. Fast-twitch muscles contribute greatly to work at this level, stimulating their growth and development while also stressing the body's ability to tolerate and remove lactate. High volume of anaerobic endurance training is the most likely cause of overtraining in the serious athlete, so must be approached with caution and followed by extended recovery.

Power work is seldom needed.

• **Power (Zone 5c)** Power training has limited value for the multisport athlete, with the possible exception of those who are greatly lacking in the capacity to develop muscle mass or recruit fast-twitch muscles when speed is needed. Duration at this intensity is a matter of seconds, and maximal effort is required to realize a benefit. Power workouts use only a few short, explosive intervals separated by long recoveries. Two or more days of recovery are often necessary following one of these sessions as damage to muscle tissue is likely.

Figure 4.2 illustrates one way in which these six intensity zones are combined into an annual training program. This is meant only as an example of mixing intensities to build fitness. The actual blend you use to design a program depends on your individual strengths and weaknesses and the type of races for which you are training. In Chapters 7, 8 and 9 you will learn how to make these decisions.

FIGURE 4.2
Relative contributions of the six training intensities to the total annual training volume typical of triathlon. Actual intensity volumes will vary based on individual needs and the nature of the goal races.

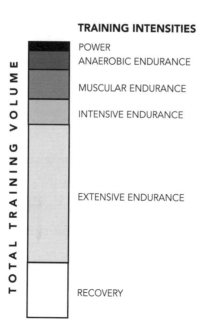

TRAINING INTENSITIES

POWER
ANAEROBIC ENDURANCE
MUSCULAR ENDURANCE
INTENSIVE ENDURANCE
EXTENSIVE ENDURANCE
RECOVERY

TOTAL TRAINING VOLUME

MEASURING INTENSITY

How do you know which intensity zone you are in? Due to the prevalence of heart-rate monitors in the last few years, endurance athletes have come to think of the heart as the best, and perhaps only, indicator of intensity. Such an exaggerated emphasis on heart rate has caused many to forget that it is not the heart rate that limits performance in races and training. As previously explained, fatigue occurs mostly in the muscles, not the cardiovascular system. The beating of the heart is merely one way to peek into the body to see what is happening. At best, heart rate is an indirect measure of intensity, and not a very sensitive one. There are others that should also be used whenever possible to measure how intensely you are swimming, biking and running. Just as with heart rate, each has shortcomings. By employing two or more every time you work out, you will accurately gauge intensity and reap the desired training benefits.

Heart rate is
over-emphasized.

• **Pace.** In the "old" days of triathlon (circa 1980), training intensity was based primarily on pace. "I ran five miles at a seven-minute pace," was a common way of describing a workout. We still use this method, but less importance is given to it. That's too bad, because it is an effective measure that is easily refined based on recent races or time trials.

Using standards — such as your average mile pace for a recent 10km race — allows you to easily define intensity. The problem, of course, is that when swimming or running you don't know intensity instantaneously, but have to wait until a given distance is covered, such as a pool lap or mileage marker, in order to determine pace. The exception is when riding and using a handlebar computer with a speed mode. This is not a perfect situation on the bike either, for wind and small hills have a tremendous effect on speed.

Determining intensity
from pace is based on
standard times.

For the experienced athlete, pace is still the best gauge of swimming intensity, and must also be a consideration in running workouts. For cycling it has less benefit. Tables 4.1 and 4.2 provide standards for the six training zones described above for swimming and running.

Pace is best for swimming.

• **Rating of perceived exertion (RPE).** The experienced athlete has a well-developed ability to assess the level of exertion based strictly on sensations emanating from the body's many systems. This perceived exertion is one of the best indicators of intensity, and is used by all athletes, whether they are consciously aware of it or not.

Perceived exertion is quantifiable using the Borg Rating of Perceived Exertion (RPE) scale, and is frequently used by scientists to determine at what level a subject is working. Many coaches and athletes also rely on RPE as the supreme gauge of effort. Borg's RPE is applicable to any sport. It's based on scale of six to twenty with six representing no exertion at all and twenty as maximum, all-out effort with absolutely nothing held in reserve. The scale of six to twenty was chosen because this range represents about 10 percent of the heart rates experienced by a moderately fit young to middle-aged person. In other words, a score of six (resting) should parallel a heart rate of about sixty beats per minute, and twenty (maximum) a pulse of two hundred. In reality, these numbers seldom equate so nicely since heart rate varies considerably between individuals.

RPE is the simplest way to
measure effort.

To use the Borg RPE scale, give an honest appraisal to the feelings of exertion you experience while working out, and assign it a number on the scale (see Table 4.3). As you

TABLE 4.1

Estimated swimming zones by 100-meter or 100-yard pace based on a 1000-meter or 1000-yard time trial.

Your time for 1000m/yds	Estimated swimming zones by 100m/yd pace (in min:sec)						
	1 zone	2 zone	3 zone	4 zone	5a zone	5b zone	5c zone
9:35-9:45	1:13+	1:09-1:12	1:04-1:08	1:01-1:03	:58-1:00	:54-:57	:53-max
9:46-9:55	1:15+	1:11-1:14	1:06-1:10	1:02-1:05	:59-1:01	:55-:58	:54-max
9:56-10:06	1:16+	1:12-1:15	1:07-1:11	1:03-1:06	1:00-1:02	:56-:59	:55-max
10:07-10:17	1:17+	1:13-1:16	1:08-1:12	1:04-1:07	1:01-1:03	:57-1:00	:56-max
10:18-10:28	1:18+	1:14-1:17	1:09-1:13	1:05-1:08	1:02-1:04	:58-1:01	:57-max
10:29-10:40	1:20+	1:15-1:19	1:10-1:14	1:06-1:09	1:03-1:05	:58-1:02	:57-max
10:41-10:53	1:22+	1:17-1:21	1:12-1:16	1:08-1:11	1:05-1:07	1:00-1:04	:59-max
10:54-11:06	1:23+	1:19-1:22	1:13-1:18	1:09-1:12	1:06-1:08	1:01-1:05	1:00-max
11:07-11:18	1:24+	1:20-1:23	1:14-1:19	1:10-1:13	1:07-1:09	1:02-1:06	1:01-max
11:19-11:32	1:26+	1:21-1:25	1:15-1:20	1:11-1:14	1:08-1:10	1:03-1:07	1:02-max
11:33-11:47	1:28+	1:23-1:27	1:17-1:22	1:13-1:16	1:10-1:12	1:05-1:09	1:04-max
11:48-12:03	1:29+	1:24-1:28	1:18-1:23	1:14-1:17	1:11-1:13	1:06-1:10	1:05-max
12:04-12:17	1:32+	1:26-1:31	1:20-1:25	1:16-1:19	1:13-1:15	1:07-1:12	1:06-max
12:18-12:30	1:33+	1:28-1:32	1:22-1:27	1:17-1:21	1:14-1:16	1:08-1:13	1:07-max
12:31-12:52	1:35+	1:30-1:34	1:24-1:29	1:19-1:23	1:16-1:18	1:10-1:15	1:09-max
12:53-13:02	1:38+	1:32-1:37	1:26-1:31	1:21-1:25	1:18-1:20	1:12-1:17	1:11-max
13:03-13:28	1:40+	1:34-1:39	1:28-1:33	1:23-1:27	1:20-1:22	1:14-1:19	1:13-max
13:29-13:47	1:41+	1:36-1:40	1:29-1:35	1:24-1:28	1:21-1:23	1:15-1:20	1:14-max
13:48-14:08	1:45+	1:39-1:44	1:32-1:38	1:27-1:31	1:23-1:26	1:17-1:22	1:16-max
14:09-14:30	1:46+	1:40-1:45	1:33-1:39	1:28-1:32	1:24-1:27	1:18-1:23	1:17-max
14:31-14:51	1:50+	1:44-1:49	1:36-1:43	1:31-1:35	1:27-1:30	1:21-1:26	1:20-max
14:52-15:13	1:52+	1:46-1:51	1:39-1:45	1:33-1:38	1:29-1:32	1:23-1:28	1:22-max
15:14-15:42	1:56+	1:49-1:55	1:42-1:48	1:36-1:41	1:32-1:35	1:25-1:31	1:24-max
15:43-16:08	1:58+	1:52-1:57	1:44-1:51	1:38-1:43	1:34-1:37	1:27-1:33	1:26-max
16:09-16:38	2:02+	1:55-2:01	1:47-1:54	1:41-1:46	1:37-1:40	1:30-1:36	1:29-max
16:39-17:06	2:04+	1:57-2:03	1:49-1:56	1:43-1:48	1:39-1:42	1:32-1:38	1:31-max
17:07-17:38	2:09+	2:02-2:08	1:53-2:01	1:47-1:52	1:43-1:46	1:35-1:42	1:34-max
17:39-18:12	2:13+	2:05-2:12	1:57-2:04	1:50-1:56	1:46-1:49	1:38-1:45	1:37-max
18:13-18:48	2:18+	2:10-2:17	2:01-2:09	1:54-2:00	1:50-1:53	1:42-1:49	1:41-max
18:49-19:26	2:21+	2:13-2:20	2:04-2:12	1:57-2:03	1:53-1:56	1:44-1:52	1:43-max
19:27-20:06	2:26+	2:18-2:25	2:08-2:17	2:01-2:07	1:56-2:00	1:48-1:55	1:47-max
20:07-20:50	2:31+	2:22-2:30	2:12-2:21	2:05-2:11	2:00-2:04	1:52-1:59	1:51-max
20:51-21:37	2:37+	2:28-2:36	2:18-2:27	2:10-2:17	2:05-2:09	1:56-2:04	1:55-max
21:38-22:27	2:42+	2:33-2:41	2:22-2:32	2:14-2:21	2:09-2:13	2:00-2:08	1:59-max
22:28-23:22	2:48+	2:38-2:47	2:27-2:37	2:19-2:26	2:14-2:18	2:04-2:13	2:03-max
23:23-24:31	2:55+	2:45-2:54	2:34-2:44	2:25-2:33	2:20-2:24	2:10-2:19	2:09-max
24:32-25:21	3:02+	2:52-3:01	2:40-2:51	2:31-2:39	2:25-2:30	2:15-2:24	2:14-max

TABLE 4.2

Estimated running zones by mile pace based on a 5km or 10km time in a running race (not triathlon split).

Your time for		Estimated running zones by mile pace (in min:sec)						
5km	10km	1 zone	2 zone	3 zone	4 zone	5a zone	5b zone	5c zone
14:15	30:00	6:38+	5:52-6:37	5:27-5:51	5:09-5:26	4:59-5:08	4:37-4:58	4:36-max
14:45	31:00	6:50+	6:02-6:49	5:37-6:01	5:18-5:36	5:07-5:17	4:45-5:06	4:44-max
15:15	32:00	7:02+	6:13-7:01	5:47-6:12	5:27-5:46	5:16-5:26	4:53-5:15	4:52-max
15:45	33:00	7:13+	6:23-7:12	5:56-6:22	5:36-5:55	5:25-5:35	5:01-5:24	5:00-max
16:10	34:00	7:25+	6:33-7:24	6:06-6:32	5:45-6:05	5:34-5:44	5:10-5:33	5:07-max
16:45	35:00	7:36+	6:43-7:35	6:15-6:42	5:54-6:14	5:42-5:53	5:18-5:41	5:17-max
17:07	36:00	7:48+	6:54-7:47	6:25-6:53	6:03-6:24	5:51-6:02	5:26-5:50	5:25-max
17:35	37:00	8:00+	7:04-7:59	6:34-7:03	6:12-6:33	6:00-6:11	5:34-5:59	5:33-max
18:05	38:00	8:11+	7:14-8:10	6:44-7:13	6:21-6:43	6:09-6:20	5:42-6:08	5:41-max
18:30	39:00	8:23+	7:24-8:22	6:53-7:23	6:30-6:52	6:17-6:29	5:50-6:16	5:49-max
19:00	40:00	8:34+	7:35-8:33	7:03-7:34	6:39-7:02	6:26-6:38	5:58-6:25	5:57-max
19:30	41:00	8:46+	7:45-8:45	7:12-7:44	6:48-7:11	6:35-6:47	6:06-6:34	6:05-max
19:55	42:00	8:58+	7:55-8:57	7:22-7:54	6:57-7:21	6:44-6:56	6:14-6:43	6:13-max
20:25	43:00	9:09+	8:05-9:08	7:31-8:04	7:06-7:30	6:52-7:05	6:22-6:51	6:21-max
20:50	44:00	9:21+	8:16-9:20	7:41-8:15	7:15-7:40	7:01-7:14	6:31-7:00	6:30-max
21:20	45:00	9:32+	8:26-9:31	7:51-8:25	7:24-7:50	7:10-7:23	6:39-7:09	6:38-max
21:50	46:00	9:44+	8:36-9:43	8:00-8:35	7:33-7:59	7:18-7:32	6:47-7:17	6:46-max
22:15	47:00	9:56+	8:47-9:55	8:10-8:46	7:42-8:09	7:27-7:41	6:55-7:26	6:54-max
22:42	48:00	10:07+	8:57-10:06	8:19-8:56	7:51-8:18	7:36-7:50	7:03-7:35	7:02-max
23:10	49:00	10:19+	9:07-10:18	8:29-9:06	8:00-8:28	7:45-7:59	7:11-7:44	7:10-max
23:38	50:00	10:31+	9:17-10:30	8:38-9:16	8:09-8:37	7:53-8:08	7:19-7:52	7:18-max
24:05	51:00	10:42+	9:28-10:41	8:48-9:27	8:18-8:47	8:02-8:17	7:27-8:01	7:26-max
24:35	52:00	10:54+	9:38-10:53	8:57-9:37	8:27-8:56	8:11-8:26	7:35-8:10	7:34-max
25:00	53:00	11:05+	9:48-11:04	9:07-9:47	8:36-9:06	8:20-8:35	7:43-8:19	7:42-max
25:25	54:00	11:17+	9:58-11:16	9:16-9:57	8:45-9:15	8:28-8:44	7:52-8:27	7:51-max
25:55	55:00	11:29+	10:09-11:28	9:26-10:08	8:54-9:25	8:37-8:53	8:00-8:36	7:59-max
26:30	56:00	11:40+	10:19-11:39	9:36-10:18	9:03-9:35	8:46-9:02	8:08-8:45	8:07-max
26:50	57:00	11:52+	10:29-11:51	9:45-10:28	9:12-9:44	8:54-9:11	8:16-8:53	8:15-max
27:20	58:00	12:03+	10:39-12:02	9:55-10:38	9:21-9:54	9:03-9:20	8:24-9:02	8:23-max
27:45	59:00	12:15+	10:50-12:14	10:04-10:49	9:30-10:03	9:12-9:29	8:32-9:11	8:31-max
28:15	60:00	12:27+	11:00-12:26	10:14-10:59	9:39-10:13	9:21-9:38	8:40-9:20	8:39-max

increase or decrease the pace, RPE will also change reflecting greater or lesser stress. The major problem when using RPE is the tendency of athletes to underestimate their exertion level to appear tough or brave. Moral value judgments should not accompany effort decisions. It should be a cold and scientific endeavor.

• **Power.** Power = force x distance/time. In everyday language, power is the ability to apply your muscular strength. On the bike, if you are able to increase the gear size while cadence remains constant, power goes up. Or, with the same gear size you turn the cranks faster, power also increases. Currently it's not feasible to directly measure power in swimming or running, although the day may come when it is, probably sooner for running. A few multisport athletes, however, are now using power to regulate cycling intensity.

Power is the quick application of strength.

Power is more closely related to speed than is any other measure discussed here, and is, therefore, a good predictor of performance. The more power you can generate, the higher the likelihood that you will get good results in races. For example, according to one study, the amount of power generated during a two-minute test is a better indicator of time-trial ability on the bike than is aerobic capacity (VO_2 max).

TABLE 4.3

The Borg Rating of Perceived Exertion (RPE) Scale and training zones.

	Zone	RPE	Description
1	Recovery	6	
1	Recovery	7	Very, very light
1	Recovery	8	
2	Extensive endurance	9	Very light
2	Extensive endurance	10	
2	Extensive endurance	11	Fairly light
3	Intensive endurance	12	
3	Intensive endurance	13	Somewhat hard
3	Intensive endurance	14	
4	Threshold	15	Hard
5a	Threshold	16	
5b	Anaerobic endurance	17	Very hard
5b	Anaerobic endurance	18	
5c	Power	19	Very, very hard
5c	Power	20	

The problem in measuring intensity using power
...devices currently
...er (800/522-
...ermany: 011-
...indoor train-
...ner. The simi-
...ntendo system
...ar control unit
...rses while rac-
...In addition to
...ed, heart rate,
...average power
...out $1100, the
...any serious ath-
...ower training.

The RacerMate CompuTrainer makes indoor training with power possible.

...echnik) is a crank and chain ring assembly, and so
...he road or indoors. On a handlebar unit similar to
...heart rate, cadence, speed, time, distance, average
...eed. The SRM is also capable of downloading into
...models of SRM available for road bikes. The stan-
...us-or-minus 5 watts and sells for about $2400. The

The SRM Powermeter shows power on the road.

...within
...arger stor-
...ut $4100. In the
...to see competition
...falling prices make train-
ing with power on the bike less expensive.

Training with power, just as training with pace, RPE or a heart rate monitor, requires training zones based on a per-

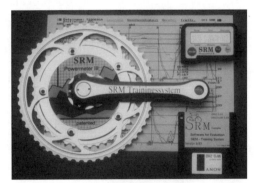

The SRM Powermeter displays on a handlebar control unit and records for later down- loading to a computer power, heart rate, cadence, speed, time, distance, average heart rate, average power, average cadence and average speed. Such devices are the wave of the future and will change the way cyclists train.

sonal standard. Power achieved at lactate threshold serves as such a standard. The next chapter will describe how to determine your lactate threshold power (LTP). The unit of measurement in which power is usually expressed is the "watt," named after James Watt, who invented the steam engine in 1769. Table 4.4 suggests power training zones based on LTP for use with the CompuTrainer or SRM.

		TABLE 4.4

Estimated power training zones for cycling based on lactate threshold power (LTP)

	Zone	Watts as % of LTP
1	Recovery	<40%
2	Extensive endurance	40-79%
3	Intensive endurance	80-87%
4	Sub-threshold	88-99%
5a	Super-threshold	100-104%
5b	Anaerobic endurance	105-149%
5c	Power	150%+

• **Lactate.** If the lactate threshold is such an important phenomenon, why not simply measure blood lactate to gauge intensity? Until recently, it wasn't practical to check lactate levels in the real world of multisport athletes at the pool or on the road. The only equipment available required electricity, was expensive and cumbersome, and better suited for lab use. A couple of years ago, however, the AccuSport Portable Lactate Analyzer (888/474-5239) was introduced at about $500 making it possible to measure lactate from a drop of blood drawn from the finger. Such testing is still rather sophisticated and is more reliable in the hands of an experienced technician or coach.

Lactate can now be measured in workouts.

Lactate measurement does not provide instantaneous feedback in the same way that power, pace and RPE do since a minute or two are needed to draw and analyze the blood.

The AccuSport portable lactate analyzer.

At a couple of dollars per analysis, frequent measurement, even with a portable analyzer, is impractical. So lactate measurement is best used in a testing situation such as confirming lactate threshold, measuring improvement, determining economy of movement or setting up a bike for optimal efficiency.

• **Heart rate.** In the 1980s, the introduction of the wireless heart-rate monitor brought a profound change in the way athletes in all sports trained. Until then, since intensity could not be directly measured, volume was generally considered the key to race fitness. Using the monitor taught us that by varying intensity across a broad spectrum of heart rates, great benefits were possible. We learned how to improve recovery by using the monitor to slow us down. It also taught us that more intense workouts were often possible. The monitor not only allowed us to accurately determine intensity, but also provided a way of measuring progress and gauging effort in a long race such as the Ironman.

At first the heart-rate monitor was a "gee whiz" toy. It was fun to see what happened to heart rate under varying conditions, but the numbers didn't really mean much. By the late 1980s, some coaches and athletes were starting to get a handle on effective ways of employing heart rate in training. Today nearly all multisport athletes have heart-rate monitors, and most are fairly sophisticated in their use.

As previously mentioned, the problem now is that heart rate-based training has become so pervasive that athletes too often believe that heart rate is the determining factor in how they train and race. Too many have become slaves to their heart-rate monitors, and other skills for measuring intensity are fading. Heart rate is but one window through which we can peek into the exercising body. Relying on it to the exclusion of all other measures of intensity can be as detrimental to your training as not having any gauge of effort at all.

On the other hand, when used intelligently the heart-rate monitor can improve fitness and race performance. Sometimes low motivation, high enthusiasm, competition, loss of focus and poor judgment get in the way of smart training. At times like these the heart-rate monitor is like having a coach along for the workout. With a good working knowledge of heart rate and skill in using other intensity measures, mixed with a little common sense resulting from experience, a monitor can help determine if you're working too hard or not hard enough, if recovery is complete and how fitness is progressing. Later chapters will address these issues in detail.

Just as with the other measures of intensity discussed above, heart-rate training zones are best tied to the standard of lactate threshold. Often maximum heart rate is used for this, but that presents some problems. Attempting to achieve the highest heart rate possible in a workout requires extremely high motivation — as in a gun to the head. In addition, for some individuals, exercising at such an intensity may not be safe. LT is also a better indicator of what the body is experiencing, and is highly variable between athletes. For example, your LT heart rate (LTHR) may occur at 85 percent of maximum heart rate while another athlete's may happen at 92 percent. If both of you train at 90 percent of maximum, one is deeply anaerobic and working quite hard, but the other is cruising along mostly aerobically. Percentages of maximum heart rate just aren't as precise as basing zones on LTHR.

The heart-rate monitor changed training.

Over-reliance on heart rate is counterproductive.

Use LT to set training zones.

TABLE 4.5

Cycling Heart Rate Zones

Find your lactate threshold heart rate (bold) in the "5a Zone" column.
Read across to left and right for training zones.

1 Zone	2 Zone	3 Zone	4 Zone	5a Zone	5b Zone	5c Zone
	Extensive	Intensive	Sub-	Super-	Anaerobic	
Recovery	Endurance	Endurance	Threshold	Threshold	Endurance	Power
90-108	109-122	123-128	129-136	**137**-140	141-145	146-150
91-109	110-123	124-129	130-137	**138**-141	142-146	147-151
91-109	110-124	125-130	131-138	**139**-142	143-147	148-152
92-110	111-125	126-130	131-139	**140**-143	144-147	148-153
92-111	112-125	126-131	132-140	**141**-144	145-148	149-154
93-112	113-126	127-132	133-141	**142**-145	146-149	150-155
94-112	113-127	128-133	134-142	**143**-145	146-150	151-156
94-113	114-128	129-134	135-143	**144**-147	148-151	152-157
95-114	115-129	130-135	136-144	**145**-148	149-152	153-158
95-115	116-130	131-136	137-145	**146**-149	150-154	155-159
97-116	117-131	132-137	138-146	**147**-150	151-155	156-161
97-117	118-132	133-138	139-147	**148**-151	152-156	157-162
98-118	119-133	134-139	140-148	**149**-152	153-157	158-163
98-119	120-134	135-140	141-149	**150**-153	154-158	159-164
99-120	121-134	135-141	142-150	**151**-154	155-159	160-165
100-121	122-135	136-142	143-151	**152**-155	156-160	161-166
100-122	123-136	137-142	143-152	**153**-156	157-161	162-167
101-123	124-137	138-143	144-153	**154**-157	158-162	163-168
101-124	125-138	139-144	145-154	**155**-158	159-163	164-169
102-125	126-138	139-145	146-155	**156**-159	160-164	165-170
103-126	127-140	141-146	147-156	**157**-160	161-165	166-171
104-127	128-141	142-147	148-157	**158**-161	162-167	168-173
104-128	129-142	143-148	149-158	**159**-162	163-168	169-174
105-129	130-143	144-148	149-159	**160**-163	164-169	170-175
106-129	130-143	144-150	151-160	**161**-164	165-170	171-176
106-130	131-144	145-151	152-161	**162**-165	166-171	172-177
107-131	132-145	146-152	153-162	**163**-166	167-172	173-178
107-132	133-146	147-153	154-163	**164**-167	168-173	174-179
108-133	134-147	148-154	155-164	**165**-168	169-174	175-180
109-134	135-148	149-154	155-165	**166**-169	170-175	176-181
109-135	136-149	150-155	156-166	**167**-170	171-176	177-182
110-136	137-150	151-156	157-167	**168**-171	172-177	178-183
111-137	138-151	152-157	158-168	**169**-172	173-178	179-185
112-138	139-151	152-158	159-169	**170**-173	174-179	180-186
112-139	140-152	153-160	161-170	**171**-174	175-180	181-187
113-140	141-153	154-160	161-171	**172**-175	176-181	182-188
113-141	142-154	155-161	162-172	**173**-176	177-182	183-189
114-142	143-155	156-162	163-173	**174**-177	178-183	184-190
115-143	144-156	157-163	164-174	**175**-178	179-184	185-191
115-144	145-157	158-164	165-175	**176**-179	180-185	186-192
116-145	146-158	159-165	166-176	**177**-180	181-186	187-193
116-146	147-159	160-166	167-177	**178**-181	182-187	188-194
117-147	148-160	161-166	167-178	**179**-182	183-188	189-195
118-148	149-160	161-167	168-179	**180**-183	184-190	191-197
119-149	150-161	162-168	169-180	**181**-184	185-191	192-198
119-150	151-162	163-170	171-181	**182**-185	186-192	193-199
120-151	152-163	164-171	172-182	**183**-186	187-193	194-200
121-152	153-164	165-172	173-183	**184**-187	188-194	195-201
121-153	154-165	166-172	173-184	**185**-188	191-195	196-202
122-154	155-166	167-173	174-185	**186**-189	190-196	197-203
122-155	156-167	168-174	175-186	**187**-190	191-197	198-204
123-156	157-168	169-175	176-187	**188**-191	192-198	199-205
124-157	158-169	170-176	177-188	**189**-192	193-199	200-206
124-158	159-170	171-177	178-189	**190**-193	194-200	201-207
125-159	160-170	171-178	179-190	**191**-194	195-201	202-208
125-160	161-171	172-178	179-191	**192**-195	196-202	203-209
126-161	162-172	173-179	180-192	**193**-196	197-203	204-210
127-162	163-173	174-180	181-193	**194**-197	198-204	205-211
127-163	164-174	175-181	182-194	**195**-198	199-205	206-212

TABLE 4.6

Running Heart Rate Zones

Find your lactate threshold heart rate (bold) in the "5a Zone" column.
Read across to left and right for training zones.

1 Zone	2 Zone	3 Zone	4 Zone	5a Zone	5b Zone	5c Zone
Recovery	Extensive Endurance	Intensive Endurance	Sub-Threshold	Super-Threshold	Anaerobic Endurance	Power
93-119	120-126	127-133	134-139	**140**-143	144-149	150-156
94-119	120-127	128-134	135-140	**141**-144	145-150	151-157
95-120	121-129	130-135	136-141	**142**-145	146-151	152-158
95-121	122-130	131-136	137-142	**143**-146	147-152	153-159
96-122	123-131	132-137	138-143	**144**-147	148-153	154-160
96-123	124-132	133-138	139-144	**145**-148	149-154	155-161
97-124	125-133	134-139	140-145	**146**-149	150-155	156-162
97-124	125-134	135-140	141-146	**147**-150	151-156	157-163
98-125	126-135	136-141	142-147	**148**-151	152-157	158-164
99-126	127-135	136-142	143-148	**149**-152	153-158	159-165
99-127	128-136	137-143	144-149	**150**-153	154-158	159-166
100-128	129-137	138-144	145-150	**151**-154	155-159	160-167
100-129	130-138	139-145	146-151	**152**-155	156-160	161-168
101-130	131-139	140-146	147-152	**153**-156	157-161	162-169
102-131	132-140	141-147	148-153	**154**-157	158-162	163-170
103-131	132-141	142-148	149-154	**155**-158	159-164	165-172
103-132	133-142	143-149	150-155	**156**-159	160-165	166-173
104-133	134-143	144-150	151-156	**157**-160	161-166	167-174
105-134	135-143	144-151	152-157	**158**-161	162-167	168-175
105-135	136-144	145-152	153-158	**159**-162	163-168	169-176
106-136	137-145	146-153	154-159	**160**-163	164-169	170-177
106-136	137-146	147-154	155-160	**161**-164	165-170	171-178
107-137	138-147	148-155	156-161	**162**-165	166-171	172-179
108-138	139-148	149-155	156-162	**163**-166	167-172	173-180
109-139	140-149	150-156	157-163	**164**-167	168-174	175-182
109-140	141-150	151-157	158-164	**165**-168	169-175	176-183
110-141	142-151	152-158	159-165	**166**-169	170-176	177-184
111-141	142-152	153-159	160-166	**167**-170	171-177	178-185
111-142	143-153	154-160	161-167	**168**-171	172-178	179-186
112-143	144-154	155-161	162-168	**169**-172	173-179	180-187
112-144	145-155	156-162	163-169	**170**-173	174-179	180-188
113-145	146-156	157-163	164-170	**171**-174	175-180	181-189
114-145	146-156	157-164	165-171	**172**-175	176-182	183-191
115-146	147-157	158-165	166-172	**173**-176	177-183	184-192
115-147	148-157	158-166	167-173	**174**-177	178-184	185-193
116-148	149-158	159-167	168-174	**175**-178	179-185	186-194
117-149	150-159	160-168	169-175	**176**-179	180-186	187-195
117-150	151-160	161-169	170-176	**177**-180	181-187	188-196
118-151	152-161	162-170	171-177	**178**-181	182-188	189-197
118-152	153-162	163-171	172-178	**179**-182	183-189	190-198
119-153	154-163	164-172	173-179	**180**-183	184-190	191-199
120-154	155-164	165-173	174-180	**181**-184	185-192	193-201
121-154	155-165	166-174	175-181	**182**-185	186-193	194-202
121-155	156-166	167-175	176-182	**183**-186	187-194	195-203
122-156	157-167	168-176	177-183	**184**-187	188-195	196-204
123-157	158-168	169-177	178-184	**185**-188	189-196	197-205
123-158	159-169	170-178	179-185	**186**-189	190-197	198-206
124-159	160-170	171-179	180-186	**187**-190	191-198	199-207
124-159	160-170	171-179	180-187	**188**-191	192-199	200-208
125-160	161-171	172-180	181-188	**189**-192	193-200	201-209
126-161	152-172	173-181	182-189	**190**-193	194-201	202-210
126-162	163-173	174-182	183-190	**191**-194	195-201	202-211
127-163	164-174	175-183	184-191	**192**-195	196-202	203-212
127-164	165-175	176-184	185-192	**193**-196	197-203	204-213
128-165	166-176	177-185	186-193	**194**-197	198-204	205-214
129-165	166-177	178-186	187-194	**195**-198	199-205	206-215
129-166	167-178	179-187	188-195	**196**-199	200-206	207-216
130-167	168-178	179-188	189-196	**197**-198	199-207	208-217
130-168	169-179	180-189	190-197	**198**-201	202-208	209-218
131-169	170-180	181-190	191-198	**199**-202	203-209	210-219
132-170	171-181	182-191	192-199	**200**-203	204-210	211-220

Finding LTHR requires some precision, but don't let that scare you away. It's actually a simple procedure and is described in the next chapter.

Just as with lactate threshold, heart-rate zones vary by sport since there are differences in the amount of muscle used and the effects of gravity. For most triathletes, LTHR is highest for running and lowest for swimming with cycling in between. Lactate production also varies with the activity. This means that each sport must have its own set of heart-rate values. Tables 4.5 and 4.6 provide heart rate training zones for cycling and running. Swimming is not included since training with a heart-rate monitor is difficult in the water. Pace and RPE are the best measures of intensity for swimming.

Heart rate training zones vary by sport.

HIGH-INTENSITY TRAINING IN THE REAL WORLD

The road to fitness generally takes one of two routes. For the multisport athlete with lots of time, high volume may bring excellent performances. Pro triathletes and duathletes typically train twenty-five to thirty hours per week. The downside of such training is the risk of injury and exhaustion leading to overtraining. To deal with this problem, those who make triathlon their occupation often train in blocks of time greater than the seven-day week. Nine- or ten-day "weeks" allow them to space the workouts and recover.

For the athlete with a full-time job, a family, a home to maintain, and a myriad of other responsibilities, such volume and calendar manipulations are not an option. High intensity scheduled around a seven-day week is. But it's not risk-free as overtraining is just as likely, perhaps more so, when anaerobic workouts dominate the training routine in such a short period of time. There are limits to how many high-effort sessions can be managed in a week without eventually breaking down.

For most multisport athletes, high-intensity training, when used intelligently, offers the possibility of a breakthrough in fitness. Most can only do three or four of these break-through efforts in a week; more may lead to overtraining, injury, illness or burnout. The most important information you can learn about yourself as a serious triathlete is how many breakthroughs you can do in a week and how much recovery time is needed after them. Once this is determined, planning a week of training is a snap.

REFERENCES

Anderson, O. 1996. German study confirms major shifts in intensity work far better than big upswings in mileage. *Running Research News* 12 (9): 1-5.

Borg, G. 1985. *An Introduction to Borg's RPE-Scale.* Ithaca, NY: Mouvement Publications.

DiCarlo, L.J., et al. 1991. Peak heart rates during maximal running and swimming: Implications for exercise prescription. *International Journal of Sports Medicine* 12: 309-312.

Dunbar, C.C., et al. 1992. The validity of regulating exercise intensity by ratings of perceived exertion. *Medicine and Science in Sports and Exercise* 24: 94-99.

Friel, J. 1996. *The Cyclist's Training Bible.* Boulder, CO: VeloPress.

Gibbons, E.S. 1987. The significance of anaerobic threshold in exercise prescription. *Journal of Sports Medicine* 27: 357-361.

Goforth, H.W., et al. 1994. Simultaneous enhancement of aerobic and anaerobic capacity. *Medicine and Science in Sports and Exercise* 26 (5): 171.

Hagberg, J.M. 1984. Physiological implications of the lactate threshold. *International Journal of Sports Medicine* 5: 106-109.

Ivy, J.L., et al. 1980. Muscle respiratory capacity and fiber type as determinants of the lactate threshold. *Journal of Applied Physiology* 48: 523-527.

MacLaren, C.P., et al. 1989. A review of metabolic and physiologic factors in fatigue. *Exercise and Sports Science Review* 17: 29.

McArdle, W., F. Katch and V. Katch. 1996. *Exercise Physiology.* Baltimore, MD: Williams & Wilkins.

Niles, R. 1991. Power as a determinant of endurance performance. Unpublished study at Sonoma State University.

Riegel, P. 1981. Athletic records and human endurance. *American Scientist* 69: 285-290.

Romijn, J.A., et al. 1993. Regulation of endogenous fat and carbohydrate metabolism in relation to exercise intensity and duration. *American Journal of Physiology* 265: E380.

Weltman, A. 1995. *The Blood Lactate Response to Exercise.* Champaign, IL: Human Kinetics.

Weston, A.R., et al. 1997. Skeletal muscle buffering capacity and endurance performance after high-intensity interval training by well-trained cyclists. *European Journal of Applied Physiology* 75: 7-13.

Wilmore, J. and D. Costill. 1994. *Physiology of Sport and Exercise.* Champaign, IL: Human Kinetics.

TRAINING WITH A PURPOSE

How much time do you have available to train? After subtracting 40 hours for working and another 56 for sleeping from your 168-hour weekly allotment, you're left with 72. Of those remaining hours, more than half, perhaps 50, are accounted for in basic activities such as meal preparation, eating, personal care, home maintenance, transportation and shopping for necessities. That leaves 22 "free" hours each week for most of us. According to John Robinson and Geoffrey Godbey in Time for Life (Penn State Press, 1997), the average American spends 15 of those hours watching television and the remainder socializing with others including family.

It's doubtful that you put in 15 hours, or whatever weekly time you have left over, staring at the tube or you wouldn't compete in multisport events. After all, multisport does require a rather hefty time commitment. But more than likely, you don't have as many hours to train as you want, and the situation probably won't change in the foreseeable future. It's imperative, therefore, that the time you do have available — whether it's 15 hours or five — is spent wisely by doing workouts that have a direct and beneficial impact on race performance.

That's the purpose of the next two chapters: to determine exactly what your training needs are and the optimal ways to address them. Chapter 5 will show how to determine your fitness and progress, and Chapter 6 examines the implications of the abilities and limiters discovered. With a solid understanding of personal training needs, you'll be ready to begin planning for better race performances in Part IV.

ASSESSING FITNESS

"The focus must be on individual workouts — not on miles per week."
— MARK SISSON, AUTHOR OF *TRAINING AND RACING BIATHLONS*

I n a way, training for triathlon or duathlon is similar to investing money. When you have a few spare dollars and want to increase them, you look for good investments. You consider several options and compare many factors, especially the potential rate of return and the risk of losing your money. The objective is to get the greatest growth possible with the lowest level of risk. Generally, these two factors — growth and risk — work in opposition. When the potential growth rate is high, so is the risk of losing everything. At low levels of growth, risk is minimal. The trick in investing is seeking a balance between growth and risk. To make that decision, you must understand yourself and your financial status quite well: How much money do you have to invest? How much risk are you willing to take? How much can you afford to lose?

In a similar way, growth and risk play a role in multisport training. The precious resource you have to invest in training is time. The goal is to invest it wisely so that the fitness return you get is sizable. The greatest rate of growth comes from high-intensity, high-volume training. You could simply work out for an hour or two a day in each sport including lots of intervals, hills, repetitions and races. But this is also the riskiest combination as the potential for injury, overtraining, illness and burnout, all of which leave you with less fitness than when you started, is great.

Just as with financial investing, it is important to understand your present fitness needs. The purpose of this chapter is to help you make wise training investments of your limited time so that you get a good growth rate while minimizing risk. Wise training investments also require knowing your fitness status:

Growth and risk play a role in athletic training.

- How much time do you have to invest in training?
- In which areas of multisport performance are you weakest?
- In which areas are you the strongest?
- How intensely should you swim, bike and run?
- Are you making progress toward fitness goals?

Knowing the answers to these questions makes training a simple process of devoting precious road and pool time to those needs that give you the greatest fitness return for your investment while keeping risk manageable by swimming, cycling and running at appropriate intensities.

One way to find the answers to these questions is with race results. For example, if you've done the same race under similar conditions in previous years, how do your times compare? Are you faster or slower now? Comparing your time splits with those of others in the same race category also reveals quite a lot. If you ranked fifth in the swim in your age group, eighth on the bike, and tenth on the run, you have a fair idea of which sports need the most work (cycling and, especially running), and the least (swimming). Of course, these assessment methods assume that race conditions stay the same from year to year, and that your age group was large enough to offer a good sample. This method also requires that you race often enough to measure progress, but there are few, if any, races in the winter in most parts of the country when many "investment" decisions must be made.

One way to resolve this dilemma is to periodically measure your fitness against a standard, such as a graded exercise test or time trial. These aren't perfect, however, as conditions change. Many variables, such as the test venue, weather, warm-up procedures and food and drink intake must be controlled. When done carefully and regularly, the personal information gathered is invaluable for making training decisions.

Race results provide valuable clues for training.

Testing can help with training assessment.

PERSONAL PROFILE

The first step in making training decisions is knowing yourself, especially your proficiencies and natural physical abilities. It's important that you are totally honest in these ranking exercises. The results will help design your training program and must be based on reliable information.

Begin by scoring your swim, bike and run proficiencies using the following scale. The score you choose for each sport is subjective and based on a long-term comparison with others in your race category or age group. A score of five means that you are

Grade your multisport proficiencies.

among the best, three indicates *average* for your category, and one places you *at the bottom* of the category.

Compared with my race category, I'm among the...					
Sport	**worst**		**average**		**best**
Swimming	1	2	3	4	5
Biking	1	2	3	4	5
Running	1	2	3	4	5

Now complete and score the Natural-Abilities Profile on the next page. Then return to the next paragraph to find out what this means for your training.

NATURAL ABILITIES

Some were born multisport athletes. Their parents blessed them with the physiology necessary to excel in swimming, biking and running. Others were born to excel as soccer players, high jumpers or pianists. Many of us have chosen to swim, bike and run regardless of the genetic hand dealt to us. Passion for the sport means a lot and overcomes many physiological shortcomings.

Success in any sport is determined by the right mix of three basic abilities:

- Endurance — the ability to resist fatigue.
- Force — the ability to use muscular strength.
- Speed — the ability to move quickly.

Abilities common to all sports.

For example, an Olympic weight lifter must generate a tremendous amount of force, needs a fair amount of speed, and very little endurance. A pole vaulter needs tremendous speed, a moderate amount of force, and little endurance. A marathon runner doesn't need much force, only a little speed, but great endurance. Every sport is unique in terms of the mix of these three elements and, therefore, requires unique methods of training.

Triathlon and duathlon put a premium on endurance, but force development for hills and rough open water, and speed for short-distance races and finishing kicks are also needed. This unique combination of abilities is one of the reasons that triathlon and duathlon are such difficult sports for which to train. A multisport athlete can't just put in a lot of miles to develop huge endurance and disregard force and speed. It takes some mix of all three abilities to excel.

Addressing the abilities required for multisport is complex.

The Natural Abilities Profile you completed provides a snapshot of your individ-

What are your natural abilities?

ual capabilities for the three elements of fitness for multisport. A "score" of four or five for one of the abilities indicates a strength area. If all of your scores are four or five you undoubtedly have been a good athlete in many sports. A score of three or less indicates a weakness, one that may partly be due to heredity and partly to training. You can't change your genes, but you can change your training, if necessary. That's what you will read about in the next chapter.

Triathlete Natural Abilities Profile

Read each statement below and decide if you agree or disagree as it applies to you. Check the appropriate answer. If unsure, go with your initial feeling.

(A=Agree   D=Disagree)

A   D

___ ___ 1. I prefer to ride in a bigger gear with a lower cadence than most of my training partners.

___ ___ 2. The shorter the race, the better I perform.

___ ___ 3. As the intervals get shorter, I get better.

___ ___ 4. I'm stronger at the end of long workouts than my training partners.

___ ___ 5. I can squat and/or leg press more weight than most in my category.

___ ___ 6. I prefer long races.

___ ___ 7. I run and bike in the hills better than most in my age group.

___ ___ 8. I enjoy high-volume training weeks.

___ ___ 9. My running stride is short and quick.

___ ___ 10. I have always been better at sprints than at endurance.

___ ___ 11. In most sports, I've finished stronger than most others.

___ ___ 12. I'm more muscular than most triathletes of my age and sex.

___ ___ 13. I'm better at swimming in rough water than most others in my age group.

___ ___ 14. I prefer workouts that are short, but fast.

___ ___ 15. I'm confident of my endurance at the start of long races.

SCORING: For each of the following sets of statements, count the number of "Agree" answers you checked.

Statement numbers

1, 5, 7, 12, 13: Number of "Agrees" _____ Force score

2, 3, 9, 10, 14: Number of "Agrees" _____ Speed score

4, 6, 8, 11, 15: Number of "Agrees" _____ Endurance score

Mental Skills Profile

Read each statement below and choose an appropriate answer from these possibilities:

1=Never 2=Rarely 3=Sometimes 4=Frequently 5=Usually 6=Always

___ 1. I believe my potential as an athlete is excellent.

___ 2. I train consistently and eagerly.

___ 3. When things don't go well in a race I stay positive.

___ 4. In hard races I can imagine myself doing well.

___ 5. Before races I remain positive and upbeat.

___ 6. I think of myself more as a success than as a failure.

___ 7. Before races I'm able to erase self-doubt.

___ 8. The morning of a race I awake enthusiastically.

___ 9. I learn something from races when I don't do well.

___ 10. I can see myself handling tough race situations.

___ 11. I'm able to race at near my ability level.

___ 12. I can easily picture myself training and racing.

___ 13. Staying focused during long races is easy for me.

___ 14. I stay in tune with my exertion levels in races.

___ 15. I mentally rehearse skills and tactics before races.

___ 16. I'm good at concentrating as a race progresses.

___ 17. I make sacrifices to attain my goals.

___ 18. Before an important race I can visualize doing well.

___ 19. I look forward to workouts.

___ 20. When I visualize myself racing, it almost feels real.

___ 21. I think of myself as a tough competitor.

___ 22. In races I tune out distractions.

___ 23. I set high goals for myself.

___ 24. I like the challenge of a hard race.

___ 25. When the race becomes difficult I concentrate even better.

___ 26. In races I am mentally tough.

___ 27. I can relax my muscles before races.

___ 28. I stay positive despite late race starts, bad weather, poor officiating, etc.

___ 29. My confidence stays high the week after a bad race.

___ 30. I strive to be the best athlete I can be.

SCORING: Add up the numerical answers you gave for each of the following sets of statements.

Statement numbers	Score*			Total	Ranking	*Score
2, 8, 17, 19, 23, 30:	Total _____	Motivation _____		32-36	Excellent	5
1, 6, 11, 21, 26, 29:	Total _____	Confidence _____		27-31	Good	4
3, 5, 9, 24, 27, 28:	Total _____	Thought habits _____		21-26	Average	3
7, 13, 14, 16, 22, 25:	Total _____	Focus _____		16-20	Fair	2
4, 10, 12, 15, 18, 20:	Total _____	Visualization _____		6-15	Poor	1

PERFORMANCE TESTING

The best indicator of race fitness is racing. If there was a short race every month or so and the course and weather never changed, performance testing might be unnecessary. Such is never the case, however, so periodically measuring your fitness in race-specific ways is needed to gauge progress. When done correctly, testing indicates if your training is working and provides clues as to weaknesses that need more attention. Testing also helps to locate your lactate threshold, which, as discussed in the previous chapter, is key to regulating workout intensity.

Self-testing provides training clues.

The trick is to make the tests dependable by repeating the procedures exactly the same way each time. Small variations in such areas as warm-up, weather, equipment and eating all contribute to and possibly confound the measured results. One way to control such variables is to have your testing done by a local sports medicine clinic or in a university laboratory, but the expense makes this impractical for most. Self-testing with care and a high degree of precision is a reasonable alternative.

Precise testing is necessary for meaningful results.

Besides dependability and repeatability, the tests used must also measure elements of fitness related to multisport success. In addition, short-duration tests are preferable so as not to leave you tired for several days afterwards. Repeating the tests in each sport every three to six weeks during non-race periods of the year will keep you appraised of progress or lack thereof.

Two types of tests are recommended. The first is called a graded exercise test and involves monitoring heart rate and work output as the effort gradually rises until fatigue prevents further increases in effort. Graded exercise tests are done throughout the year, but are most effective early in the season during the general preparatory period of training. The other type of test is a short time trial done at race intensity and measured as elapsed time. Time trials are best used to measure progress in the last several weeks before racing begins.

Measure progress with graded exercise tests and time trials.

On the accompanying pages are descriptions of graded exercise tests and time trials for swimming, biking and running. Again, bear in mind that it's critical that the many potential variables, such as equipment and warm-up, are kept constant from one testing session to the next. Equipment selection and calibration is critical in bike and run graded exercise testing. If you don't have a CompuTrainer or other calibratable indoor trainer or a reliable treadmill, you're better off conducting these tests outdoors.

Testing is not perfect.

As fitness approaches your potential, results change little from one test to the next, perhaps as little as one percent or less. At such times, fitness may even appear to slide backwards due to the small variables that slip past you and confound the results.

Swimming Graded Exercise Test in Pool

Preparation

1. An assistant is needed to record lap times, heart rates, ratings of perceived exertion and to control recovery intervals. You will also need a pace clock near the pool. It's best to conduct the test when the pool is not crowded and the water relatively calm. If possible, use the same pool for retests. If not possible, the other pool should be the same length, either 25 meters or 25 yards.

2. Do not eat for two hours before the test. It's generally best if the previous day was light exercise or a rest day. Warm up for 10-20 minutes before the test. Note in your log what the warm-up procedure was.

3. If at any time you feel lightheaded or nauseous, stop the test immediately. You are not looking for a maximum heart rate on the test, but it's necessary to attain a very high effort level.

Test

1. The test is a series of increasingly faster 100-meter/yard repeats with 20-second recovery intervals.

2. Swim the first repeat at a very slow speed and low effort, a RPE of about 7. Your assistant records the time for the repeat and monitors the 20-second recovery interval. As soon as you finish, tell how great the exertion was using the RPE scale below, look at the pace clock, count your pulse at the throat for 10 seconds, report this number to the assistant who records it along side the repeat time, and prepare for the next send off on the assistant's command. It's a good idea to do a couple of practice repeats during the warm-up to become comfortable with the procedure. A heart rate monitor will make the test more accurate and may be used if the chest strap stays snugly positioned. Place this RPE scale where it can be seen at the end of each repeat:

6		14	
7	Very, very light	15	Hard
8		16	
9	Very light	17	Very hard
10		18	
11	Fairly light	19	Very, very hard
12		20	
13	Somewhat hard		

3. On each subsequent repeat, increase the speed and effort slightly so that your repeat times get faster by increments of about 2-3 seconds.

4. The data collected will look something like this:

Time (sec)	RPE	Heart Rate (beats/10 sec)
88	7	15
86	8	16
84	10	18
82	12	20
79	13	23
77	15	25
74	17	26
72	19	27

Bike Graded Exercise Test on CompuTrainer

Preparation

1. An assistant is needed to record information.
2. Do not eat for two hours before the test. It's generally best if the previous day was light exercise or a rest day. Warm up for 10-20 minutes before the test. Note in your log what the warm-up procedure was.
3. If at any time you feel lightheaded or nauseous, stop the test immediately. You are not looking for a maximum heart rate on the test, but it's necessary to attain a very high effort level.
4. Ride on the CompuTrainer for about 10 minutes at a light to moderate effort to warm up the equipment, and then calibrate. Reinsert Nintendo stereo jack into handlebar control unit.
5. Set "Program" to "Road Races/Courses" program 70.
6. Indicate a course of 10 miles length (you won't use all of it).
7. Input body weight plus bike weight.
8. Turn "Drafting" off.

Test

1. Throughout the test you will maintain a predetermined power level (plus or minus 5 watts) as displayed on the television screen. Start at 50 to 100 watts and increase by 20 watts every minute until you can no longer continue. Stay seated throughout the test. Shift gears at any time.
2. At the end of each minute tell your assistant how great your exertion is using the RPE scale (place this where it can be seen):

6			14	
7	Very, very light		15	Hard
8			16	
9	Very light		17	Very hard
10			18	
11	Fairly light		19	Very, very hard
12			20	
13	Somewhat hard			

3. Your assistant records your power output level, exertion rating and heart rate at the end of each minute and instructs you to increase power to the next level.
4. The assistant also listens closely to your breathing to detect when it first becomes labored. This point is marked as "VT" for ventilatory threshold.
5. Continue until you can no longer hold the power level for at least 15 seconds.
6. The data collected should look something like this:

Power (watts)	Heart Rate (bpm)	Exertion (RPE)	
100	110	9	
120	118	11	
140	125	12	
160	135	13	
180	142	14	
200	147	15	
220	153	17	VT
240	156	19	
260	159	20	

Bike Graded Exercise Test on Road

Preparation

1. In a large parking lot or undeveloped housing area with finished streets that allows a circular course of about a half mile, locate landmarks such as light poles or place cones to indicate the course. Do not attempt this test if there is traffic or if parked cars block any portion of the course. It may be best to conduct this test early in the morning. Try to use the same course and bike for retests.

2. An assistant with a stopwatch is needed to record lap splits and heart rates.

3. Do not eat for two hours before the test. It's generally best if the previous day was light exercise or a rest day. Warm up for 10-20 minutes before the test. Note in your log what the warm-up procedure was.

4. If at any time you feel lightheaded or nauseous, stop the test immediately. You are not looking for a maximum heart rate on the test, but it's necessary to attain a very high effort level.

Test

1. Start the test at a very slow speed — 13-15 mph. Every lap, increase speed by about 1 mph until you are eventually forced to stop because you can't go any faster. This may take eight to 12 laps of the course.

2. Once the test starts, your assistant records your time and heart rate for each lap

3. A few yards before passing by your assistant, call out your heart rate. The assistant will record this, along with your last lap split time in seconds. The data collected will look something like this:

Time (sec)	Heart Rate (bpm)
120	117
110	123
104	128
99	124
92	139
88	144
82	149
76	152
71	155

Run Graded Exercise Test on Treadmill

Preparation

1. Use a treadmill that accurately displays speed and has a top speed exceeding your best one-mile time or has variable incline. If the treadmill's top speed does not exceed your ability, set it at a sufficient grade to make the fastest speed quite difficult. Note this grade in your log.
2. An assistant is needed to record information and operate the treadmill. He/she stands so as to easily reach the speed and stop controls on the treadmill panel.
3. Do not eat for two hours before the test. It's generally best if the previous day was light exercise or a rest day. Warm-up for 10-20 minutes before the test. Note in your log what the warm-up procedure was.
4. If at any time you feel lightheaded or nauseous, stop the test immediately. You are not looking for a maximum heart rate on the test, but it's necessary to attain a very high effort level.

Test

1. Start at a slow speed such as 6 mph and increase by 0.2 mph every minute until you can no longer continue.
2. At the end of each minute tell your assistant how great your exertion is using the RPE scale (place this where it can be seen):

6		14	
7	Very, very light	15	Hard
8		16	
9	Very light	17	Very hard
10		18	
11	Fairly light	19	Very, very hard
12		20	
13	Somewhat hard		

3. Your assistant records your speed, exertion rating and heart rate at the end of each minute and increases the treadmill's speed to the next level (+0.2 mph).
4. The assistant listens closely to your breathing to detect when it first becomes labored marking this point as "VT" for ventilatory threshold.
5. Continue until you can no longer hold the speed, and then slow the treadmill gradually to a walking pace.
6. The data collected should look something like this:

Speed (mph)	Heart Rate (bpm)	Exertion (RPE)	
8.2	147	12	
8.4	154	13	
8.6	161	13	
8.8	166	14	
9.0	172	15	
9.2	179	17	VT
9.4	182	19	
9.6	185	20	

Run Graded Exercise Test on Track

Preparation

1. On a 400-meter or 440-yard running track, locate a starting mark and a half-lap mark.
2. An assistant with a stopwatch is needed to record splits and heart rates.
3. Do not eat for two hours before the test. It's generally best if the previous day was light exercise or a rest day. Warm up for 10-20 minutes before the test. Note in your log what the warm-up procedure was.
4. If at any time you feel lightheaded or nauseous, stop the test immediately. You are not looking for a maximum heart rate on the test, but it's necessary to attain a very high effort level.

Test

1. Start the test at a very slow speed — 70-80 seconds for a half lap. Every half lap, slightly increase running speed until you are eventually forced to stop because you can't go any faster. This may take six to 10 full laps of the track.
2. Once the test starts, your assistant jogs back and forth across the track meeting you at exactly the half way point for each lap.
3. Two or three steps before passing by your assistant, call out your heart rate. The assistant will note this, call out your last half-lap split time in seconds and record both numbers. Then pick up the pace slightly so that you run the next half lap about 3 to 5 seconds faster than the previous one. The data collected will look something like this:

Time (sec)	Heart Rate (bpm)	
78	127	
75	132	
70	137	
66	143	
61	149	
57	153	
52	159	VT
48	162	

4. Both you and your assistant should pay close attention to your breathing. When it becomes labored for the first time (a lot of air being moved), the assistant should note the heart rate at that point on the data sheet. This is your "ventilatory threshold" (VT).

Even with the best testing, there is still the necessity to listen to your body and have a subjective sense of progress. Fitness testing is not perfect.

If you are new to racing, or have coronary risk factors such as a family history of heart disease, a high total-cholesterol-to-HDL ratio, high blood pressure, a heart murmur or frequent dizziness or chest discomfort after exercise, you should only conduct such a test in a laboratory or clinic under the close supervision of a doctor.

UNDERSTANDING TEST RESULTS

Regular testing, especially during the preparatory periods of training that precede important races, is effective for measuring fitness changes. Each test provides unique indicators of progress. Time trials, since they resemble the stresses of racing, are most effective in the last few weeks before racing, while graded exercise tests offer valuable insights earlier in the season. Of the two types of graded exercise tests for biking and running, those on a CompuTrainer and on the treadmill are generally more comprehensive since ratings of perceived exertion are possible and work output is more controllable than tests on the road or track. As previously mentioned, however, test repeatability is important to mea-

---

SPECIAL ELEMENT 5.8

Swim Time Trial in Pool

Preparation

1. This test is conducted in a 25-yard or 25-meter pool. The only equipment needed is a stopwatch and possibly a heart-rate monitor ("suspenders" may be necessary to keep the chest strap in place while swimming).
2. Do not eat for two hours before the test. It's generally best if the previous day was light exercise or a rest day. Warm up for 10-20 minutes as if preparing for a race. Note in your log what the warm-up procedure was.
3. If at any time you feel lightheaded or nauseous, stop the test immediately. You are not looking for a maximum heart rate on the test, but rather the fastest time you can now swim.

Test

1. Immediately following the warm-up, swim 1000 meters or yards at race effort. Start your stopwatch at the beginning of the time trial and stop it as you finish.
2. On finishing, count your pulse for 10 seconds. If you are using a heart-rate monitor, this is not necessary.
3. Cool down or continue with the planned workout.
4. Determine your average 100 time by dividing your finish time by 10 and converting the time to minutes and seconds (17 minutes ÷ 10 = 1.7 = 1 minute, 42 seconds). Record the time, average 100 time and heart rate in your training log for future reference.

surement, making calibration of equipment critical. If you are not confident of the accuracy of the equipment available to you, road and track tests are probably the better options.

Graded exercise tests and time trials provide information on three aspects of fitness: lactate threshold, endurance and velocity. Testing also provides subjective insights into your potential for race performance, such as the ability to control pace, cope with physical stress and readiness to race.

Testing offers insights on lactate threshold, endurance and velocity.

LACTATE THRESHOLD MEASUREMENT

Graded exercise tests are effective for estimating lactate threshold heart rate (bike and run), lactate threshold power (bike), and lactate threshold pace (swim). For the novice multisport athlete, or those who have been away from serious training for some time, improvement is evident in gradually rising heart rates at lactate threshold (LT) over the course of several weeks of spaced testing. For the experienced and fit athlete, advancing fitness is noted not in a higher heart rate at LT, but rather in faster pace, velocity and greater power output at

There are different LT measures.

SPECIAL ELEMENT 5.9

Bike Time Trial on Road

Preparation

1. Find a flat, 5-kilometer stretch of road that has no turns or stop streets, and little traffic. Mark or note landmarks at the ends of this stretch of road. If 5km is not convenient, any distance in the range of 2.5 to 4 miles may be used if the course remains constant from one test to the next.
2. Wear a heart-rate monitor and stopwatch.
3. Do not eat for two hours before the test. It's generally best if the previous day was light exercise or a rest day. Warm-up for 10-20 minutes as if preparing for a race. Note in your log what the warm-up procedure was.
4. If at any time you feel lightheaded or nauseous, stop the test immediately. You are not looking for a maximum heart rate on the test, but rather the fastest time you can now ride for 10km.

Test

1. Immediately following the warm-up, ride 10km at race effort. Ride 5km out, turn around and return to the starting point. Start your stopwatch at the beginning of the time trial and stop it as you finish.
2. On finishing, note your heart rate. If your heart-rate monitor has an average function, note what it was later.
3. Cool down or continue with the planned workout.
4. Record the time, average and highest heart rate observed in your training log for future reference.

lactate threshold. Understand that LT is different for each sport and unique to the individual.

The first step in assessment, once testing is complete, is the estimation of LT heart rate, power and pace. This is done by observing four indicators of LT: RPE, ventilatory threshold, time above LT and power percentage.

How to estimate LT.

For the fit and experienced athlete, LT typically arrives when RPE is in the range of fifteen to seventeen. So a rough indication is quickly made by noting the heart rates, power and paces that are within this range of exertion ratings. The point at which your LT occurs may be further refined by noting your assistant's estimation of "VT." If this falls in the range of fifteen to seventeen RPE, it's probably close to your LT. In addition, an athlete will typically not be able to continue for more than five minutes once LT has occurred, so your LT is likely within the last five data points collected in the graded exercise test. On the CompuTrainer, with power used as an output measure, LT is also estimated by multiplying the highest power achieved on the test by 0.85.

By comparing all of these indicators, you should now have an estimate of lactate threshold for each sport. You can confirm it by observing other indicators during workouts such as your perceptions of the onset of an anaerobic state marked by heavy breathing and the build up of lactate. Of course, the results of subsequent retests will also help to confirm or modify your lactate threshold estimate.

AEROBIC AND ANAEROBIC ENDURANCE MEASUREMENT

Graded exercise tests are only valuable as comparative tools. In other words, they show how you're doing in relation to your previous tests. The first time you complete this battery of tests, you establish standards or baselines against which subsequent tests are compared to determine fitness progress. Greater endurance, both aerobic and anaerobic, result from producing greater outputs, such as velocity, with the same effort. What this indicates is that you are becoming more economical as a swimmer, cyclist or runner as less oxygen and fuel are used to produce movement. Sparing of fuel means better endurance.

Economy of movement means less effort.

Graphing allows you to easily compare the data from graded exercise tests. Using grid paper, produce XY graphs for each test. Then each time within the same season that you are tested, put the results on the appropriate graph. Improving fitness is evident when the slope of retests moves to the right and more data points are collected at the upper end of a test.

• **Swim-graded exercise test in pool.** Put swim repeat times on the horizontal axis and pulse counts multiplied by six to convert to beats per minute on the vertical axis.

Place the data points on these coordinates to create the graph. Figure 5.1 shows the results of two swim tests. Test No. 1 was done at the start of an eight-week training period; Test No. 2 shows progress at the end of that period. Notice on Test No. 2 that the slope of the line is now moved to the right indicating faster times at nearly the same heart rates, and, therefore, greater potential for endurance. Also note that LT remained constant at about 150 bpm on each test, but that on the Test #2 there are three data points beyond LT instead of only two as on Test No. 1. This means that the individual now has also improved anaerobic endurance.

How to graph a swim test.

• **Bike-graded exercise test on CompuTrainer.** Graphing the results of a bike test done on the CompuTrainer compares heart rate (vertical axis) to power (horizontal axis). Figure 5.2 illustrates a situation that often occurs during the base-building period of the season when the emphasis is on endurance and little training is devoted to anaerobic endurance. Notice how the lines are separated below LT, but converge above it. Aerobic fitness improved as anaerobic fitness remained constant. As this athlete progresses to the intensity-building period of training, anaerobic endurance should improve as noted by the test graphs separating at the upper end, and if aerobic endurance is maintained, the lines below LT should remain separated.

How to graph a bike test.

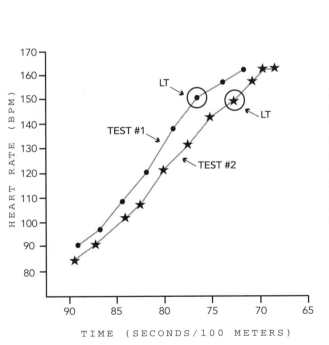

FIGURE 5.1
Graph of two swim-graded exercise tests.

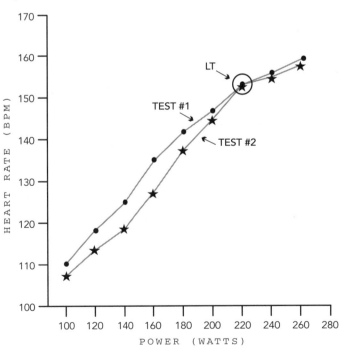

FIGURE 5.2
Graph of two bike-graded exercise tests on CompuTrainer.

• Run-graded exercise test on treadmill. Figure 5.3 shows unusual test results that you may experience. Following a four-week training period, this athlete is not improved aerobically. By itself that is not unusual, but if the athlete feels as if fitness has improved, and indeed, running workouts seem to confirm this, the problem may be a treadmill that is not properly calibrated. That's common if you use health club treadmills that get many hours of use each day. Without reliable equipment, testing is best done on the roads or track. Such test results could also mean unusual occurrences in your life in the last few hours or days before the test, such as poor sleep, a changed diet or additional stresses.

How to graph a run test.

FIGURE 5.3
Graph of two run-graded exercise tests on treadmill.

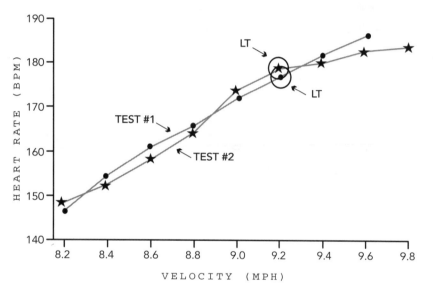

Notice also that the final heart rate achieved is not as high on Test No. 2 as on Test No. 1, although an additional minute was run at the upper end. This sometimes leads athletes to mistakenly believe that they are in worse condition. The inability to achieve a near-maximum heart rate is fairly common once high levels of fitness are achieved later in the season. Any time you can swim, bike or run faster at a lower heart rate, your fitness is improved.

VELOCITY MEASUREMENT

Testing means little if race times don't improve. In the final analysis, faster swim, bike and run velocities are why we train. Short of racing, the best way to determine progress in this all-important area is with time trials. Race velocity is the primary focus of the intensity-building period of training in the last few weeks before important races. At the start of this period, and again every three to six weeks during it, are when time trials are used. Once a period of frequent racing begins, testing is no longer necessary as the races provide important clues about fitness.

Time trials are used in the intensity-building period.

Don't expect great increases in velocity during this period of training, especially if you are a seasoned triathlete or duathlete. A 5-percent improvement from one test to the next is considerable. Half or even less of that is a more reasonable expectation in a few weeks time.

Your time trial results can be used as a gauge of what to expect in a race. Here's how to make a rough estimate for sprint- and international-distance races. We know that as the distance doubles, pace slows about 5 percent. For example, if your 1.5-mile run time trial was done in ten minutes (6:40 pace per mile), you could expect to run a 5km at about a seven-minute pace (6:40 ¥ 0.05 = 0:20; 6:40 + 0:20 = 7:00), or in a time of about 21:40. But, of course, during a triathlon, you'll have to run slower than you would in a running race, so expect to slow down approximately another 5 percent (7:20 pace, or about 22:45). So as the distance doubles, expect your velocity in the race to diminish by about 10 percent. This system of prognosticating has limited value, especially as the distance increases by more than a factor of two, but it provides a rough estimate of what you might expect if you haven't raced for some time.

How to convert time trial results to race pace predictions.

The better use of time trials is as a periodic indicator of progress in your ability to maintain a fast pace. Comparing past records of time trials at various points in the season from one year to the next is a good gauge of long-term improvement.

ASSESSMENT

Testing is of no value unless the information gained is used to improve your training or confirm that you are training in an appropriate manner. For example, you may learn from the three graded exercise tests that swimming and running are steadily improving, but that your cycling is not. This should cause you to rethink what you're doing on the bike. Perhaps you need to ride more to improve the aerobic end of the graph, or start high-intensity training to boost the anaerobic side. In the same way, the time trials may indicate the need for a change, such as more race-specific training.

Testing confirms or shows a need to change training.

Periodic assessment of race performance and fitness is a valuable tool in knowing how to train for steady improvement. The next chapter takes a closer look at how to go about correcting whatever you may have discovered is holding you back from better racing.

REFERENCES

Bouchard, C. and G. Lortie. 1984. Heredity and endurance performance. *Sports Medicine* 1: 38-94.

Costill, D. 1989. Predicting athletic potential: The value of laboratory testing. *Sports Medicine Digest* 11 (11): 7.

Daniels, J. 1989. Physiological characteristics of champion male athletes. *Research Quarterly* 45: 342-348.

Droghetti, P., et al. 1985. Noninvasive determination of the anaerobic threshold in canoeing, cross-country skiing, cycling, roller and ice skating, rowing and walking.

European Journal of Applied Physiology 53: 299-303.

Francis, K.T., et al. 1989. The relationship between anaerobic threshold and heart rate linearity during cycle ergometry. *European Journal of Applied Physiology* 59: 273-277.

Friel, J. 1996. *The Cyclist's Training Bible.* Boulder, CO: VeloPress.

Gibbons, E.S. 1987. The significance of anaerobic threshold in exercise prescription. *Journal of Sports Medicine* 27: 357-361.

Hagberg, J.M. 1984. Physiological implications of the lactate threshold. *International Journal of Sports Medicine* 5: 106-109.

Hendy, H.M. and B.J. Boyer. 1995. Specificity in the relationship between training and performance in triathlons. *Perception and Motor Skills* 81 (3) 1231-1240.

Kuipers, H., et al. 1988. Comparison of heart rate as a non-invasive determination of anaerobic threshold with lactate threshold when cycling. *European Journal of Applied Physiology* 58: 303-3-6.

Noakes, T.D. 1988. Implications of exercise testing for prediction of athletic performance: A contemporary perspective. *Medicine and Science in Sports and Exercise* 20 (4): 319-330.

Schneider, D.A., et al. 1990. Ventilarory threshold and maximal oxygen uptake during cycling and running in triathletes. *Medicine and Science in Sports and Exercise* 22 (2): 257-264.

Simon, J., et al. 1986. Plasma lactate and ventilation thresholds in trained and untrained cyclists. *Journal of Applied Physiology* 60: 777-781.

Sleivert, G.G. and H.A. Wenger. 1993. Physiological predictors of short-course triathlon performance. *Medicine and Science in Sports and Exercise* 25 (7): 871-876.

Sleivert, G.G. and D.S. Rowlands. 1996. Physical and physiological factors associated with success in the triathlon. *Sports Medicine* 22 (1): 8-18.

Steed, J.C., et al. 1994. Ratings of perceived exertion (RPE) as markers of blood lactate concentration during rowing. *Medicine and Science in Sports and Exercise* 26: 797-803.

Wakayoshi, K., et al. 1993. Does critical swimming velocity represent exercise intensity at maximal lactate steady state? *Medicine and Science in Sports and Exercise* 25 (5): S366.

Weltman, A. 1995. *The Blood Lactate Response to Exercise.* Champaign, IL: Human Kinetics.

BUILDING FITNESS

*"I train as a means to an objective, and that objective is
to race faster the next time than I did the last time...."*
— KAREN SMYERS, PROFESSIONAL TRIATHLETE

Have you ever observed a house under construction for several weeks? If so, you
know there's a well-defined order in which the many tasks of building are completed. First, the foundation is constructed of a durable material such as concrete. Great
care is taken at this stage to ensure that the foundation is level, square and solidly stable.
A haphazardly built foundation means the finished house will be of poor quality. Next,
the wall and roof framing are put up. This goes quickly, and as it's done, the house begins
to take shape. With just a little imagination, you can even picture what it will look like
when done. Finally, after the plumbing and electrical are installed, walls are enclosed and
the finish work begins with windows, doors, cabinets, floor covers and a multitude of
progressively smaller tasks completed. Eventually, all the work is done, and if each stage
of the construction was performed carefully, the house will provide shelter and a home
for many years to come with only minor maintenance along the way.

It's remarkable how similar the paradigm of house building is to multisport fitness
building. In triathlon and duathlon, training begins by first establishing a foundation of
the most basic physical needs, and then progresses to carefully constructing smaller,
more refined fitness aspects that match the "blueprint" requirements of racing. Building
a solid base foundation takes years, but if it's done correctly, such fitness is easy to maintain. Too often, novice athletes want to speed up or even skip the foundation-building
phase of training. Even experienced athletes are tempted to do this in order to get on
with the intense training that produces final race shape. But just as with a poor house

**Building on fitness is
similar to building a house.**

foundation, slighting the base-development period means a low-quality finished product. The stronger the base, the more solid and long-lasting the final fitness is.

On the other hand, developing only the foundation without ever doing the "finish work," means that one's race potential is never realized. A season of training must include all of the phases of construction at just the right times to bring a high-level of race fitness when it's needed.

Timing is critical for the stages of fitness building.

In the previous chapter you began developing the blueprints for a better race season by learning more about yourself. This chapter further develops the blueprint by determining exactly what is holding you back from better racing, and introduces the tasks to accomplish in building improved multisport fitness. Then Part IV finalizes the blueprints by showing you how to organize your training so the tasks are completed in an order and to a magnitude which produces peak race fitness.

LIMITERS

In Chapter 5 your strengths and weaknesses were identified using the Natural Abilities Profile. At the bottom of the profile page you came up with a score for some of the factors related to multisport success. You also ranked your swimming, biking and running proficiencies. A score of three or lower on any of these items indicates a weakness, while those scored as a four or five may be interpreted as strengths.

Let's examine just your weaknesses for a moment, as these are holding you back. Or are they? What if you gave yourself a score of "one" on swimming, but you only race in duathlons. While swimming is no less of a weakness, it is not limiting your race success in this case. That's a rather gross example. But how about if your endurance score was "three," and you know that for half-Ironman and longer races, you struggle just to finish. That's certainly a weakness. If, however, you concentrate on sprint-distance races, endurance may not be such a big deal. In this case, endurance is a weakness, but it is not limiting your performance. So it's not a concern, unless, of course, you decide to train for a longer race.

Limiters are race-specific weaknesses.

It's important to know which weaknesses are holding you back for the types of races you do. These race-specific weaknesses are your "limiters." As shown, a little weakness in endurance is not a limiter if you don't do long races. In the same way, a force weakness may not be a limiter unless you compete in hilly, windy or rough-water events.

This chapter focuses on how to improve your limiters in the areas of swim, bike and run proficiencies, and the physical abilities necessary for successful racing. Later chapters will address mental skills and other miscellaneous factors that may limit performance.

TRAINING BASIC ABILITIES

Let's shift the direction of this discussion to get a better understanding of the abilities of endurance, force and speed that have been frequently referred to. Having a good grasp of what they are all about is important to designing your training program starting in the next chapter.

You have probably noticed that some athletes seem to excel in long races, but are less competitive in short races. Then there are riders who thrive in the hills leading your training group every time the terrain goes vertical, but into the wind on flat ground they struggle. What you're observing here is individual mixes of the basic abilities of endurance, force and speed resulting from a unique combination of genetics and training.

Each athlete has a unique set of abilities.

The basic abilities are crucial to optimal multisport performance. For the experienced athlete, every year must begin with the development of endurance, force and speed before progressing to the more advanced aspects of race fitness. In the first two or three years of a novice athlete's career, training must primarily consist of these abilities in workouts and little else. Resist the temptation to dive into the high-effort workouts such as intervals until the basic abilities are well established.

Rebuild the basic abilities at the start of each new season.

It may help to understand the abilities of racing to think of fitness as represented by a triangle with the basic abilities anchoring its corners, just as a house foundation does. In addition, knowing how the terms are used, and how the abilities are developed in training may prove helpful before starting to design your training program.

The various abilities related to multisport fitness are developed at different times of the year following a periodization plan as described in Chapter 3. In review, figure 6.2 summarizes those periods using the terms found in the following discussions about training.

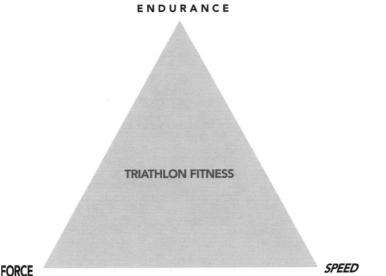

FIGURE 6.1
Basic abilities triangle.

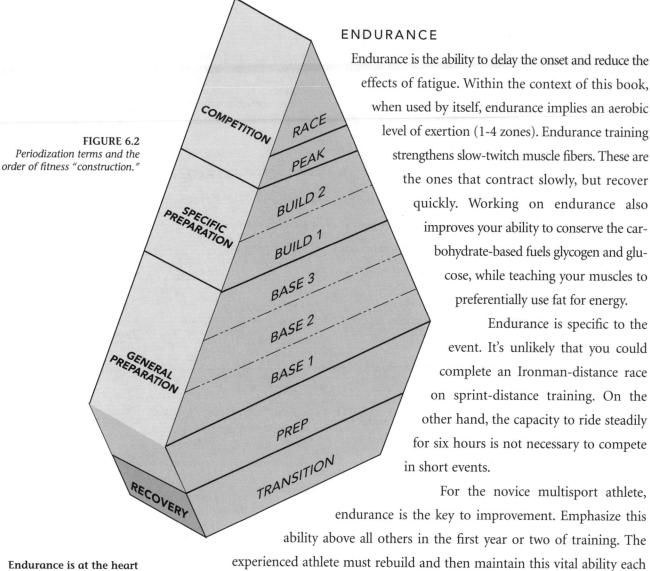

FIGURE 6.2
Periodization terms and the order of fitness "construction."

ENDURANCE

Endurance is the ability to delay the onset and reduce the effects of fatigue. Within the context of this book, when used by itself, endurance implies an aerobic level of exertion (1-4 zones). Endurance training strengthens slow-twitch muscle fibers. These are the ones that contract slowly, but recover quickly. Working on endurance also improves your ability to conserve the carbohydrate-based fuels glycogen and glucose, while teaching your muscles to preferentially use fat for energy.

Endurance is specific to the event. It's unlikely that you could complete an Ironman-distance race on sprint-distance training. On the other hand, the capacity to ride steadily for six hours is not necessary to compete in short events.

For the novice multisport athlete, endurance is the key to improvement. Emphasize this ability above all others in the first year or two of training. The experienced athlete must rebuild and then maintain this vital ability each season. A high level of endurance takes a relatively long time to mature.

Endurance is at the heart of multisport training.

As with the other abilities, endurance is optimally developed by starting with general endurance training and progressing to more race-specific workouts. This means that to build endurance, start by developing a sound cardiorespiratory system (heart, lungs and blood) with a broad range of general, or cross-training, modes such as cross-country skiing, rowing and aerobics classes in addition to swimming, biking and running. In the Prep and Base 1 periods such workouts are done at low intensity, mostly in the 1 to 3 zones. Later in the Base 2 and 3 and Build periods, training becomes more specific as cross-training is reduced or eliminated and workouts gradually begin simulating races, at first in terms of duration, and later of intensity. Figure 6.3 illustrates this progression of general-to-specific training.

Training progresses from general to specific during the season.

Endurance is improved not only by long duration swim, bike and run workouts, but also by consistent, chronic exposure to the activity. In other words, the weekly volume of training plays a role in the development of endurance, although not as great as workout duration. Great care is needed when increasing duration and volume since the body is not capable of rapid change when it comes to endurance adaptations. Plan on taking months and years to increase endurance, rather than days or weeks.

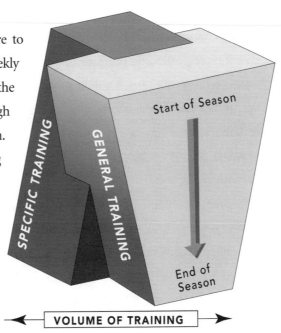

FIGURE 6.3
As the season progresses, training becomes increasingly specific to triathlon racing.

Endurance improves over a long time.

FORCE

Force is the ability to overcome resistance. In multisport, force production relates to how well you do in rough water, on hills and into the wind. It also plays a role in muscular economy. When the slow-twitch muscles are strengthened, faster paces are produced at aerobic efforts thus sparing glycogen and glucose, which are in short supply.

Strong muscles improve fuel economy.

Just as with endurance, force development progresses from general to specific throughout the training year. It begins in the Prep and Base periods of the early season with weight training or other forms of general resistance work such as with stretch cords, body-weight exercises and special equipment. By the end of Base 1, general body-strength development should be maximal allowing you to begin more triathlon- and duathlon-specific force training in the pool and on the road. At this point, many young athletes stop lifting weights since they are capable of easily maintaining strength with specific training. Older athletes and many women, however, should continue general strength work throughout most of the remainder of the season, although at a reduced level, since they seem less capable of retaining their strength gains. Chapter 13 provides greater detail on general strength training in the weight room.

Force training begins with progressive resistance work such as weights.

SPEED

Speed is the ability to move effectively while swimming, biking or running. It is not used here to mean how fast your race times or pace are, although those are related issues. Effective movement leads to faster race times and comes in many forms. In swimming it is a hydrodynamic position in the water that produces speed. In cycling and running, leg turnover rate is critical. Some portions of this ability may be genetic; in other words, you may have been born with certain muscle types, tendon attachment points and limb lengths that favor effective movement. It's possible, however, to improve speed. Several scientific studies have demonstrated that swim technique and leg turnover are trainable given the right types of workouts and consistency of purpose in training.

As with force, speed development improves economy. Regularly incorporating drills into swim, bike and run workouts teaches big and small muscles exactly when to contract and when to relax. As the muscles involved in forward movement are activated with precise harmony, economy improves and precious little fuel is wasted. Speed training begins in the Base period and is maintained throughout the remainder of the season.

Chapter 8 provides several workouts for improving speed, and Chapter 12 describes how to improve swim, bike and run skills that ultimately lead to greater speed.

TRAINING ADVANCED ABILITIES

The basic abilities of endurance, force and speed at the corners of the fitness triangle diagrammed in figure 6.1 are only the foundation for our construction project. The sides of the triangle represent the wall and roof framing. In the parlance of endurance training, the framing is constructed of muscular endurance, anaerobic endurance and power. These are the advanced abilities the athlete emphasizes in the later periods of training with only ten weeks or so remaining until the most important races. Figure 6.4 shows how these abilities are situated in relation to the foundational abilities. Each advanced ability results from the development of the basic abilities on either end of it, but are further refined with training specific to that ability.

MUSCULAR ENDURANCE

Muscular endurance is the ability of the muscles to maintain a relatively high force load for a prolonged time. It is a combination of force and endurance abilities. A high level of muscular endurance results from adaptation of the mechanical properties of the muscles to resist fatigue, an elevated lactate threshold and tolerance of lactate that slowly accumulates at such intensities. Muscular endurance is a critical ability for the multisport athlete. Toward the end of the swim, bike and run legs of a race, this ability keeps the pace high. With the run usually coming last in races, muscular endurance for running is especially important since fatigue is cumulative throughout the event.

Muscular-endurance work should begin in the Base 2 period with sustained efforts

---

Speed is a trainable ability.

The timing of contraction and relaxation of muscle is crucial to speed.

The advanced racing abilities grow from the basic abilities.

Muscular endurance is necessary for multisport success.

of several minutes in the 3 zone. Training gradually progresses by Base 3 to include mostly aerobic interval workouts in the 4 and 5a zones. The work intervals lengthen as the recovery intervals remain quite short, about a third or fourth of the work-interval duration. By the Build periods, steady-state, non-stop efforts of twenty to forty minutes in the 4 and 5a zones are done. The effort of these workouts is much like "controlled" time trialing and is tremendously effective in boosting both aerobic and anaerobic fitness with little risk of overtraining. Throughout the Race period, muscular-endurance is maintained.

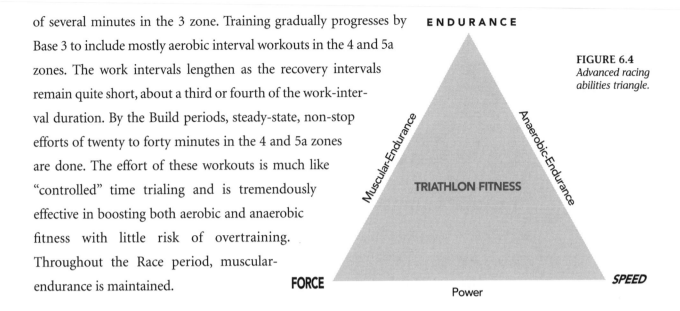

FIGURE 6.4
Advanced racing abilities triangle.

ANAEROBIC ENDURANCE

As a blending of speed and endurance, anaerobic endurance is the ability to resist fatigue at very high efforts when arm or leg turnover is rapid. An athlete with excellent anaerobic endurance has good tolerance for lactate and performs well in short-distance events and head-to-head competitions with frequent speed surges. For the athlete who specializes in long-distance events, such as half-Ironman or longer, anaerobic endurance is of less importance.

Muscular endurance training is done at about lactate threshold.

There are two types of anaerobic-endurance workouts. One is based on aerobic capacity-developing intervals done in the 5b zone. At the start of the Build period of training, the experienced athlete should phase into interval training to increase aerobic capacity. The intervals are two to six minutes long with recoveries, at first, approximately equal to the work interval for running and cycling, and less than that for swimming. As the season progresses and fitness improves, the work interval length is decreased.

Shorter repetitions of thirty seconds to two minutes duration at 5c intensity, are effective for developing the capacity to manage extremely high levels of lactate. Recovery intervals are two to three times the length of the work interval for lactate tolerance repetitions with swimming having the shortest recoveries and running the longest. The idea is to produce a maximal effort that creates large amounts of lactic acid, recover and repeat the process several times. The early onset of fatigue from overly short recoveries will inhibit maximum effort and reduce lactic acid production. For the shorter-distance race specialist, lactate tolerance work in the Build 2 and Peak periods trains the body to remove lactate from the blood and to buffer its usual effects.

Anaerobic-endurance training is based on intervals.

Anaerobic-endurance training is quite stressful and should not be a part of the

Short repetitions at 5c train lactate tolerance.

novice's regimen. Develop both speed and endurance with at least two years of training before regularly attempting these workouts. The likely results of too much anaerobic-endurance work, too soon is burnout and overtraining.

POWER

Power is the ability to apply maximum force quickly. It results from having high levels of the basic abilities of force and speed. Well developed power, or a lack of it, is obvious on short, steep hills, in fast swim starts and in sudden pace changes such as when initiating a finishing sprint.

Since it includes both speed and force components, power is dependent on the nervous system to send strong signals, and on the muscles to contract maximally. For this reason, improvements in power come from short, all-out efforts into the 5c zone followed by very long recovery intervals to allow the nervous system and muscles to fully recover. These repetitions are quite brief — less than thirty seconds. Heart rate monitors are of no use in power training; use RPE, pace, or on the bike, a power-measuring device of some sort.

Short, maximum efforts train power.

Attempting to improve power while fatigued is counterproductive. Such training is, therefore, best done when rested and early in a training session when the nervous system and muscles are most responsive.

LIMITERS AND RACING

Let's return to the discussion of limiters, which was previously defined as race-specific weaknesses. By now you should have a good idea of what your physical-ability limiters are. The basic abilities of endurance, force and speed were easily identified. The advanced abilities are somewhat more difficult to recognize. But since the advanced abilities are based on the combination of the basic abilities, a weakness in the latter produces a weakness in the former. For example, if your endurance is weak it will prevent both muscular endurance and anaerobic endurance from reaching their potential. If endurance is good, but force is lacking, muscular endurance and power are negatively effected. Poor speed means low power and inferior anaerobic endurance.

Advanced ability limiters result from basic ability limiters.

As mentioned, the types of races you do determine what strengths are needed and how your weaknesses limit you. So matching your abilities to the demands of the event are critical for success. Let's examine how that works.

TABLE 6.1

Summary of triathlon abilities

Ability	Period*	Frequency per Sport*	Duration**	Intervals Work	Intervals Recovery***	Intensity Zones	Benefit	Example
Endurance	Prep Base 1,2,3 Build 1,2 Peak	1-2/week	20'-6 hrs	N/A	N/A	1-3	a. Delay fatigue b. Build slow twitch c. Fuel economy	Swim 60' steady Bike 3 hrs flat course Run 90'
Force	Base 2,3 Build 1	1/week	4'-60'	30"-60"	1:2	4-5b	a. Muscular strength b. Muscular economy	Swim with paddles Bike hills seated Run hilly course
Speed	Base 1,2,3 Build 1,2 Peak Race	1-2/week	1'-6' of intervals	10"-30"	1:2-5	5a-5c	a. Arm/leg turnover b. Muscular economy	Swim 10x25 on 1' Bike 12x30" (90" RI) Run 8x20" (90" RI)
Muscular Endurance	Base 2,3 Build 1,2 Peak Race	1/week	a. 18'-60' of intervals b. 20'-40' steady state	6'-12'	3-4:1	4-5a	a. Strength endurance b. Race-pace comfort c. Boost LT d. Lactate tolerance	Swim 6x400m on 8' Bike 4x6' (2' RI) Run 20' steady state
Anaerobic Endurance	Build 1,2 Peak Race	1/week	a. 12'-30' of intervals b. 3'-12' of intervals	2'-6' 30"-2'	2:1-2 1:2-3	5b 5c	a. Elevate VO2 max b. Sustain high effort c. Lactate tolerance	Swim 6x200m on 4' Bike 5x5' (5' RI) Run 5x400m (400m RI)
Power	Build 2 Peak Race	1/week	1'-6' of intervals	10"-30"	1:2-3	5c	a. Muscular power b. Fast starts c. Climb short hills	Swim 12x25 on 1' Bike 6x30" on hill (60" RI) Run 4x150m (250m RI)

* Varies with individual, period and sport.
**Applies to portion of workout that develops the ability.
*** Work-interval-to-recovery-interval ratio (example: 3:1 means rest for 1 min for every 3 min of work time).
Note: Recovery intervals typically are shortest for swimming and longest for running.
Abbreviations: ' = minute, " = second, hrs = hours, RI = recovery interval, m = meters, LT = lactate threshold.

RACE PRESCRIPTION

Races vary not only in course length, but also in terrain. Matching your physical fitness to the demands of the most important events for which you are training produces the best results.

The longer the race is, the more it favors the basic abilities. Conversely, the shorter the race, the more important the advanced abilities are. In preparing for an Ironman-distance race, endurance is paramount, but force is also necessary to deal with hills or even just undulating terrain, and good fuel economy resulting from speed training conserves energy. Muscular endurance plays a role, but training for anaerobic endurance and power is of questionable value.

In the same way, a sprint-distance race favors the advanced abilities, especially anaerobic endurance and power. That doesn't mean that endurance and force aren't needed, just not to the same extent as the ultra- and long-course athletes. Speed training is critical for short races, but muscular endurance also plays a role.

Sprint- and Ironman-distance races are easy to define in terms of the abilities needed. Race distances between these extremes demand a blending of basic and advanced abilities with the half-Ironman favoring basic abilities and international distance benefiting somewhat more from advanced abilities.

So training for an important event means first deciding what is important for success, and then improving your limiters in those areas while maintaining the strengths also necessary for success.

SWIM, BIKE AND RUN LIMITERS

Of course, you can have a limiter in one sport, but it's not in another. For example, you may have developed a high level of muscular endurance for cycling from years spent in bike racing, but your muscular endurance for running is holding you back. Considering the three sports, the six abilities and the most important races on your schedule, there are numerous possible combinations of limiters unique to you. The most important decision before designing a training program is to identify those limiters. In the next two chapters you'll prepare a training plan based on what you decide.

There are other ways to improve a limiter for swimming, biking or running besides training with specific fitness abilities in mind. Here are a few "non-training" suggestions to improve a flagging proficiency. Chapter 12 will describe many of these in greater detail.

Long races favor the basic abilities.

Short races favor the advanced abilities.

Limiters are unique to the sport and to the race profile.

"Non-training" fixes for proficiency limiters.

Swimming

• Train with a masters swim team.

• Take swim lessons.

• Focus on form, not fitness, in workouts.

• Attend a swim camp.

• Swim shorter workouts more frequently.

• Videotape your swim stroke and analyze it.

• Videotape a proficient swimmer and study his or her mechanics.

Biking

• Lift weights, especially squats, step ups or leg press.

• Ride shorter workouts more frequently.

• Purchase a bike that fits correctly.

• Ride regularly with a group of multisport athletes.

• Frequently ride a fixed-gear bike in the Base period.

• Improve ability to spin smoothly.

• Have bike set up evaluated by a coach or experienced rider.

• Buy "fast" equipment such as aero' bars or disc wheels.

Running

• Run with a group.

• Run shorter workouts more frequently.

• Refine running technique.

• Build running-specific leg strength with weights.

• Have your running gait analyzed by a coach.

• Buy shoes that fit your exact structural needs.

OTHER LIMITERS

Besides the ability and proficiency limiters discussed in this and the previous chapter, there are other factors that may also hold you back from achieving your race goals. One of the most critical is a lack of time to train. This is perhaps the most common limiter for multisport athletes, especially those who compete in long- and ultra-distance races. If this is a limiter for you, when designing a program bear in mind that specificity of training becomes increasingly important as the hours available to work out diminish. In other words, when time is scarce, your training must closely simulate racing, so as volume declines, workout intensity increases. The next chapter will help you decide how many hours are reasonable to expect in training for races of different distances.

Scarce training time is a common limiter.

Triathlon Assessment

Score each of the following racing abilities and miscellaneous factors on a scale of 1 to 5 using the following guidelines. Circle the selection that best describes you in relation to your competition.

1 = among the worst in my race category

3 = about the same as others in my race category

5 = among the best in my race category

Abilities/Techniques	Swim					Bike					Run				
Endurance	1	2	3	4	5	1	2	3	4	5	1	2	3	4	5
Force	1	2	3	4	5	1	2	3	4	5	1	2	3	4	5
Speed	1	2	3	4	5	1	2	3	4	5	1	2	3	4	5
Muscular Endurance	1	2	3	4	5	1	2	3	4	5	1	2	3	4	5
Anaerobic Endurance	1	2	3	4	5	1	2	3	4	5	1	2	3	4	5
Power	1	2	3	4	5	1	2	3	4	5	1	2	3	4	5
Technique	1	2	3	4	5	1	2	3	4	5	1	2	3	4	5

Miscellaneous Factors															
Time to train	1	2	3	4	5	1	2	3	4	5	1	2	3	4	5
Injuries	1	2	3	4	5	1	2	3	4	5	1	2	3	4	5
Health	1	2	3	4	5	1	2	3	4	5	1	2	3	4	5
Body strength	1	2	3	4	5	1	2	3	4	5	1	2	3	4	5
Flexibility	1	2	3	4	5	1	2	3	4	5	1	2	3	4	5
Mental skills	1	2	3	4	5	1	2	3	4	5	1	2	3	4	5
Nutrition	1	2	3	4	5	1	2	3	4	5	1	2	3	4	5
Body composition	1	2	3	4	5	1	2	3	4	5	1	2	3	4	5

Miscellaneous limiters and where to find them.

Other common miscellaneous limiters are poor swim, bike or run techniques; frequent injuries and poor health (discussed in Chapter 11); a general lack of muscular strength or flexibility (Chapter 13); unique age, sex or experience needs (Chapter 14); and mediocre nutrition or excess body fat (Chapter 16). Before completing the Annual Training Plan in the following chapter, it may help to first read any of the preceding chapters that relate to your miscellaneous limiters. Chapter 14, dealing with unique age, sex or experience needs, should definitely be read before commencing, if this is a concern of yours.

FINAL ASSESSMENT

By now you should have established a pretty clear idea of what your limiters are. Before starting to plan your season, let's summarize them. This will make the planning process more meaningful. Take a few minutes to complete the accompanying "Triathlete Assessment" form before going to the next chapter.

REFERENCES

Bompa, T. 1994. *Theory and Methodology of Training*. Dubuque, IA: Kendall/Hunt Publishing.

Butts, N.K., et al. Correlations between VO$_2$ max and performance times of recreational triathletes. *Journal or Sports Medicine and Physical Fitness* 31 (3): 339-344.

Freeman, W. 1991. *Peak When It Counts*. Mountain View, CA: TAFNEWS Press.

Friel, J. 1996. *The Cyclist's Training Bible*. Boulder, CO: VeloPress.

Maglischo, E. 1982. *Swimming Faster*. Mountain View, CA: Mayfield Publishing Co.

Martin, D.E. and P.N. Coe. 1991. *Training Distance Runners*. Champaign, IL: Leisure Press.

Sleamaker, R. 1989. *Serious Training for Serious Athletes*. Champaign, IL: Leisure Press.

part four

PLANNING

There are no "secrets" to success in athletics regardless of what you may hear. Although some elite athletes and coaches believe they have discovered the "one true way" to train, there is nothing new under the sun. Intervals of many types have been extensively used since the 1920s; fartlek training has been around for ninety years; periodization was born in the 1960s; long, slow distance was all the rage twenty years ago; tempo training was common in the early 1900s; post-World War I athletes regularly recorded high volume; and the list could go on and on. In studying the greatest endurance athletes of all time, one inescapable fact stands out: No two trained exactly the same way. In fact, the training methods of history's most talented swimmers, cyclists and runners cover the spectrum of possibilities. Some trained only long and slow, others favored sprint workouts, several employed long intervals, many preferred a mix of regimens, a few found hill work effective while others stayed only on flat ground. You name it, and someone's already done it.

No, there are no secrets when it comes to training. There always has been, and probably always will be, five ingredients for success in sport:

1. Purpose: Know exactly what your goal is.

2. Passion: Have a burning desire to achieve it.

3. Planning: Determine how you'll go about achieving it.

4. Perspiration: Work hard following your plan to achieve it.

5. Perseverance: Don't let anything get in the way of achieving it.

The purpose of the next three chapters is to help you with the third P — planning. In Chapter 7 you'll develop a one-year training plan. Chapter 8 describes how to lay out a week of training. And Chapter 9 provides examples of plans for races of different distances.

PLANNING
A YEAR

"Just as the farmer's field must lie fallow every winter, so does the human body, mind and spirit need a rest, with time to reflect, recover and rejuvenate."
— ROB SLEAMAKER, AUTHOR OF *SERIOUS TRAINING FOR SERIOUS ATHLETES*

In this chapter you'll design an annual training plan. The best time of year to do this is a few weeks following the end of your last race period of the preceding season, when you're ready to start preparing for the next season. If you're already well into the season, but have just purchased this book, it's still a good idea to plan where you're going the rest of the year. Better late than never.

This chapter will take you through a simple six-step process of annual planning that will have you on the way to a better season before you even work up a sweat. It's amazing what having direction will do for your fitness. This will require some writing, so you'll need a pencil. Don't work in ink as you'll undoubtedly need to make changes later. The Annual Training Plan worksheets are in Appendix A. Make a copy of the appropriate one before starting to work. Chapter 9 provides sample plans, should you need an example.

While planning your season in advance can lead to better race performance, the danger in following such a methodical process is that you'll become so engrossed in procedure that you'll fail to think in a realistic way. Your purpose is not simply to write a plan, but to race better than ever before. At the end of a successful season you'll realize how important having a written plan was.

Writing and following an annual training plan is somewhat like climbing a mountain. Before taking the first step it's a good idea to ask questions and do some

Better racing is the purpose of planning.

planning: What equipment is needed? What's the likely weather? What routes are best? The answers to these and other questions will help you devise a plan to reach the summit. The plan will probably take into account your previous climbs on other mountains. You may also talk with others who have climbed this particular mountain to find out their experiences. They may help you know what problems are likely along the way so you're prepared to deal with them.

Finally, you decide on the route, estimated time, clothing, food and equipment needs, and start the arduous trek. While ascending the mountain you stop occasionally to look at the peak and check progress. Along the way, you may decide to change the route based on unexpected conditions, such as bad weather or obstacles. Arriving at the peak, you're elated. Looking back down you remember all of the problems overcome along the way, and especially how planning gave you direction.

So it is with planning for a peak racing season. Planning is the master key to success. It is most likely to get you to the top when you approach the planning process with adequate information regarding the known best routes and potential pitfalls. Hopefully, your previous training experiences, those of your training partners and the other chapters in this book will supply that information.

Planning is the key to success.

Remind yourself throughout the remainder of this chapter that you are not writing an annual plan to impress anyone, or to simply feel organized. The purpose is to create a useful and dynamic guide for your training. In the coming months, you will refer to the plan regularly to make decisions about your training. The plan will help you to keep an eye on the goal and not get lost in just working out and going to races. A training plan is dynamic in that you will frequently modify it as new situations arise.

THE ANNUAL TRAINING PLAN

It's time to get started planning. The six steps you'll complete in this chapter are:

Step 1: Determine season goals

Step 2: Establish supporting objectives

Step 3: Set annual training hours

Step 4: Prioritize races

Step 5: Divide year into periods

Step 6: Assign weekly hours

In Chapter 8 you will complete the plan by assigning weekly workouts based on abilities. This probably sounds like a lot to accomplish. It is, but the system set out here will make it easy to do.

Appendix A has annual planning worksheets for the years 1999-2003. You should complete the appropriate worksheet as you read this and the next chapter. Notice that there are several parts to the Training Plan. At the top left of the page are spaces for "Annual Hours," "Season Goals" and "Training Objectives." Down the left side are rows for each week of the year with the week number and date of the Monday of each week indicated. There are also columns to list the "Races," their priorities ("Pri"), the specific periodization "Period" and training "Hours" for each week. The small boxes down the right side are used to indicate categories of workouts by abilities as listed at the top of the page. You may recognize the "Swim," "Bike" and "Run" subheadings as the abilities discussed in the previous two chapters. Chapter 8 takes you through this last part.

STEP 1: DETERMINE SEASON GOALS

Let's start with the destination. What racing goals do you want to accomplish this season? Perhaps you want to finish a half Ironman-distance race, improve on your time in a particular race, or qualify for Ironman Hawaii. Studies have shown that clearly defined goals improve one's ability to achieve them, just as the successful mountain climber always has the peak in the back of his or her mind. If you don't know where you want to go, by the end of the season you will have gone nowhere.

Clear goals contribute to success.

Don't get goals confused with dreams. Athletes often dream about what they want to accomplish. That's healthy. Without dreams there is no vision for the future and no long-range incentives. Dreams can become realities, but they are so big they take longer than one season to accomplish. If you reasonably can achieve it this season, no matter how big it may seem, it's no longer a dream — it's a goal.

Dreams take more than one season to attain.

Let's be realistically optimistic. If you had trouble finishing international-distance races last season, winning your age group at an Ironman is probably a dream, not a goal. "But," you say, "if you don't set high goals, you never achieve anything." That's true, but the problem with using dreams as annual goals is that since you know down deep you really aren't capable of achieving it this season, there's little commitment to the training required. A challenging goal will stretch you to the limits, and may require you to take some risks, but you can imagine accomplishing it in the next few months. Ask yourself: "If I do everything right, can I achieve this goal this year?" If you can't even conceive of attaining it this year, making it a goal is just window dressing. If you can, it's a good goal. Otherwise, it's a dream. Hang on to it for the more distant future, establish this and the coming years' goals to lead you to it, and eventually the dream will become a goal.

Goals lead to dreams.

There are four principles your goals should adhere to:

Principle 1. Your goal must be *measurable*. How will you know if you are getting closer to it? How do business people know if they are achieving their financial goals? They count their money, of course. Rather than using vague phrases such as "get better" in your goal statement, you might specifically say, "Complete Such-and-Such Race in less than 2:18."

Principles of goal setting.

Principle 2. Your goal must be under *your* control. A successful person doesn't set goals based on other people. "Win my age group in the XYZ race," sounds like a measurable goal, but what if the world champion in your age group shows up? You have no control over who races, what kind of shape they're in, or if they are "training through" or peaking for a given race. You only have a measure of control over yourself, your training and your motivation. There are some goals that are obviously measurable, and yet on the cusp of your control. For example, qualifying for Ironman Hawaii certainly takes a major commitment on your part, and yet is also determined by who shows up at the qualifier. You can improve how much control you have over such a goal by determining what finishing time you think it will take to qualify, probably based on previous year's results, and then aiming at that specific time.

Principle 3. Your goal must *stretch* you. A goal that is too easy is the same as having no goal. "Finish the Stinkyville sprint-distance race" isn't much of a challenge for an experienced multisport athlete. But qualifying for the national championship may really stretch you.

Principle 4: Your goal must be stated in the *positive*. A major league baseball catcher once told his pitcher, "Whatever you do, don't throw it low and outside to this batter." Guess where the pitcher threw it. Home run. Your goal must keep you focused on what you want to happen, not what you want to avoid. What do you suppose happens to a triathlete who sets a goal such as, "Don't swim off course in the Podunkville triathlon"? Chances are the swim is poor because there wasn't a focus on what he or she was *supposed* to do. In the same way, "Don't get a running injury," isn't as good a goal as "Lower the risk of injury by running only when recovered." The latter tells you what to do, rather than what not to do.

With few exceptions, the goal should also be racing-outcome oriented. For example, don't set a goal of climbing better. That's an objective, as we'll see shortly. Instead, commit to certain bike split in a hilly race. A possible exception has to do with major obstacles that have held you back in the past, such as overtraining, injury, burnout or health problems. While these aren't exactly race specific, they may play a big part in your season's success and enjoyment. The following are examples of racing-oriented goals.

EXAMPLES OF GOALS

Goal: Break 2:30 at the national championship.

Goal: Run 10km in less than 40 minutes in the Boulder Peak Triathlon.

Goal: Race for first in my age group in all A-priority races.

Goal: Qualify for Ironman Hawaii with a sub-5:00 time at Desert Sun Triathlon.

Goal: Improve on my USA Triathlon national age-group ranking for last year.

After determining your first goal, you may have one or two others that are important to you. Give them the same consideration as you did the first goal. Stop at three goals so things don't get too complicated in the coming months. List all of your goals at the top of the Annual Training Plan.

STEP 2: ESTABLISH TRAINING OBJECTIVES

In the previous two chapters you determined your strengths and weaknesses, and at the end of Chapter 6 you completed the "Triathlete Assessment" form (page 86). Look back at that form now to refresh your memory. What are your strengths and weaknesses?

Chapter 6 described the concept of limiters. These are the key race-specific weaknesses holding you back from being successful in certain events. Chapter 6 also explained that different abilities were required for different types of races. By comparing your weaknesses with the race's requirements you know your limiters. For example, a long, hilly race requires good force for climbing hills and a high level of endurance. A weakness in either of these areas means you have a limiter for this race that must improve for success.

Read your first season goal. Do any of your weaknesses (score of three or lower on the Triathlete Assessment) present a limiter for this goal? If so, you will need to work specifically to improve that limiter for the coming season. Chapters 8 and 9 provide the details of how to do that.

Knowing your limiters is crucial to success.

Written objectives challenge you to improve a limiter by a certain time. They are specific and measurable tasks you must accomplish in order to achieve the season goal. There are several ways to measure the progress of your objectives. Chapter 5 presented graded exercise tests and time trials you could conduct to gauge improvement, but low-priority races and workouts also serve as good progress indicators. Write training objectives in a manner similar to that used to write your season goals. Set time limits

Objectives are tasks that lead to goals.

for each objective. Most objectives are measured in some precise way, such as a certain time, but some may be subjective. For example, checking improvement of mental skills often relies on sensing that you are more confident or focused.

Timing of the objectives is critical to overall success. To accomplish the goal, the training objective must be achieved by a certain point in the season. Too late is as good as never when it comes to races.

By the time you are done with this part of the Annual Training Plan, you will probably have three to five training objectives listed. These are the short-term standards against which you will measure progress toward goals. If they are appropriate to your limiters and accomplished on time, your goals should be within reach.

EXAMPLES OF LIMITERS AND TRAINING OBJECTIVES BY GOAL

Goal: Break 2:30 at the national championship.

Limiter: Bike muscular endurance

Training Objectives:

1. Elevate lactate threshold power to 220 watts on graded exercise test by July 6.

2. Complete 4 x 10km each under 15:15 with five-minute recoveries by August 3.

Goal: Run 10km in less than 40 minutes in the Boulder Peak Triathlon.

Limiters: Leg speed and muscular endurance

Training Objectives:

1. Run comfortably at a cadence of 90 rpm by May 31.

2. Run a 10km road race in 37:30 or faster by July 20.

Goal: Race for first in my age group in all A-priority races.

Limiter: Mental skills, especially confidence

Training Objectives:

1. Read *Mental Training for Peak Performance* and complete all exercises by February 1.

2. Feel more confident and focused in spring races and group workouts.

Goal: Qualify for Ironman Hawaii with a sub-five-hour at Desert Sun Triathlon.

Limiters: Swim technique, bike force, run endurance

Training Objectives:

1. Squat 250 pounds four times by January 5.

2. Complete a Total Immersion Swim Camp by February 1.

3. Feel stronger climbing hills by May 1.

4. Run 2 hours at an average pace of 7:30 following a 2-hour ride by June 22.

Goal: Improve on my USA Triathlon national age-group ranking for last year.

<u>Limiter:</u> Time available to train

<u>Training Objectives:</u>

1. During Base period, complete longer workouts on weekend.

2. During Build period, schedule group interval workouts in my weekly calendar.

3. Throughout the season, swim with the 5:30 am masters group.

STEP 3: SET ANNUAL TRAINING HOURS

The number of hours you train in the coming season — including swimming, cycling running, weights and cross-training — determines a large part of your training work load. Too high an annual volume is likely to result in overtraining; too low and fitness is lost. Setting annual training hours is one of the most critical decisions you make about training.

Work load is partly determined by volume.

Volume is best expressed in terms of hours rather than distance, such as miles or yards. Training with volume based on distance encourages you to repeat the same bike and run courses week after week. It also causes you to compare your time on a given course today with what it was last week, and to "beat" the previous time. While gauging progress periodically on standard courses is effective, training this way day after day is counterproductive. Using time, however, as a basis for training volume allows you to go wherever you want, so long as you finish within a given time. Your rides are more enjoyable due to the variety and lack of concern about today's speed or pace.

Volume is best based on time rather than distance.

To determine your annual hours, start by adding up the hours you have trained in the previous twelve months. For the coming season, a small increase in volume, in the range of 10 to 15 percent, may be necessary if you are training for a longer-distance race this year than you have done in the past. If you have been training and racing successfully at the same distances for the past season or two, there is little reason to increase volume. There may even be seasons in which your annual hours must decrease due to greater responsibilities at work or lifestyle changes.

How do you determine annual hours if you haven't kept track of time in the past? Many athletes keep a record of the distances they have covered. If you have such a record, divide the totals by what you guess the average speeds were. For example, you may estimate that you swam 2500 meters per hour, biked at eighteen miles per hour and ran seven miles per hour on average for the year. If you have also cross-trained and lifted weights, estimate how many hours you put into those activities in the past year. By adding all of the estimates together, you have a ballpark figure for your annual training hours.

Even without records of annual miles or hours trained, try coming up with an estimate by simply guessing your average weekly volumes in each sport. That will give you a starting point.

Looking back over the last three years, you can probably see trends related to training volume. For example, did you race better in the high-volume years, or worse? Were you overtrained or undertrained at previous volume levels? There were undoubtedly other factors in your performance at those times, but this may help you to decide on the training volume for the coming season.

Table 7.1 offers a general guideline of the annual hours typical of athletes by race distance and age. *This is not a required volume.* There are many athletes with years of racing experience who put in far fewer miles than those suggested here for their category and yet race quite well. Training volume is most effective for developing endurance. With endurance already established by years of training, the emphasis can be shifted away from volume and toward intensity.

Examine performance in previous years at given volume levels.

	TABLE 7.1

Suggested annual training hours based on distance of targeted races or age.

Race Distance/Age	Annual Hours
Ironman	600-1200
Half Ironman	500-700
International	400-600
Sprint	300-500
Juniors	200-350

When in doubt, choose a lower volume.

Carefully limiting the number of hours you train produces better results than struggling through an overly ambitious volume. If you have a full-time job, a family, a home to maintain and other responsibilities, be realistic — don't expect to train with the same volume as the pros. Training *is* their job.

If, however, you have not been competitive in the past, endurance is a limiter, and you fall well below the suggested annual hours for the longest races you have targeted for this season, consider increasing your volume to approach the lower figure in your race range so long as this is not more than a 15-percent increase. Otherwise, increases in your annual hours from year to year are best in the range of 5 to 10 percent.

Many professional business people have limitations imposed on their training time by travel and work responsibilities rather than inherent training capacity. Determining annual hours in this case is based strictly on what is available.

Time available for training is a consideration.

Write your annual training hours at the top of the Annual Training Plan. Later you'll use that figure to assign weekly training hours.

STEP 4: PRIORITIZE RACES

For this step, a list of your planned races is needed. If the race schedule hasn't been published yet, go back to last year's race calendar and guess which days they'll be on. Races usually stay on the same weekends from year to year. Later on, when the race dates are announced, you may need to make some changes. That's one reason for completing the plan in pencil.

On the Annual Training Plan, list all of the races you intend to do by writing them into the "Races" column in the appropriate date rows. Remember that the date indicated in the first column is the Monday of a given week, and the week includes the following Saturday and Sunday. This should be an inclusive list of tentative races, so list all that you may do, even if you're not sure now. You may decide later on not to do some of them, but for now assume you'll do them all. Then categorize the races into A, B and C priorities using the criteria below.

A-PRIORITY RACES

Pick out the three or four races most important to you this year. No more than four. Two A races on the same weekend count as one race. An A race isn't necessarily the one that gets the most press or has the biggest prize purse. It could be the Nowhereville Triathlon, but if you live in Nowhereville, that could be the big race of the year for you.

Assign an A priority to three or four races.

The A races are the most important on the schedule, and all training is designed around them. The purpose of training is to build up to and then peak for the A races.

It's best that these races be clumped together in two- or three-week blocks or widely separated by eight or more weeks. For example, two of the races may fall into a three-week period in May with a non-race week between them, and the other two on back-to-back weekends in August. Then again, two may occur in May, one in July, and the other in September. The idea is that in order to come to a peak for each of these most important races, a period of several weeks is needed to rebuild race fitness. During this time between A races you will still race, but won't experience top form because training volume and intensity has again increased.

Widely spacing A races produces best results.

For most athletes, it's best that the single most important race of the year (the "Mother of All A Races") is scheduled for the second half of the season when fitness is likely the highest of the year.

If your A races aren't neatly spaced or grouped as described here, don't worry. Season priorities are not determined by the calendar, but rather by goals. A schedule, however, that doesn't conveniently space the races makes planning and coming to a peak much more difficult.

In the "Pri" column write in "A" for all of your A-priority races. Remember, no more than four.

B-PRIORITY RACES

These are important races at which you want to do well, but they're not as critical as the A races. You'll rest for a few days before each of them, but not build to a peak. Select as many as 12 of these, and as with the A events, two B races on the same weekend count as one race.

In the Pri column write in "B" for all of these races.

B-priority races are important, but you don't peak for them.

C-PRIORITY RACES

You now have up to 16 weeks dedicated to either A or B races. That's most of the season, and probably more than you will do. All other races on the list are C-priority. C races are done for experience, as hard workouts, as tests of progress, for fun or as tune-ups for A races. You will "train through" these races with no peaking and minimal rest before. It's not unusual to decide at the last moment not to do one of these low-priority events. If your heart isn't in it, you'd be better off training that day.

Be careful with C races as they are the ones in which you're most likely to have a bad experience or go over the edge into a state of overtraining since you may be tired and have low motivation to perform well. They are also usually associated with haphazard racing and confused incentives. Every race scheduled should have a purpose, so decide before a C race what you want to get out of it. If unsure, consider not doing it.

Have a reason for doing C-priority races.

The more experienced you are as a multisport athlete, the fewer C races you should do. Conversely, juniors and novices should do several to gain experience.

Race priorities have nothing to do with how hard you push yourself in a given event, as some athletes believe. With few exceptions, effort is always high in races. You don't go all out in A races and loaf in C races. Rather, the difference between A, B and C races is how you prepare for them. Due to the greater rest and the peaking process, A races usually yield better performances than C races.

The difference between race priorities is preparation, not effort.

STEP 5: DIVIDE YEAR INTO PERIODS

Now that the times in the year when you want to come into top form are known (the A-race weeks), annual periodization is possible. Periodization was described in Chapters 3 and 6. Figure 7.1 summarizes those discussions in terms of the suggested time spans and purposes of each period.

If you are a junior, master or elite athlete, you should read the appropriate section in Chapter 14 before preceding as you may need to alter the periodization routine described here.

Find your first A race on the schedule, and in the Period column write in "Race" next to it. This first Race period extends throughout your one- to three-week clumping of A races. Count up the page two weeks from Race and write in "Peak" in the Period column. If the A race is a sprint- or international-distance event, work backward four weeks from Peak and indicate "Build 2." When training for an Ironman-distance race, the Build periods are omitted to concentrate on the most basic abilities. Periodization for half-Ironman races depends on your experience level. If you have done several races of this distance and are comfortable with them, continue to include the Build periods. Otherwise, omit the Build periods and concentrate on Base.

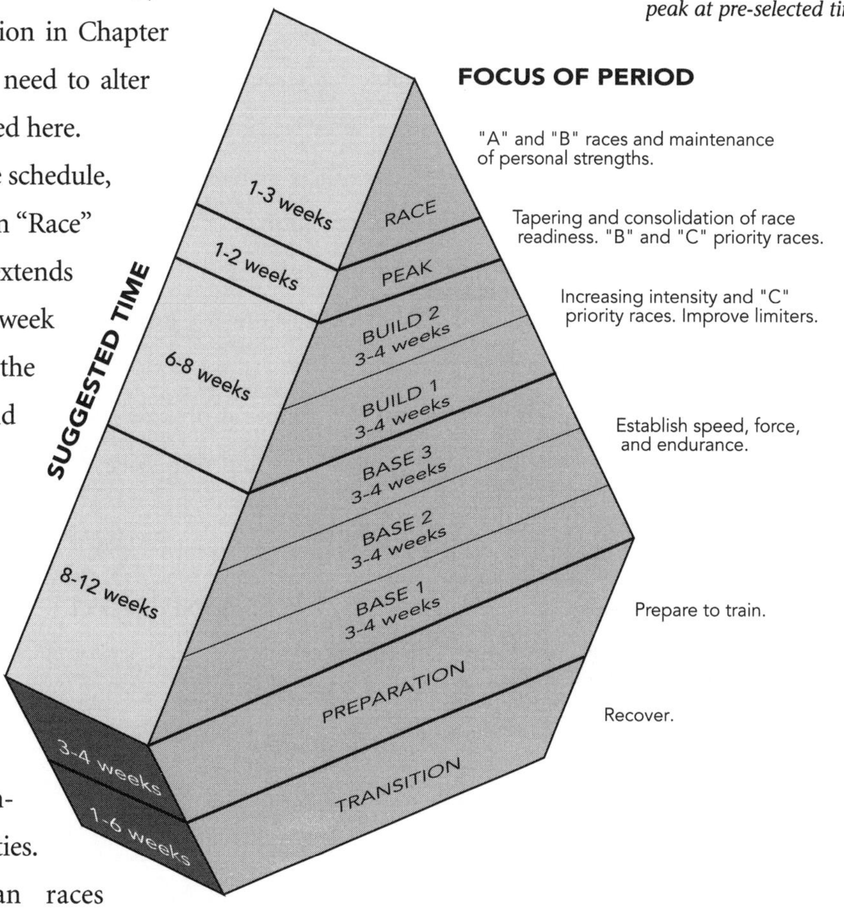
FOCUS OF PERIOD
SUGGESTED TIME
1-3 weeks
1-2 weeks
6-8 weeks
8-12 weeks
3-4 weeks
1-6 weeks
RACE
PEAK
BUILD 2 3-4 weeks
BUILD 1 3-4 weeks
BASE 3 3-4 weeks
BASE 2 3-4 weeks
BASE 1 3-4 weeks
PREPARATION
TRANSITION
"A" and "B" races and maintenance of personal strengths.
Tapering and consolidation of race readiness. "B" and "C" priority races.
Increasing intensity and "C" priority races. Improve limiters.
Establish speed, force, and endurance.
Prepare to train.
Recover.

FIGURE 7.1
Using training periods to peak at pre-selected times.

Using weekly durations as indicated in figure 7.1, do the same for Build 1, Base 3, Base 2, Base 1, Prep and Transition. The first peak of the year is now scheduled.

Go to your second A race or clumping of A races, and write in "Race" as you did above. Count backwards two weeks and write in "Peak" again. Using the same criteria for race distances explained above, count back four weeks for Build 2 and another four for Build 1. Also include a "Transition" week following the first Race period, and before Build 1. When training for sprint- and international-distance races, it's not necessary to repeat the Base period unless you have had a long break from training following the first Race period.

It's unlikely that the Build-Peak period between your two Race periods will work out to exactly 11 weeks. Once you have the second Peak period and a Transition week scheduled, if you have six weeks remaining, plan on a three-week Build 2 and a three-week Build 1. If there are seven weeks you could schedule a four-week Build 1 and a three-week Build 2, depending on your needs. Of course, if your next scheduled race is at the Ironman, or possibly half-Ironman distance, use Base 2 and Base 3 instead. In some schedules, there may only be time for one period, in which case it's probably best as a Build 1 or Base 3 since these periods do a better job of maintaining your endurance.

The one-week Transition after your first Race period is to allow for recovery before cranking up the training again, and to prevent burnout later in the season. This always pays off with higher enthusiasm for training and greater fitness for late-season races. Following the last Race period of the season schedule a longer Transition period.

If this step in the planning process seems confusing, look ahead to Chapter 9 where case studies with easy and not-so-easy annual plans are described. These may help to clear up the confusion.

STEP 6: ASSIGN WEEKLY HOURS

Throughout the season there is a stair-step pattern of increasing and decreasing volume and intensity as you build to a peak. Figure 7.2 illustrates this. The purpose of this pattern is to make sure your endurance is maintained, but to permit increases in intensity without overly stressing your body's systems.

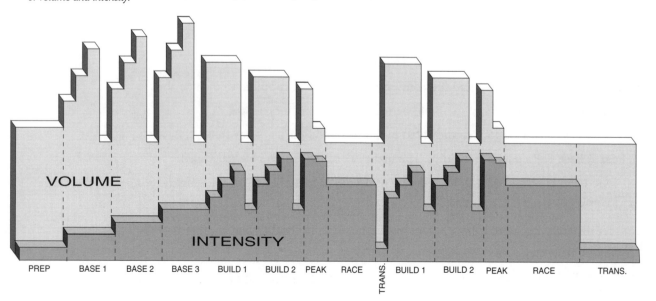

TABLE 7.2

Weekly Training Hours

Period	Week	200	250	300	350	400	450	500	550	600	650	700	750	800	850	900	950	1000	1050	1100	1150	1200
												Annual hours										
Prep	All	3.5	4.0	5.0	6.0	7.0	7.5	8.5	9.0	10.0	11.0	12.0	12.5	13.5	14.5	15.0	16.0	17.0	17.5	18.5	19.5	20.0
Base 1	1	4.0	5.0	6.0	7.0	8.0	9.0	10.0	11.0	12.0	12.5	14.0	14.5	15.5	16.5	17.5	18.5	19.5	20.5	21.5	22.5	23.5
	2	5.0	6.0	7.0	8.5	9.5	10.5	12.0	13.0	14.5	15.5	16.5	18.0	19.0	20.0	21.5	22.5	24.0	25.0	26.0	27.5	28.5
	3	5.5	6.5	8.0	9.5	10.5	12.0	13.5	14.5	16.0	17.5	18.5	20.0	21.5	22.5	24.0	25.5	26.5	28.0	29.5	30.5	32.0
	4	3.0	3.5	4.0	5.0	5.5	6.5	7.0	8.0	8.5	9.0	10.0	10.5	11.5	12.0	12.5	13.5	14.0	14.5	15.5	16.0	17.0
Base 2	1	4.0	5.5	6.5	7.5	8.5	9.5	10.5	11.5	12.5	13.0	14.5	16.0	17.0	18.0	19.0	20.0	21.0	22.0	23.0	24.0	25.0
	2	5.0	6.5	7.5	9.0	10.0	11.5	12.5	14.0	15.0	16.5	17.5	19.0	20.0	21.5	22.5	24.0	25.0	26.5	27.5	29.0	30.0
	3	5.5	7.0	8.5	10.0	11.0	12.5	14.0	15.5	17.0	18.0	19.5	21.0	22.5	24.0	25.0	26.5	28.0	29.5	31.0	32.0	33.5
	4	3.0	3.5	4.5	5.0	5.5	6.5	7.0	8.0	8.5	9.0	10.0	10.5	11.5	12.0	12.5	13.5	14.0	15.0	15.5	16.0	17.0
Base 3	1	4.5	5.5	7.0	8.0	9.0	10.0	11.0	12.5	13.5	14.5	15.5	17.0	18.0	19.0	20.0	21.0	22.5	23.5	25.0	25.5	27.0
	2	5.0	6.5	8.0	9.5	10.5	12.0	13.5	14.5	16.0	17.0	18.5	20.0	21.5	23.0	24.0	25.0	26.5	28.0	29.5	30.5	32.0
	3	6.0	7.5	9.0	10.5	11.5	13.0	15.0	16.5	18.0	19.0	20.5	22.0	23.5	25.0	26.5	28.0	29.5	31.0	32.5	33.5	35.0
	4	3.0	3.5	4.5	5.0	5.5	6.5	7.0	8.0	8.5	9.0	10.0	10.5	11.5	12.0	12.5	13.5	14.0	15.0	15.5	16.0	17.0
Build 1	1	5.0	6.5	8.0	9.0	10.0	11.5	12.5	14.0	15.5	16.0	17.5	19.0	20.5	21.5	22.5	24.0	25.0	26.5	28.0	29.0	30.0
	2	5.0	6.5	8.0	9.0	10.0	11.5	12.5	14.0	15.5	16.0	17.5	19.0	20.5	21.5	22.5	24.0	25.0	26.5	28.0	29.0	30.0
	3	5.0	6.5	8.0	9.0	10.0	11.5	12.5	14.0	15.5	16.0	17.5	19.0	20.5	21.5	22.5	24.0	25.0	26.5	28.0	29.0	30.0
	4	3.0	3.5	4.5	5.0	5.5	6.5	7.0	8.0	8.5	9.0	10.0	10.5	11.5	12.0	12.5	13.5	14.0	15.0	15.5	16.0	17.0
Build 2	1	5.0	6.0	7.0	8.5	9.5	10.5	12.0	13.0	14.5	15.5	16.5	18.0	19.0	20.5	21.5	22.5	24.0	25.0	26.5	27.0	28.5
	2	5.0	6.0	7.0	8.5	9.5	10.5	12.0	13.0	14.5	15.5	16.5	18.0	19.0	20.5	21.5	22.5	24.0	25.0	26.5	27.0	28.5
	3	5.0	6.0	7.0	8.5	9.5	10.5	12.0	13.0	14.5	15.5	16.5	18.0	19.0	20.5	21.5	22.5	24.0	25.0	26.5	27.0	28.5
	4	3.0	3.5	4.5	5.0	5.5	6.5	7.0	8.0	8.5	9.0	10.0	10.5	11.5	12.0	12.5	13.5	14.0	15.0	15.5	16.0	17.0
Peak	1	4.0	5.5	6.5	7.5	8.5	9.5	10.5	11.5	13.0	13.5	14.5	16.0	17.0	18.0	19.0	20.0	21.0	22.0	23.5	24.0	25.0
	2	3.5	4.0	5.0	6.0	6.5	7.5	8.5	9.5	10.0	11.0	11.5	12.5	13.5	14.5	15.0	16.0	17.0	17.5	18.5	19.0	20.0
Race	All	3.0	3.5	4.5	5.0	5.5	6.5	7.0	8.0	8.5	9.0	10.0	10.5	11.5	12.0	12.5	13.5	14.0	15.0	15.5	16.0	17.0

Now that you know annual hours and have divided the year into periods, you are ready to assign weekly training hours — the volume portion of your season. Find the column in table 7.2 that corresponds with your Annual Hours at the top of the Annual Training Plan. In that column are weekly hours in half-hour increments. On the left side of the table are all of the periods and the weeks within each. By reading across and down, determine the number of hours for each week, and write those in the appropriate rows under the Hours column on the Annual Training Plan.

You've now completed the Annual Training Plan with the exception of the Swim, Bike and Run workouts portion. That's the next chapter.

REFERENCES

Bompa, T. 1988. Physiological intensity values employed to plan endurance training. *New Studies in Athletics* 3 (4): 37-52.

Bompa, T. 1994. *Theory and Methodology of Training*. Dubuque, IA: Kendall/Hunt Publishing.

Costill, D., et al. 1991. Adaptations to swimming training: Influence of training volume. *Medicine and Science in Sports and Exercise* 23: 371-377.

Friel, J. 1996. *The Cyclist's Training Bible*. Boulder, CO: VeloPress.

Maglischo, E. 1982. *Swimming Faster*. Mountain View, CA: Mayfield Publishing.

Martin, D. and P. Coe. 1991. *Training Distance Runners*. Champaign, IL: Leisure Press.

VanHandel, P.J. 1991. The science of sport training for cycling, part I. *Conditioning for Cycling* 1(1): 8-11.

VanHandel, P.J. 1991. The science of sport training for cycling, part II. *Conditioning for Cycling* 1(2): 18-23.

VanHandel, P.J. 1991. Planning a comprehensive training program. *Conditioning for Cycling* 1(3): 4-12.

PLANNING A WEEK

"All too often, athletes — particularly young ones — equate improvements in performance solely with hard physical training.... It's really only part of the picture."

— ROD CEDARO, EXERCISE PHYSIOLOGIST

If there's one lesson you must get from this book, it's that training should have a purpose based on your unique needs. Haphazard training may bring results sporadically, but to reach the highest level of racing fitness at the right times, carefully planned workouts are necessary. Before starting any training session, from the easiest to the most difficult, one simple question requires an answer: What is the purpose of this workout? If that question goes unanswered, there's a high likelihood that little progress is made in the swim, bike or run session. The answer to this question relates to your objectives, goals, strengths and limiters. You are either trying to improve some specific aspect of physical and/or mental fitness, or you are maintaining. Another possibility, and one that's too often overlooked by athletes, is that the planned workout's purpose is active recovery. Other purposes are testing and race simulation. Deciding in advance what benefit the workout will provide, and reviewing its purpose before starting, is critical to peaking at the right moments in the season. Of course, this is predicated on first having a well-conceived plan.

> **Purposeful training produces peak fitness at the right times.**

The purpose of this chapter is understanding and applying the principles of workout scheduling. The first task in accomplishing this is the completion of the Annual Training Plan started in Chapter 7. With it complete, by the time you finish the present chapter, you will have determined the key workouts for each week of the season, and have a good understanding of how they blend into a weekly schedule. As mentioned before, all work on the Annual Training Plan is done in pencil as changes are usually necessary during the year. Keep the completed Annual Training Plan with your training diary and review it weekly as you prepare for the next training week. Later, in Chapter 15, you will learn how to use the diary in conjunction with your Annual Training Plan to produce a comprehensive daily and weekly schedule.

STEP 7: SCHEDULE WEEKLY WORKOUTS

The last chapter led you through the first six steps in designing your season using the Annual Training Plan. By now you should have completed the sections of the Plan titled Annual Hours, Season Goals, Training Objectives, Races, Priorities (Pri), Period and Hours. Now you have reached the meat of the plan — the workout categories.

Across the top right of the Annual Training Plan are the headings Swim, Bike and Run, and below each are six columns titled with the abilities discussed in previous chapters (Endurance, Force, Speed, Muscular Endurance, Anaerobic Endurance and Power) and a column for Testing. In this step, you will assign workouts in these categories to each week of the season. Then, when you are ready to start a given week, you will determine which specific workouts will most benefit each of the abilities. Appendixes B, C, D and E list workouts by each of the abilities from which you can choose the appropriate one for a given day. This listing of workouts is by no means exhaustive. There are many other possibilities, including the combination of workouts into a unique session that challenges more than one ability.

WEIGHTS

Weight training especially benefits cycling.

Before getting started on the swim, bike and run workout sections, however, notice that there is a column to their left headed "Weights." In this column you can note the phases of weight-room strength training for the season. This is a sometimes-neglected aspect of training for multisport, especially by athletes whose limiter is force. Measurable results, especially on the bike, are initially quite evident from this type of training. Newcomers to weight training are usually amazed at how strong they feel on hills in the spring after a winter of weights.

The details of the five strength phases are discussed in Chapter 13, but with a little information you can complete the Weights column now by penciling in the abbreviations for the various phases. Here's how to determine the duration of each phase. If you're a bit confused, flip ahead to Chapter 9 for examples of completed Annual Training Plans.

• **Anatomical Adaptation (AA) phase**. If no strength work has been done in the last four weeks, include four to six weeks of AA at the outset of your training year, preferably during the Preparation period at the start of the season. If there are less than four weeks since weight training stopped, assign two to four weeks of AA during Prep.

• **Maximum Strength (MS) phase.** If force, especially on the bike, is a limiter, schedule the next six weeks to MS. Otherwise, just four weeks of MS. This is usually best in the Base 1 period of the season.

• **Power-Endurance (PE) phase.** If you compete primarily in short events such as sprint-distance races, or both force and speed are limiters for any of the three sports, assign the next six weeks to PE. Otherwise, schedule four weeks for PE.

• **Muscular-Endurance (ME) phase.** If muscular endurance is a limiter for any of the three sports, schedule six weeks of ME. If not a limiter, plan on four weeks of ME. Muscular-endurance takes longer to develop than the other strength qualities, but is fortified by swim, bike and run training.

• **Strength Maintenance (SM) phase.** At this point in the year, about the time Build 1 begins, many athletes in their 20s and even into their early 30s may stop weight training. Most masters and women, however, are well advised to maintain their strength gains from the winter months throughout most of the remaining season. Schedule no weight training during the week of A races.

PERIODIZATION OF WORKOUTS

The following will help you complete the Swim, Bike and Run sections of the Annual Training Plan. Let's begin with the recovery and rest (R & R) weeks since those are usually neglected, but are in some ways the most important. If there is any confusion on how to mark the Annual Training Plan, see the examples in Chapter 9. Masters, those new to multisport and elite athletes should read the appropriate part of Chapter 14, if not already read, before continuing.

Masters, novices and elites read Chapter 9 before proceeding.

• **R & R Weeks.** Every fourth week during the Base and Build periods is reserved for recovery and rest from the accumulated fatigue of the previous three weeks. Without such regular unloading of fatigue, fitness won't progress for long. You have already partially incorporated R & R by assigning reduced weekly hours during the fourth weeks of Base and Build based on Table 7.2. Now we'll assign the workouts to those low-volume weeks.

R & R weeks help prevent overtraining, burnout, illness and injury.

For each of the R & R weeks, place an "X" under the Endurance and Speed columns for each sport. In the Base and Build periods, put an X under the Testing column if there is not a race. Other than the possibility of one strength session, that's all for those weeks. The idea is to recover from the collected stress, feel rested by week's end, maintain endurance, speed and strength, and test progress once rested. In the Build and Peak periods there may be a B or C race at week's end that serves as a test. Chapter 5 and Appendixes B, C and D describe tests you may do during R & R weeks.

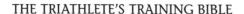

Now you are ready to complete workout categories for the other, "non-R & R" weeks of the year by indicating which abilities will be targeted. Later, when you are ready to choose the exact workouts for a given week, Appendixes B, C, D and E will help you select the proper ones based on the abilities targeted here.

• **Preparation.** Place an X in the Endurance and Speed columns for each week of the Preparation period for each sport. Endurance training during this period concentrates on improving the endurance characteristics of the heart, blood and lungs, referred to collectively as the cardiorespiratory system. Cross-training is an option during this period, especially when poor weather interferes with bike and run sessions, but since multisport already is so diverse, swimming, cycling and running may otherwise continue normally. Also place an X under Testing in the first and last weeks of the Preparation period.

The Prep period is a time of "training to train."

• **Base 1.** Again, mark the Endurance and Speed columns for each week of the Base 1 period. During this period, endurance workouts are longer and speed work increases. Weather is often the determining factor for the bike and run training done now. A mountain-bike ride, cross-country ski or snowshoe trip are excellent alternatives during this period when the weather makes road work difficult. A good indoor bike trainer and a treadmill are also excellent tools to train on throughout the Base period when you can't get on the roads.

Base 1 improves endurance and max strength.

• **Base 2.** Place an X in the Endurance, Force, Speed and Muscular-Endurance columns for each non-R & R week of the Base 2 period. As you can see in the suggested workouts for this period in Appendixes B, C and D, muscular-endurance is done at moderate intensities and force training is in the initial stages as the strength gained in the just-completed weights MS phase begins the conversion to swim-, bike- and run-specific force. Endurance workouts continue to increase in duration.

Force and muscular endurance are introduced in Base 2.

• **Base 3.** Mark the Endurance, Strength, Speed and Muscular-Endurance columns for each week of the Base 3 period, other than R & R weeks. Training volume reaches a maximum level during this period. Intensity has also risen slightly with the addition of more force and muscular endurance work.

In Base 3 volume reaches the annual high point.

• **Build 1 and Build 2.** Schedule workouts for Endurance and Muscular Endurance for each non-R & R week of the Build 1 and Build 2 period. Also select your greatest limiter for each sport and mark that column. If unsure which limiter to schedule, choose Strength for the bike and run, and Anaerobic Endurance for swimming. If Power or Anaerobic Endurance are not selected for a sport, also mark Speed for that sport. In this period, work on two abilities is often combined in one workout session.

In the Build periods, volume is reduced as intensity rises.

Races count as workouts, too. A sprint-distance race may take the place of an Anaerobic Endurance or Power workout. Hilly races are substitutes for Force, and international- and half Ironman-distance events are both Muscular Endurance and Endurance workouts. Early season races in the Build 1 period are best as C-priority. The week of B-priority races, schedule only one ability in one sport. Remember that you're training through C-priority races, meaning that there is no extensive rest before the race. Schedule each Build 1 and Build 2 period on your Annual Training Plan in this same way.

• **Peak.** Place an X in the Endurance and Muscular Endurance columns for each sport. If the race you are peaking for is an international-distance race or shorter, also mark your remaining greatest limiter for just one sport for each week of the Peak period. If unsure of your next limiter, select Anaerobic Endurance in your weakest sport. If Anaerobic Endurance or Power are not marked, also mark Speed. If the race is a half Ironman or an Ironman, schedule only Speed in addition to Endurance and Muscular Endurance for each sport. Races may be substituted for workouts using the same criteria as in the Build period. C races in the Peak period are excellent tune-ups for the approaching A races as they get you back into a racing mode again. There should only be two high-intensity workouts (4 and 5 zones) each week of Peak. Remember that high-intensity bike and run workouts are combined into one workout. Mark all Peak periods in this same way.

In Peak, volume drops again as race intensity is emphasized.

• **Race.** During each week of this period, either race or, when there is no race, complete a race-effort simulation such as a "brick," a combined bike and run session, and an Anaerobic Endurance swim. Mark Power for each sport. All Race periods are marked in the same manner. R & R weeks with a B-priority race at the end may be treated like Race weeks. In Race weeks the race provides the "workout" for other abilities.

A little power work in the Race period maintains "sharpness."

• **Transition.** Don't mark anything. This is an unstructured period that is meant to recharge your mental and physical "batteries." You should, however, stay active, especially in sports that you enjoy other than swimming, biking and running. These could be team games such as soccer, basketball, volleyball or hockey; or endurance activities including cross-country skiing, power hiking or in-line skating. Don't become a couch potato, but also don't train seriously. Take several days off, and rest as much as you can.

The Transition period is a time of mental and physical recovery.

BREAK THROUGH AND RECOVERY WORKOUTS

The only workouts you have scheduled so far are those meant to challenge or maintain your racing abilities. Those that challenge you are called "Break Through" — or "BT" — workouts. The difficulty of any given BT workout will vary by period. For example, a session with lots of three-zone time challenges your muscular endurance in the Base period. In the Peak

BT workouts challenge your fitness.

period, however, this same workout would probably not be considered very challenging. In the same way, a long endurance session in Base 1 may really tax you, but later on, once your endurance is well established, such a swim, bike or run places little demand on your body.

Recovery workouts that are placed between such difficult BT sessions are not scheduled on the Annual Training Plan, but they are obviously an integral part of any program and should be included frequently. Appendixes B, C and D offer suggestions for such workouts, and the following section on weekly training patterns describes how to incorporate them into your training.

WEEKLY TRAINING ROUTINES

Now that your Annual Training Plan is complete, the only issues left to decide at the start of each week are which specific workouts to do, on which days to do them, and how long to make them. That's no small thing. You could have the best possible plan, but if workouts are not blended in such a way as to allow for both recovery and adaptation, then it's all for nothing. The problem is that both long- and short-duration workouts must be combined with workouts that are of high and low intensity in three sports in addition to other training modes such as weights.

Chapter 15 provides a weekly training journal format on which to record the days' scheduled workouts and their results. For now let's examine ways to determine each day's routine.

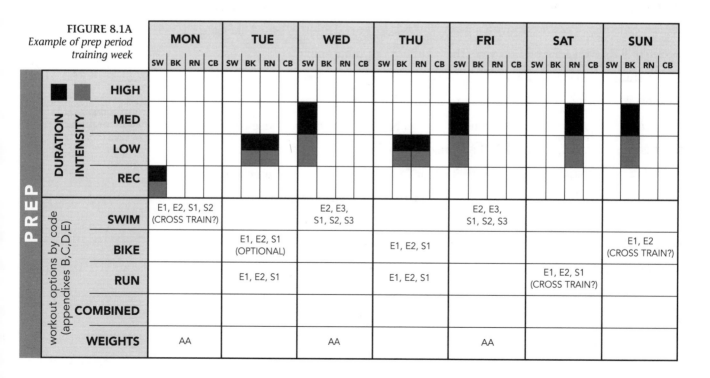

FIGURE 8.1A
Example of prep period training week

PATTERNS

Figure 8.1 illustrates one possible pattern for blending volume and intensity for each week of the year's training periods including R & R and Race weeks. These are examples only as there are too many individual variables, such as different combinations of limiters and time available for training, to provide patterns that work for every athlete. Use these as a guide to help you design your own patterns.

FIGURE 8.1B
Example of Base 1 period training week

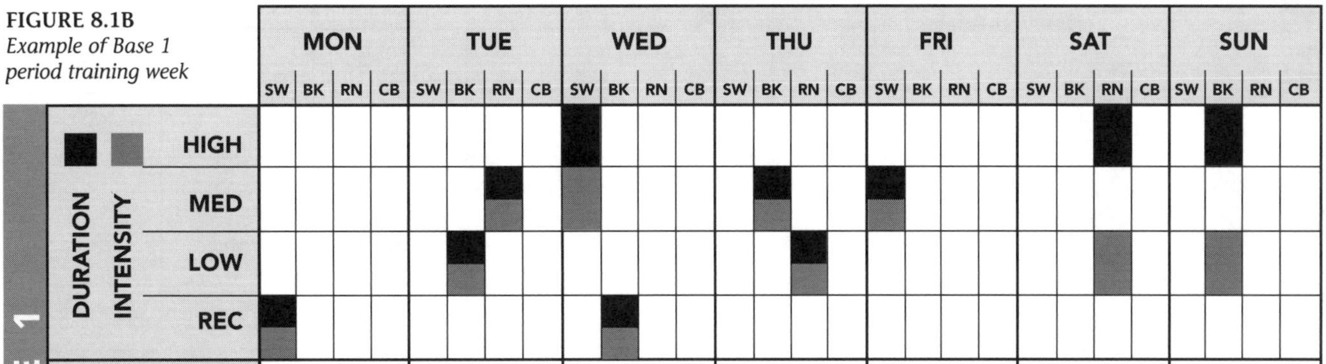

		MON				TUE				WED				THU				FRI				SAT				SUN			
		SW	BK	RN	CB	SW	BK	RN	CB	SW	BK	RN	CB	SW	BK	RN	CB	SW	BK	RN	CB	SW	BK	RN	CB	SW	BK	RN	CB

BASE 1 — DURATION / INTENSITY: HIGH, MED, LOW, REC

workout options by code (appendixes B,C,D,E):

	MON	TUE	WED	THU	FRI	SAT	SUN
SWIM	E1, E2, S1, S2		E2, E3, S3		E2, E3, S3		
BIKE		E2, S1, S2	E1	E3, S1, S2			E2
RUN		E3, S1, S2		E2, S1, S2		E2	
COMBINED							
WEIGHTS	MS				MS		

FIGURE 8.1C
Example of Base 2 period training week

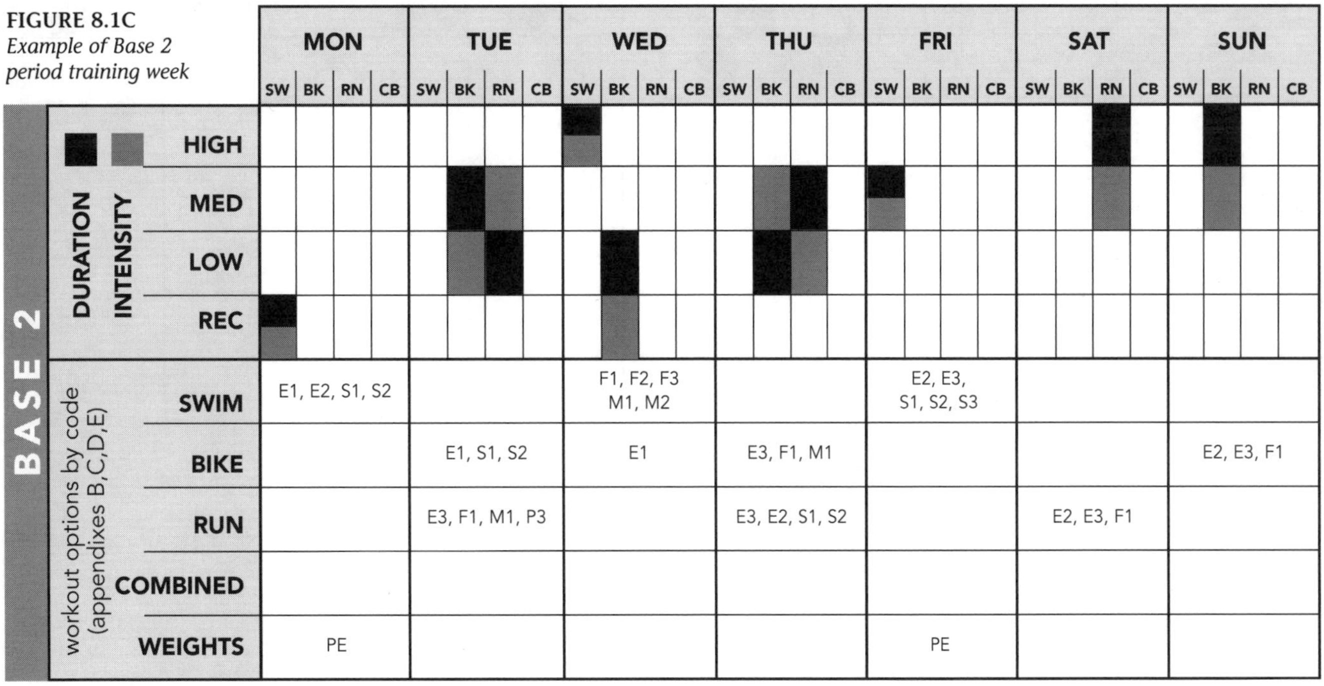

		MON				TUE				WED				THU				FRI				SAT				SUN			
		SW	BK	RN	CB	SW	BK	RN	CB	SW	BK	RN	CB	SW	BK	RN	CB	SW	BK	RN	CB	SW	BK	RN	CB	SW	BK	RN	CB

BASE 2 — DURATION / INTENSITY: HIGH, MED, LOW, REC

workout options by code (appendixes B,C,D,E):

	MON	TUE	WED	THU	FRI	SAT	SUN
SWIM	E1, E2, S1, S2		F1, F2, F3 M1, M2		E2, E3, S1, S2, S3		
BIKE		E1, S1, S2	E1	E3, F1, M1			E2, E3, F1
RUN		E3, F1, M1, P3		E3, E2, S1, S2		E2, E3, F1	
COMBINED							
WEIGHTS	PE				PE		

FIGURE 8.1D
Example of Base 3 period training week

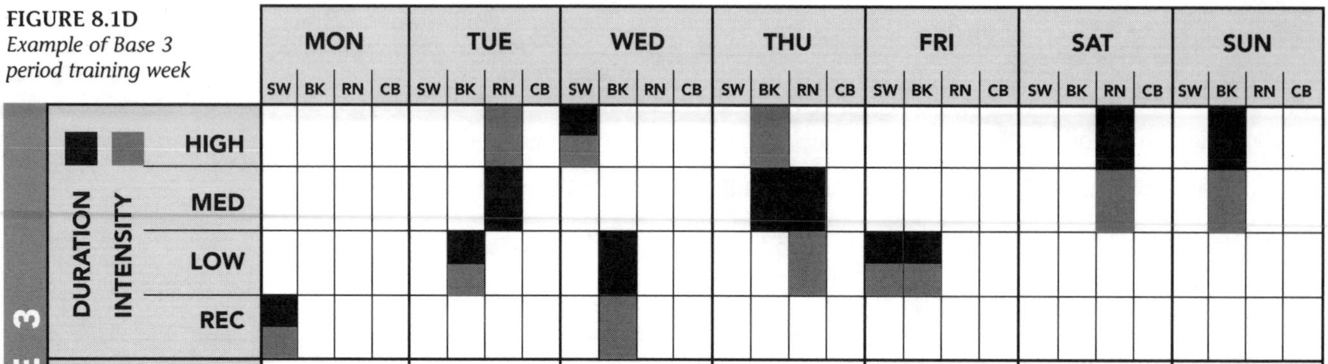

			MON				TUE				WED				THU				FRI				SAT				SUN			
			SW	BK	RN	CB	SW	BK	RN	CB	SW	BK	RN	CB	SW	BK	RN	CB	SW	BK	RN	CB	SW	BK	RN	CB	SW	BK	RN	CB
BASE 3	DURATION / INTENSITY	**HIGH**									■					■										■				■	
		MED							■							■											■				■	
		LOW						■					■					■			■											
		REC	■																													
	workout options by code (appendixes B,C,D,E)	**SWIM**	E1, E2, S1, S2								F1, F2, F3, M1, M2, M3								E2, E3, S1, S2, S3											
		BIKE					E2, S1, S2				E1				F1, F2, M1, M2				E2, S1, S2								E1, E2, E3, F1, F2			
		RUN					F1, F2, M1, M2, P3								E2, S1, S2								E2, E3, F1, F2							
		COMBINED																					E1, E2, F1 (OPTIONAL)							
		WEIGHTS	ME																											

FIGURE 8.1E
Example of Base period rest and recovery week

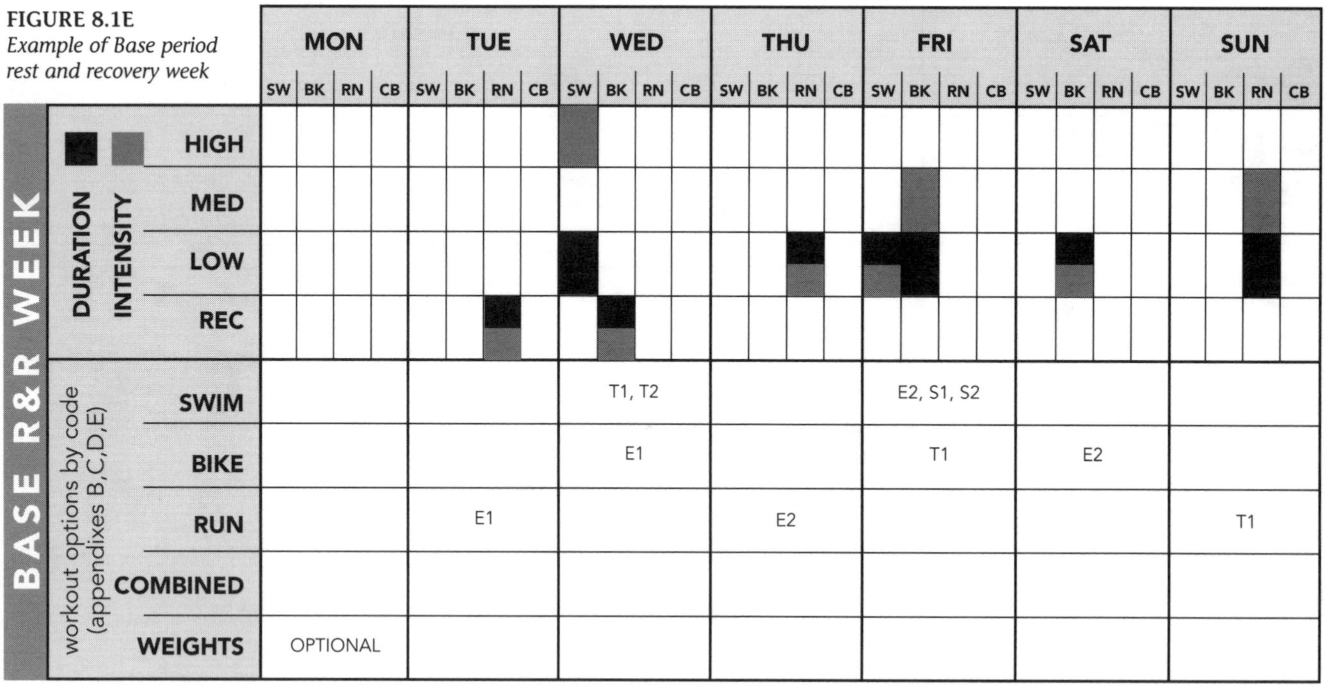

			MON				TUE				WED				THU				FRI				SAT				SUN			
			SW	BK	RN	CB	SW	BK	RN	CB	SW	BK	RN	CB	SW	BK	RN	CB	SW	BK	RN	CB	SW	BK	RN	CB	SW	BK	RN	CB
BASE R&R WEEK	DURATION / INTENSITY	**HIGH**									■																				
		MED																		■										■	
		LOW									■				■					■				■					■	
		REC							■			■																		
	workout options by code (appendixes B,C,D,E)	**SWIM**									T1, T2								E2, S1, S2											
		BIKE									E1								T1				E2							
		RUN					E1								E2												T1			
		COMBINED																												
		WEIGHTS	OPTIONAL																											

FIGURE 8.1F
Example of Build 1 training week.

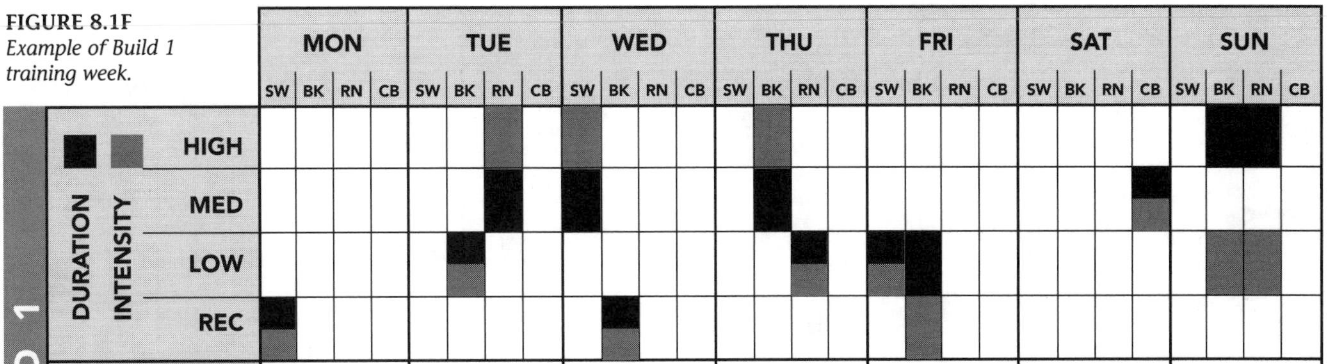

Build 1 — intensity grid (DURATION / INTENSITY: HIGH, MED, LOW, REC) across MON–SUN (SW, BK, RN, CB).

workout options by code (appendixes B, C, D, E):

	MON	TUE	WED	THU	FRI	SAT	SUN
SWIM	E1, E2, S1, S2		F1, F2, F3, M1 M2, M3, A1, P1		E2, S1, S2, S3		
BIKE		E2, S3	E1	F1, F2, M2, M3, M4, A1, A2, A3, P1	E1		ALTERNATE WEEKS E2
RUN		F2, F3, M2, M3, M4, A1, A2, A3, P1		E2, S1, S2			ALTERNATE WEEKS E2
COMBINED						E1, E2, F1, S1	
WEIGHTS	SM						

FIGURE 8.1G
Example of Build 2 training week

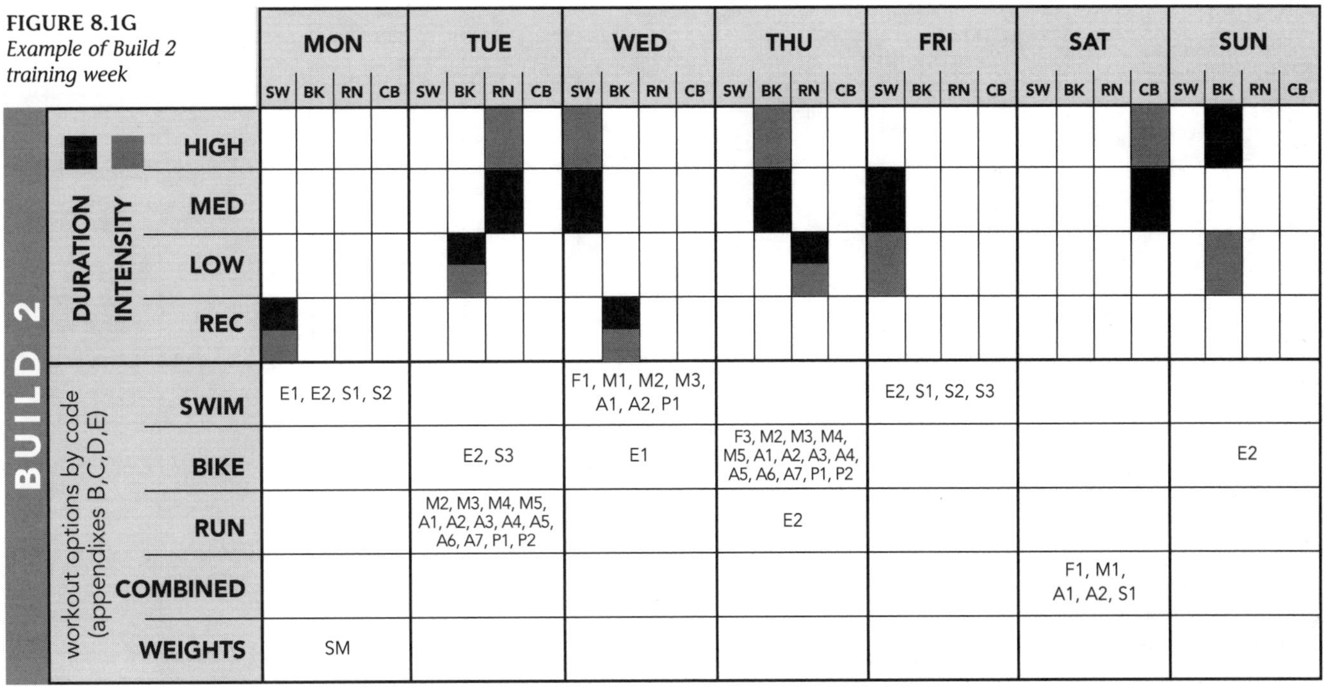

Build 2 — intensity grid (DURATION / INTENSITY: HIGH, MED, LOW, REC) across MON–SUN (SW, BK, RN, CB).

workout options by code (appendixes B, C, D, E):

	MON	TUE	WED	THU	FRI	SAT	SUN
SWIM	E1, E2, S1, S2		F1, M1, M2, M3, A1, A2, P1		E2, S1, S2, S3		
BIKE		E2, S3	E1	F3, M2, M3, M4, M5, A1, A2, A3, A4, A5, A6, A7, P1, P2			E2
RUN		M2, M3, M4, M5, A1, A2, A3, A4, A5, A6, A7, P1, P2		E2			
COMBINED						F1, M1, A1, A2, S1	
WEIGHTS	SM						

FIGURE 8.1H
Example of Build period rest and recovery week.

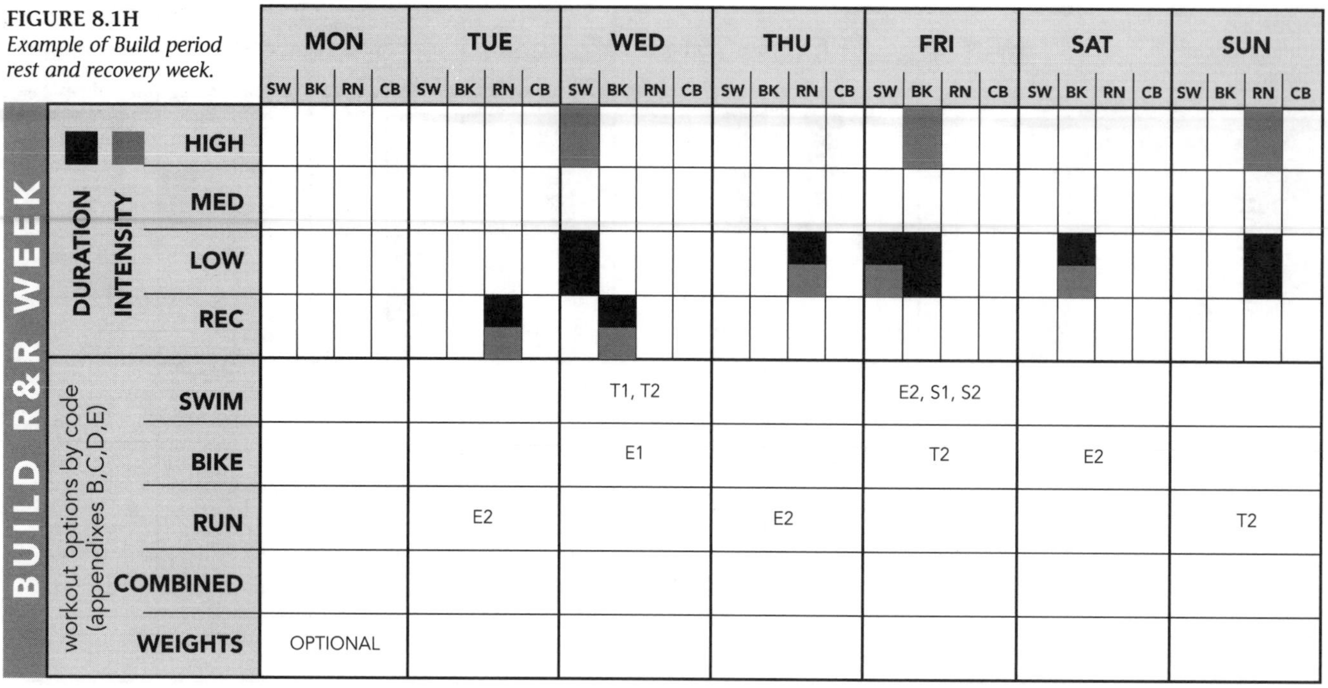

BUILD R&R WEEK		MON				TUE				WED				THU				FRI				SAT				SUN			
		SW	BK	RN	CB	SW	BK	RN	CB	SW	BK	RN	CB	SW	BK	RN	CB	SW	BK	RN	CB	SW	BK	RN	CB	SW	BK	RN	CB
DURATION / INTENSITY	HIGH									■										■								■	
	MED																												
	LOW									■						■			■				■					■	
	REC						■				■																		
workout options by code (appendixes B,C,D,E)	SWIM									T1, T2								E2, S1, S2											
	BIKE										E1								T2				E2							
	RUN					E2									E2													T2	
	COMBINED																												
	WEIGHTS	OPTIONAL																											

FIGURE 8.1I
Example of Peak period training week.

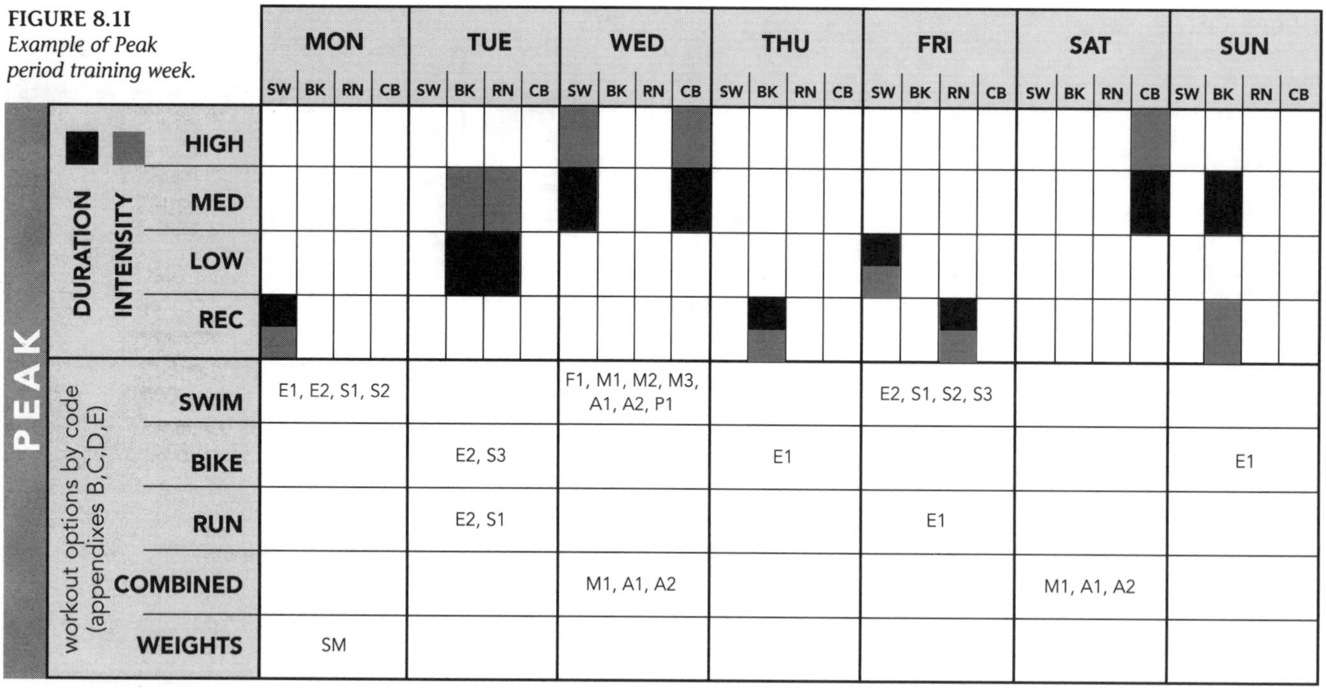

PEAK		MON				TUE				WED				THU				FRI				SAT				SUN			
		SW	BK	RN	CB	SW	BK	RN	CB	SW	BK	RN	CB	SW	BK	RN	CB	SW	BK	RN	CB	SW	BK	RN	CB	SW	BK	RN	CB
DURATION / INTENSITY	HIGH									■																	■		
	MED						■	■		■			■												■		■		
	LOW						■	■											■										
	REC	■												■						■									
workout options by code (appendixes B,C,D,E)	SWIM	E1, E2, S1, S2								F1, M1, M2, M3, A1, A2, P1								E2, S1, S2, S3											
	BIKE					E2, S3								E1														E1	
	RUN					E2, S1												E1											
	COMBINED									M1, A1, A2												M1, A1, A2							
	WEIGHTS	SM																											

FIGURE 8.1J
Example of Race period week with race on Saturday.

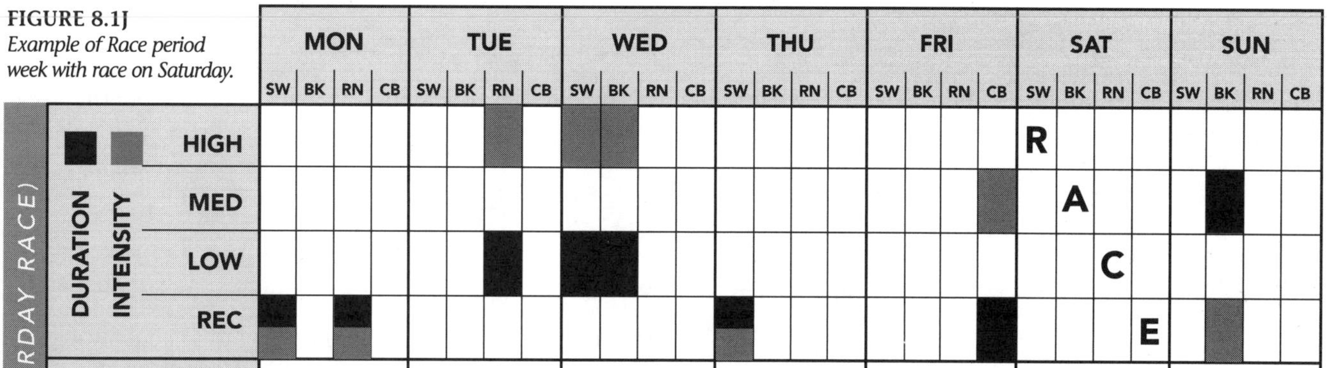

RACE (SATURDAY RACE)			MON				TUE				WED				THU				FRI				SAT				SUN			
			SW	BK	RN	CB	SW	BK	RN	CB	SW	BK	RN	CB	SW	BK	RN	CB	SW	BK	RN	CB	SW	BK	RN	CB	SW	BK	RN	CB
DURATION / INTENSITY	HIGH								■		■	■												R							
	MED																						■	A					■		
	LOW								■		■	■													C						
	REC		■		■										■						■				E			■		
workout options by code (appendixes B,C,D,E)	SWIM		E1, E2, S1, S2									S3, P1				E1, E2, S1, S2 (OR DAY OFF)															
	BIKE											S3, P1																	E1		
	RUN		E1, E2					S1, S2, P1																							
	COMBINED																			S1				RACE							
	WEIGHTS																														

FIGURE 8.1K
Example of Race period week with race on Sunday

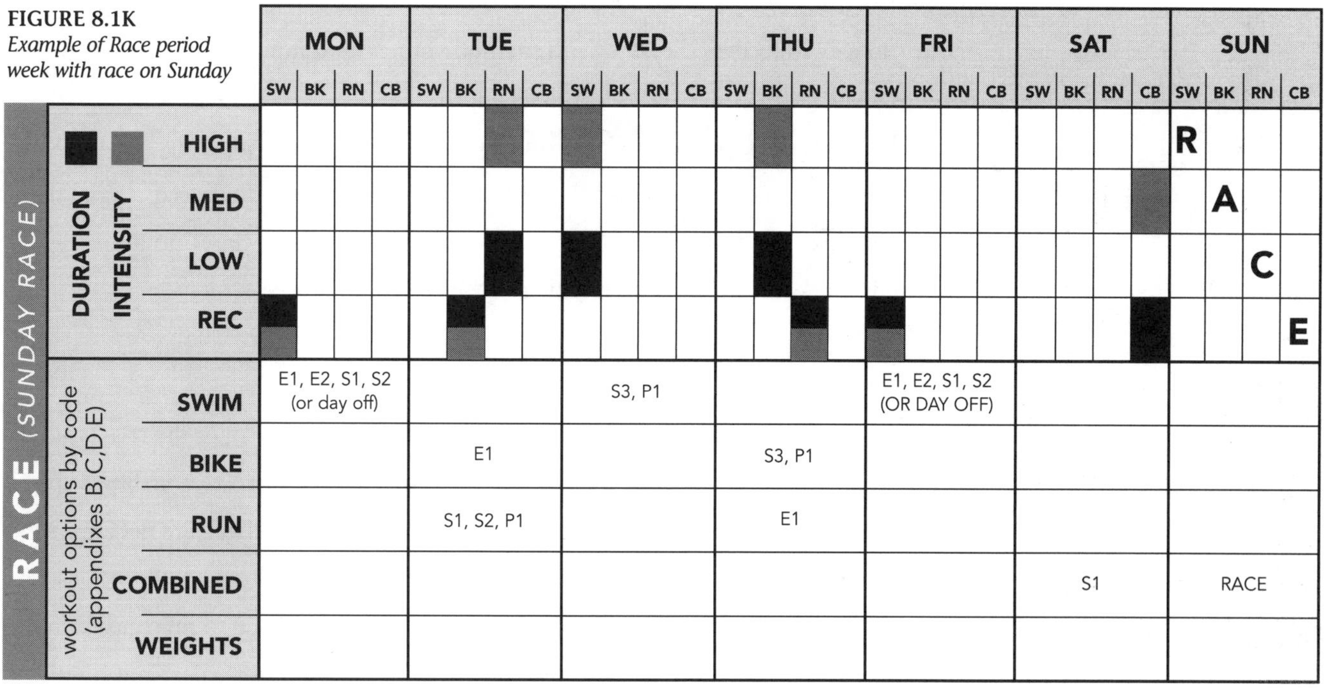

RACE (SUNDAY RACE)			MON				TUE				WED				THU				FRI				SAT				SUN			
			SW	BK	RN	CB	SW	BK	RN	CB	SW	BK	RN	CB	SW	BK	RN	CB	SW	BK	RN	CB	SW	BK	RN	CB	SW	BK	RN	CB
DURATION / INTENSITY	HIGH								■				■				■											R			
	MED																										■		A		
	LOW								■				■					■												C	
	REC		■					■									■		■								■				E
workout options by code (appendixes B,C,D,E)	SWIM		E1, E2, S1, S2 (or day off)									S3, P1								E1, E2, S1, S2 (OR DAY OFF)											
	BIKE							E1								S3, P1															
	RUN							S1, S2, P1								E1															
	COMBINED																							S1				RACE			
	WEIGHTS																														

On Figure 8.1, volume and intensity are indicated as high, medium, low or recovery. Obviously, what is high volume for one athlete may be low for another, so these levels are meaningful only to you. Recovery days are active recovery (very light workout), or passive (day off) depending on your experience level. Novices usually benefit from taking the day off entirely.

Scheduling BT workouts is a balancing act with the creation of appropriate levels of adaptation-causing stress on one side, and recovery, when the adaptation actually occurs, on the other. Within a given week there are two commonly accepted ways of doing this. One is the standard hard-day, easy-day approach. With this pattern, a BT day is followed by a recovery day. Another widely used pattern in triathlon is "block" training in which two, or even three, BT workouts are placed back to back followed by days of recovery and maintenance. Triathlon favors block training since three sports stress different muscle groups on back-to-back workout days. A BT run on one day, for example, can usually be followed by a BT swim the next. Many multisport athletes find that they can even do two BT sessions on the same day in different sports if one, usually the second of the day, is less intense, such as a Muscular-Endurance workout, or if one is a swim. Individual differences in the capacity to recover dictate which method you use and how densely spaced the BT sessions are. Figure 8.1 illustrates the block approach.

Block training is common in multisport.

The "Workout Options by Code" on Figure 8.1 are based on Appendixes B, C, D and E. You may want to create other workouts to better fit your individual needs. Write these down and assign codes to them. These codes are used as short-hand notations when scheduling workouts in your training diary at the start of the week.

DAILY HOURS

In general, triathlon exaggerates a proficiency for cycling since that leg of the race typically makes up about half of a triathlon finishing time. Therefore, it seems reasonable to spend about half of your training time on the bike. In the real world of training, that's not always the case, although cycling should usually make up the largest portion. There are exceptions. For example, triathletes living in the more northern latitudes find it difficult to ride outside in the winter due to cold and snow. In the more equatorial latitudes, summer heat and humidity also favor indoor training. In addition, work responsibilities may force training to early morning or late evening when there is insufficient light for riding outdoors. For these reasons, a quality indoor bike trainer is of paramount importance for the multisport athlete with high aspirations, but even with one of these, cycling volume will certainly suffer during such periods of indoor riding. That's just the way it is, and the creative athlete takes it in stride while mak-

Bike workouts make up the greatest portion of training time.

TABLE 8.1

Daily training hours
(May be two-a-day workouts, or three-a-day for elites)

Weekly Hours	Suggested Daily Hours						
3:00	1:30	0:45	0:45	Off	Off	Off	Off
3:30	1:30	1:00	1:00	Off	Off	Off	Off
4:00	1:30	1:00	1:00	0:30	Off	Off	Off
4:30	1:30	1:00	0:45	0:45	0:30	Off	Off
5:00	1:30	1:00	1:00	1:00	0:30	Off	Off
5:30	1:30	1:15	1:00	1:00	0:45	Off	Off
6:00	1:30	1:15	1:00	1:00	0:45	0:30	Off
6:30	1:30	1:15	1:00	1:00	1:00	0:45	Off
7:00	1:30	1:30	1:15	1:00	1:00	0:45	Off
7:30	2:00	1:30	1:15	1:00	1:00	0:45	Off
8:00	2:00	1:30	1:15	1:15	1:00	1:00	Off
8:30	2:00	1:30	1:15	1:15	1:00	1:00	0:30
9:00	2:00	1:30	1:30	1:15	1:00	1:00	0:45
9:30	2:30	1:30	1:30	1:15	1:00	1:00	0:45
10:00	2:30	2:00	1:30	1:15	1:00	1:00	0:45
10:30	2:30	2:00	1:30	1:30	1:00	1:00	1:00
11:00	2:30	2:00	1:30	1:30	1:30	1:00	1:00
11:30	3:00	2:00	1:30	1:30	1:30	1:00	1:00
12:00	3:00	2:00	2:00	1:30	1:30	1:00	1:00
12:30	3:30	2:00	2:00	1:30	1:30	1:00	1:00
13:00	3:30	2:30	2:00	1:30	1:30	1:00	1:00
13:30	3:30	2:30	2:00	2:00	1:30	1:00	1:00
14:00	4:00	2:30	2:00	2:00	1:30	1:00	1:00
14:30	4:00	2:30	2:00	2:00	1:30	1:30	1:00
15:00	4:00	2:30	2:30	2:00	1:30	1:30	1:00
15:30	4:00	2:30	2:30	2:00	2:00	1:30	1:00
16:00	4:00	3:00	2:30	2:00	2:00	1:30	1:00
16:30	4:00	3:00	2:30	2:30	2:00	1:30	1:00
17:00	4:00	3:00	2:30	2:30	2:00	2:00	1:00
17:30	4:30	3:00	2:30	2:30	2:00	2:00	1:00
18:00	4:30	3:00	3:00	2:30	2:30	2:00	1:00
18:30	4:30	3:00	3:00	2:30	2:30	2:00	1:00
19:00	4:30	3:30	3:00	2:30	2:30	2:00	1:00
19:30	4:30	3:30	3:00	3:00	2:30	2:00	1:00
20:00	4:30	3:30	3:00	3:00	2:30	2:30	1:00
20:30	5:00	3:30	3:00	3:00	2:30	2:30	1:00
21:00	5:00	3:30	3:30	3:00	2:30	2:30	1:00
21:30	5:00	3:30	3:30	3:00	3:00	2:30	1:00
22:00	5:00	4:00	3:30	3:00	3:00	2:30	1:00
22:30	5:00	4:00	3:30	3:30	3:00	2:30	1:00
23:00	5:00	4:00	3:30	3:30	3:00	2:30	1:30
23:30	5:30	4:00	3:30	3:30	3:00	2:30	1:30
24:00	5:30	4:00	4:00	3:30	3:00	2:30	1:30
24:30	5:30	4:00	4:00	3:30	3:30	2:30	1:30
25:00	5:30	4:30	4:00	3:30	3:30	2:30	1:30
25:30	5:30	4:30	4:00	4:00	3:30	2:30	1:30
26:00	6:00	4:30	4:00	4:00	3:30	2:30	1:30
26:30	6:00	4:30	4:00	4:00	3:30	3:00	1:30
27:00	6:00	4:30	4:30	4:00	3:30	3:00	1:30
27:30	6:00	4:30	4:30	4:00	4:00	3:00	1:30
28:00	6:00	5:00	4:30	4:00	4:00	3:00	1:30
28:30	6:00	5:00	4:30	4:30	4:00	3:00	1:30
29:00	6:00	5:00	4:30	4:30	4:00	3:30	1:30
29:30	6:00	5:00	4:30	4:30	4:00	3:30	2:00
30:00	6:00	5:00	5:00	4:30	4:00	3:30	2:00
30:30	6:00	5:00	5:00	4:30	4:30	3:30	2:00
31:00	6:00	5:30	5:00	4:30	4:30	3:30	2:00
31:30	6:00	5:30	5:00	5:00	4:30	3:30	2:00
32:00	6:00	5:30	5:00	5:00	4:30	4:00	2:00
32:30	6:00	5:30	5:30	5:00	4:30	4:00	2:00
33:00	6:00	5:30	5:30	5:00	5:00	4:00	2:00
33:30	6:00	6:00	5:30	5:00	5:00	4:00	2:00
34:00	6:00	6:00	5:30	5:00	5:00	4:30	2:00
34:30	6:00	6:00	5:30	5:30	5:00	4:30	2:00
35:00	6:00	6:00	5:30	5:30	5:00	5:00	2:00

Annual hours may be adjusted seasonally.

ing training adjustments for these conditions.

Since bike workouts are longer than swim or run workouts, when weather or other such hurdles force riding indoors, weekly training volume also needs to decrease. Knowing in advance what may interfere with riding on the roads, make changes in your annual hours to allow for this. If you live in Minnesota, for example, you may plan on training at 350 annual hours in the winter when nearly all cycling is indoors, and at 450 hours in the summer when outdoor riding is possible.

Another exception to spending half of one's training time on the bike involves the athlete who is already a highly proficient cyclist, but has a major limiter in either swimming or running. In such situations, workout volume shifts from time on the bike to the limiting sport.

In the Hours column of your Annual Training Plan you've indicated the volume for each week of the season. All that remains is to decide how those hours are spread during the week. Table 8.1 offers a *suggested* break down. In the left-hand column note the hours you have scheduled for the first week of the season. By reading across to the right, the weekly hours are broken into daily amounts. For example, find "12:00" in the Weekly Hours column. To the right are seven daily hours, one for each day of the week, adding up to 12:00: 3:00, 2:00, 2:00, 1:30, 1:30, 1:00 and 1:00. So the longest workout, or total training for a given day that week, is three hours. The daily hours may be divided between two workouts in the same day, especially in the Base period when volume is high. In fact, there are some advantages to working out two times a day, such as an increase in quality for each workout. These daily hours include all the training you do — swimming, biking, running, weights, and any other cross-training activities.

How to divide weekly hours for each day.

COMBINED WORKOUTS

If you count the BT workouts scheduled for some weeks of your Annual Training Plan, you will see that there are frequently four or five of them, especially in the Build periods. Preparing for races beyond the international distance, or for your maximum performance at any distance, practically requires training twice a day to fit everything in. Three workouts in a day are seldom, if ever, necessary, however. Only the elite athlete who races for a living and has few time demands should seriously consider regular doses of three-a-days. For most serious recreational athletes who have jobs, families, homes and other responsibilities, such a frequency of training is quite likely to lead to overtraining, burnout, illness or injury. Two good workouts are always better than three mediocre ones.

Training three times in a day is not necessary.

Besides two-a-days, it's frequently beneficial in the Build periods to combine workouts in two abilities into one session. Not only does this make better use of available time, but it also more closely simulates the stresses of multisport racing. The two ways to accomplish this are with bricks, as described in Appendix E, and multi-ability sessions detailed in Appendixes C and D called *AE Intervals + Threshold*.

BRICKS

Once the basic abilities of Endurance, Force and Speed are established, combined bike and run workouts, known as bricks, play an increasingly important role in training. Bricks take on many forms including those that enhance aerobic endurance, race pacing, anaerobic endurance, hill strength and even the final equipment check before a race. Selecting the proper brick from Appendix E is based on understanding what the demands of an approaching A- or B-priority race are, and matching the workout to it.

Bricks are key workouts in the Build periods.

MULTI-ABILITY

In the Build and Peak periods it is often necessary to combine two abilities for a single sport into one session. This makes better use of time, and also produces stress levels that more closely simulate racing. A general rule of thumb is to combine either Endurance or Muscular Endurance with Force, Speed, Anaerobic Endurance or Power. When doing this, the less-intense ability of Endurance or Muscular Endurance should follow the higher-intensity ability within the workout. So, for example, a combined run workout, following a warm-up, could start with intervals on the track that challenge Anaerobic Endurance, and then progress to a steady run at near lactate threshold for Muscular Endurance. Such a session is excellent for developing the type of fitness necessary for the run that finishes a race.

Combining abilities within a single workout uses time effectively and simulates race stress.

REFERENCES

Bompa, T. 1988. Physiological intensity values employed to plan endurance training. *New Studies in Athletics* 3(4): 37-52.

Burke, E. 1995. *Serious Cycling.* Champaign, IL: Human Kinetics.

Daniels, J., et al. 1984. Interval training and performance. *Sports Medicine* 1: 327-334.

Faria, I.E. 1984. Applied physiology of cycling, *Sports Medicine* 1: 187-204.

Friel, J. 1996. *The Cyclist's Training Bible.* Boulder, CO: VeloPress.

Guezennec, C.Y., et al. 1996. Increase in energy cost of running at the end of a triathlon. *European Journal of Applied Physiology* 73 (5): 440-445.

Knuttgen, H.G., et al. 1973. Physical conditioning through interval training with young male adults. *Medicine and Science in Sports* 5: 220-226.

Laughlin, T. and J. Delves. 1996. *Total Immersion*. New York: Simon & Schuster.

Okkels, T. 1983. The effect of interval- and tempo-training on performance and skeletal muscle in well-trained runners. *Twelfth European Track Coaches Congress* (Acoteias, Portugal): 1-9.

Maglischo, E.W. 1982. *Swimming Faster*. Palo Alto, CA: Mayfield Publishing.

VanHandel, P.J. 1987. Specificity of training: Establishing pace, frequency, and duration of training sessions. *Bike Tech* 6 (3): 6-12.

PLANNING TO RACE

*"The feeling I get at the starting line is that it's over —
all the hard work and training are over. The race is the fun part."*

— JULIE MOSS, PROFESSIONAL TRIATHLETE

The previous two chapters provided annual and weekly tools for planning a peak performance. These tools along with the information presented in Chapters 3 through 6 make up the *science* of self-coaching for multisport. The less definitive and more difficult part to learn is the *art* of self-coaching. This aspect refers to detecting, scrutinizing and remodeling the many variables that go into designing a season. Sometimes such decisions require careful thought and evaluation. Other times they are simply gut-level feelings born of experience. Many successful athletes, especially those who have trained a long time, operate entirely within this visceral arena. This is not to say that the art of training can't be learned in an academic sense.

One way of developing comprehensive self-coaching skills is to study how others have put together their annual and weekly plans. The case studies that follow are all based on real-world athletes with high aspirations, limited time and great commitment. Their stories may help you see other options for setting up your season. As you read, look especially for ways in which they bent the "rules" described in the previous chapters in order to meet unique sets of circumstances. Their plans as presented here are not necessarily the only possibilities, but they are sound and potentially effective. Regardless of your goal-race distance, reading all of these case studies may offer insights into the process of planning.

DM is a 42-year-old surgeon from Florida who has competed in triathlon for four years. Prior to this he was a runner, but recurrent injuries eventually led him to swimming and cycling as cross-training activities, and finally to triathlon. Running injuries

Sprint-Distance Triathlon

continue to plague DM whenever he increases his mileage too quickly, or repeatedly runs on back-to-back days.

Due to the summer heat in Florida, most of DM's races are in the spring and fall, with the latter being his primary race season. As a surgeon, he has a tight daily schedule and can seldom train more than 10 hours per week. Even that is not possible in some weeks. His annual training plan as illustrated in Figure 9.1 is based on 450 annual hours. But since his maximal, weekly volume is more a matter of how many hours he has available, rather than how many he can physically handle, the weekly hours have all been truncated at 10. This means there is no increase in volume as is typical of the Base period. To use a volume level that built to 10 weekly hours as a high point in the third week of Base 3, as is suggested in Table 7.2, would leave him considerably undertrained since he's capable of handling more than 10 hours weekly.

Available hours often dictate training volume.

DM has planned for two peaks with the fall peak the most important. His season goals are based on the fall sprint-race series and the national championship. By trying to maintain peak race form for four weeks from week 43 to 46, DM is stretching it, but since the week-46 race is the last important one of the season, there is no reason to do otherwise.

An extended Peak period may be possible at season end.

Weight-room strength is not a problem for DM, but he has been unable to convert this to on-bike strength since taking up triathlon. This is evidenced by his inability to turn a high gear at race cadence. So bike muscular endurance is emphasized in his annual plan, and these workouts will include many cruise interval and threshold sessions in which he repeatedly shifts between a "comfortable" gear and the next higher one in 30- to 60-second bouts. In the brief periods he is in the higher gear, he will attempt to maintain the same cadence of the lower gear. Such training should improve his ability to drive a bigger gear.

Other limiters for DM, besides bike force and time available for training, are swimming and running anaerobic endurance. Since anaerobic endurance comes around rather quickly once aerobic endurance, force, speed and muscular endurance are developed, high intensity intervals are only scheduled for the Build periods.

Anaerobic endurance responds quickly to training.

Figure 9.2 shows how a typical week in the Prep period is organized. Notice that DM has only planned one bike workout in this period. That's because weight training takes the place of riding during this period. The benefit of greater force appears to have a more direct application to cycling than to swimming and running, with swim performance having the second closest relationship to high force development. Once the Base period begins, weight-room workouts are cut back to two per week and more time on the bike is included.

Weight training most benefits cycling.

FIGURE 9.1

Athlete: DM
Annual Hours: 450
Season Goals:
1 TOP 5 FINISH IN SPRINT SERIES
2 BREAK 1 HOUR AT NATIONALS.
3
Training Objectives:
1 INCREASE BIKE LT POWER 15% BY WK 40
2 RUN 19-MINUTE 5K BY WK 36.
3 REMAIN INJURY FREE.
4 SWIM 800 METERS IN <8 MIN BY WK 19.
5

Abilities column key (each discipline): E = Endurance, F = Force reduced Endur, S = Speed Skills, M = Muscular Endur, A = Anaerobic Endur, P = Power Endur, T = Testing

Wk#	Mon	Races	Pri	Period	Hours	Wts	Sw							Bk							Rn						
							E	F	S	M	A	P	T	E	F	S	M	A	P	T	E	F	S	M	A	P	T
1	Jan-04			PREP	7.5	AA	X		X					X		X					X		X				
2	Jan-11				7.5	AA	X		X				X	X		X				X	X		X				X
3	Jan-18			BASE1	9.0	MS	X		X					X		X					X		X				
4	Jan-25				10.0		X		X					X		X					X		X				
5	Feb-01				10.0		X		X					X		X					X		X				
6	Feb-08				6.5		X		X				X	X		X				X	X		X				X
7	Feb-15			BASE2	9.5	ME	X	X	X	X				X	X	X	X				X	X	X	X			
8	Feb-22				10.0		X	X	X	X				X	X	X	X				X	X	X	X			
9	Mar-01				10.0		X	X	X	X				X	X	X	X				X	X	X	X			
10	Mar-08				6.5		X		X				X	X		X				X	X		X				X
11	Mar-15			BUILD1	10.0	SM	X			X	X			X			X	X			X			X	X		
12	Mar-22				10.0		X			X	X			X			X	X			X			X	X		
13	Mar-29				6.5		X			X			X	X			X			X	X			X			X
14	Apr-05			BUILD2	10.0		X			X	X			X			X	X			X			X	X		
15	Apr-12				10.0		X			X	X			X			X	X			X			X	X		
16	Apr-19	5K ROAD RACE	C		6.5		X		X					X		X					X		X				
17	Apr-26	INT'L DISTANCE	B	PEAK	9.5		X			X	X			X			X	X			X			X	X		
18	May-03				7.5		X			X				X			X				X			X			
19	May-10	SPRINT DISTANCE	A	RACE	6.5	O					X							X						X			
20	May-17			TRAN	—	O																					
21	May-24			BASE1	9.0	MS	X		X					X		X					X		X				
22	May-31				10.0		X		X					X		X					X		X				
23	Jun-07				10.0		X		X					X		X					X		X				
24	Jun-14				6.5		X		X				X	X		X				X	X		X				X
25	Jun-21			BASE2	9.5	PE	X	X	X	X				X	X	X	X				X	X	X	X			
26	Jun-28				10.0		X	X	X	X				X	X	X	X				X	X	X	X			
27	Jul-05				10.0		X	X	X	X				X	X	X	X				X	X	X	X			
28	Jul-12				6.5		X		X				X	X		X				X	X		X				X
29	Jul-19			BASE3	10.0	ME	X	X	X	X				X	X	X	X				X	X	X	X			
30	Jul-26						X	X	X	X				X	X	X	X				X	X	X	X			
31	Aug-02						X	X	X	X				X	X	X	X				X	X	X	X			
32	Aug-09				6.5		X		X				X	X		X				X	X		X				X
33	Aug-16			BUILD1	10.0	SM	X			X	X			X			X	X			X			X	X		
34	Aug-23						X			X	X			X			X	X			X			X	X		
35	Aug-30	SPRINT DISTANCE	C				X			X	X			X			X	X			X			X	X		
36	Sep-06	5K ROAD RACE	C		6.5		X		X					X		X					X		X				
37	Sep-13			BUILD2	10.0		X			X	X			X			X	X			X			X	X		
38	Sep-20	SPRINT DISTANCE	C				X			X	X			X			X	X			X			X	X		
39	Sep-27						X			X	X			X			X	X			X			X	X		
40	Oct-04				6.5		X		X				X	X		X				X	X		X				X
41	Oct-11	SPRINT DISTANCE	B	PEAK	9.5		X			X	X			X			X	X			X			X	X		
42	Oct-18	SPRINT DISTANCE	B		7.5		X			X	X			X			X	X			X			X	X		
43	Oct-25	SPRINT DISTANCE	A	RACE	6.5	O				X							X							X			
44	Nov-01	SPRINT DISTANCE	B		7.5	SM				X							X							X			
45	Nov-08	SPRINT NATS	A		6.5	O				X							X							X			
46	Nov-15	SPRINT DISTANCE	B		7.5	SM				X							X							X			
47	Nov-22			BUILD1	10.0		X			X	X			X			X	X			X			X	X		
48	Nov-29						X			X	X			X			X	X			X			X	X		
49	Dec-06						X		X				X	X		X				X	X		X				X
50	Dec-13	SPRINT DISTANCE	C		6.5		X		X					X		X					X		X				
51	Dec-20			TRAN	—	O																					
52	Dec-27				—	O																					

FIGURE 9.2
Week #1 for DM.

	MON		TUE		WED		THU		FRI		SAT		SUN	
WORKOUT 1	WTS AA	:45	RUN E1	:45	SWIM S1, E2	:45	RUN S1	:45	SWIM S1, E2	:45	RUN E1	1:00	BIKE E1	1:30
WORKOUT 2					WTS AA	:45			WTS AA	:45				

FIGURE 9.3
Week #39 for DM.

	MON		TUE		WED		THU		FRI		SAT		SUN	
WORKOUT 1	SWIM S1, E1	:45	RUN E1	:45	SWIM M1, A1	:45	RUN A2	1:00	SWIM S1, E2	:45	CMB M1	1:30	BIKE E2	2:00
WORKOUT 2	WTS SM	:30	BIKE P1	1:00	BIKE E1	1:00								

Maximize fitness each intensity zone.

Notice in Figure 9.2 that most all of the aerobic workouts are zone 1. In the early stages of fitness building it's important to become as fast as possible at a low effort before progressing to the next, higher intensity zone. This ensures comprehensive fitness development.

Figure 9.3 illustrates a challenge commonly faced by endurance athletes: a week including high-intensity workouts following a week that ended with a race. For DM, attempting to do an anaerobic-endurance running workout on Tuesday of this week would greatly increase his risk of injury. Therefore his track session is moved to Thursday with the higher intensity bike workout on Tuesday. The Tuesday bike session is a power workout. DM will start this workout and assess his capacity to finish it as he progresses. Should he not feel that his body is recovered enough for powerful movements yet, he will not attempt to complete the repetitions, and will simply ride easily in the 1 zone for the remainder of the hour.

The hours in both illustrated weeks are varied from what is suggested in Table 8.1 in order to better fit DM's unique needs.

INTERNATIONAL-DISTANCE DUATHLON

EW is a 53-year-old, part-time fitness director at a health club. She has competed in duathlons and running for four years, but started cycling competitively seven years ago. This greater experience on the bike is evident in her race splits.

Year-round strength training is necessary for some.

At 1.74 pounds per inch, EW is quite lean, even for an athlete, and as is sometimes the case when body mass is low, force development is her major limiter. Year-round weight training, especially with an emphasis on it in the Prep and Base periods is a necessity for her to achieve her aggressive goals as listed at the top of her annual training plan in Figure 9.4.

FIGURE 9.4

Athlete: EW
Annual Hours: 350 (WKS 1-12), 450 (WKS 13-52)
Season Goals:
1 PLACE TOP 10 AT DUATHLON NATS.
2 QUALIFY FOR DUATHLON WORLDS.
3 RUN UNDER 25 MINUTES FOR 5K.
Training Objectives:
1 FINISH HALF MARATHON IN WK 12.
2 DO 6 STEP UPS WITH 75+ lbs BY WK 6.
3 2ND 5K WITHIN 1 MIN OF 1ST IN A & B RACES.
4 COMPLETE 40K TT IN <1:11 BY WK 45.
5

Column key — each discipline (Swim, Bike, Run) subdivided: E = Endurance, F = Force, S = Speed skill, M = Muscular Endurance, A = Anaerobic Endurance, P = Power, T = Testing.

Wk#–Mon	Races	Pri	Period	Hours	Weights	Sw-E	Sw-F	Sw-S	Sw-M	Sw-A	Sw-P	Sw-T	Bk-E	Bk-F	Bk-S	Bk-M	Bk-A	Bk-P	Bk-T	Rn-E	Rn-F	Rn-S	Rn-M	Rn-A	Rn-P	Rn-T
1-Nov-02			BASE1	8.5	MS								X	X						X	X					
2-Nov-09			↓	9.5									X	X						X	X					
3-Nov-16			↓	5.0									X		X					X		X				X
4-Nov-23			BASE2	9.0									X	X						X	X	X				
5-Nov-30			↓	10.0									X	X						X	X	X				
6-Dec-07			↓	5.0									X		X					X		X				X
7-Dec-14			BASE3	9.5	PE								X	X						X	X	X				
8-Dec-21			↓	10.5									X	X						X	X	X				
9-Dec-28			↓	5.0									X		X					X		X				
10-Jan-04			PEAK	7.5									X	X						X	X					
11-Jan-11			↓	6.0									X		X					X		X				
12-Jan-18	HALF MARATHON	A	RACE	5.0	O									X												X
13-Jan-25			TRAN	–	O																					
14-Feb-01			BASE2	9.5	MS								X	X	X	X				X	X	X	X			
15-Feb-08			↓	11.5									X	X	X	X				X	X	X	X			
16-Feb-15			↓	12.5									X	X	X	X				X	X	X	X			
17-Feb-22	15K ROAD RACE	C	↓	6.5									X		X					X		X				
18-Mar-01			BASE3	10.0	ME								X	X	X	X				X	X	X	X			
19-Mar-08			↓	12.0									X	X	X	X				X	X	X	X			
20-Mar-15			↓	13.0									X	X	X	X				X	X	X	X			
21-Mar-22	INT'L DU	C	↓	6.5									X		X					X		X				
22-Mar-29	5K ROAD RACE	C	BUILD1	11.5	SM								X	X	X	X				X	X	X	X			
23-Apr-05			↓	11.5									X	X	X	X				X	X	X	X			
24-Apr-12	10K ROAD RACE		↓	6.5									X		X					X		X				
25-Apr-19			BUILD2	10.5									X	X	X	X				X	X		X	X		
26-Apr-26			↓	10.5									X	X	X	X				X	X		X	X		
27-May-03	INT'L DU	B	↓	6.5									X		X					X		X				
28-May-10			BUILD2	10.5									X	X	X	X				X	X		X	X		
29-May-17	INT'L DU		↓	6.5									X		X					X		X				
30-May-24	TEAM TRI	C	PEAK	9.5									X	X	X					X			X	X		
31-May-31			↓	7.5									X	X	X					X			X	X		
32-Jun-07	DU NATS	A	RACE	6.5	O													X						X		
33-Jun-14			TRAN	–	O																					
34-Jun-21			BASE3	12.0	SM								X	X	X	X				X	X	X	X			
35-Jun-28			↓	6.5									X		X					X		X				X
36-Jul-05			BUILD1	11.5									X	X	X	X				X	X	X	X			
37-Jul-12			↓	11.5									X	X	X	X				X	X	X	X			
38-Jul-19	INT'L DU	B	↓	6.5									X		X					X		X				
39-Jul-26			BUILD2	10.5									X	X	X	X				X	X		X	X		
40-Aug-02	INT'L DU	C	↓	10.5									X	X	X	X				X	X		X	X		
41-Aug-09			↓	6.5									X		X			X		X		X				X
42-Aug-16			BUILD2	10.5									X	X	X	X				X	X		X	X		
43-Aug-23			↓	10.5									X	X	X	X				X	X		X	X		
44-Aug-30			↓	6.5									X		X					X		X				X
45-Sep-06	40K TT	B	PEAK	9.5									X	X	X	X				X		X	X			
46-Sep-13			↓	7.5									X	X	X	X				X		X	X			
47-Sep-20	INT'L DU	A	RACE	6.5	O													X						X		
48-Sep-27	5K ROAD RACE	B	↓	↓	O													X								X
49-Oct-04	5K ROAD RACE	B	↓	↓	O													X								X
50-Oct-11			TRAN	–	O																					
51-Oct-18			↓	–	O																					
52-Oct-25			↓	–	O																					

Although EW will not attend the duathlon world championship this year due to a schedule conflict, qualifying is still a strong incentive and would indicate her ability as a duathlete. In the previous year she made Team USA and participated in the world championship by qualifying at a regional race, but she has never competed in the duathlon nationals. The following year she is aiming for a medal at nationals and a top five at world's. In that year, EW will "age-up" to the 55-59 age group, and even loftier goals are on the agenda for that season.

It's usually unrealistic to set goals based on performance in relation to others since you never know who might show at a race and what their fitness might be. In this case, however, EW knows all of the players, and can count on them being in top form for national and world championships as they have been at these races in the past. So, in a way, EW has fairly well-known quantities with which to compare her performances. And since the championship courses are never the same two years in a row, the competitors are the only variable that remains somewhat constant.

Besides force, the other limiter EW must improve is running muscular endurance. A duathlete's muscular endurance for running is suspect when the second-5km, average pace is more than 20 seconds slower than the first. Improving this vital element of duathlon fitness involves boosting running endurance and force development separately and then combining them in workouts such as cruise intervals and threshold runs. Following this with tempo bricks makes the ability more race specific. Figure 9.5 illustrates how this process is begun in an early week of EW's training season. Notice that on Saturday of week 7 she is doing a two-hour, "M1" run workout. The first 75 minutes of this workout is done in the 1 and 2 zones with the last 45 minutes continuous in the 3 zone. Figure 9.6 shows how this ability reaches it's final form with a two-hour, "M1" brick. This "graduate-level" workout starts with a 30-minute run building from the 1 to the 3 zone. The 60-minute bike portion includes a 10km time trial at the goal effort for her next A-priority race that follows in week 47. The final 30-minute run includes a 15-minute effort at goal race pace. Late in the season this workout will seem less intimidating than if it was done prior to the development of the prerequisite abilities.

Week 43 has a lot of intensity built into it with bike hill repeats on Tuesday, run hill intervals on Thursday and the brick on Saturday. So on Wednesday, EW may cut the bike ride short, and on Thursday may replace the bike "jumps" with an "E1" ride. These decisions are made shortly after starting the workouts and assessing the level of recovery. Typically, recovery is somewhat improved later in the season as fitness reaches its highest levels of the year. Early in the year such a week may not be possible for EW.

FIGURE 9.5
Week #7 for EW.

	MON		TUE		WED		THU		FRI		SAT		SUN	
WORKOUT 1	RUN S1	:45	RUN E1	1:00	RUN F1	1:30	RUN E1	:30	OFF		RUN M1	2:00	BIKE E1	2:00
WORKOUT 2	WTS PE	:45					WTS PE	:45						

FIGURE 9.6
Week #43 for EW.

	MON		TUE		WED		THU		FRI		SAT		SUN	
WORKOUT 1	RUN E1	:30	RUN E2	:45	BIKE E1	1:30	RUN A4	:45	OFF		CMB M1	2:00	BIKE E2	2:30
WORKOUT 2	WTS SM	:30	BIKE F3	1:00			BIKE S3	1:00						

INTERNATIONAL-DISTANCE TRIATHLON

LT is a 29-year-old, second-year professional triathlete. Life as a neopro is not easy, so LT works part time to make ends meet financially. Her husband is a coach at the local college and quite supportive of her career. They have no children.

In college LT was an All-American runner at 800 meters with a 2:06 personal best, so her running speed is excellent. Prior to this season, she had never run for more than about 75 minutes in a workout, and most were far shorter, so her endurance is questionable. Some disproportionate slowing as the distance gets longer is evident in her other personal best times: 35:30 for 10km, 16:30 for 5km and 2:11 for an international-distance triathlon. Excellent speed, however, is a good starting place for a career in endurance sports.

Endurance can be developed easier than speed.

Other limiters that impact her major goal of qualifying for the national team for the world championship as an elite athlete are swim speed, bike force and bike-handling skills in a pack (many of her most important races are draft-legal). These limiters are primarily the result of being new to triathlon — she's in her third season — and having no background in swimming or cycling. While experience will correct these deficiencies given enough time, speeding the process up is necessary this year as she is rapidly approaching her assumed physiological peak period in her early 30s as an endurance athlete. In addition, her long-term goal is contending for a spot on the national team for the Olympics in three years, so the improvement curve must be steep.

Probably because she is new to the sport, confidence is also holding her back. If LT is to make the world's team and continue growing, frequent success is necessary. To build greater confidence, several C-priority running races and local international-distance

FIGURE 9.7

Athlete: LT
Annual Hours: 550
Season Goals:
1 QUALIFY FOR WORLDS TEAM.
2 SWIM SUB-23 MIN. FOR 1500m.
3 RUN SUB-38 MIN. FOR 10K IN A RACE.

Training Objectives:
1 SWIM 1K IN <15:14 BY WK 18.
2 LEG PRESS 320+ POUNDS BY WK 10.
3 RIDE IN PACK 7 TIMES BY WK 29, 16 BY WK 45.
4 EASILY RUN 90+ MIN BY WK 18.
5 COMPLETE 3 CRASH WEEKS IN 6 WEEKS BY 43.

Ability column legend — each discipline (Swim, Bike, Run) has columns: E = Endurance, F = Force, S = Speed, M = Muscular Endurance, A = Anaerobic Endurance, P = Power, T = Testing. The first column is Weights.

Wk# Mon	Races	Pri	Period	Hours	Wt
1-Jan-06			PREP	9.0	AA
2-Jan-13					
3-Jan-20					
4-Jan-27					
5-Feb-03					
6-Feb-10					
7-Feb-17			BASE 1	11.0	MS
8-Feb-24				13.0	
9-Mar-03				14.5	
10-Mar-10				8.0	
11-Mar-17			BASE 2	12.5	PE
12-Mar-24				14.0	
13-Mar-31				15.5	
14-Apr-07	5K ROAD RACE	C		8.0	
15-Apr-14			BASE 3	12.5	ME
16-Apr-21	INT'L DU	C		14.5	
17-Apr-28				16.5	
18-May-05	INT'L TRI	B		8.0	
19-May-12	SPRINT TRI	B	BUILD 1	14.0	SM
20-May-19					
21-May-26	5K ROAD RACE	C			
22-Jun-02	INT'L DU	B		8.0	
23-Jun-09			BUILD 2	13.0	
24-Jun-16	10K ROAD RACE	C			
25-Jun-23					
26-Jun-30	INT'L TRI	C		8.0	
27-Jul-07			PEAK	11.5	
28-Jul-14	INT'L TRI	B		9.5	
29-Jul-21	TRI NATS, INT'L	A	RACE	8.0	O
30-Jul-28			TRAN	-	O
31-Aug-04			BASE 2	15.5	SM
32-Aug-11	INT'L TRI	B		8.0	
33-Aug-18			BASE 3	12.5	
34-Aug-25				14.5	
35-Sep-01	10K ROAD RACE	C		16.5	
36-Sep-08	INT'L DU	B		8.0	
37-Sep-15			BUILD 1	14.0	
38-Sep-22			CRASH	14.0	O
39-Sep-29	5K ROAD RACE	C	R&R	7.0	O
40-Oct-06			BUILD 2	13.0	SM
41-Oct-13	10K ROAD RACE	C	CRASH	13.0	O
42-Oct-20	6K XC RACE	C	R&R	7.0	SM
43-Oct-27			CRASH	13.0	O
44-Nov-03			R&R	7.0	O
45-Nov-10	8K ROAD RACE	C	PEAK	11.5	O
46-Nov-17	TRI WORLDS, INT'L	A	RACE	8.0	O
47-Nov-24			TRAN	-	
48-Dec-01				-	
49-Dec-08				-	
50-Dec-15				-	
51-Dec-22					
52-Dec-29					

triathlons are sprinkled throughout her annual training plan, as shown in Figure 9.7. She is likely to win these, which will boost confidence, while she gains valuable race experience at the same time. A well-established professional triathlete need not race this frequently, especially in low-key events, and may pick and choose competitions. Other than world's, one or two races in foreign countries will be sought to gain experience at traveling and competing, in addition to two or three major national events. Since her finances are tight, LT will need to convince the national governing body that she is a good investment for the future. Success in races is the only way to do this.

> Success breeds confidence.

Notice in Figure 9.7 that her season is rather long starting with an event in early April and going well into late November. The chance of burnout is quite high when a racing season lasts for 32 weeks as hers does. R & R weeks and Transition periods are critical in this situation. Also due to the season's length, LT will return to base training in week 31 to shore up the most basic elements of fitness before building to a second peak for Worlds.

> Frequent rest is a necessity in a long season.

Figure 9.8 shows how she will blend a typical B-priority, race-week schedule with an R & R week. The week is treated much as a race week, except more caution is evident since she will have just finished a three-week Build 1 period at relatively high volume and intensity. The race at week's end is an international-distance event that she should complete in about 2:15. The extra 30 minutes allocated to that race includes warm-up and cool-down time.

> Blending race and R & R weeks.

In order to reach as high a level of fitness as possible for the World Championship, LT will incorporate three "crash" weeks into her late season preparation in weeks 38, 41 and 43. (Crash weeks are described in greater detail in Chapter 14.) If done correctly, a crash week will dramatically boost fitness. If done recklessly, such a schedule is likely to cause injury. The likelihood of overtraining is possible, but not overwhelming since the increased training intensity only lasts for a week and is followed by a greater-than-normal reduction in volume. Also, there is only a one-week build up to crash weeks 38 and 41, so that R & R weeks are spaced just three weeks apart. The last crash week (43) is preceded and followed by R & R weeks. One study showed that with elite athletes more than two weeks of crash-type training is necessary to cause overtraining.

> Overtraining may result from more than two weeks of overreaching.

FIGURE 9.8 *Week #22 for LT.*	**MON**		**TUE**		**WED**		**THU**		**FRI**		**SAT**		**SUN**	
WORKOUT 1	WTS SM	:30	RUN P1	:45	SWIM P1	:30	BIKE P1	1:00	OFF		CMB S1	:45	RACE	2:45
WORKOUT 2			BIKE E1	:45	BIKE E1	1:00								

Figure 9.9 illustrates a crash week. LT is cautious with swim intensity this week since a still-developing swim stroke is fragile and could easily break down. At this stage in swimming, fitness at the expense of form is not a good trade off. For the same reason, swimming first on double workout days is a good idea. The hours from Table 8.1 have been redistributed to better fit her needs. Note that Friday is a recovery day. A little caution following a run-emphasis brick on Thursday and a hilly run on Saturday is wise in such weeks since running injuries are the most common problem faced in a crash week. Monday also is reduced-intensity day since she will have raced cross-country on the prior Saturday. You don't want to start a crash week tired.

The risk of injury from excessive running is high in a crash week.

FIGURE 9.9 Week #43 for LT.	MON		TUE		WED		THU		FRI		SAT		SUN	
WORKOUT 1	SWIM S1, S2	1:00	RUN M5	:45	SWIM F3, N2	1:00	SWIM E2	:30	SWIM S1, S2	:45	RUN F2	1:30	SWIM S1, E2	:30
WORKOUT 2			BIKE S3	1:00	BIKE M3	1:30	CMB M1	1:30	BIKE E1	1:00			CMB A1	2:00

HALF-IRONMAN-DISTANCE TRIATHLON

HP is a 35-year-old, executive director of a small, non-profit organization who works about 35 hours per week on a flexible schedule. He is married and has a teenage son. His athletic experience includes 20 years of running and five years of triathlon. HP's previous best race times include a 2:15 international-distance and a 5:12 half-Ironman.

Although HP has perhaps 15 to 20 hours available for training each week, the physical stress such levels have caused in the past mean that such volume is not appropriate for him. His annual training plan, therefore, calls for 500 annual hours. That means his highest weekly volume of the year is about 15 hours, but much of it is in the range of 12 to 13 hours.

Sometimes it's not hours available, but hours possible.

HP's mental skills are excellent, especially his motivation to excel. Sometimes such enthusiasm can lead to obsessive training, but he has a good working knowledge of the science of training from years of reading, which serves as a moderating factor.

To achieve his goals listed at the top of the annual training plan, HP must improve three limiters: running muscular endurance, climbing force on the bike and swimming technique. He has determined that there are five objectives he must work toward in order to strengthen his limiters and ultimately achieve his half-Ironman time goals.

Since the week-46 half Ironman is on a hilly course, much of the season is spent developing greater bike force, so weight training will continue year round. In addition, he will do hilly bike rides frequently throughout the year as indicated by the frequent "Force"

Athlete: HP
Annual Hours: 500
Season Goals:
1 BREAK 5:00 AT GULF COAST (WK #27)
2 BREAK 5:10 AT CLERMONT (WK #46)
3
Training Objectives:
1 Swim 500m UNDER 8MIN BY WK #31.
2 LEG PRESS 6×450 lbs BY WK #8.
3 FASTER BIKE SPLIT THAN LAST YEAR IN WK #38.
4 RUN 10K UNDER 38:30 IN WK #20.
5 FASTER RUN SPLIT THAN LAST YEAR IN WK #38.

FIGURE 9.10

Column key (each of Swim / Bike / Run has these seven ability columns):
E = Endurance · F = Force · S = Speed · M = Muscular Endurance · A = Anaerobic Endurance · P = Power · T = Testing

Wk# Mon	Races	Pri	Period	Hours	Wts	S·E	S·F	S·S	S·M	S·A	S·P	S·T	B·E	B·F	B·S	B·M	B·A	B·P	B·T	R·E	R·F	R·S	R·M	R·A	R·P	R·T
1-Nov-02			PREP	8.5	AA	X	X					X	X	X					X	X	X					X
2-Nov-09						X	X						X	X						X	X					
3-Nov-16						X	X						X	X						X	X					
4-Nov-23			↓	↓	↓	X	X					X	X	X					X	X	X					X
5-Nov-30			BASE 1	10.0	MS	X	X						X	X						X	X					
6-Dec-07				12.0		X	X						X	X						X	X					
7-Dec-14				13.5		X	X						X	X						X	X					
8-Dec-21				7.0		X	X					X	X	X					X	X	X					X
9-Dec-28			BASE 2	10.5	PE	X	X	X					X	X	X					X	X	X				
10-Jan-04	(SWIM CAMP)			12.5		X	X	X					X	X	X					X	X	X				
11-Jan-11				14.0		X	X	X					X	X	X					X	X	X				
12-Jan-18				7.0		X	X	X				X	X	X	X				X	X	X	X				X
13-Jan-25			BASE 3	11.0	ME	X	X	X	X				X	X	X	X				X	X	X	X			
14-Feb-01				13.5		X	X	X	X				X	X	X	X				X	X	X	X			
15-Feb-08				15.0		X	X	X	X				X	X	X	X				X	X	X	X			
16-Feb-15			↓	7.0	↓	X	X	X	X			X	X	X	X	X			X	X	X	X	X			X
17-Feb-22			BUILD 1	12.5	SM	X		X	X	X			X	X	X	X				X		X	X	X		
18-Mar-01						X		X	X	X			X	X	X	X				X		X	X	X		
19-Mar-08			↓			X		X	X	X			X	X	X	X				X		X	X	X		
20-Mar-15	10K ROAD RACE	C	↓	7.0		X		X	X	X		X	X	X	X	X			X	X		X	X	X		X
21-Mar-22			BUILD 2	12.0		X		X	X	X			X	X	X	X				X		X	X	X		
22-Mar-29						X		X	X	X			X	X	X	X				X		X	X	X		
23-Apr-05						X		X	X	X			X	X	X	X				X		X	X	X		
24-Apr-12	SPRINT TRI	C		7.0		X		X	X				X		X	X				X		X	X			
25-Apr-19	INT'L TRI	B	PEAK	10.5	O	X		X	X				X		X	X				X		X	X			
26-Apr-26			↓	8.5	SM	X		X	X				X		X	X				X		X	X			
27-May-03	HALF IRONMAN	A	RACE	7.0	O		X			X					X			X			X			X		
28-May-10	SPRINT TRI	B	↓	7.0	SM		X			X					X			X			X			X		
29-May-17			TRAN	—	O																					
30-May-24			BASE 3	13.5	SM	X	X	X	X				X	X	X	X				X	X	X	X			
31-May-31				15.0		X	X	X	X				X	X	X	X				X	X	X	X			
32-Jun-07			↓	7.0		X	X	X	X			X	X	X	X	X			X	X	X	X	X			X
33-Jun-14			BUILD 1	12.5		X		X	X	X			X	X	X	X				X		X	X	X		
34-Jun-21			↓			X		X	X	X			X	X	X	X				X		X	X	X		
35-Jun-28	SPRINT TRI	B	↓	7.0		X		X	X				X		X	X				X		X	X			
36-Jul-05	INT'L DU	B	PEAK	8.5		X		X	X				X	X		X				X		X	X			
37-Jul-12			↓	↓		X		X	X				X		X	X				X		X	X			
38-Jul-19	INT'L TRI	A	RACE	7.0	O		X			X					X			X			X			X		
39-Jul-26			BASE 3	13.5	SM	X	X	X	X				X	X	X	X				X	X	X	X			
40-Aug-02			↓	15.0		X	X	X	X				X	X	X	X				X	X	X	X			
41-Aug-09	INT'L DU	B	↓	7.0	↓	X		X					X			X				X		X				
42-Aug-16			BUILD 1	12.5	O	X		X	X	X			X	X	X	X				X		X	X	X		
43-Aug-23						X		X	X	X			X	X	X	X				X		X	X	X		
44-Aug-30	SPRINT TRI	C	↓	7.0		X		X	X				X		X	X				X		X	X			
45-Sep-06			PEAK	8.5		X		X	X				X		X	X				X		X	X			
46-Sep-13	HALF IRONMAN	A	RACE	7.0			X			X					X			X			X			X		
47-Sep-20			TRAN	—																						
48-Sep-27				—																						
49-Oct-04				—																						
50-Oct-11			↓	—																						
51-Oct-18																										
52-Oct-25																										

workouts under the bike column. Sometimes these hilly workouts are combined with other abilities. Such is the case in the sample week-23 schedule. Notice that on Thursday he is doing a one-hour, "M3" ride. This is a cruise-interval session done on a hill while remaining seated. Also that week HP will complete a three-hour brick. The emphasis of this workout will be on a one-hour ride on a hilly course followed by a two-hour run. This is the last brick before his first peak of the season, so it will be conducted as a "dress rehearsal" for the race. This means that the workout intensity, bike set up, running shoes, sports nutrition and feeding schedule are exactly what is intended for the race.

Dress rehearsals build race confidence and identify potential problems.

Throughout the season, HP includes swim drills frequently and does an "extra" swim on Saturdays that focuses on technique. If time is tight on Saturday, the swim session is moved to Sunday. These weekend workouts include drills specific to his needs and short, race-effort repetitions in which he applies what he's learning in the drills. Short bouts of swimming, for example, 25 to 50 meters/yards, with long recoveries allow for total concentration on skills at race speed. Frequent swim drilling without applying the skills at anticipated race velocity is of little value.

Apply skills at race speed to develop mastery.

Figure 9.12 shows how HP will rest while maintaining fitness the week of his last race of the year. Notice that the annual training plan calls for seven hours that week, but that his weekly duration actually adds up to five hours. And, of course, there is a race at the end of the week that he should complete in a little more than five hours, based on his goal of 5:10. In addition, there is a pre-race warm up. In all, his actual time for the week will total about 10 hours and 30 minutes. Weekly hours in race weeks are highly dependent on the type of race planned. The volume scheduled for these weeks is only a rough guideline intended to keep volume minimal.

Race-week hours are rough guidelines.

FIGURE 9.11
Week #23 for HP.

	MON		TUE		WED		THU		FRI		SAT		SUN	
WORKOUT 1	SWIM S1, S2	:45	RUN M5	:45	SWIM S3, M1,A1	1:00	RUN S1	:45	SWIM S3, E2	:45	SWIM S1, E2	:45	BIKE E2	2:00
WORKOUT 2	WTS SM	:30	BIKE S3, E2	1:00			BIKE M3	1:00			CMB F1	3:00		

FIGURE 9.12
Week #46 for HP.

	MON		TUE		WED		THU		FRI		SAT		SUN	
WORKOUT 1	SWIM S1, E2	:45	RUN P1	:45	SWIM P1	:30	RUN E1	:30	OFF		CMB S1	:45	RACE	5:30
WORKOUT 2			BIKE E1	1:00			BIKE P1	:45						

Also notice in week 46 that HP does a Power workout in one sport each on Tuesday, Wednesday and Thursday of the week. The purposes of such workouts are to maintain the ability to call on and use fast-twitch muscles, keep blood volume high and feel mentally ready to go fast. Total rest in a race week with only easy distance frequently results in feelings of "flatness" on race day. Along the same line, doing a brief workout with short, high-intensity efforts the day before the race encourages sharpness on race day while relieving nagging concerns about whether enough training has been done the last few days. Many triathletes find that taking a day off 48 hours prior to the race is effective for ensuring recovery.

Too much rest sometimes causes feelings of being flat.

IRONMAN-DISTANCE TRIATHLON

JH is a 46-year-old mortgage broker who is married and has two high-school-aged children. He has competed in triathlons for six years, mostly at the international and half-Ironman distances.

Last year JH completed his first ultra-distance race at Ironman Canada in Penticton, British Columbia. On minimal training his time was 11:05, primarily the result of strong swim and bike portions. His run was mostly a walk in that race as he posted a marathon split of 4:07. In Penticton, his swimming was strong and he did well on the bike climbs. At 140 pounds, his strength-to-weight ratio is excellent for climbing, and good swimming results from his days as a collegiate swimmer.

Running endurance has always been his major limiter, although he has good anaerobic endurance and leg speed as evidenced by his sub-18-minute, 5km-run race times. He attempted a marathon two years ago, but did not finish. The following year he ran a 3:20, which, based on his 10km time of 37:20, is at least 25 minutes slower than his potential, based on prediction tables. To achieve his goals of qualifying for Ironman Hawaii and finishing in 10:30 or better, JH must, first of all, improve his running endurance. Also needed is greater bike force on the windy portions of the Hawaii course, for although he's a good climber — due largely to his small size — his ability to drive a high gear into the wind is lacking.

Endurance and force are the two major requirements of Ironman Hawaii.

JH's international-distance race times are around 2:08. Multiplying this by 4.67 to 5.0 yields an estimated range for the Ironman of 9:57 to 10:40, so his sub-10:30 goal seems reasonable. Projected splits for his Ironman are a 1:05 swim, 5:40 bike, 3:35 run and 10-minute transitions. Assuming he will slow down 20 percent on the marathon leg from his best performance in a run-only marathon race, he is capable of running the 3:35 final split if he can set a 2:55-marathon personal best. His annual training plan as illustrated in Figure 9.13 has JH aiming for a marathon in week 12 with that objective in mind.

Ironman time can be estimated from international-distance times.

FIGURE 9.13

Athlete: JH
Annual Hours: 450 (WKS 1–12), 550 (WKS 14–50)
Season Goals:
1 QUALIFY FOR IRONMAN HAWAII
2 10:30 OR FASTER AT IRONMAN
3
Training Objectives:
1 RUN MARATHON (WK 12) FASTER THAN 2:55.
2 LEG PRESS 410+ POUNDS 6 TIMES BY WK 17.
3 WK 25 RACE BIKE SPLIT FASTER THAN 1:04.
4 SPEND MORE TIME WITH FAMILY IN R&R WKS.
5 COMPLETE AT LEAST 3, 5+ HOUR BRICKS (WKS 42–48)

						Swim							Bike							Run						
Wk# Mon	Races	Pri	Period	Hours	Weights	End	For	SS	ME	AnE	Pwr	Test	End	For	SS	ME	AnE	Pwr	Test	End	For	SS	ME	AnE	Pwr	Test
1-Nov-02			BASE1	10.5	MS	X	X						X	X						X	X					
2-Nov-09				12.0		X	X						X	X						X	X					
3-Nov-16			↓	6.5		X	X						X	X						X	X					X
4-Nov-23			BASE2	11.5	↓	X	X						X	X						X	X	X				
5-Nov-30				12.5	PE	X	X						X	X						X	X	X				
6-Dec-07			↓	6.5		X	X						X	X						X	X	X				
7-Dec-14			BASE3	12.0		X	X						X	X						X	X	X				
8-Dec-21				13.0		X	X						X	X						X	X	X	X			
9-Dec-28			↓	6.5	ME	X	X						X	X						X	X					
10-Jan-04			PEAK	9.5		X	X						X	X						X	X	X				
11-Jan-11			↓	7.5	↓	X	X						X	X						X		X	X			
12-Jan-18	MARATHON	A	RACE	6.5	O		X							X												X
13-Jan-25			TRAN	—	O																					
14-Feb-01			BASE2	12.5	MS	X	X	X	X				X	X	X	X				X	X	X	X			
15-Feb-08				14.0		X	X	X	X				X	X	X	X				X	X	X	X			
16-Feb-15				15.5		X	X	X	X				X	X	X	X				X	X	X	X			
17-Feb-22			↓	8.0	↓	X	X	X				X	X	X	X				X	X	X	X				X
18-Mar-01			BASE3	12.5	PE	X	X	X	X				X	X	X	X				X	X	X	X			
19-Mar-08				14.5		X	X	X	X				X	X	X	X				X	X	X	X			
20-Mar-15				16.5		X	X	X	X				X	X	X	X				X	X	X	X			
21-Mar-22	INT'L DU	C	↓	8.0	↓	X	X					X	X	X					X	X	X					X
22-Mar-29			BUILD1	14.0	SM	X			X	X			X			X	X			X		X	X			
23-Apr-05						X			X	X			X			X	X			X		X	X			
24-Apr-12			↓			X			X	X			X		X	X				X		X	X			
25-Apr-19	INT'L TRI	B	↓	8.0		X	X						X	X						X	X					
26-Apr-26			BUILD2	13.0		X			X	X			X			X	X			X			X			
27-May-03						X			X	X			X			X	X			X			X			
28-May-10	INT'L TRI	C	↓			X			X	X			X			X	X			X			X			
29-May-17			↓	8.0		X					X		X					X		X					X	
30-May-24			PEAK	11.5		X		X	X				X		X	X				X		X				
31-May-31			↓	9.5	↓	X		X	X				X		X	X				X		X	X			
32-Jun-07	½ IRONMAN (Q)	A	RACE	8.0	O				X							X							X			
33-Jun-14			TRAN	—	O																					
34-Jun-21			BASE1	11.0	MS	X	X						X	X	X					X		X				
35-Jun-28				13.0		X	X						X	X	X					X		X				
36-Jul-05				14.5		X	X						X	X	X					X		X				
37-Jul-12	INT'L TRI	C	↓	8.0	↓	X	X						X	X						X		X				X
38-Jul-19			BASE2	12.5	SM	X	X	X	X				X	X	X	X				X	X	X	X			
39-Jul-26				14.0		X	X	X	X				X	X	X	X				X	X	X	X			
40-Aug-02	½ IRONMAN	B		15.5		X	X	X	X				X	X	X	X				X	X	X	X			
41-Aug-09			↓	8.0		X					X		X	X				X		X	X				X	
42-Aug-16			BASE3	12.5		X	X	X	X				X	X	X	X				X	X	X	X			
43-Aug-23				14.5		X	X	X	X				X	X	X	X				X	X	X	X			
44-Aug-30			↓	8.0		X	X					X	X	X						X	X					X
45-Sep-06			BASE3	14.5		X	X	X	X				X	X	X	X				X	X	X	X			
46-Sep-13				16.5		X	X	X	X				X	X	X	X				X	X	X	X			
47-Sep-20			↓	8.0		X	X					X	X	X					X	X	X					X
48-Sep-27			PEAK	11.5		X		X	X				X	X	X	X				X		X	X			
49-Oct-04			↓	9.5	↓	X		X	X				X	X	X	X				X		X	X			
50-Oct-11	IRONMAN	A	RACE	8.0+	O				X							X							X			
51-Oct-18			TRAN	—																						
52-Oct-25			↓	—																						

In preparing for this marathon (weeks 1-12), his training time is mostly devoted to running with swimming and cycling in a maintenance mode. Since marathon training does not take as many hours as Ironman training, his annual volume for weeks 1-12 are based on 450 hours, but starting in week 14 it escalates to 550 hours. Once his running endurance is established, assuming the marathon goes well, the emphasis of his training will shift primarily toward cycling as running fitness is maintained.

Annual hours may vary during the season based on needs.

Since the biggest challenges facing the runner training for a personal-best marathon are injury prevention and overtraining avoidance, training is scheduled in three-week periods, instead of the more usual four, during the endurance build-up with the third week set aside for rest and recovery. Weeks 42 through 47 of final preparation for the Ironman are scheduled in the same manner for the same reasons. There is a four-week Prep period preceding Base 1 that starts in week 1.

Best to avoid injury and overtraining with extra rest.

As anyone who has ever contemplated Ironman Hawaii knows, the biggest challenge is qualifying. The half Ironman in week 32 is the qualifier for which JH is aiming. This is his second peak of the season. There is also a qualifier at the international distance in week 25. He will not be ready for a peak performance by week 25, but this race will serve as a good assessment race and give him a preview of what the competition is likely to be in week 32. That should serve as excellent motivation for the final seven weeks before the qualifier. The week-25 race could also hurt his confidence, however, if his performance is relatively poor and he sees little chance for the necessary improvement. So it is imperative that the weekend before this race that great caution with intensity and duration is exercised. Consequently, it may be wise to reduce the volume of week 24 regardless of what the tables say.

There should be few, if any, races in the last 12 weeks before an Ironman event as competition cuts into training on both sides of the race due to the need to have some degree of rest before and recovery after. So the week-40 half Ironman is tentative and may well be skipped if training is not progressing at the desired level. If it is, this race will serve as an excellent indicator of progress since he's done it before. Backing off of training in the days preceding this race is probably necessary, so the weekly hours are tentative. Since this race is followed by an R & R week, there is adequate opportunity to recover before returning to Ironman-specific training.

It is best to not race in the last 12 weeks before an Ironman.

Weeks 39, 46 and 49 are shown in Figures 9.14, 9.15 and 9.16 to provide examples of how Ironman training is scheduled in the early weeks of endurance development in Base 2, during the Ironman-specific training of Base 3 and in the penultimate week when training volume is greatly reduced, but fitness is maintained. Remember that JH's

Improved endurance comes from duration, not frequency of training.

strengths are swimming and climbing hills on the bike, and that his greatest limiter is running endurance. In light of that it may be surprising that his weekly running volume is only about four hours. The reason for this is that once three or four weekly workouts are achieved, the greatest improvement in endurance comes not from doing more workouts, but from extending the length of one of those workouts. Increasing run frequency is likely to cause injury.

Use the tables and figures only as suggested guidelines.

Note that in Figure 9.15 (week 46), the suggested hours from Table 8.1 are rearranged so that the brick is the longest workout at five hours, instead of the four hours as proposed in the Table. Remember that Table 8.1 and Figures 8.1 are only suggestions, and it is often necessary to modify them.

CASE STUDIES SUMMARY

Notice that each of the athletes in these case studies made changes from the guidelines previously described in order to meet their specific needs. Such modifications represent one aspect of the art of training and are often necessary if successful training and racing are to happen. Don't be afraid to bend the rules, but have a reason for doing so. That reason could be that it just felt right given your unique circumstances. If the change worked — great! If not, learn from your experience.

FIGURE 9.14
Week #39 for JH.

	MON		TUE		WED		THU		FRI		SAT		SUN	
WORKOUT 1	SWIM S1, E2	:30	RUN S1, M1	:45	SWIM S1, M2, F3	1:00	RUN E1	:45	SWIM S1, E1	1:00	RUN F1	2:30	BIKE M1, E3	3:45
WORKOUT 2	WTS SM	:30	BIKE S1, E2	:45	BIKE E1	1:00	BIKE F1	1:15					RUN E3	:15

FIGURE 9.15
Week #46 for JH.

	MON		TUE		WED		THU		FRI		SAT		SUN	
WORKOUT 1	SWIM S1, E1	:45	RUN S1, M2	1:00	SWIM F1, E2	1:15	RUN E1	1:00	SWIM S1, E1	1:00	CMB F1	5:00	BIKE E1	2:30
WORKOUT 2	WTS SM	:30	BIKE S1, E2	1:00	BIKE E1	1:00	BIKE M2	1:30						

FIGURE 9.16
Week #49 for JH.

	MON		TUE		WED		THU		FRI		SAT		SUN	
WORKOUT 1	SWIM S1, E1	:45	RUN S1	:45	SWIM F1	1:00	BIKE E1	1:00	SWIM S1, E2	:30	CMB M1	1:30	BIKE E1	:45
WORKOUT 2	WTS SM	:30	BIKE E2	:45	CMB A1	1:30			RUN E1	:30				

RACING AND RECOVERY

Back in the 1950s and 1960s there was a television program called "The Ed Sullivan Show." It was the last of the old vaudeville shows offering a variety of short acts that had been so popular in the early 20th century. One of the show's favorite repeat performers was a juggler who would spin and balance a plate on a long pole. His act involved keeping several plates spinning at the same time and constantly starting more while maintaining the spin on those that slowed down and threatened to crash to the floor. Each time he came on the program he tried to keep more plates spinning than on his previous performances. He had nothing on multisport athletes.

We are masters at keeping lots of plates spinning while avoiding calamity. We balance family, career, home upkeep, relationships and community responsibilities, while swimming, biking, running and lifting weights all with the intended purpose of producing peak racing fitness. Few of us get paid for doing all of this.

The real reward we all seek is the perfect race — the one in which we feel strong and in control with each leg of the race a personal best. For that elusive reward we endure workouts that most "normal" people never even imagine are possible. Unfortunately, some of us occasionally get caught up in spinning more and more plates and allow some to crash to the floor. This is most common in the week of a race and at times when we are so driven to succeed that recovery isn't an option.

Part V looks at the times when less training means more fitness. Chapter 10 shows how to plan your taper during race week and expend your energy during the race. Chapter 11 examines how to avoid the problems that come from not allowing your body to recover. Knowing how to reduce the number of spinning plates at these times avoids calamity and produces triathlon and duathlon success.

RACING

"Race day is harvest time; that's when you reap the benefits."
— MARK ALLEN

This is it! The first A-priority race of the year has finally arrived. All of the blood, sweat and tears of weeks, months and years of training have brought you to this point. Your fitness is at its highest level of the young season, and you are ready to go.

Wouldn't it be a shame to ruin all of this in the last few days before the race? Many an athlete has done just that by training in inappropriate ways in the final week of the big race. The most common error for serious multisport athletes is continuing to train at a high work load in the mistaken belief that fitness is improved only by hard work. It isn't so. Fitness improves during rest. In fact, it's unlikely that any highly stressful training done in the last week can cause physiological changes along the lines of what was accomplished in the Base and Build periods. Better to rest.

Rest has its shortcomings, too. Several studies have shown that total rest causes a steady loss of fitness (see Table 3.1). Some place between your normal training work load and inactivity is an appropriate amount of training for race week. This chapter examines that issue and takes you through final race-day preparation, the race itself and post-race activities.

"Extra" training does not mean more fitness in a race week.

RACE WEEK

Another way some athletes approach race week is to treat it as a "slough-off" week in which they piddle around with little effort since they believe that nothing of physiological value happens except rest. While it's true that rest is the major objective of this week, there are some other benefits to be gained that will produce improved performance. In fact, what you do in the week of a big race is every bit as important as what you do in any other prior week of preparation. When done right, a taper week peaks speed and power, boosts confidence

Peak speed and power in a race week.

and allows for rest. Let's examine how to plan for a peak performance by counting down the days leading to an A-priority race.

SIX DAYS BEFORE RACE

Take it easy today.

If the race is on a Sunday, six days before is Monday. This is a good day for a zone 1, active-recovery swim or bike ride since the day before was probably a brief race-effort simulation coming at the end of a Peak-period week. Don't lift weights today, or any day this week. Now is not the time to further tear down muscle tissue or even attempt to maintain strength. If you find yourself exceptionally tired from the previous day's workout, taking this day off altogether may be wise. Regardless, don't do anything that is stressful.

Prepare bike for race.

This is a good day to get your bike tuned and set up for the race. All rides this week are best done on your race set up to ensure that everything is in working order and that you're comfortable with position. The one exception is race tires. These are best saved until the day before the race to protect them from cuts and tiny slivers that could go unnoticed. When installing your race tires this week, check them for potential problems.

Match eating to activity level.

As with all days in this week, be cautious with how much you eat. Due to the decreased workload you need fewer calories, but the tendency is to eat normally. By the end of the week you may have gained an extra pound or so primarily due to the storage of water, but avoid adding body fat.

THREE TO FIVE DAYS BEFORE RACE

Several university studies have demonstrated that a moderate and decreasing amount of high intensity during a taper week produces better endurance performances than either total rest or easy, slow training. The reason for this is that rest improves glycogen stores, increases aerobic enzyme levels and activity, boosts blood volume and allows for connective-tissue repair. High-intensity training maintains or even improves muscle-recruitment patterns. Not doing any high intensity in this week is likely to leave you feeling "flat" and even a little awkward at faster paces on race day. The speed and power aspects of fitness are lost first when work load is reduced, so these must be paramount in race week.

Combine low volume with high intensity on these days.

Brief bursts of intense movement with long recoveries, such as those common to the power workouts in Appendices B, C, D and E, are effective for these days. Within one session each day, include three to five repetitions at near maximum effort as described in the appropriate workout. Figures 8.1j, 8.1k, 9.8 and 9.12 provide suggested workouts and patterns for these days.

TWO DAYS BEFORE RACE

This is Thursday for a Saturday race or Friday for a Sunday race. Take today off from training or include a short swim. It should be your more restful day of the week. If traveling to the race, now or the night before is the time to pack your bike. Travel is quite stressful, so anything you can do to lessen its psychological and physical impact is beneficial. A travel checklist that includes everything you want to take reduces your fear of forgetting something such as your helmet or running shoes. Another stress reliever is traveling with a non-racing friend or spouse who can deal with the inevitable hassles as they arise. In airports and at hotels, use a push cart or pay a porter to lug your bike around.

Travel today for races within two time zones.

Besides staying as calm and relaxed as you can today, eat food that you're accus-

---

SPECIAL ELEMENT 10.1

Travel Checklist

To reduce stress and the possibility of forgetting something, use this checklist when packing your bags to travel to a race.

Swim
___ Swim suit
___ Goggles (2 pair)
___ Defogger
___ Wetsuit
___ No-stick spray/lube
___ Swim cap
___ Stretch cord

Bike
___ Bike
___ Shoes
___ Special pedals
___ Shorts
___ Gloves
___ Helmet
___ Pump
___ Tools
___ Lubricant
___ Spare tire/tube
___ Handlebar computer
___ Race wheels

___ Water bottles
___ Lock and cable

Run
___ Race shoes
___ Training shoes
___ Shorts
___ Singlet
___ Visor/hat
___ Orthotics

Transition
___ Towel
___ Marker

Miscellaneous
___ Tights
___ Socks
___ Skin lubricant
___ Sunscreen
___ Jacket
___ Sunglasses

___ Clear lenses
___ Backpack
___ Toiletries kit
___ Raincoat
___ Sports drink mix
___ Food/energy bars/gels
___ First aid kit
___ Safety pins
___ Training log
___ USAT license
___ Race confirmation
___ Race number
___ Parking permit
___ Race info packet
___ Airline tickets
___ Bike passes
___ Duct tape
___ Jog bra
___ Eyeglasses or contacts
___ Heart-rate monitor
___ Post-race sandals

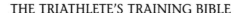

tomed to (you may need to carry some), drink plenty of water (not sports drinks) throughout the day and go to bed at a time that is normal for you.

DAY BEFORE RACE

This morning is the last time to work out before the race. It's also a good time to check out the swim venue from the shore as the sun is rising as it will be on race morning. Keep today's workout short and include some brief bouts of high intensity. A bike-run combined workout done on the run course for the race is an excellent final workout, if possible. Keep the workout short with perhaps a 30-minute bike ride and a 15-minute run. All you want to do is get warmed up, throw in a few accelerations to faster-than-goal race pace, and then stop and stretch. Following this workout, check all bolts on your bike for tightness.

Check out swim site and do a short brick.

Following a normal breakfast, check off the pre-race activities at a comfortable pace. Avoid rushing through the process. Keep everything in perspective today by minimizing the significance of the inevitable day-before-the-race hassles. Pick up your race packet and attend the pre-race meeting, if there is one. Drive the bike course paying special attention to hills and the likely gearing needed, mile marks, pavement surface, turn-around points, corners and weather nuances such as wind direction and shade. Back in the hotel room, fasten the race number on your belt or singlet and bike. Lay out race-day clothes and pack your race bag using the checklist.

Complete the many pre-race tasks calmly and without hurrying.

After all race activities are taken care of, get your mind off of the race, avoid crowds of nervous athletes and stay off of your legs and out of the sun. Some possible activities include going to a movie, taking a bus tour of the area, renting a videotape and reading. Throughout the day, continue to sip from a bottle of water (not a sports drink), and don't allow hunger to set in. But in the same spirit of avoiding extreme changes, don't overeat today. Have dinner a bit on the early side avoiding caffeine, alcohol and roughage. Don't experiment with the local cuisine today. Eat foods that are normal for you the day before the race.

Rest and get your mind off of the race.

Following dinner, get away from other competitors to slow your mind and body down even more as you prepare to sleep. Watch television or read in a quiet room with low light. Don't dwell on the "what-ifs" of tomorrow's race. Whenever race thoughts pop into your mind, replace them by recalling recent successes you have had in workouts or races. Place a bottle of water next to the bed and turn in at a normal time. Sleeping pills are likely to leave you groggy, but a melatonin capsule an hour before bed time may help. Don't do this unless you've experimented with melatonin in training or before a C-priority race. It's a good idea to talk with your medical-care provider before using melatonin.

Prepare your mind and body for sleep.

RACE DAY

If you've prepared well throughout the week, there's little that can physically go wrong today. At this point it's simply a matter of following a detailed procedure — a ritual — that you have done scores of times before now. An A-priority is not the time to experiment with new pre-race rituals; stick with what you know works.

Pre-race rituals are important because they allow you to operate without thinking as you mentally and physically steel yourself for the coming race. There is a confident, focused and business-like countenance about the successful athlete's pre-race ritual from the moment of waking until the starting pistol fires. If you don't have a ritual established, use the C-priority races on your schedule to refine one that exactly fits your needs and personality. The following suggestions may help accomplish that.

WAKING, EATING, TRAVELING AND PREPARING

Sports psychologist Brent Rushall in "Psyching for Sports" suggests that on race day you should start calmly and confidently following these guidelines:

- Awake with the gentle sound of a subdued alarm clock, not a startling ring. If you're a heavy sleeper, ask your roommate to handle the wake-up chore.
- Prepare a drink that you like and are accustomed to, such as tea or coffee. This may mean carrying a small hot-water-making device with you, staying in a hotel that provides these in the rooms, or simply walking to the lobby where coffee or tea is already made.
- Starting from the moment you awake, smile and think positive thoughts about the race and how well you feel.
- Stretch and breathe deeply.
- As your mood becomes more buoyant, dress while quietly repeating positive self-affirmations about your well-established ability.
- Replace anxiety-producing thoughts about the race with positive thoughts about recent successes. Have a mental "list" of these prepared and well practiced.

Before leaving your room, use the toilet. If your body isn't accustomed to bowel movements first thing in the morning, train it to do so by going to the bathroom every morning before working out. A warm drink or a little food may help with this. Eventually it will become natural.

Eat a pre-race meal two to three hours before your warm-up will start. The purpose of this feeding is to restock liver glycogen stores that have been depleted during your overnight fast. This should be about 200 calories from predominantly low-fiber, low-glycemic-index carbohydrate (see Chapter 16 for the glycemic index) such as applesauce with no added sugar, baby food or fruit. Besides choosing foods that are known to agree with you, it's a good idea to use products you can bring with you, or are available in grocery or convenience stores any place you may travel.

Eat two to three hours pre-race for early starts.

Eat and drink nothing else following this meal except water until your warm-up begins. At that time you can begin using a sports drink. If you're not warming up, save the sports drink until 10 minutes before the race start.

If the race starts later in the day, eat four to five hours before and include some fat. This could be something such as eggs, dairy or bacon. The extra circulating fat will spare glycogen and leave you with a satisfied feeling throughout the wait for the race.

Eat four to five hours pre-race for a late-day start.

Slightly overdress for the weather conditions that greet you on race morning. You can always remove extra layers. That's better than being chilled and assists with warm-up. The bottom layer is race clothes that are appropriate for the expected weather, but prepare for sudden changes. If the weather is unstable, you may want to carry "contingency" clothing in a bag to the race site with you. This could include a light rain jacket, arm covers, tights, lightweight gloves and a headband that covers the ears. While you are at it, put a roll of toilet paper from the hotel bathroom into your bag just in case the portable toilets run out. Return what you don't use after the race.

Overdress for the race.

Before leaving, ask the hotel's front desk attendant for a late check-out so that you have time to come back to the room and shower. Most will gladly allow this if the requested time is reasonable.

Depart for the race site early enough to allow for a traffic jam as all of the racers funnel into the parking area. Also allow ample time for standing in line for body marking, finding your rack, pumping up tires, checking out the transition, talking with old acquaintances, visiting the toilets several times and warming up.

Allow plenty of time for travel.

When you arrive at the transition area, rack your bike and position equipment as you always do. Don't try anything new today. Visit the toilet. Acquaint yourself with landmarks for your rack such as its position relative to tress, light poles, pavement marking, signs or other permanent markers. *Visit the toilet.* Walk to the swim and bike finishes and locate your transition stall from those perspectives. *Visit the toilet.* Rehearse the best route from each to your rack two or three times. And, of course, *visit the toilet.*

Don't forget to visit the toilet.

START-LINE STRESS

That your bladder sphincter is becoming difficult to control while your body attempts to shed water is a sure sign of the anxiety known as "start-line stress." These are also the symptoms of the genetic and ancient "fight or flight" preparation the human body goes through whenever it senses a threat. Only now the threat is not a saber-toothed tiger, but rather a race.

The body is ready to fight or flee.

This state of arousal can have a beneficial or detrimental affect on performance depending on the sport. Extremely high arousal is beneficial for power movements requiring only gross motor skills, such as the kick-off in football or the clean and jerk in Olympic power lifting. On the other hand, very low arousal is needed by the golfer attempting to putt for par. The multisport athlete will reap rewards by keeping arousal at a more moderate level between these extremes. If arousal is too great, energy is wasted and pacing strategies fall apart early in the race. Low arousal results in a lethargic and unmotivated performance. Figure 10.1 illustrates the "inverted-U" relationship between arousal and performance, and the indicators of the extremes of arousal.

Arousal can help or hinder.

For most athletes, the greater concern is overly high arousal. Reducing it to optimal levels requires the development of coping skills. The refinement of such skills is one of the reasons for the inexperienced athlete to participate in many C-priority races. Those who have been around the sport for years will have already mastered them. Some examples of arousal-lowering skills include:

How to reduce inappropriate arousal.

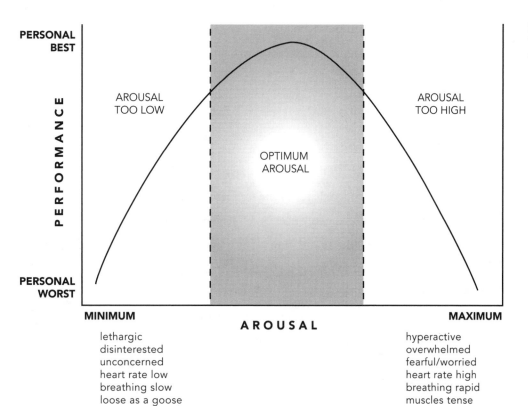

FIGURE 10.1
The relationship between arousal and performance.

- Physically slow down movements and relax muscles by "shaking out" the tension. Breathe slower and use your heart-rate monitor as a biofeedback device to slow your pulse.
- Mentally slow down by replacing negative, fearful thoughts with positive ones that emphasize recent successes.
- Allow your body to go on "autopilot" throughout the warm-up as your mind dissociates and "plays" with other stimuli such as music, conversation, hobbies, scenery, or anything else that interests you.
- Learn to trust your training and racing experience in order to allow you to perform at near maximal ability without undue effort or pain. Know that when the start pistol fires, you'll simply flip a "switch" and race as you always have.
- Mentally separate yourself from thoughts of winning and losing. Race like a child by simply enjoying the challenge and the event.
- Don't race against others; you have no control over whether you are better than them or not. You can only control your effort and skill.
- Forget about race outcomes. Think only about the here and now.
- Act as if you were calm. Look at others who appear relaxed and emulate their appearance.
- Act as if this is merely another workout with friends.
- Remind yourself that no matter what happens, only good will come from the race. If it's a personal best — great! If not, you'll learn something from the experience that will make you better next time. The difference between winning and losing is that when you lose, you learn something.

WARM UP

Warming up has several benefits for race performance. It starts the flow of fatty acids to the muscles for use as fuel while simultaneously reducing dependence on your limited stores of carbohydrate-based glycogen. It raises the temperature of the working muscles. The capacity of muscles to produce energy rises by 13 percent for every degree Celsius of temperature rise. Heart stroke volume and lung capacity increase with warming up. The production of lactate is reduced following a warm-up meaning that you are less likely to go anaerobic at the start. It opens capillaries to allow more oxygen into the muscles. Warming up sensitizes the nervous system for smoother movements so that you waste less energy at the start of the race. And finally, perceived exertion is lower following warm-up.

There are many warm-up benefits.

Scientific studies have supported the value of warming up when it duplicates the movements of the sport and doesn't cause undue fatigue. A few studies have even shown that a passive warm-up , such as a hot bath or massage, may even have some benefit, but not nearly as much as an active warm-up.

On race day, start warming up early enough so that you can take care of minor problems that may arise at the last minute, such as your bike not shifting smoothly or leaky goggles. For international-distance races and shorter, this might mean beginning some 45 to 60 minutes before your start time. For longer races, shorten the warm-up. Most competitors should do little or no warm-up before an Ironman-distance race.

Other factors that influence warm-up duration are your fitness level and the weather. The more endurance base you have built up, the longer your warm-up may be. For example, if your longest workout of any type is two hours and the race will probably take you three hours, a warm-up is not advised. Under such conditions, you are better served by saving your fuel and merely starting slowly on each leg of the race. In cool weather, more warm-up is needed, but if the water is also cold, stay out of it and use stretch cords or calisthenics to warm up. In hot weather, decrease the length of the bike, and especially, the run warm-up portions. If it's a wet and rainy day, shorten or omit the bike warm-up.

It's usually best to warm up in the reverse order of the event. So for a standard swim-bike-run triathlon, start with the run warm-up, then the bike and finally the swim. Duathletes warm up on the bike first and the run last.

Devote 10 to 15 minutes to each sport by beginning at a low effort and heart rate (1 zone) and slowly increasing to the 2 or 3 zone, depending on how you feel. Finish with two to four, 10- to 30-second accelerations to race pace with long recoveries. Stretch briefly after each sport warm-up is completed.

If possible, end your warm-up no more than five minutes before you start. When this isn't possible, and the wait will be much longer, make the race-paced accelerations of the last warm-up portion longer — perhaps 45 to 60 seconds, instead of 10 to 30 seconds. These longer efforts will provide a greater "depth" of warm-up, and the long wait for the start will allow for the removal of any lactate created.

Whatever warm-up procedure you use, practice the various portions of it weekly before your most intense swim, bike and run workouts in the Build, Peak and Race periods of your season. It should become such a natural thing to do that you warm up without even thinking about it.

THE START

In the last five minutes or so before the start, review your race strategy. This usually has to do with pacing, target heart-rate zones and maximum allowable efforts. This latter point is

---

Plan warm-up time according to race duration.

Weather and fitness also determine warm-up duration.

Warm up 10 to 15 minutes in each sport in reverse order.

Adjust the intensity of the warm-up to the anticipated wait for the start.

TABLE 10.1A

Suggested warm up for an experienced triathlete before an international-distance triathlon.

Time (minutes)	Activity
10	Run. Slowly increase intensity from 1 to 2 or 3 zone.
5	Run 2-4 x 10-30 seconds at race effort/pace with long, easy recoveries.
5	Return to transition area. Stretch calves and hamstrings. Walk bike out of transition (or set up trainer).
10	Bike. Slowly increase intensity from 1 to 2 or 3 zone.
5	On bike do 2-4 x 10-30 seconds at race effort/pace with long, easy recoveries.
5	Return to transition area. Stretch quads and low back. Make sure that everything in transition is in order. Put on wetsuit, if applicable and walk to swim start.
10	Swim. Slowly increase pace from 1 to 2 or 3 zone.
5	Swim 2-4 x 10 to 30 seconds at race-start effort/pace with long, easy recoveries.
5	Report to start area and stretch shoulders.
total 60	

TABLE 10.1B

Suggested warm up for an experienced duathlete before an international-distance duathlon.

Time (minutes)	Activity
10	Bike on road or trainer. Slowly increase intensity from 1 to 2 or 3 zone.
5	On bike do 2-4 x 10-30 seconds at race effort/pace with long, easy recoveries.
5	Return to transition area. Stretch quads and low back. Put on running shoes.
10	Run. Slowly increase intensity from 1 to 2 or 3 zone.
5	Run 2-4 x 10-30 seconds at race effort/pace with long, easy recoveries.
5	Return to transition area to make sure that everything is in order.
5	Report to start area and stretch calves and hamstrings.
total 45	

of special significance for long races such as half Ironman or Ironman in which going anaerobic may result in a DNF (Did Not Finish). Among elite athletes, race strategy may include position relative to other athletes at various times in the race. For draft-legal bike legs in some professional events, the swim can easily mean the difference between placing well and finishing well out of the money. In such cases, a strong commitment to doing whatever it takes in the swim to stay near the front is necessary and should be reviewed before the start.

Review race strategy before the start.

If swimming is your weakest sport, or if you are new to triathlon, start on the outer edge or at the back of your wave group. Front row and central positions are best left for those who swim strongly. After the initial sprint, settle into your planned effort and look for others to draft on while frequently checking your pre-selected navigation landmarks. In the last two minutes or so of the swim, mentally rehearse your upcoming transition by going through the exact steps in your mind: getting to your transition stall, removing the wetsuit, putting on shoes, sunglasses and helmet, and exiting the transition.

Know your pre-selected swim landmarks.

At the start of the bike leg, begin in a lower gear than you plan to race in. This gear is determined before the race based on the terrain exiting the transition area, and set before the start. During the first three to five minutes, steadily increase the gear size. Pay special attention to hydration and fuel while on the bike. Some athletes even set their wristwatch alarms to sound every 10 to 15 minutes to remind them to drink and eat. Just as at the end of the swim, with a couple of minutes left in the bike portion, review the steps of your next transition. With the transition area in sight near the end of the ride, shift to an easier gear and spin more. Unless you are leading and there is a bike prime prize, avoid the temptation to race another athlete to the dismount line. Always make it a habit to remove your helmet only at your transition stall. That will prevent silly penalties.

Use the bike leg to hydrate and refuel.

Start the run by listening to your breathing while ignoring your legs. They will always tell you that you are going too slowly, which is erroneous at this point in the race. Initially, your stride will be shorter than normal, but will slowly lengthen without the need to force it. During the run, and, indeed, throughout the entire race, forget about outcomes such as finishing in a certain time, placing or winning. Race only in the here and now. That involves continually checking form and vital signs such as breathing and muscle tension.

Listen to your breathing at the start of the run.

Relaxation is a crucial element for success in racing. Too much muscle tension wastes energy. If this is a problem for you, a personal cue word such as "relax" should be repeated throughout the race whenever you sense tension building. You may even want to tape your cue word to the handlebars as a constant reminder, and, of course, it should be practiced in Break Through workouts. Whenever you think the cue word, it should trigger a relaxation response in your non-working muscles.

Optimal relaxation produces the best races.

POST-RACE

Should you cool down after the race? Unless it was a sprint- or international-distance event, and you have an excellent base of aerobic fitness, there is no reason to cool down by jogging or riding. It further depletes your body of fuel and increases the stress on damaged muscles needlessly prolonging recovery in the coming days. You are better off walking around for a few minutes while drinking fluids and restocking spent fuel sites. The usual reason given for a cooldown is the removal of lactic acid, but it is gone in a few minutes post-race with or without a cooldown. And besides, lactic acid is not a cause for muscle soreness, nor does it impact long-term recovery.

Cooldown is usually unnecessary following a race.

The first priority after crossing the finish line is to replace fluid losses and, secondarily, spent fuel. Water replacement is enhanced if sodium is included in the drink or in accompanying salty foods.

Fluids and fuel are the highest priorities for recovery.

Walking around, drinking, eating and swapping lies with friends is all that's needed after a race.

REFERENCES

Anderson, O. 1995. Things your parents forgot to tell you about tapering. *Running Research News* 11 (7): 1-8.

Astrand, P.O. and K. Rohdahl. 1977. *Textbook of Work Physiology.* New York: McGraw-Hill.

Bonen, A. and A. Belcastro. 1976. Comparison of self-selected recovery methods on lactic acid removal rates. *Medicine and Science in Sports and Exercise* 8: 176-178.

deVries, H.A. 1959. Effects of various warm-up procedures on 100-yard times of competitive swimmers. *Research Quarterly* 30: 11-20.

Dimsdale, J, et al. 1984. Postexercise peril: Plasma catecholamines and exercise. *Journal of the American Medical Association* 251: 630-632.

Hemmert, M.K., et al. 1985. Effect of plasma volume on exercise stroke volume in normally active and endurance-trained men. Paper presented at the American College of Sports Medicine annual meeting.

Hermiston, R.T. and M.E. O'Brien. 1972. The effects of three types of warm-up on the total oxygen cost of a short treadmill run. In A.W. Taylor (ed.), *Training: Scientific Basis and Application.* Springfield, IL: Charles C. Thomas.

Houmard, J., et al. 1991. The effect of warm-up on responses to intense exercise. *International Journal of Sports Medicine* 12 (5): 400-403.

Houmard, J., et al. 1994. The effects of taper on performance in distance runners. *Medicine and Science in Sports and Exercise* 26 (5): 624-631.

Houmard, J. and R. Johns. 1994. Effects of taper on swim performance. *Sports Medicine* 17: 224-232.

Karvonen, J. 1992. Importance of warm-up and cool down on exercise performance. In J. Karvonen (ed.), *Medicine in Sports Training and Coaching*. Dasel, Germany: Karger.

Keul, J., et al. 1972. *Energy Metabolism of Human Muscle*. Baltimore: University Park Press.

Maglischo, E.W. 1982. *Swimming Faster*. Mountain View, CA: Mayfield Publishing.

Martin, D.E. and P.N. Coe. 1997. *Better Training for Distance Runners*. Champaign, IL: Human Kinetics.

McArdle, W.D., F. Katch and V. Katch. 1996. *Exercise Physiology*. Baltimore, MD: Williams & Wilkins.

Noakes, T. 1991. *The Lore of Running*. Champaign, IL: Leisure Press.

Nose, H., et al. 1988. Involvement of sodium retention hormones during hydration in humans. *Journal of Applied Physiology* 65: 325-331.

Robinson, S. 1963. Temperature regulation in exercise. *Pediatrics* 32: 691-702.

Rushall, B. 1979. *Psyching in Sport. The Psychological Preparation for Serious Competition in Sport*. London: Pelham Books.

RECOVERY

"I've learned to back off when I need to."
— MARK ALLEN

The need for balance in life is undeniable. For every high there must be a low. For every fast workout, a slow one must soon follow. When at a peak and feeling invincible, you are only one training mistake from losing it all. Failure to maintain balance, especially by shortchanging recovery, will nearly always result in a breakdown that interrupts training consistency and brings a loss of fitness.

Chronic fatigue is not the purpose of training, as some exercise-addicted multi-sport athletes believe. Increasing fatigue is normal as the volume or intensity of training rises, but it must be unloaded frequently to maintain fitness growth. Failure to do so is a training mistake.

Chronic fatigue is not normal.

Fitness growth results not from the quantity of exercise, but rather from the capacities of the mind and body for restoration. The athlete who recovers the fastest is able to complete the most high-quality workouts. Quick recovery from fatigue is the key. To those who master this concept, who moderate motivation with patience and who balance intensity with intelligence, go the medals.

This chapter first examines what happens when recovery is denied. Then it introduces basic concepts for wisely incorporating recovery into your training program.

RECOVERY-RELATED PROBLEMS

With rare exception, the setbacks we experience in training are of our own making. Our motivation to excel is exceeded only by our inability to listen to our bodies. The result is often overtraining, illness or injury.

OVERTRAINING

Overtraining is best described as a decreased work capacity resulting from an imbalance between training and rest. In the real world of multisport, decreasing performance and nagging exhaustion that no longer respond to short-term rest is the best indicator of training gone awry. It is also known by coaches and athletes as "staleness." When faced with this dilemma, athletes are likely to increase training as to get the needed time off. They are apt to put in more miles, or do more intervals, or both. It's a rare multisport athlete who rests more when things aren't going well.

Poor performance coupled with exhaustion may indicate overtraining.

Of course, poor races don't always result from too much training. You could be "overliving" by burning the candle at both ends. A 50-hour-per-week job, two kids to raise, a mortgage and other responsibilities all take their toll on physical and psychological energy. Training is simply the most easily controlled cause. You sure aren't going to call the boss to ask for the day off since you suspect overtraining. Nor will you tell the kids to get themselves to the scout meeting. Life goes on. At such times, the smartest option is to train less and rest more.

"Overliving" may also bring on an overtrained state.

Figure 11.1 shows what happens when recovery is denied and motivation goes unbridled. Notice that as the training load increases, fitness also increases, up to your personal limit. At that point fitness declines despite an increasing work load. Training beyond your present capacity causes a loss of fitness.

Increased training loads eventually leading to overtraining come from one or more of three common training excesses: 1) workouts too long (excess duration); 2) exertion too high, too often (excess intensity); and 3) too many workouts in too little time (excess

FIGURE 11.1
The overtraining curve.

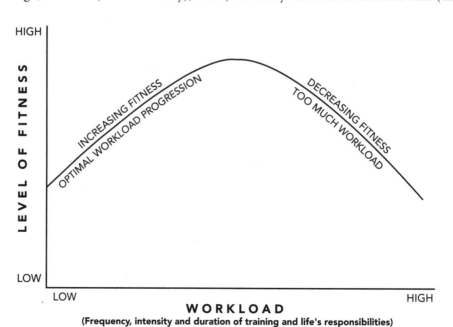

frequency). Probably the most common cause in competitive endurance athletes is excess intensity. Depending on the distance, multisport events are somewhere in the neighborhood of 90-percent aerobic and 10-percent anaerobic. Training should reflect that relationship. Placing excessive emphasis on anaerobic training for week after week is a sure way to overtrain. That's why the Build period of training is limited to six weeks of high intensity plus two recovery weeks.

Excessive intensity is a common cause of overtraining.

• **Overtraining indicators.** The body responds to the overtrained state by issuing warnings in many forms (see Table 11.1 Overtraining Indicators). In part, these reactions are the body's way of preventing death by making further increases in stress volume all but impossible.

Overtraining is the body's fail-safe system.

Many elite athletes will have blood chemistry testing done in the Prep or early Base periods of training to establish a healthy baseline for later comparison should training go awry. When they aren't responding normally to training during other periods of the season, they have blood drawn and tested again to see if there have been significant changes, such as a decrease in the amount of serum iron or an increase in allergy indicators. This goes beyond the needs of most serious, age-group athletes. If you are training poorly and have other indicators from Table 11.1, blood testing will only offer knowledge about the condition, and rarely a treatment method. Blood testing is helpful, however, when performance is poor, but there are no other indicators of a problem. In either case, the problem is dealt with by resting more and training less.

None of the items listed in Table 11.1, or even those deduced from blood testing, is a "sure" indicator. Abnormalities may exist in perfectly healthy athletes who are in top shape. In dealing with overtraining there are no absolutes. You are looking

TABLE 11.1

Overtraining indicators

<u>Behavioral</u>
Apathy
Lethargy
Poor concentration
Sleep pattern changes
Irritability
Decreased libido
Clumsiness
Increased thirst
Sluggishness
Craving for sugar

<u>Physical</u>
Reduced performance
Weight change
Morning heart rate change
Muscle soreness
Swollen lymph glands
Diarrhea
Injury
Infection
Amenorrhea
Decreased exercise heart rate
Slow-healing cuts

Blood testing may confirm overtraining.

for a preponderance of evidence to confirm what you already suspect.

• **Stages of overtraining.** There are three stages on the road to becoming over-trained. The first stage is "overload." This is a normal part of the process of increasing the training volume or intensity beyond what you are used to in order to cause the body to adapt. If great enough, but within manageable limits, it results in overcompensation as described in Chapter 3. During this stage it's typical to experience short-term fatigue, but generally you will feel great and may have outstanding race results. But also during this stage it's common to feel as if your body is invincible. You can do anything you want. That belief often leads to the next stage.

In the second stage, "overreaching," you begin to train at abnormally high load levels for a period of two weeks or more. Extending the length of the higher-intensity Build period, or even increasing the amount of anaerobic training in this period, is a common cause of overreaching. Now, for the first time, your performance noticeably decreases. Usually this happens in workouts before it shows up in races where high motivation often pulls you through. Fatigue becomes longer lasting than in the overload stage, but with a few days of rest it is still reversible. The problem is that you decide what's needed is still more difficult training, which brings on the third stage.

The third and final stage is a full-blown overtraining syndrome. Fatigue is now chronic — it's with you like a shadow. You're tired on awaking and throughout the day, on the job or in class, and yet have trouble sleeping normally at night. Your body is exhausted.

• **The geography of overtraining.** The challenge is, that in order to get to the "Peak of Fitness," you must occasionally travel through the "Valley of Fatigue" dangerously close to the "Edge of Overtraining." Figure 11.2 shows how increasing the training load causes a decline in fitness and brings you closer to the Edge. The decline in fitness is evident to anyone who has ever completed a maximum effort race on Saturday and tried to race again on Sunday. The second time around, it isn't quite as easy.

The idea is to go the Edge infrequently, and then back off. "Infrequently" means once every four weeks or so. After three weeks of load increases, you need to allow for recovery and adaptation. Some athletes, especially masters and novices, may need to recover more frequently, perhaps after only two weeks. To do more is to fall over the Edge and start the downward spiral through overreaching to overtraining.

As the body enters the Valley of Fatigue, overtraining indicators rear their ugly heads. You may experience poor sleep quality, excessive fatigue or muscle soreness on a continuing basis. Once in the Valley, indicators may be minor in number and severity, but with too great an increase or too prolonged a period of stress, you teeter on the Edge

Sidebar notes (left margin):

Overloading the body is a normal part of training.

Overreaching is common but risky.

Overtraining is marked by exhaustion.

Go to the Edge only once every three or four weeks.

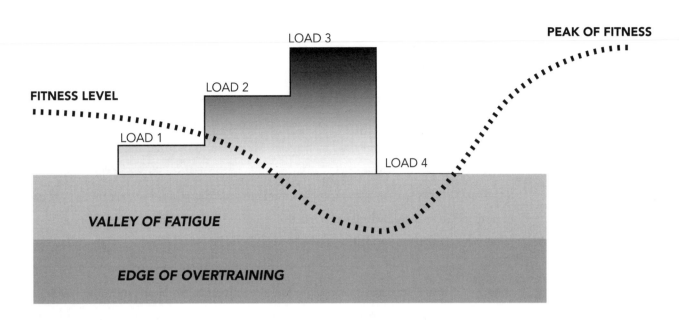

of overtraining. At this point, you wisely reduce training (Load 4 in Figure 11.2) and rest more. Rest brings adaptation marked by fitness increasing to a level exceeding the starting level four weeks before. By repeating this process several times, you eventually reach the Peak of Fitness.

FIGURE 11.2
Valley of fatigue.

If you fall over the edge into overtraining, the only option is rest. At the first signs of overtraining, take 48 hours of complete rest, and then try a brief recovery workout. If you're still not feeling peppy, take another 48 hours off and repeat the test workout. It could take five to eight weeks of this to fully beat back overtraining, at a great loss of fitness.

Recovering from overtraining requires extended rest.

• **The art of training.** The art of training is knowing where the Edge of Overtraining is for you. Highly motivated, young or novice athletes are less likely to recognize having crossed the line than are seasoned competitors. That's why many serious athletes are better off training under the guidance of a coach.

Smart training requires constantly assessing your readiness to train. Chapter 15 provides a training diary format with suggested daily indicators to rate. Judiciously tracking these indicators will help you pay closer attention to the body's daily messages. By learning to listen closely to your body, you will become adept at going to the Edge safely.

Listen to your body.

Unfortunately, there is no sure-fire formula for knowing when you have done too much and are starting to overreach. The best prevention is the judicious use of rest and recovery. Just as workouts must vary between hard and easy, so must weeks and months vary. It's far better to be undertrained and eager, than to be overtrained. When in doubt, leave it out.

ILLNESS

You would think that a lot of training is healthy and might help you avoid illness. Unfortunately, that's not the case. Those who work out frequently are more likely to catch a bug than those who work out occasionally.

High volume training is associated with illness.

A study of runners in the Los Angeles Marathon found that those running more than 60 miles per week were twice as susceptible to respiratory illness as those who ran less than 20 miles weekly. Runners who completed the marathon were six times as likely to be ill in the week following the race as those who trained hard for the race and for some reason did not run it.

• **Illness and timing.** The six hours following a high-intensity workout (4 or 5 zones) or race is the most critical phase for remaining healthy as the immune system is depressed and less capable of fighting off disease. This six-hour period is a good time to avoid people and public places. Washing your hands frequently if you have contact with others or with public facilities during this time is also a good idea for staying healthy. Develop the habit of touching your face only with your left hand and touching objects, such as doors and telephones, with your right. New Zealand's former world duathlon champion Matt Brick, a physician by training, following races would wear a surgical mask on airplanes for this reason.

Be cautious for the six hours after a race.

• **Neck check.** What should you do when a cold or flu bug gets you down? Should you continue to train as normal, cut back or stop altogether? Doing a "neck check" will help you decide. With above-the-neck symptoms such as a runny nose, sneezing or a scratchy throat, start your workout, but reduce the intensity to the 1 or 2 zones only and keep the duration shorter than usual. You will probably begin to feel better once warmed up, but if you feel worse after the first few minutes, stop and head home. If the symptoms are below the neck, such as chest cold, chills, coughing up matter, achy muscles or a fever, don't even start. You've probably got an acute viral infection. Exercising intensely in this condition will increase the severity of the illness and can even cause extreme complications, including death.

Don't train with symptoms below the neck.

These below-the-neck symptoms are sometimes accompanied by the Coxsackie virus that can invade the heart muscle causing arrhythmia and other complications. I can speak from experience on this one. In November 1994, I caught a bad cold with several below-the-neck symptoms including fever, achy muscles and coughing up mucous. Five months later I had a full-blown Coxsackie virus in my heart. After spending most of the year inactive, I was finally able to start training again. No race or any amount of fitness is worth paying such a price. Don't take these symptoms lightly. Suspect Coxsackie virus is present whenever you have a respiratory infection with indicators below the neck.

• **Recuperating**. After the illness has abated, you are likely to be run down for some time. One study found that there is a 15-percent reduction in muscle strength that may last for up to a month following a bout of the flu. Aerobic capacity is also reduced for up to three months, and muscles become acidic at lower levels of intensity during this time. This means you will feel weak when working out even though the acute stage is past. It's probably wise, following a below-the-neck illness, to return to the Base period of training for two days for every day you had symptoms. That means an emphasis on re-establishing aerobic endurance, strength and technique, while avoiding intervals or extended anaerobic effort.

Return to base training following a serious illness.

Trying to "push" past the flu will likely make your condition worse and cause it to last longer. It's best to get rid of the illness as soon as possible by allowing your limited energy reserves to go into fighting the disease rather than adapting your body to the stresses of training.

INJURIES

There is nothing worse than an injury. It's not bad enough that fitness is slipping away, but so much of an athlete's psyche is intertwined with physical activity that depression often sets in. No one wants to be around a lame athlete.

Some people are "fragile" and especially prone to injuries. Runners call this "glass legs." Such athletes get hurt doing what others find routine. It's more than a nuisance for those so afflicted. One study found that in triathletes, the most common injuries occur in the lower leg and ankle, knee, back, thigh and shoulder. Other studies have shown that triathletes have an injury rate of 75 percent, but among those training for an Ironman-distance race, the rate is 91 percent. Here are some prevention tips that may help keep injury-prone you out of the doctor's office.

• **Equipment selection**. Using equipment that fits correctly and is meant for your needs is paramount to staying injury-free. Riding a bike that is too big or too small is an invitation to an injury. This is especially a problem for small women who often ride bikes designed for men, and for juniors riding bikes they will "grow in to." Bike fit is not only important to injury prevention, but also to performance. Shop around when in the market for a new bike, and ask lots of questions. If you are less than 63 inches tall or more than 74 inches tall, or if your arm or leg lengths are disproportionate to your height, a custom bike is the way to go.

Tall or short people may need custom-made bikes.

Suspect your running shoes at the first sign of discomfort or pain below the waist.

A common mistake is trying to get too many miles from shoes. Some triathletes and duathletes may only get 200 miles from their favorite model, while others may run for 500 before needing replacements. While the outer sole is what most examine, it's really the midsole and heel cup that should be closely monitored. If injury resulting from shoe breakdown is a common problem for you, learn what the limits of your favorite style are and keep a cumulative record of their miles in your diary. When halfway through their anticipated life span, regardless of how they look, buy a second pair and start breaking them in.

Another error is buying shoes that are wrong for your foot. Running shoes are quite technical, and are likely to cause injuries if you don't have the condition for which the shoes were meant. For example, shoes designed to control excessive pronation are excellent for those with such a foot type, but if you underpronate, these shoes may set you up for Achilles tendonitis, iliotibial band syndrome, stress fracture, or any of a number of other serious injuries. The best way to avoid such problems is to buy only shoes that are known to work for you, or to shop at a store where knowledgeable runners can help you make the right choice. It often helps the sales person if you take your old running shoes to the store with you when shopping.

• **Run and swim technique.** Repeating the same improper movement pattern hundreds or thousands of times under a load is often the cause of leg injury in running and shoulder problems in swimming. Expert videoanalysis or performing under the watchful eye of an experienced athlete or coach, coupled with lots of practice, can correct such mistakes. Realize, however, that we are not all built exactly the same way, and that some individual variance is necessary. Chapter 12 offers technique suggestions for running and swimming.

• **Bike set up.** Just as with running and swimming, having poor biomechanics on the bike can easily injure a joint, especially the knee. Once you have the right equipment, ask an experienced multisport athlete, bike shop employee or coach to take a look at your position and offer suggestions for improvement. Be especially concerned with saddle fore-aft position and height. See Chapter 12 for more details on bike set up.

• **Training.** The most likely times to get injured are the two or three days after very long or very intense workouts and races. Running at these times is especially risky and is best done slowly and on a soft surface such as grass, if at all. Swimming and cycling are often better choices at such times for the injury-prone. Post-race training should be brief and easy, or days off. In the same manner, two or three weeks of high-work load training are best followed by a week of reduced volume and intensity. This is difficult to do when your cardiovascular and energy-production systems are willing and able to handle

Shoe breakdown is a common injury cause.

Buy running shoes designed for your foot type.

Poor technique may cause injury.

Improper bike set up may cause knee injury.

Reducing the work load at key times lowers injury risk.

more, but such restraint will keep your more fragile musculo-skeletal system injury-free.

• **Strength and stretching**. For most of us, our weakest link is the muscle-tendon junction. This is where tears and strains are likely to occur. Many muscle-tendon problems can be prevented early in the season by gradually improving the muscle's strength and range of motion. One study estimated that up to 80 percent of all running injuries resulted from muscle weakness, muscular imbalance or lack of flexibility. These are sometimes neglected areas for endurance athletes. Going for a swim, bike or run is fun, but grunting through a combined strength and stretching session in the gym seems like drudgery. Hang in there, and you will reap the benefits. On the other hand, excessive strength development or stretching is sometimes the cause of injury. Maintain a moderate approach in both of these areas. See Chapter 13 for more details on strength and stretching.

A conservative approach is necessary with strength and flexibility development.

• **Listen**. Learn to tell the difference between sore muscles that come from a high-quality effort and sore joints or tendons. Pinpoint any unusual discomfort and try to put the sensation into words. Don't just say "my knee hurts." Is it above or below the kneecap? Front or back of the knee? Is it a sharp pain or a dull ache? Does it hurt only while swimming, cycling or running, or all the time? Is the pain worse going up stairs, or down? Investigate shoes, bike set-up, running surfaces and training or technique changes. Such probing may lead you to the cause of the injury and its treatment. These are also the sorts of questions you are asked if you must seek professional help.

Methodically analyzing injuries often leads to the cause.

If all of these suggestions fail, you still develop an injury and the pain isn't gone with five days of reduced activity, it's time to see a health-care provider. Don't put it off. Injuries are easier to turn around in the early stages than later on when they have become chronic. During convalescence, increase your volume in the sports that are unaffected by the injury. Healing is speeded up by exercise.

RECOVERY TIMING AND TECHNIQUE

What happens inside the muscles during an intense exercise is not a pretty sight. If you could look into your legs with a microscope after a race, what you would see looks like a battleground. The muscles appear as if a miniature bomb has exploded, with torn and jagged cell membranes evident and leaking fluids. The damage can vary from slight to extreme depending on how great the stress was. Under extreme conditions, it's unlikely the energy, muscles and nervous system will be ready for such an effort again soon. Not until the cells are repaired, the energy stores rebuilt, and cellular chemistry returns to normal is another all-out effort possible. Your fitness depends on how long that process takes.

Intense exercise damages muscle cells.

Much of the time needed for recovery has to do with creating new muscle protein to repair the damage. Research conducted at McMaster University in Hamilton, Ontario, and at the Washington University School of Medicine in St. Louis, found that this protein resynthesis process takes several hours. The study used young, experienced weight lifters and maximal efforts followed by observation of the muscles' repair process. Reconstruction work started almost immediately following the workout. Four hours after the damaging weight session, protein activity was increased about 50 percent. By 24 hours post-workout it reached a peak of 109 percent of normal. Protein resynthesis was back to normal, indicating that repair was complete, 36 hours after the hard workout.

While this study used exhaustive strength training to measure recovery time, the results are probably similar to what could be expected following a race or intense workout.

RECOVERY PHASES

The recovery process can be divided into three distinct phases in relation to the workout — before and during, immediately following, and long term. If the recovery process in each phase is carefully observed, damage is minimized and repair is accelerated allowing the next quality session to occur sooner.

Warm-up speeds recovery.

• **Recovery before and during the workout.** Recovery actually starts with a warm-up before the workout or race that will cause the damage, not after. A good warm-up before starting to train intensely helps limit damage by:

- Thinning body fluids to allow easier muscle contractions.
- Opening capillaries to bring more oxygen to muscles.
- Raising muscle temperature so that contractions take less effort.
- Conserving carbohydrate and releasing fat for fuel.

Refueling during workouts speeds recovery.

The recovery process should continue during the workout with the on-going replacement of carbohydrate-based energy stores. By drinking 18 to 24 ounces of a sports drink every hour, the training session is less stressful on the body, and the recovery of the energy-production system later on is enhanced. There are individual differences in how well carbohydrate drinks are tolerated and emptied from the stomach. Find a sports drink that tastes good and doesn't upset your stomach when working intensely. Before a race, make sure you have plenty of what works on your bike, and have prepared for whatever is offered at the aid stations by using it in training. Making the drink more concentrated than is recommended on the label may cause you to dehydrate during a race as body fluids are shunted to the gut to digest the concentrated carbohydrate. Races and workouts that last more than one hour are most likely to benefit from a sports drink. In races lasting longer than about four or five hours, solid food is also recommended.

Recovery continues with a brief cool-down. The cool-down should be a mirror image of the warm-up, ending with easy effort in the 1 zone for several minutes.

• **Recovery immediately following the workout.** As soon as you finish, the most important thing you can do to speed recovery is to replace the carbohydrate and protein just used for fuel. A long and difficult workout or race can deplete nearly all of your stored glycogen, a carbohydrate-based energy source, and use several grams of muscle-bound protein. In the first 30 minutes after workouts, your body is several times more capable of absorbing and replenishing those fuels than at any other time.

At this time, you probably don't want to use the same sports drink you used on the bike. It's not potent enough and doesn't include protein. You need something designed for recovery. There are several such products now on the market. As long as you like the taste and can get about 15-20 grams of protein and 80 grams or so of carbohydrate from one of them, it will meet your recovery needs. Dr. Owen Anderson in *Running Research News* suggests making a recovery "homebrew" by adding five tablespoons of table sugar to 16 ounces of skim milk. It's probably best not to use a high glycemic index carbohydrate, such as a sugary drink without protein, (see Chapter 16 for the glycemic index) as some scientists believe that this may reduce the body's release of growth hormone, further slowing the recovery process. Whatever you use, drink all of it within the first 30 minutes after finishing.

• **Long-term recovery.** For six to nine hours after a breakthrough (BT) workout, you must actively seek recovery by using one or more specific techniques. The most basic method is sleep. Nothing beats a nap for rejuvenation as growth hormone is released in pulses starting about 30 minutes into slumber. In addition to a 30- to 60-minute, post-workout nap, seven to nine hours of sleep are needed each night. Other recovery methods are unique to each individual, so you will need to experiment with several of these to find the ones that work best for you. The accompanying sidebar, Recovery Techniques, offers several suggestions. By employing some of the specific techniques described here you can accelerate the recovery process and return to action sooner. Figure 11.3 illustrates how this happens.

INDIVIDUALIZATION OF RECOVERY

You will find that some recovery techniques work better for you than do others. You may also discover that a training partner doing the same workouts as you and following the same recovery protocol springs back at a different rate, either slower or faster. This goes back to the principle of individualization discussed in Chapter 3. While there are many physiological similarities between athletes, each is unique and responds in his or her own way to any given set of cir-

Use a carbohydrate-protein drink immediately following a Break Through workout.

Down the recovery drink within 30 minutes of finishing.

Sleep offers the best form of recovery.

Optimal recovery techniques vary with the individual.

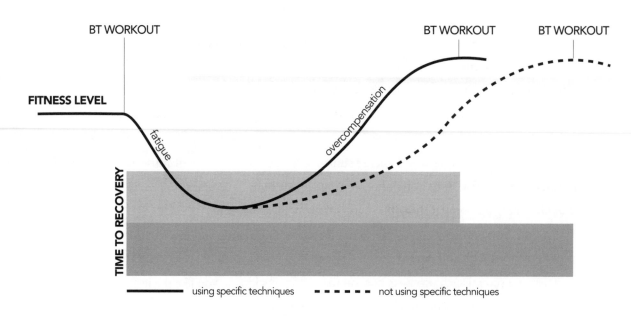

BT WORKOUT   BT WORKOUT   BT WORKOUT

FITNESS LEVEL

fatigue

overcompensation

TIME TO RECOVERY

—————— using specific techniques   - - - - - not using specific techniques

FIGURE 11.3
Recovery time with and without specific techniques.

cumstances. You must experiment to discover the best recovery techniques for you.

There are several individual factors effecting recovery. Younger multisport athletes, especially 18 to 22 years old, recover faster than older athletes. The more race-experienced an athlete is, the quicker he or she recovers. If fitness is high, recovery is speeded up. Females were shown in one study to recover faster than males. Other factors influencing the rate of recovery are climate, diet and psychological stress.

How do you know if you are recovering? The best indicator is performance in races and Break Through workouts, but these are the worst times to find out that you are not ready. Typical signs that recovery is fully complete include a positive attitude, feelings of

Look for signs of recovery.

health, a desire to train intensely again, high quality sleep, normal resting and exercise heart rates, and balanced emotions. If any of these are lacking, continue the recovery process. By closely monitoring such signs you should eventually determine not only the best techniques, but also the typical time needed to bounce back from different types of workouts and races.

RECOVERY IN THE REAL WORLD

If you are following the periodization program suggested in Part IV, there will occasionally be periods when you experience an increasing load of fatigue. Despite your best recovery efforts, you will not unload all of the fatigue between planned workouts and will go into

Be careful with the "creative" use of fatigue.

some Break Through workouts a bit heavy legged and lacking power. Don't expect full recovery for every workout, all the time. In fact, a little fatigue at the right times in workouts can bring fitness benefits in the form of "supercompensation" — an increased level of overcompensation. This can better prepare you for peak performances. You just don't want

Recovery techniques

Most of these techniques speed recovery by slightly increasing the heart rate, increasing blood flow to the muscles, accelerating the inflow of nutrients, reducing soreness, lowering blood pressure and relaxing the nervous system.

HOT SHOWER OR BATH

Immediately following the cool-down and recovery drink, take a hot shower or bath for 10 to 15 minutes. Do not linger, especially in the bathtub, as you will dehydrate even more.

ACTIVE RECOVERY

For the experienced triathlete, one of the best recovery methods is to pedal or swim easily for 15 to 30 minutes several hours after the workout and before going to bed. The intensity should be extremely light with heart rate below the 1 zone.

MASSAGE

Other than sleep, most triathletes find a massage by a professional massage therapist is the most effective recovery technique. A post-race massage should employ long, flushing strokes to speed the removal of the waste products of exercise. Deep massage at this time may actually increase muscle trauma. After 36 hours, the therapist may apply greater point pressure, working more deeply.

Due to the expense of massage, some athletes prefer self-massage. Following a hot bath or shower, stroke the muscles for 20 to 30 minutes working away from the extremities and toward the heart.

SAUNA

Several hours following a workout or race you may find that a dry sauna speeds recovery. Do not use a steam room for recovery as it will have the opposite effect. Stay in the sauna for no more than 10 minutes and begin drinking fluids as soon as you are done.

RELAX AND STRETCH

Be lazy for several hours. Your body wants quality rest. Provide it by staying off your feet whenever possible. Never stand when you can lean against something. Sit down whenever possible. Better yet, lay on the floor with your feet elevated against a wall or furniture. Sit on the floor and stretch gently. Overused muscles tighten and can't seem to relax on their own. This is best right after a hot bath or sauna, and just before going to bed.

WALK IN A PARK OR FOREST

A few hours after finishing the workout or race, a short, slow walk in a heavily vegetated area such as a park or forest seems to speed recovery for some. Abundant oxygen and the aroma of grass, trees and other plants is soothing.

OTHER METHODS

The sports program of the former Soviet Union made a science of recovery and employed several techniques with their athletes that may or may not be available to you. Many are also unproved in the scientific literature. They included electromuscular stimulation, ultrasound, barometric chambers, sport psychology and pharmacological supplements including vitamins, minerals and adaptogens such as ginseng. These require expert guidance.

❖

this to occur more often than about every third or fourth week, depending on your ability to avoid overtraining, illness and injury. A recovery week should immediately follow a period in which fatigue played a major role in the training load.

REFERENCES

Bompa, T. 1994. *Theory and Methodology of Training.* Dubuque, IA: Kendall/Hunt.

Brenner, I.K.M. 1994. Infection in athletes. *Sports Medicine* 17 (2): 86-107.

Brunner, R. and B. Tabachnik. 1990. *Soviet Training and Recovery Methods.* Sport Focus Publishing.

Cade, J.R., et al. 1991. Dietary intervention and training in swimmers. *European Journal of Applied Physiology* 63: 210-215,

David, A.S., et al. 1988. Post-viral fatigue syndrome: Time for a new approach. *British Medical Journal* 296: 696-699.

Dragan, I. and I. Stonescu. 1978. *Organism recovery following training.* Bucharest: Sport-Turism.

Driver, H.S., et al. 1994. Prolonged endurance exercise and sleep disruption. *Medicine and Science in Sports and Exercise* 26 (7): 903-907.

Farber, H.W., et al. 1991. The endurance triathlon: Metabolic changes after each event and during recovery. *Medicine and Science in Sports and Exercise* 23 (8): 959-965.

Fitzgerald, L. 1988. Exercise and the immune system. *Immunology Today* 9 (11): 337-339.

Fry, R.W., et al. 1991. Overtraining in athletes: An update. *Sports Medicine* 12 (1): 32-65.

Fry, R.W. and D. Keast. 1991. Overtraining in athletes. *Sports Medicine* 12 (1): 32-65.

Heath, G.W., et al. 1992. Exercise and upper respiratory tract infections: Is there a relationship? *Sports Medicine* 14 (6): 353-365.

Hoffman-Goetz, L. and B.K. Peterson. 1994. Exercise and the immune system: A model of the stress response? *Immunology Today* 15 (8): 382-387.

Hooper, S.L. and L.T. MacKinnon. 1995. Monitoring overtraining in athletes: Recommendations. *Sports Medicine* 20 (5): 321-327.

Hooper, S.L., et al. 1995. Markers for monitoring overtraining and recovery. *Medicine and Science in Sports and Exercise* 27 (1): 106-112.

Keast, D., et al. 1988. Exercise and the immune response. *Sports Medicine* 5: 248-267.

Korkia, D.S., et al. 1994. An epidemiological investigation of training and injury patterns in British triathletes. *British Journal of Sports Medicine* 28: 191-196.

Kuipers, H. and H.A. Keizer. 1988. Overtraining in elite athletes: Review and directions for the future. *Sports Medicine* 6: 79-92.

Lehmann, M., et al. 1993. Overtraining in endurance athletes: A brief review. *Medicine and Science in Sports and Exercise* 25(7): 854-862.

MacDougal, J.D., et al. 1995. The time course for elevated muscle protein synthesis following heavy resistance exercise. *Canadian Journal of Applied Physiology* 20 (4): 480486.

Masten, et al. 1990. Different short-term effects of protein and carbohydrate intake on TSH, GH, insulin and glucagon. *Scandinavian Journal of Clinical and Laboratory Investigation* 50 (11): 801-805.

Milne, C. 1991. The tired athlete. *New Zealand Journal of Sports Medicine* 19 (3): 42-44.

Newham, D.J., et al. 1982. Muscle pain and tenderness after exercise. *Australian Journal of Sports Medicine and Exercise Science* 14: 129-131.

Nieman, D.C., et al. 1990. Infectious episodes in runners before and after the Los Angeles Marathon. *Journal of Sports Medicine and Physical Fitness* 30: 316-328.

O'Toole, M.L. 1992. Prevention and treatment of injuries to runners. *Medicine and Science in Sports and Exercise* 24 (9): S360-363.

O'Toole, M.L., et al. 1989. Overuse injuries in ultraendurance triathletes. *American Journal of Sports Medicine* 17: 514-518.

Reuter, B.H. and G. Wright. 1996. Overuse injury prevention in triathletes. *Strength and Conditioning* 18 (6): 11-14.

Sharp, N.C.C. and Y. Koutedakis. 1992. Sport and the overtraining syndrome. *British Medical Journal* 48 (3): 518-533.

Stone, M., et al. 1991. Overtraining: A review of the signs, symptoms, and possible causes, *Journal of Applied Sport Sciences* 5 (1): 35-50.

Tipton, C.M., et al. 1975. The influence of physical activity on ligaments and tendons. *Medicine and Science in Sports and Exercise* 7: 165-175.

Urhausen, A., et al. 1995. Blood hormones as markers of training stress and overtraining. *Sports Medicine* 20: 251-276.

THE COMPETITIVE EDGE

Up to this point, we've examined the role of the more obvious contributors to fitness: training principles; intensity; limiters; planning and periodization; swim, bike and run workouts; tapering; and recovery. While these factors certainly play a role in the attainment of peak fitness, there are many others. In fact, it's unrealistic to divide certain parts of your life and say only these particular things have a bearing on race performance. When you go to the starting line, all of the physical and psychological components of your recent lifestyle have shaped your readiness for that moment.

This part examines a few of those components that play an important role in your race readiness, but may be overlooked, including physical skills, muscle strength and flexibility, the needs of unique subgroups, the training diary and diet. Our purpose in this part is to refine these aspects of your training and lifestyle in order to gain a competitive edge.

SKILLS

*"Fitness is something that happens to you
while you're practicing good technique."*

— TERRY LAUGHLIN, SWIM COACH

There are three goals multisport athletes typically seek: the capacity to go farther,
the ability to go faster, and the capability to go farther and faster without breaking down. Of these, the most common single goal is to swim, bike and run faster for a
given distance. In fact, faster race times are the reason most of us train.

What can you do to get faster? The answer is simple: Increase how quickly you
can move your arms and legs, or how much distance you can cover in each stroke or
stride, or some combination of both. In other words, velocity is a product of cadence
and stroke/stride length. In running, for example, if you develop the quickness to take
more strides per minute while the length of each stays the same, you will run faster. Or
if you build the strength to take a longer stride with the same cadence, running times
will improve.

Let's examine this relationship more closely, again using running as the medium. If
you run a 5km race with an average step length of 1.5 meters and an average cadence of
170 steps per minute, your finish time is 19 minutes, 36 seconds. But if you take three
more steps per minute and step length stays the same, you finish 20 seconds faster. Or, if
you increase the length of each step by 0.025 meters (about one inch) and stride rate
remains at 170, your time is improved by 19 seconds. If you are able to accomplish both
the faster stride rate and a longer stride, you lop off 39 seconds and have a new personal best of 18:57. Small changes in technique can produce significant results.

Of course, running with a stride that is both longer and faster means that you must
develop the fitness to maintain such an effort. As described in previous chapters, improving the basic abilities of endurance, strength and speed, and the more advanced abilities of

**Velocity results from
cadence and stroke/
stride length.**

Improved fitness is necessary to support increases in cadence and stroke/stride length.

muscular endurance, anaerobic endurance and power will lead you to this goal of greater race velocity. Another way of looking at the necessary fitness components uses the terms of science: Great race fitness results from a large *aerobic capacity* (VO_2 max), a high *lactate threshold* as a percentage of aerobic capacity, and an excellent *economy* of movement.

Aerobic capacity (how much oxygen the body processes at maximal work) and lactate threshold (the level of submaximal work at which lactate begins to accumulate in the blood) are generally well understood by endurance athletes. You may not be as familiar with economy, but it is critical to understanding how improving skills may reap greater rewards for you than working strictly on aerobic capacity and lactate threshold. In fact, your performance in multisport may be limited more by your skills than by what we commonly think of as "fitness."

ECONOMY

In 1969, Australian Derek Clayton set the world record for the marathon at 2:08:34 — a record that was not broken until 1981. What is surprising about Clayton's feat is that he had a VO_2 max of only 69.7 ml/min/kg (milliliters of oxygen used per minute per kilogram of body weight). That is rather pedestrian for a world-class athlete and pales in comparison to the aerobic capacities of many of his running contemporaries such as Craig Virgin (81.1), Gary Tuttle (82.7), Don Kardong (77.4) and Bill Rodgers (78.5). None of these runners came close to Clayton's time despite having remarkably "big engines." The reason for Clayton's success was his economy. He simply wasted less energy when he ran than did the others.

Economy can "make up" for aerobic capacity.

The concept of economy is important, all the more so if your parents didn't bless you with a large aerobic capacity. Just as Derek Clayton did, you can enhance your performance by learning to swim, bike and run in an efficient manner. Let's examine economy more closely, especially the ways to improve it.

UNDERSTANDING ECONOMY

Economy simply refers to how much oxygen you use while swimming, biking and running. Since oxygen usage is an indirect indicator of the amount of fuel burned, and economy is a measure of fuel expenditure in relation to work (like miles per gallon in a car), knowing how much oxygen an athlete uses at various velocities reveals how economical he or she is. Fuel efficiency in one sport, however, does not indicate economy in others. You may use fuel like a small, economy car while running, but be a "gas guzzler" on the bike.

The more economical you are, the faster you can travel at any given effort level. For example, let's say you currently run an eight-minute pace at an oxygen cost of 50 ml/min/kg, but through training you improve economy by 2 percent. That means you could now run at an eight-minute pace at 49 ml/min/kg, so it would feel easier. Or you could run at the same 50 ml/min/kg, but your pace would have improved to 7:50 — a 10-second increase in velocity for every mile run. Over the course of a 10km, that results in more than a one-minute improvement in time. So small changes in economy can produce rather dramatic changes in performance.

Improved economy means faster times.

It's also important to note that the longer the race is, the more important economy becomes. In a sprint-distance race you may get away with squandering fuel since the event is so short and you may be able to simply "muscle" your way through it. That's not possible in an Ironman-distance event where the fuel consumption rate often means the difference between a personal best and not finishing.

It's sometimes easy to spot the economical athletes as they make swimming, biking and running look effortless. This is especially true in swimming since water is more dense than air and severely penalizes extraneous, wasteful movements. An accomplished swimmer seems to glide through the water. Such a swimmer makes it look so easy that when you check lap splits, you may be surprised at how fast he or she is moving. In the same way, an uneconomical swimmer's thrashing and struggling technique is obvious.

Economy can sometimes be observed.

Good economy isn't always so apparent since there are several less conspicuous factors that effect it. For example, science has shown that endurance athletes endowed with lots of slow-twitch muscle fibers are somewhat more economical than those who have an abundance of fast-twitch fibers. Body size may also effect economy. Small people are generally found to have better economies than bigger athletes. These are factors outside of your control, but there are other variables effecting economy that you can mitigate to improve energy consumption, such as:

- Excess body weight
- Psychological stress
- Equipment (for example, bike and running shoes) weight and shape
- The amount of frontal area exposed to water or wind
- Subtle variances in technique

IMPROVING ECONOMY

This last point, subtle variances in technique, is worth further discussion. By consciously modifying your movement patterns to resemble those of elite swimmers, cyclists and runners who typically have excellent economies, it may be possible to improve your fuel usage. Unfortunately, scientific studies nearly always find that changing technique has little or no positive effect on economy. It's important to understand, however, that testing in economy research is usually limited by such factors as the length of a school semester and the motivation of the subjects, often college students, to continue training. So in the typical study, testing to measure improvement in economy is generally carried out a few days or weeks following the prescribed changes. But the body's adjustment to such changes may take months to fully realize since many slowly occurring adaptations are required of the nervous system and muscles before appreciable gains are measurable. At first, during that period of adaptation, economy may even worsen.

Form changes take months of practice before economy improves.

Experience tells us that it is possible to boost economy, even in elite athletes. One case in point is that of American miler Steve Scott who in the early 1980s, at the height of his running career, broke the American record for the mile after improving his economy by a whopping 5 percent.

There are three principles you must adhere to in your training if economy is to steadily and rapidly improve. The first is to practice the new technique frequently. If your swimming skill needs correction, getting in the pool only once a week is not enough. Three swims spaced evenly throughout the week is probably a minimum, and more is better. The second principle is that once the new skill is mastered at slower velocities, to regularly practice it at goal race pace. These goal race-pace repetitions are kept quite short — on the order of 20 to 30 seconds — to allow for total concentration on the new skill, and to prevent fatigue from interfering as the new movements are practiced.

Three principles for learning new skills.

The last principle is perhaps the most important: Complex skills are best learned when the desired movement pattern is broken down into manageable units which are mastered individually before gradually combining them into more complex movements. Essentially, this means that technique drills are best for helping you learn new skills. Improved economy of movement results from training the nervous system to choose the best pathways to the exact muscles that need activating. The more times this is done, the better the nervous system becomes at producing the desired movement pattern. This can be compared to making a path across open land. If enough people frequently take the exact same shortcut, a path results. This is obvious on most college campuses where students have produced "economical" pathways irrespective of sidewalks in order to cut the distance between destinations.

Frequent repetition of inappropriate movement patterns builds bad habits by destroying the fragile pathways you try to build with drills. To fully develop the new skills, it's important to let go of old patterns and fully commit to the new. At first this will inevitably result in poorer performance and frustration. You must realize that this is merely a stage of learning that you must go through in order to ultimately improve. The best time in the training year to develop new skills is during the Prep and early Base periods, but there is no time like the present for getting started.

Expect decreased performance while learning new skills.

SWIM SKILLS

The energy cost of a 150-pound triathlete running a kilometer is about 70 kilocalories. But when swimming that same kilometer, assuming the athlete's economy is about the same, 280 kilocalories are expended. Why does swimming require so much more energy? The answer is that water is nearly a thousand times more dense than air. Water is a formidable barrier for the human shape to move through. Unfortunately for triathletes, we weren't given the shape and instincts of fish; we're land-based animals and try to apply what works in that world whenever we enter the world of fish. Those land-based skills are seldom effective in water. To become an effective and economical swimmer, you must change the way you think about movement in the watery world. Let's examine the necessary changes.

Land-based skills are ineffective in the water.

Essentially, there are two ways to swim faster. The first is to decrease drag by streamlining body position. The second is to increase propulsion by improving aerobic and anaerobic fitness. Of these two, scientific studies have found that reducing drag has the potential to produce the greatest gains. Drag is the retarding force created by turbulence around the body as it moves through water. The more streamlined the body is, the lower the resulting drag force.

One swimming authority estimates that the opportunity for triathlon performance improvement by reducing drag is more than twice as great as focusing on propulsive effort. Our land-based instincts tell us the opposite, so we spend countless hours in the pool struggling to become more fit to fight drag while paying only lip service to the skills of swimming.

Reducing drag is the surest way to improve swimming.

On land, humans discover that running with an increased cadence leads to faster times, so we take that knowledge with us into the water. The problem is, this solution doesn't work in the water. The faster we try to move our arms, the more the water pushes back against us. The solution is to go to the other variable by increasing stroke length, and, for some triathletes, decreasing stroke rate. Again, research has shown that the swimmers with the longest strokes are the most economical and produce the best results. A good indicator of improving economy in swimming is how many strokes are taken in a given length. Reducing your stroke count is the surest way to a new swimming personal-best time.

A long stroke and low cadence produce the most economical stroke.

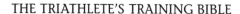

Goal: Reduce strokes per length.

Develop the habit of counting strokes for a length of the pool, and set a goal of taking 10 percent fewer. Once you've achieved that lower stroke-count goal, which you will if you concentrate on form rather than "fitness," extend the time you can maintain it. When you can hold it for more than two minutes, it's time to set a new stroke-count goal and start over again.

The best path to faster swim times comes from improving drag-reducing skills so that you are more "fishlike" and "slippery" — not from high yardage and propulsion-increasing battles with the water. Instead of trying to overpower the water, develop the skills to slice through it with the least amount of energy expended. The best way to achieve these skills is by having a smart coach on deck. That's not always feasible, so let's look at what you can do on your own to improve economy in the water.

REDUCING DRAG

Terry Laughlin is perhaps the leading authority in the U.S. on swimming drag reduction for triathletes. Through his Total Immersion swim camps, video, workbook, drill guide, magazine articles and book, he has consistently promoted the concept that better swimming results from mastering three simple techniques. The successes of his students prove that his methods work. Here are his three techniques and one basic drill for each. There are many more drills Laughlin recommends. (For more information on Total Immersion products call 800/609-7946, or set your Web browser for http://www.totalimmersion.swim.com.)

Sinking hips is the biggest challenge of triathletes.

• **Swim "downhill."** The most common swimming complaint heard from rock-hard triathletes is that they sink in the water. Actually, what sinks is the hips and legs as the upper body has natural buoyancy due to the lungs. When the lower body sinks, drag forces increase since more of the body is exposed to the approaching water. Just as aerodynamics on the bike require greatly reducing frontal area, economical hydrodynamics depends on a small frontal area, as shown in Figure 12.1.

FIGURE 12.1
Swimmer A presents a large frontal area as he swims through a large "tube," due to his sinking hips and legs. Swimmer B disrupts little water and creates less drag as a result of a more streamlined position.

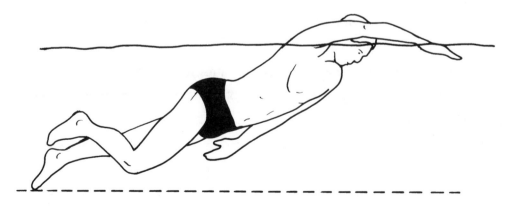

Your head controls your hip and leg position relative to the surface of the water. When the head comes up, the legs go down. So if you swim with the face lifted looking at the far end of the pool, your hips and legs sink and are no longer following your torso through the "tube" it has created in the water. This is like dragging an anchor around behind you. Your only option is to work harder to increase the propulsive force, thus wasting a lot of energy — not very economical.

If, however, you look slightly downward while "leaning" on your chest, the hips and legs come up and follow your torso through the tube. When done correctly, only a small portion of the back of the head will show above water line, as will your butt. These are sure signs that you are swimming downhill, and can be readily confirmed by an observer on the deck. A video tape of swimming with and without the downhill position will clearly show you these economy traits.

The head controls hip position.

Learning to lean on the chest — "pressing the buoy" as Laughlin calls it — is the most basic skill for you to master in swimming. Until you have this down pat, there is no reason to practice other skills. One drill for developing this skill involves kicking a length of the pool without a board and the arms at your sides. While kicking in this position, keep your face looking slightly toward the pool bottom as you lean on your chest (your "buoy") pushing it down into the water. When you look up to breathe, notice that the hips and legs drop immediately, but that you can bring them back up by looking down and leaning more. Figure 12.2 illustrates this drill.

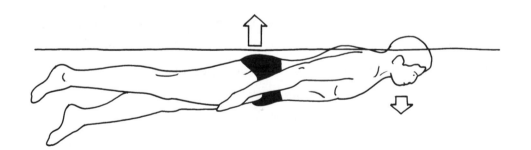

FIGURE 12.2
"Pressing the buoy." (Adapted from T. Laughlin and J. Delves, 1996, Total Immersion, with permission.)

• **Swim like a knife.** On land, we mammals move forward by keeping the line of our shoulders perpendicular to the direction of movement. This works fine in the less-dense world of air, but in water it presents a bigger frontal area and increases drag. By swimming on your side, as fish do, less energy is wasted and you go faster. This position also allows you to better use the powerful latissimus dorsi (lats) muscles on both sides of your upper back. So swimming in this position has a double benefit by reducing drag and increasing propulsive force.

Swimming on the side lessens drag and increases propulsion.

Swimming on the side requires rolling the hips and shoulders with all rotation happening around the spine. Such a maneuver feels as if you might flop over on your back and is unnatural for humans. It takes some getting use to. A drill to improve comfort in the position is "belly-to-the-wall." Swim a length of the pool lying on your left side with your left arm extended and the right arm lying on your hips as shown in Figure 12.3. The back of your head is pressed against the biceps of your outstretched arm and your face is looking up. This is a good drill to use fins with to keep the kick compact and minimize the "risk" of rolling completely onto your back. Change to your right side and kick back down the pool. Remember to keep the side of your chest (your buoy) pressed down into the water.

FIGURE 12.3
"Belly to the wall" (Adapted from T. Laughlin and J. Delves, 1996, Total Immersion, with permission.)

Once you have become comfortable with this position, practice rolling from one side to the other after a three-count pause on your side. As you roll, bring the top arm and hand slowly up your side like taking your hand out of a pocket. Notice that if this arm is swung out in front of your center of gravity, you immediately flop over onto your chest and belly. As your hand reaches your shoulder, initiate a roll to the prone position with your hips, and then bring your hands together with the arms outstretched. Hold this position for a three-count while pressing the buoy just as in the first drill. Then again using the hips to initiate movement, roll to the other side for a count of three.

• **Swim taller.** In watching elite swimmers, one thing stands out clearly: They fully extend their hand and arm in the reach phase that allows them to swim quite fast with strokes that seem long and unhurried. This results in a lower stroke rate, but a longer stroke, which, as we've seen, is associated with reduced drag and improved economy. They also kick from the hip with minimal bending of the knee further lengthening their position in the water. This also reduces drag by keeping the legs within the tube described above.

Reach — glide — stroke is a characteristic pattern of elite swimmers.

Swimming with a long stroke, including a reach and glide, while staying on your side requires constant practice to make it a habit. Stroke counting to ensure a low number of strokes per length is one way of checking how you are doing. A drill to refine this skill involves swimming a length while using only one arm as the other one is fully extended in the reach position as shown in Figure 12.4. As the "propulsive" arm starts its stroke, you roll onto your side as in the previous skill, and stretch as far as you can with the reaching arm. At the conclusion of the stroke, the recovery hand returns to touch the "reach" hand as you roll back to your chest. Be sure to continue pressing your chest and face into the water throughout the drill, even when on your side. Fins may be used to help keep the legs up as you develop these upper body skills.

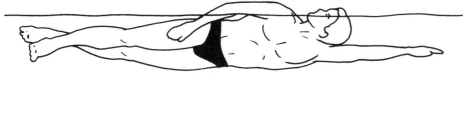

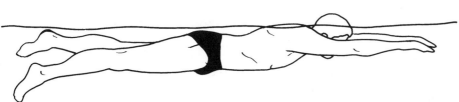

FIGURE 12.4
One-arm-only drill, (Adapted from T. Laughlin and J. Delves, 1996, Total Immersion, with permission.)

SWIM TRAINING

Your swimming is more likely to improve if you think of your pool sessions as "practices" rather than "workouts." Just as golfers spend hours on the practice tee and tennis players endlessly practice their service, triathletes must devote considerable time to technique refinement with drills and concentration on correct movement patterns. There are two ways to look at this allocation of valuable pool time for drill work. One is seasonal and has to do with the incorporation of drill work into your periodization plan. The other is within a given practice session. Here are some general guidelines for both areas to help you plan the timing of your drill work.

• **Periodization.** The Prep period is the time in each season to work exclusively on technique. One objective for this period is to correct any stroke flaws that may have found their way into your swimming mechanics by returning to the most basic drills, such as those described above and gradually making them more complex. This is also a good time to regularly meet with a knowledgeable swim coach, attend a swim camp, read a book on swimming or have someone videotape your swimming for analysis.

The Prep period is the time to return to the basics of stroke mechanics.

In the Base period, while aerobic and muscular endurance along with force are developing, continue to include a good deal of stroke work. The novice triathlete may devote nearly half of each swim practice just to refining technique.

As intensity increases in the Build and Peak periods, great care must be taken not to allow the good stroke mechanics you established in previous periods to erode. In an attempt to push velocity to a higher level, it is common to revert to a higher stroke rate, since that's what living on land tells us to do. Constantly review and refresh your muscle memory by including drills in every practice session throughout the year.

• **Practices**. The best time to work on skills is when you are fresh, at the start of a swim practice session. Developing new patterns of muscle recruitment means firing scores of small muscles in exquisite harmony for the desired movements to occur. If any of these muscles are fatigued, they will refuse to fire, or will fire or relax at the wrong times, frustrating your efforts to improve technique. Early in the practice, following a warm up, the muscles and nervous system are most receptive to learning new skills.

Include drills early in a practice session.

Near the end of a practice session, as general-body and local-muscle fatigue begin to set in, concentration on proper technique is paramount to improvement. There is no value to practicing skills by drilling and then abandoning all that you have worked on when the "fitness" portion of a swim session begins.

Total devotion to change is necessary if you are to get better. You must be prepared for a setback at first, as new and yet unrefined skills will slow you down. As you concentrate on stroke mechanics, other swimmers who you usually "beat" in interval sets will wonder what has happened to you. At these times it's important that you stay focused on your ultimate goal — swimming faster in races by wasting less energy. Attempting to "win" workouts will cost you dearly when it really counts in races.

BIKE SKILLS

In cycling, your ability to race well comes down to two variables — how you and the bike fit together, and how effectively you apply force to the pedals. If you ride a bike that doesn't fit, or if the bike set up is incorrect, you will needlessly waste energy. Once the bike is correctly adjusted to your unique biomechanical needs, most of the force application issues are resolved and all that's needed is some minor tweaking of pedaling skills.

BIKE SET UP

In setting up your bike for multisport racing, there are four concerns. In relative order from most to least important, they are: 1) safety; 2) comfort; 3) aerodynamics; and 4) power. The following guidelines are concerned mostly with safety, aerodynamics and power; small adjustments may be necessary to improve comfort.

There are three parts of the bicycle that come in contact with the rider — the seat, handlebars and pedal/cleat — that are adjusted for fit. There is not a single relationship between these three that works for everyone. Correct position can vary considerably from one person to the next, even though they appear to be the same size. Your body proportions, duration of goal races, personal style and cycling experience can change the positions suggested in the following discussion. Consider the methods described here as starting points for your eventual, correct set up. You will probably want to experiment with adjustments. Bear in mind that it's best to make changes incrementally, especially if you have ridden in one position for a long time. A half-inch change of your saddle height, while it may eventually improve your position, will at first feel strange, and is even likely to cause discomfort. One-quarter-inch adjustments weekly are probably best.

Bike set-up is unique for each rider.

Fitting the bike begins with cleats, proceeds next to the saddle, and finishes with the handlebars. Once these three are correctly positioned, you will ride more economically, which translates into faster bike splits.

• **Cleat position.** Before setting cleat position, it's important that you have the right length crank arm. Time trialing is improved by a slightly longer crank than is typically used for touring or commuting. One way to gauge this length is based on your leg-inseam length. To determine this, stand in your bare feet with a book between your legs firmly up in the crotch just as when sitting on a bike seat. While facing a wall, mark the top edge of the book on the wall, and then measure the distance from the mark to the floor. This is your inseam length. If it's 31 inches or less, your crank length is 170mm to 172.5mm. If the inseam is 31 to 33 inches, crank length is 172.5mm to 175mm. For an inseam of 33 to 35 inches, choose a crank that is 175mm to 177.5mm. Above 35 inches, a crank of 177.5mm to 180mm is best. If you are nearer the upper end of the inseam range, select the longer crank. Riders who have a limiter in force generation or climbing may find improvement with a longer crank. But bear in mind that as the crank gets longer, stress on the knee also increases. An overly long crank may result in injury.

How to determine crank-arm length.

The starting point for cleat position is placement of the pedal axle directly beneath the ball of the foot as shown in Figure 12.5. This "neutral" position works best for most riders, but some, especially those whose limiter is force or who have difficulty with climbing hills, may benefit from moving the cleat slightly toward the heel. As the cleat is moved aft, more force is transferred to the pedal, but the trade off is that cadence is slowed down. This can result in an ultimate loss of power when sudden changes in velocity are neces-

As the cleat moves aft, force increases, but cadence decreases.

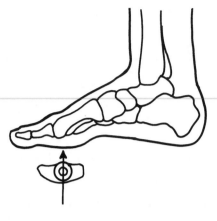

FIGURE 12.5
Cleat position, for increased force, move the cleat slightly toward the heel.

How to set cleat position.

How to adjust saddle forward and backward.

FIGURE 12.6
Neutral knee position

sary, such as when passing another rider, accelerating out of a turn or climbing a short, steep hill. Start by making a quarter-inch adjustment from neutral and see how it feels after several rides before going any further.

Find the ball of your foot with your cycling shoes on, and mark it on the lateral side of each shoe. Foot length may vary considerably, so adjust each cleat individually. On an indoor trainer, clip in to your pedals while someone checks to see if the marks are over the center of the spindles. Aligning the marks with the axles puts you in the neutral position.

• **Saddle fore-aft position.** For the aero position, your saddle adjustment depends on the length of your thigh and flexibility of your hips and lower back. To establish the neutral saddle position, put your bike on an indoor trainer and then level it using a carpenter's level on the top tube. Spin for a few minutes to warm up. Then, with the pedal in the 90 degree (3 or 9 o'clock) position, have a friend drop a plumb line from the knob on the outside of your leg just below the knee (head of the fibula). When the line intersects the pedal axle, the saddle is neutral. Figure 12.6 shows how this is done.

Moving the saddle forward of neutral up to a half-inch may make you more comfortable and improve your power and aerodynamics. One way to tell if you need such an adjustment is to check your flexibility. To do this, sit on the front of a desk with the backs of your knees against the edge. Hold on to a chair in front of you for balance, and then lean over until your chest touches your thighs. If your feet move backward in this position, you'll probably benefit from moving the saddle forward. The saddle should be parallel to the floor, or slightly tipped down at the nose for comfort.

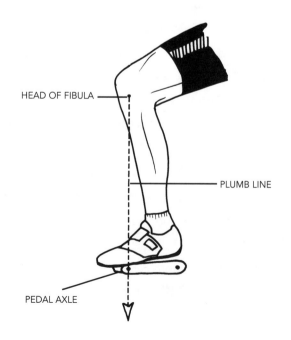

HEAD OF FIBULA

PLUMB LINE

PEDAL AXLE

• **Saddle height**. Saddle height, due to its effect on power output, is the most studied aspect of bike fit, and there are scores of formulas for determining it. Perhaps the easiest way to make this adjustment is to sit on your bike with your shoes on in the aero position. Place your heel on the pedal at the bottom of the stroke (crank arm lined up with the seat tube). To set the neutral position, adjust saddle height until your knee is straight. Notice that as the saddle goes up it also moves aft, and as it is lowered it shifts forward slightly. So you may need to make some small changes in the fore-aft setting. For every 2 centimeters (cm) it goes up, it must also go forward about 1 cm; and if you lower it 2 cm, move it aft by about 1 cm. Figure 12.7 shows how saddle height is determined.

How to set saddle height.

FIGURE 12.7
Neutral saddle height set with shoeless heel on pedal.

• **Handlebar height, reach and angle**. One of the best investments in set-up equipment that you can make is in an adjustable stem, such as the Look Ergo. This allows you to make a wide range of small changes in position to produce the exact position needed for aerodynamics and comfort without guessing what stem to buy and taking your handlebars apart. It also allows for changes throughout the season. Early in the Base period, as you are just getting back on the bike again, you will probably want the handlebars higher than they were at the end of the previous season. Then again, you may want to change your position for a sprint race in which aerodynamics is more important than comfort, or for an Ironman-distance race which demands the comfort associated with a slightly higher position.

Handlebar height may vary within the season.

In the neutral position, the top of the handlebars is about one inch below the high point of the saddle. This is determined by extending a yardstick from the saddle top out to the handlebars and leveling it with a carpenter's level. By measuring the distance between the yardstick and the handlebars, you can set stem height. Very flexible athletes, or those doing short races, may lower the handlebars by as much as an inch. Those who are less flexible, or racing in longer events, may raise it by an inch. As the handlebars are lowered, there is a corresponding need to move the saddle forward opening the angle between the thigh and trunk. If this is not done, the effort is magnified.

How to set handlebar height.

How to set handlebar reach.

Correct handlebar reach, or stem length, places your ear over your elbow in the aero position. A rough gauge of this is that the distance from the nose of the saddle to the back of the handlebars should be about one to one-and-half inches longer than the distance from the back of your elbow to the end of your extended fingers.

How to set handlebar angle.

When the up-and-down angle of the aero bars is neutral, the bottom of your hand is below the bend in the elbow, and the top of your hand is above it. Handlebar reach and angle are illustrated in Figure 12.8. As always, small adjustments from neutral may improve your comfort.

CYCLING-SPEED DRILLS

The pedaling motion appears simple, yet in an accomplished cyclist, applying force to the pedals is a complex interaction of many muscle groups that takes years to refine. During the learning process, muscles become accomplished at contracting and relaxing at exactly the right times. Once these movements are mastered, the veteran rider powers the bike more economically.

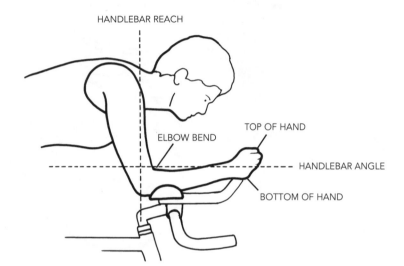

FIGURE 12.8
Handlebar reach and angle.

Even among the best cyclists, the pedaling motion is one of force application mostly in a downward direction throughout the stroke. Contrary to popular belief, good pedaling mechanics do not result from pulling the pedal up on the upstroke. What probably happens is that the rider attempts to "unweight" the pedal, but the weight of the foot and leg, and centrifugal force cause a resultant downward pressure on the pedal. Figure 12.9 shows the relative positions of the foot at various points in the stroke and the resultant forces.

Don't pull up on the pedal — unweight it.

The challenge for improving pedaling mechanics is smoothing out the direction changes in application of force at the top and bottom of the stroke. At the bottom of the stroke (positions d and e in Figure 12.9), the perceived force direction is backward, although this is only a small component of the total force applied. This movement has been described as "scraping mud from the shoes." You can get the feel for this off the bike by standing on a carpet while leaning forward on a table and sliding your foot backward as an animal would do in "pawing" the ground. As the foot scrapes, the heel comes up before the toes do.

Paw back, or scrape mud, at the bottom of the stroke.

As the foot approaches the top of the stroke (positions f, g and h in Figure 12.9), the raised heel is lowered. At the top (position h), the foot feels as if it's moving forward in the shoe when the proper technique is exaggerated. That returns the foot to the front side of the stroke, and the heel once again drops slightly as the greatest force of the entire circular movement is applied (positions a, b and c).

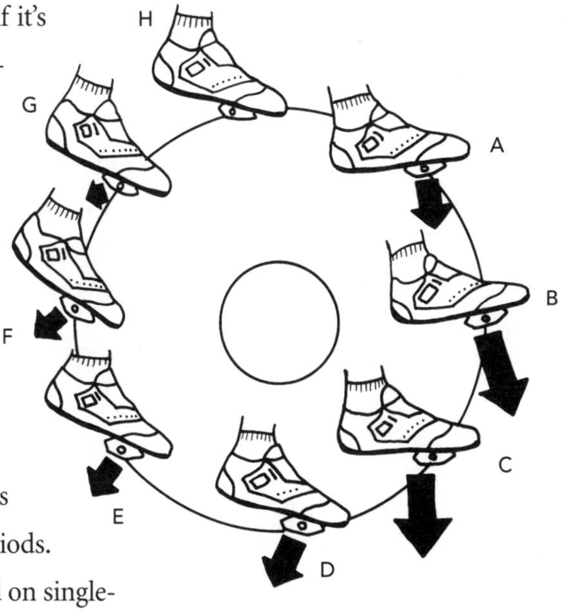

The purpose of pedaling drills is, first of all, to become aware of these three phases of the pedaling motion while practicing them, and second, to make the transition from each phase to the next as smooth and seamless as possible. Here are four ways of accomplishing these objectives. While these may be done year round, the best times to refine pedaling skills on the bike are in the Prep and Base periods.

• **Fixed gear riding**. For decades, road cyclists have trained on single-gear bikes without freewheels — called "fixed-gear" bikes — to improve pedaling mechanics. Such a bike forces your legs into a constant circular motion, and teaches your muscles where the transitions from one phase to the next are. After several weeks of fixed gear riding, the phase transitions smooth out as you learn to quit "fighting" the bike.

Be forewarned that a fixed-gear bike is dangerous to ride at first as it forces you to break old habits, such as briefly stopping the pedaling motion as you stand up or sit down. You also must learn how to pedal through turns and stop while the legs are still going around. The first few rides on a fixed-gear may best be done on an indoor trainer to get a feel for it before venturing out onto the roads for short rides. Approach all fixed-gear rides with caution as you ride slowly on flat terrain.

If you have an extra bike frame, a bike shop can set it up for you as a fixed-gear. Or they can order a "track" bike for you and install a brake on it for use on the road.

Another, and somewhat safer option, is to ride the stationary bikes used by health clubs in "spinning" classes. The large flywheels on these bikes produce an effect similar to riding on a fixed-gear bike.

• **Indoor spinning**. Ride an indoor trainer or rollers at a comfortably high cadence in a low gear. Pay particular attention to the sound your rear wheel makes. If the sound is an oscillating "whir — whir — whir," like a fan that is constantly changing speed, you have a choppy, uneven stroke that exaggerates the downstroke. You may even be shifting your body weight from side to side to accentuate the downward force. Concentrate on pedaling smoothly with no rocking of the upper body so that sound of the rear wheel is a continuous "whirrrrr." Relaxing often helps in smoothing out the pedal stroke.

FIGURE 12.9
Pedaling biomechanics — foot position and resultant force. Adapted, with permission, from "The Biomechanics of Cycling: Studies of the Pedaling Mechanics of Elite Pursuit Riders,: by P.R. Cavanagh and D.J. Sanderson, 1986. In Science of Cycling (p.95) by E.R. Burke (Ed.), 1986, Champaign, Il: Human Kinetics.

Use extreme caution when riding a fixed-gear bike.

• **Isolated-leg training.** On an indoor trainer, pedal with one leg only while the other foot rests on a chair. Alternate 20 to 60 seconds with each leg. The "dead" spots in your stroke phase transitions are made immediately obvious encouraging you to pedal smoothly to minimize them. Use a low gear and a comfortably high cadence. Allow your body to relax while doing this drill.

• **SpinScan.** If you are fortunate enough to own a CompuTrainer, pedaling in the "SpinScan" mode provides a graphic representation of your stroke on the television screen. This serves as a biofeedback device allowing you to correct obvious right-left imbalances and make minute adjustments in technique at all workloads.

RUN SKILLS

Are we born with a natural running form that is set for the rest of our lives, or can it be changed for the better? The inclination among runners is the former. Few will ever tinker with their pre-ordained running form beyond the smallest and least significant of technique points, such as a cupped hand position or relaxed facial expression. Such an attitude leads to the conclusion that the only elements of running performance worth spending time on are those related to the aerobic aspects of fitness. This seems a rather self-defeating position to take.

Indeed, based on the experiences of many formerly awkward lopers, it is possible to effectively modify running technique. But such changes require a strong desire to improve, an indomitable dedication and months of constant practice in every workout to fully realize the benefits of running more gazelle-like. If you have spent countless hours running overdistance, hills, tempo and intervals with precious little to show for it in terms of faster times, it may be time to take a long look at your technique.

With persistence, running technique will improve.

Just as with swimming and cycling, improved running skills mean your economy of movement improves with an accompanying savings in energy expended. This results in faster times in long races. Refined running skills also pay off with a lowered risk of injury. Even though this is also true of swimming and cycling, running injuries are far more pervasive, so the potential gain is much greater. In fact, a history of running-related injuries is a signal that something may be wrong with your technique.

RUNNING-SKILL FUNDAMENTALS

There are many complex actions in running, far too many to address in this chapter, so this section will examine in some detail only four which are crucial to performance in multisport, and, later on, drills that will help you to develop the skills. All are dependent on an overall body posture that provides vertical alignment of the jaw, shoulder and hip joints; a "proud" carriage with the head up and back straight; straight-ahead movement at the hip, shoulder, knee and ankle joints; an uplifted frontal waist area (butt not sticking out); and relaxation of the face and hands. Before any other running skill is addressed, these elements of good posture are necessary.

Develop an effective running posture before modifying other skill aspects.

• **High stride rate.** Count the steps of an elite runner during a race and you will probably find that he or she completes 90 or more cycles (right-foot strikes) in one minute. Combining that with a long stride is what makes them faster than the rest of us. Let's examine why you should work on leg turnover, first, if you have neither a quick cadence or a long stride.

A high stride rate is the first skill to develop.

One study revealed that when running speed doubles, stride length increases by 85 percent, but stride rate only increases by 9 percent. For example, when speeding up from a 10-minute pace to five minutes per mile, the length of a single step may expand from 18 inches to 33 inches while cycles per minute only goes from 83 to 90. The implication of this for runners is that stride rate must always be relatively high. The reason for this may be that the nervous system, which determines stride rate, has a narrower range of operation than the muscular system, which governs stride length.

It is therefore recommended that you establish comfort with a high cadence of about 90 cycles per minute before concerning yourself with how long each stride is. During this period of adjustment you will probably feel as if you are running with "baby" steps, but run with the knowledge that it is more economical to understride than to overstride. Long, slow strides have a great energy cost.

Besides greater economy, a higher stride rate also lessens the impact force at the end of each stride. This has the added benefit of reducing the risk of injury.

• **Vertical foot movement.** Nicholas Romanov, Ph.D. — formerly a Russian university professor of physical education who now lives and works in the United States — has spent two decades studying the biomechanics of running. Out of his study came what he calls the "Pose" method of teaching running technique. One of the basic tenets of Dr. Romanov's work is that the sensation the runner experiences when running correctly is that his or her feet are simply moving up and down — not swinging forward and backward. With this technique, the recovery foot is lifted toward the butt creating a small, acute angle at the knee, and thus a shorter "pendulum" of the recovery leg. The significance of this is that for the same amount of applied energy, a short pendulum moves through its arc faster than a long pendulum, which would occur if the recovery leg was nearly straight at knee. So the shorter pendulum resulting from the high foot carriage helps produce a high stride rate. In an attempt to increase running velocity, the foot must be raised higher to keep stride rate constant or increasing. Figure 12.10 illustrates the high foot-short pendulum concept.

Create a short pendulum with the recovery leg.

After the foot has been pulled up, the recovery leg begins to open at the knee as the foot is allowed to drop back down to the road making contact below or only a couple of inches in front of the body's center of gravity. From the runner's perspective, all that has happened is that the recovery foot has been pulled vertically up toward the butt and allowed to drop straight back down to the running surface.

FIGURE 12.10
Small angle of right knee in recovery phase created by right foot moving toward butt. (Adapted, with permission, from Romanov, 1994.)

According to Dr. Romanov, this movement is similar to the action of a rolling ball in which the point of support is always directly beneath the center of gravity. Such movement is very economical, and also diminishes impact forces thus reducing the risk of injury. (To order Dr. Romanov's Pose-method video, call 1-800-861-6050.)

• **Minimal support time.** The major limiter for velocity in running is how much force is applied to the ground in a brief instant. As the foot strikes the pavement, it applies a force, and since, according to Newton, for every applied force there is an equal and opposite reactive force, your body moves forward. The distance you move forward (stride length) is determined by how quickly the force was applied. Time is a major component of power. As time in contact with the ground decreases, power increases. If when your running shoe comes in contact with the road, you linger for just a split second too long, the power applied drops, thus shortening your stride. You run slower, even though you have now increased your cadence. The idea is to spend very little time with your feet planted on the ground.

Minimal ground-contact time means greater power and longer stride.

Minimal support time also means greater rebound — a free "ride." Let's see why. If you drop a tennis ball and a golf ball on hard pavement, which will bounce higher? The golf ball would because it is harder. Try it sometime and you will see that there's quite a difference in their rebound height. The reason the golf ball's hardness makes it spring back up higher is that it compresses less as it contacts the ground. The tennis ball flattens quite a bit at the point where it makes contact allowing a major portion of it's stored energy (from the fall) to be lost. In effect it stays on the ground longer than the golf ball and has less power as a result.

Your feet do the same thing as one of these balls. If you land on the heel and then roll forward to the ball of the foot before pushing off again for the next stride, your feet are lollygagging around on the ground just like the tennis ball. If, however, you land on the midfoot or forefoot, there's an almost instantaneous rebound that immediately initiates the next stride, just like the golf ball. This rebound effect comes from energy stored in your muscles as they are quickly stretched and then at once allowed to release this energy similar to a rubber band being stretched and released.

Mid- to forefoot landing provides "free" energy for running.

So landing farther forward on the foot improves your velocity by further increasing power with no effort on your part. In fact, research has revealed that most elite runners take advantage of this phenomenon. One study showed that among the swiftest runners 60 percent landed on their forefoot, 30 percent made contact at the midfoot and only 10 percent were heel strikers.

Landing forward on the foot also helps in another way. In order to land on the heel, the foot must be well in front of the body's center of gravity. Whenever a support point is placed in front of the center of gravity, forward movement is impeded. It's like hitting the "brakes" with every step. That requires an acceleration to overcome the slow down. Constantly accelerating and decelerating is quite wasteful of energy — hardly economical.

Figure 12.11 shows how a midfoot strike that minimizes time on the ground and enhances the rebound effect while staying off the brakes looks. If you are now a well-established heel striker, changing

FIGURE 12.11
Midfoot strike with left foot slightly ahead of center of gravity.

Heel striking applies the brakes with every step.

Employ caution when changing your foot strike pattern.

your form so that you land farther forward should progress slowly as this places new stresses on the feet and lower legs, stresses that could result in an injury. Save this change for the next Prep period of the training year, and at first run only on soft surfaces, such as grass, dirt or a track with plenty of time for recovery between runs.

• **Minimal vertical oscillation.** Another big waster of energy is bouncing up and down with each step. The energy stored by landing forward on the foot must be converted, as much as possible, to horizontal, not vertical, movement. Fortunately, reduced bobbing is a normal outcome of taking quicker strides. So if you get your leg speed up to around 90 cycles per minute (180 steps per minute), conversion of power is more likely to push you closer to the finish line, rather than the clouds.

Why is eliminating vertical oscillation so important? Let's look at an example. In a 10km race, if you weigh about 150 pounds and your center of gravity rises and falls two inches with every stride as you lope along, over the course of the race you will have done the work equivalent to raising about 84 tons one foot high. If instead you reduce that excess vertical oscillation of your center of gravity to one inch per step, you obviously cut the vertical component of your workload by half to something like 42 tons raised a foot high. That's a tremendous savings in energy that can be converted into forward velocity and faster running times. In fact, the cost of excessive vertical oscillation is even greater than the example indicates since more energy is also required to decelerate the two-inch fall when contact with the ground is once again made.

Not only is energy saved by reducing the bouncing associated with a long, loping stride, but also the impact forces on landing are ameliorated thus reducing the risk of running-related injury. Figure 12.12 shows a runner with excessive vertical oscillation — and other energy wasters.

Bouncing is an enormous waster of energy.

FIGURE 12.12
How Not to Run.
Note long recovery pendulum of right leg, left foot heel strike well in advance of center of gravity, and excessive vertical oscillation.

RUNNING SPEED DRILLS

Just as with swimming and cycling, drills help you develop the skills necessary for effective and economical running. Here are five.

• **Step counting.** Early in a run, count your right foot strikes for a minute. Then try to raise the count by incorporating one of the skills described above, such as vertical foot movement so that the recovery leg is more bent, by decreasing the support time or by reducing vertical oscillation. Don't simply shuffle your feet faster. This is a good one to do in the Prep and Base periods of the season when the focus is on refining your technique.

• **Hopping.** On a soft surface, such a carpet or mat, place the toes of your right foot on a 12- to 18-inch support behind you with the leg outstretched. Assume the running pose with your left knee slightly flexed and arms bent. Figure 12.13 illustrates this position. Quickly lift your left foot toward your butt, and allow it to immediately return to the floor. Keep the vertical oscillation of your center of gravity to a minimum, and instead concentrate on merely lifting and lowering the foot. Repeat with the other leg. Complete three sets of 10 hops on each leg the first time you try this one. Allow 48 hours between these exercises. Over the course of a few weeks, gradually increase the number of hops within a set to 30.

Besides teaching the up and down movement of the leg described under "Running Skill Fundamentals" above, this drill also teaches proper forefoot landing while building resiliency in the feet and lower legs. This drill should be done only in the Prep and Base periods of the season.

• **Rope jumping.** On a mat or other soft surface, jump a rope just like you did as a kid. Just as in the hopping drill, minimize the vertical oscillation concentrating instead on raising and lowering your feet and legs. This drill is especially good for strengthening the feet and lower legs as it teaches forefoot landing. Rope jumping is also an excellent warm-up before a weight workout in the Prep and Base periods.

• **Skipping.** On a soft surface such as a track or grassy field, skip for 10 to 20 seconds. Complete three to eight sets with two to three minutes of running in between. This drill is a good combination of the skills of vertical foot lift, minimal support time and minimal oscillation. It also strengthens the feet and lower legs while teaching forefoot landing. Figure 12.14 shows how to skip, in case you've forgotten. Skipping is especially effective during the Prep and Base periods when technique refinement is under

High stride rate drill.

Drill for vertical foot movement, minimal support time and minimal oscillation.

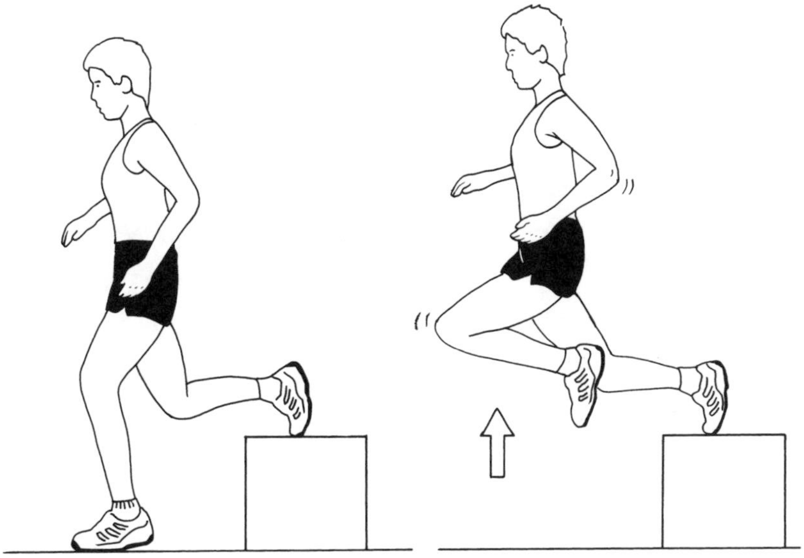

FIGURE 12.13
Hopping drill with right foot supported and left leg hopping up and down. (Adapted, with permission, from Romanov, 1994.)

Drill to strengthen forefoot landing muscles.

Drill for forefoot landing and vertical foot movement.

FIGURE 12.14
Skipping Drill.
Right leg skips as left foot remains near buttocks.

Strides combine all the skills of running into one drill.

way, but can be done year round as a part of your warm up before intervals and races.

• **Strides**. Warm up well. Then on grass, dirt or other soft surface, run 20 seconds down a very slight decline while concentrating on the skill fundamental most in need of improvement (high stride rate, vertical foot movement, short support time or minimal oscillation). These are not sprints, but are run at a velocity a little faster than 5km race pace. After each stride, walk back to the starting point taking 80 to 90 seconds to do so. Repeat three to seven times in a workout.

A variation includes barefoot strides on grass in order to exaggerate leg speed. Be sure the grassy area is free of impediments such as glass and thorns, and that there are no breaks in the skin on your feet. Another alternative is to count your right foot strikes for the 20 seconds aiming for a goal of 30. As your stride length improves, you will cover more ground in 30 foot strikes. For a third variation, include skipping instead of walking as you return to the start point.

Strides are done year round to maintain technique. They also are included in the warm up before intervals and races.

REFERENCES

Broker, J.P. and R.J. Gregor. 1996. Cycling biomechanics. In *High-Tech Cycling*, edited by E. Burke. Champaign, IL: Human Kinetics.

Cavanagh, P.R., et al. 1977. A biomechanical comparison of elite and good distance runners. *Annals of the New York Academy of Sciences* 301: 328-345.

Cavanagh, P.R. and D.J. Sanderson. 1986. The biomechanics of cycling: Studies of the pedaling mechanics of elite pursuit riders. In Burke, E. (ed.), *Science of Cycling*. Champaign, IL: Human Kinetics.

Conley, D.L. and G. Krahenbuhl. 1980. Running economy and distance running performance of highly trained athletes. *Medicine and Science in Sports and Exercise*

12 (5): 357-360.

Conley, D.L., et al. 1984. Following Steve Scott: Physiological changes accompanying training. *The Physician and Sports Medicine* 12 (1): 103-106.

Coyle, E.F., et al. 1992. Cycling efficiency is related to the percentage of type I muscle fibers. *Medicine and Science in Sports and Exercise* 24: 782.

Gonzalez, H. and M.L. Hull. 1988. Bivariate optimization of pedaling rate and crank-arm length in cycling. *Journal of Biomechanics.* 21 (10): 839-849.

Gonzalez, H. and M.L. Hull. 1989. Multivariable optimization of cycling biomechanics. *Journal of Biomechanics.* 22 (11-12): 1151-1161.

Heil, D.P., et al. 1995. Cardiorespiratory responses to seat-tube angle variation during steady-state cycling. *Medicine and Science in Sports and Exercise* 27 (5): 730-735.

Laughlin, T. and J. Delves. 1996. *Total Immersion.* New York: Simon & Schuster.

Maglischo, E.W. 1982. *Swimming Faster.* Mountain View, CA: Mayfield Publishing.

Martin, D.E. and P.N. Coe. 1997. *Better Training for Distance Runners.* Champaign, IL: Human Kinetics.

Messier, S.P. and K.J. Cirillo. 1989. Effects of a verbal and visual feedback system on running technique, perceived exertion, and running economy in female novice runners. *Medicine and Science in Sports and Exercise* 21 (2): S80.

Morgan, D.W., et al. 1989. Effects of a prolonged maximal run on running economy and running mechanics. *Medicine and Science in Sports and Exercise* 21 (2): S26.

Morgan, D.W., et al. 1994. Effect of step-length optimization on the aerobic demand of running. *Journal of Applied Physiology* 77: 245.

Noakes, T. 1991. *The Lore of Running.* Champaign, IL: Leisure Press.

O'Toole, M.L. and P.S. Douglas. 1995. Applied physiology of triathlon. *Sports Medicine* 19 (4): 251-267.

Pate, R.R and J.D Branch. 1992. Training for endurance sport. *Medicine and Science in Sports and Exercise* 24 (9): S340-S343.

Romanov, N.S. 1994. *The Pose Method of Teaching Running Technique.* Unpublished manuscript.

Svedenhag, J. and B. Sjodin. 1985. Physiological characteristics of elite male runners in- and off-season. *Canadian Journal of Applied Sport Sciences* 10 (3): 127-133.

Thomas, D.Q., et al. 1995. Changes in running economy and mechanics during a submaximal 5-km run. *Journal of Strength and Conditioning Research* 9 (3): 170-175.

Toussaint, H.M., et al. 1989. Effect of triathlon wetsuit on drag during swimming. *Medicine and Science in Sports and Exercise* 21: 325.

Toussaint, H.M. 1990. Differences in propelling efficiency between competitive and triathlon swimmers. *Medicine and Science in Sports and Exercise* 22 (3): 409-415.

Toussaint, H.M. and A.P. Hollander. 1994. Energetics of competitive swimming: Implications for training programs. *Sports Medicine* 18: 384.

Williams, K.R. 1990. Relationship between distance running biomechanics and running economy. In Cavanagh, P.R. (ed.), *Biomechanics of Distance Running*. Champaign, IL: Human Kinetics.

MUSCLES

"I don't feel like dancin'."
— TOM WARREN, AFTER WINNING THE 1979 IRONMAN

There are more than 660 muscles in the athlete's body, making up some 35 to 40 percent of the total mass. How well the muscles that provide movement for swimming, cycling and running function when contracting and relaxing is critical to performance in triathlons and duathlons. Conditioning the muscles to generate great forces while maintaining a wide range of motion leads to improved velocity and a reduced risk of injury. Weak, inflexible muscles produce little power and are likely to experience pulls and strains. Strengthening and stretching muscles has the potential to significantly improve racing.

Multisport training is a complex undertaking that takes considerable time. If you are like most triathletes and duathletes, you just don't have the luxury of training as much as you would like to. There aren't enough hours in the day to do everything, and so you are often forced to decide what is most important. On any given day, what should you do — swim, bike, run, lift weights, stretch, or combine these in some way? The answer depends on your limiters. If force, power or susceptibility to injury are holding you back from attaining your race goals, including some form of supplemental muscular training such as weightlifting and stretching may prove beneficial. Some athletes have an abundance of strength and flexibility. For these fortunate few, additional time spent lifting weights and stretching will produce few, if any, gains.

The value of lifting weights and stretching depends on limiters.

If you determine that greater strength and flexibility will help, it's still important to periodize and spend an appropriate amount of time in these supplemental activities. This chapter will provide you with the necessary tools so that the time you devote to weights and stretching is purposeful and effective. You may decide to create your own strength and flexibility program using the concepts presented here, or simply to follow the plans offered.

STRENGTH

There was a time when endurance athletes avoided strength training like the plague. Today there are still reasons why some don't strength train. Many have a great fear of gaining weight. While there are those who have a tendency to increase their muscle mass, few multisport athletes are genetically inclined to great muscle gain, especially on an endurance-based program. If two extra pounds result from weight training, the increased power typically more than offsets the mass to be carried, if the appropriate muscle groups are developed. For most triathletes, strength training does not cause any appreciable weight change.

Triathletes and duathletes, more than most other endurance athletes, are aware of what weight training can do for racing performance. This may be due to the propensity of multisport athletes to extend the boundaries of training through innovation. But the benefits of weightlifting for multisport are not based merely on a few stories of success with a few high-profile athletes; recent research studies also support the value of weight training for endurance events.

STRENGTH-TRAINING BENEFITS

Research done mostly on cyclists has demonstrated positive gains in endurance performance resulting from strength increases. Nearly all the studies find that time to exhaustion is increased, meaning the subjects could ride farther at a given intensity level after following a leg-strength program for a few weeks. The endurance improvements have typically ranged from 10 to 33 percent, depending on the intensity of the effort.

These studies don't generally find any improvement in aerobic capacity following a strength program. What may be happening is that the slow-twitch, endurance muscles are stronger from weight training and therefore able to carry more of the work load, thus requiring fewer fast-twitch, power muscles at higher efforts. Since fast-twitch muscles burn glycogen, a precious fuel in short supply in the body, and produce lactic acid as a result, endurance reaps benefits from the increased strength of the slow-twitch muscles. In effect, the lactate threshold has been raised. This is confirmed by a study done by Marcinik and colleagues at the University of Maryland in which strength-trained cyclists increased their lactate thresholds by an average of 12 percent. Strength training has also been demonstrated to improve economy — how much oxygen is needed at submaximal efforts.

Most multisport athletes soon discover, however, that weight training, especially with relatively heavy loads, seems to benefit cycling and swimming more than running, even though all are endurance sports. This apparent dichotomy is explained by Dr. Vladimir Zatsiorsky of Pennsylvania State University, a renown authority on sport bio-

Strengthening slow-twitch muscles appears to raise the lactate threshold and improve economy.

mechanics and the training of elite athletes. His work supports the notion that if the force required to produce a given movement, such as the force applied to the ground in a running stride at race effort, demands less than 20 to 25 percent of the athlete's maximum strength, then heavy weight training is of little or no value. It appears that riding a bike, especially up hill, and swimming in the dense medium of water, both require the application of relatively greater forces than does running. This helps us to understand why weightlifting benefits the cycling and swimming legs of triathlon more than the running leg. The greatest benefit of strength training to running is the prevention of injuries.

Heavy weightlifting benefits swimming and cycling more than running performance.

Whatever the mechanism of improvement is, there's little doubt that greater strength will help those who have low levels of force development, especially while climbing hills on the bike and swimming in open water.

GETTING STARTED

There are two problems for the athlete determined to improve his or her racing by lifting weights. The first is that there are many strength programs in the popular literature, each usually associated with glowing reports of improvement from elite athletes. The average triathlete or duathlete doesn't know which to follow. The second challenge is time. Given jobs, family and life in general, most age-group athletes just can't afford great blocks of time in the gym as many pros can. The program described here is one pared down to fit into the "normal" athlete's busy lifestyle while including the exercises and routine that will produce the greatest gains in the least time. Even if you could find more gym time, the benefits would not be much greater.

Too many weight-training options and too little time make strength building a challenge.

Strength training in the U.S. has been heavily influenced by body building. Using resistance exercise the same way body builders do is likely to decrease, rather than increase, endurance performance. Body builders organize training to maximize and balance muscle mass, while shaping their physiques. Function is not a concern. Endurance athletes' goals are far different, but all too often they learn the body builder's methods at their gym and employ them for lack of a better way.

The purpose of strength training for multisport is strictly functional — the application of force to the pedals or water. To accomplish this, the triathlete or duathlete needs to improve the synchronization and recruitment patterns of muscle groups — not their size and shape. This means that resistance work must not only develop the muscles, but also the central nervous system which controls muscle use.

Function, not form, is the goal of the multisport athlete.

WEIGHT-TRAINING GUIDELINES

How can you ensure that your weight-training program develops function and not simply form? The following guidelines will help, regardless of what else you may do.

• **Focus on prime movers.** Prime movers are the big muscle groups that do most of the work. For example, a prime mover for cycling is the quadriceps muscle group on the front of the thigh. Other prime movers for cycling are the hamstrings and gluteus (butt). In swimming, the prime movers are the latissimus dorsi (lats) and pectoralis (chest).

• **Prevent muscle imbalances.** Some of the injuries common to multisport athletes result from an imbalance between muscles that must work in harmony to produce a movement. For example, if the quadriceps muscle on the outside of the thigh — the vastus lateralis — is overly developed relative to the vastus medialis — the muscle above and inside the knee — a knee injury known as chondromalacia patella is likely.

• **Use multi-joint exercises whenever possible.** Biceps curls are a single-joint exercise since only the elbow joint is involved. This is the type of muscle-isolation exercise body builders do. On the other hand, squats, a basic cycling exercise, includes three joints — the hip, knee and ankle. Such exercises more closely simulate the dynamic movement patterns of the sport, and also limit time in the gym. Typically, exercises done for muscular balance are single-joint by nature. For example, the knee extension exercise — a knee-only movement — maintains the vastus lateralis-vastus medialis balance for healthy knees.

• **Mimic the positions and movements of the sport.** Position your hands and feet such that they are similar to their position in the sport. When doing leg presses on a leg-press sled, for example, the feet should be placed about the same width as the pedals. You don't ride with your feet spread 18 inches and your toes turned out at 45 degrees. Another example: When initiating the swim pull, the hand is in line with the shoulder, not 12 inches or so outside of the shoulder. Remember this when doing lat pull-downs.

• **Include the "core."** When swimming and cycling, the forces applied by your arms and legs must pass through the abdominal and low back. If these areas are weak, much of the force is dissipated and lost. A strong core means, for example, that when climbing out of the saddle, more of the force generated by pulling against the handlebars is transferred to the pedals. In swimming, a weak lower back allows the legs and hips to sink while confounding the harmony of the upper- and lower-body movements. In running, a strong core keeps the pelvis in a neutral position late in the race. If the abdominal fatigues, the front of the pelvis sags and the butt protrudes, thus shortening the stride.

• **Keep the number of exercises low.** In order to concentrate on improving specific movements, put greater focus on the sets rather than the number of exercises. This essentially means that your weight workouts will have greater depth than breadth, and therefore be likely to produce a significant improvement. Following the initial Anatomical Adaptation phase, reduce the number of exercises to those that will provide the greatest gain for the least time invested. The idea is to spend as little time in the weight room as possible, and yet still boost race performance.

• **Periodize strength training.** While a crucial period in developing force is during the early winter Maximum Strength (MS) phase, the strength developed then is subsequently converted to power endurance and muscular endurance. These are forms of strength directly applicable to triathlon and duathlon racing. The Power Endurance and Muscular Endurance phases should precede the higher-intensity Build periods of training. Once the greater efforts of swim, bike and run training commence, strength training is de-emphasized and takes on a maintenance role.

The following suggested strength program follows the above guidelines and was designed specifically for multisport athletes. If you have been training like a body builder, you may feel guilty at times using light weights, high repetitions and only a few exercises. Stay with the program and you will likely see improvements in race performance, but you won't look much different in the mirror or on the scales.

PHASES AND PERIODIZATION

There are five phases through which the triathlete and duathlete should progress in approaching the most important races of the year. The following is an explanation of each of those phases and their periodization.

• **Anatomical Adaptation (AA).** This is the initial phase of strength training that usually occurs in the late fall or early winter during the Prep period. It's purpose is to prepare the muscles and tendons for the greater loads of the Maximum Strength phase. More exercises are done at this time of year than at any other since

TABLE 13.1

Anatomical Adaptation (AA) phase

Total Sessions/Phase	8-12
Sessions/Week	2-3
Load (% 1RM)	40-60
Sets/Session	3-5
Reps/Set	20-30
Speed of Lift	Slow
Recovery (in Minutes)	1-1.5

Triathlon Exercises
(in order of completion):
1. Hip extension (squat, leg press, or step up)
2. Standing bent-arm, lat pull down
3. Hip extension (different from #1)
4. Chest press or push ups
5. Seated row
6. Personal weakness (hamstring curl, knee extension, or heel raise)
7. Abdominal with twist

Duathlon Exercises
(in order of completion):
1. Hip extension (squat, leg press, or step up)
2. Seated row
3. Hip extension (different from #1)
4. Chest press or push ups
5. Personal weakness (hamstring curl, knee extension, or heel raise)
6. Upper body choice (lat pull down or standing row)
7. Abdominal with twist

improved general body strength is a goal, and other forms of training are minimal. Machines can be used in this period, but some free-weight training is beneficial. If desired, circuit training can add an aerobic component to this phase.

In this phase, as in most others, the athlete should find that loads are increased by about 5 percent every four or five workouts. Table 13.1 provides the details.

Base 1 period.

• **Maximum Strength (MS).** The purpose of the MS phase is to improve force generation. As resistance gradually increases and repetitions decrease, more force is generated. This phase, which is usually included during the Base 1 period, is necessary to teach the central nervous system to easily recruit high numbers of muscle fibers. Care must be taken not to cause injury in this phase, especially with free-weight exercises such as the squat. Select loads conservatively at the start of this phase, and in the first set of each workout. Loads are gradually increased throughout this phase up to the following goals levels based on body weight (BW). Generally, women will aim for the lower ends of the ranges and men the upper ends. Those new to weight training should also set goals in this phase at the lower ends of these ranges.

Hip extension goals

Squat	1.3-1.7 x BW
Leg Press (sled)	2.5-2.9 x BW
Step up	0.7-0.9 x BW
Seated row goal	0.5-0.8 x BW
Standing, bent-arm lat pull goal	0.3-0.5 x BW

Only the exercises listed here with goals are done following the MS-phase routine. All other exercises, such as abdominal and personal weakness areas, continue with the AA-phase routine of light weights and 20 to 30 repetitions per set.

Once the above goals are achieved, repetitions are increased and loads remain constant. For example, a 150-pound, male triathlete doing the leg press has a goal of 435 pounds (150 x 2.9). Once he can lift this weight six times, in subsequent workouts he will increase the repetitions beyond six while keeping the load at 435 pounds. Also, once all of the goal weights are achieved, there is no reason to go beyond eight MS workouts. On the other hand, if the goal loads are not achieved even though 12 MS workouts have been completed, end the phase and go onto the next.

When to end the MS phase.

Excess MS-phase training may cause injury.

Some athletes will be tempted to do more than one hip-extension exercise, or to increase the loads beyond the goals listed above. Others will want to extend this phase beyond the recommended number of workouts in Table 13.2. Doing so is likely to result in muscle imbalances, especially in the upper leg, which may contribute to hip or knee injuries. During the MS phase, endurance performance will suffer as the legs and arms may feel "heavy." As a result, your pace for any given effort is slowed.

TABLE 13.2	
Maximum Strength (MS) phase	
Total Sessions/Phase	8-12
Sessions/Week	2
Load	BW Goal*
Sets/Session	3-6
Reps/Set	3-6+*
Speed of Lift	Slow-Mod*
Recovery (in Minutes)	2-4*

*Note: Only **bold** exercises follow this guideline. All others continue AA guidelines.*

Triathlon Exercises (in order of completion):
1. **Hip extension (squat, leg press, or step up)**
2. **Seated row**
3. Abdominal with twist
4. Personal weakness (hamstring curl, knee extension, or heel raise)
5. **Standing bent-arm, lat pull down**

Duathlon Exercises (in order of completion):
1. **Hip extension (squat, leg press, or step up)**
2. **Seated row**
3. Abdominal with twist
4. Personal weakness (hamstring curl, knee extension, or heel raise)
5. Upper body choice (lat pull down, standing row, chest press, push ups)

TABLE 13.3	
Power Endurance (PE) phase	
Total Sessions/Phase	6-8
Sessions/Week	1-2
Load (% 1RM)	40-60*
Sets/Session	2-3*
Reps/Set	8-15*
Speed of Lift	Fast*
Recovery (in Minutes)	3-5*

*Note: Only **bold** exercises follow this guideline. All others continue AA guidelines.*

Triathlon Exercises (in order of completion):
1. **Hip extension (squat, leg press, or step up)**
2. **Seated row**
3. Abdominal with twist
4. Personal weakness (hamstring curl, knee extension, or heel raise)
5. Standing bent-arm, lat pull down

Duathlon Exercises (in order of completion):
1. **Hip extension (squat, leg press, or step up)**
2. **Seated row**
3. Abdominal with twist
4. Personal weakness (hamstring curl, knee extension, or heel raise)
5. Upper body choice (lat pull down, standing row, chest press, push ups)

• **Power Endurance (PE).** The purpose of this phase is to develop the capacity to quickly recruit most of the fibers for a movement, and to sustain their use at a high power output. Examples of this in a race situation might be attacking short, steep hills on the bike, or the sprint at the start of an open-water swim.

High power results from producing the greatest possible force in the shortest possible time. It may be expressed as **power = force x velocity**. This means that speed of

Explosive movement is necessary in the PE phase.

movement is critical to improving power, so the lifting portions of all exercises are done with an explosive movement. Be careful not to move so quickly that you risk injury. Do not "throw" the weight, but rather move quickly with the load completely under control. The weight is always lowered slowly. When the ability to quickly move diminishes, the exercise is stopped regardless of the number of repetitions completed. A proper warm up is critical before a PE workout.

Base 2 period.

The PE phase generally starts in the Base 2 period, and may extend into Base 3 depending on how long the MS phase lasted. Table 13.3 provides the details.

• **Muscular Endurance (ME).** Muscular endurance is at the heart of training for endurance sports, and ME-phase lifting greatly benefits riders whose race endurance is lacking. The purpose is to extend the ability to manage fatigue at high-load levels by increasing capillary density and the number and size of mitochondria — energy production sites within the muscles. Circuit training may be used during this phase, if preferred.

Base 3-Build 1 periods.

The ME phase is usually scheduled for the Base 3 period and may continue into Build 1. The routine of the ME phase is detailed in Table 13.4.

TABLE 13.4

Muscular Endurance (ME) phase

Total Sessions/Phase	4-8
Sessions/Week	1
Load (% 1RM)	30-50*
Sets/Session	1-3*
Reps/Set	40-60*
Speed of Lift	Mod*
Recovery (in Minutes)	1-2*

*Note: Only **bold** exercises follow this guideline. All others continue AA guidelines.

Triathlon Exercises (in order of completion):
1. **Hip extension (squat, leg press, or step up)**
2. **Seated row**
3. Abdominal with twist
4. Personal weakness (hamstring curl, knee extension, or heel raise)
5. **Standing bent-arm, lat pull down**

Duathlon Exercises (in order of completion):
1. **Hip extension (squat, leg press, or step up)**
2. **Seated row**
3. Abdominal with twist
4. Personal weakness (hamstring curl, knee extension, or heel raise)
5. Upper body choice (lat pull down, standing row, chest press, push ups)

• **Strength Maintenance (SM).** This phase maintains the basic strength established in the previous phases while hills, intervals, open-water swims and steady-state efforts maintain power and muscular endurance. Stopping all resistance training at this point may cause a gradual loss of strength throughout the season. Maintenance of strength is particularly important for women and masters. Some athletes, particularly males in their twen-

TABLE 13.5

Strength Maintenance (SM) phase

Total Sessions/Phase	Indefinite
Sessions/Week	1
Load (% 1RM)	60, 80 (last set)*
Sets/Session	2-3*
Reps/Set	6-12*
Speed of Lift	Mod*
Recovery (in Minutes)	1-2*

*Note: Only **bold** exercises follow this guideline. All others continue AA guidelines.

Triathlon Exercises
(in order of completion):
1. **Hip extension (squat, leg press, or step up)**
2. **Seated row**
3. Abdominal with twist
4. Personal weakness (hamstring curl, knee extension, or heel raise)
5. **Standing bent-arm, lat pull down**

Duathlon Exercises
(in order of completion):
1. **Hip extension (squat, leg press, or step up)**
2. **Seated row**
3. Abdominal with twist
4. Personal weakness (hamstring curl, knee extension, or heel raise)
5. Upper body choice (lat pull down, standing row, chest press, push ups)

ties, seem capable of maintaining adequate levels of strength, and may not need to continue weight training throughout the Build, Peak and Race periods.

In the SM phase, only the last set is meant to stress the muscles. This set is done at about 80 percent of your one-repetition maximum. The one or two sets that provide warm up for this last set are accomplished at about 60 percent of one-repetition maximum. The details of the SM phase are listed in Table 13.5.

Hip-extension training (squats, step-ups or leg presses) is optional during the maintenance phase. If you find hip-extension exercises help your racing, continue doing them. If, however, working the legs only deepens your fatigue level, eliminate them. Continuing to work on core muscles and personal weakness areas will maintain your strength needs. Starting seven days before A-priority races eliminate all strength training to allow for peaking.

DETERMINING LOAD

Perhaps the most critical aspect of the above tables is the load selected for each phase. While they suggest loads based on the maximum you can lift for a single repetition (1RM), that's not always the best way to determine weight due to the possibility of injury, especially to the back, and of prolonged soreness eliminating most, if not all, training for two or three days following such an effort.

Another way to decide how much weight to use is to initially estimate the load based on experience, and then make adjustments as the phase progresses. Always start with less than you think is possible for the goal number of repetitions, and add more later, but cautiously.

Build-Peak-Race periods.

Should you work the legs in the SM phase?

Estimate loads based on experience.

One-repetition maximums may also be estimated from a higher number of reps done to failure. Start by doing a warm-up set of 10 repetitions with a light weight. Then select a resistance you can lift at least four times, but no more than 10. You may need to experiment for a couple of sets. If you do, rest for at least five minutes between attempts. To find your predicted one-repetition maximum, divide the weight lifted by the factor below that corresponds with the number of repetitions completed:

Estimate loads based on multiple reps.

Repetitions	Factor
4	0.917
5	0.889
6	0.861
7	0.833
8	0.805
9	0.778
10	0.750

Either exercise machines or free weights may be used in all phases. Most athletes employ both, depending on the exercise. During the MS and PE phases, free weights are likely to bring greater results than machines since barbells and dumbbells are better for developing the small muscles that aid balance. If you use free weights in these phases, also include them in the latter sessions of the AA phase. Again, be cautious whenever using barbells and dumbbells, especially with rapid movement. Never "throw" the weight, but always keep it under control. Injury is likely when lifting weights, especially in these two phases. If you're taller than 72 inches or shorter than 63 inches, you may find it difficult to use some exercise machines; in this case, free weights are again preferable.

Should you use free weights or machines?

MISCELLANEOUS

In carrying out a strength-development program, there are several other considerations.

• **Experience level.** If you are in the first two years of strength training, emphasize perfecting movement patterns while bolstering connective tissue, and place less emphasis on high loads and fast movement. Veteran athletes are less likely to sustain injury during the high-risk Maximum Strength and Power Endurance phases than are novices. Still, caution must guide all weight workouts, even for the seasoned athlete.

• **Warm up and cool down.** Before an individual strength workout, warm up with five to 10 minutes of easy aerobic activity. Running, rowing, stair climbing or cycling are good choices. Following a weight session, spin on a stationary bike with a light resistance at a comfortably high cadence such 90 rpm for five to 10 minutes. Use little effort and allow your body to relax. Do not run immediately following a strength workout as this raises your risk of injury.

• **Phasing in.** As you move into a new phase of strength training, blend the prior and new phases for a week. For example, when going from AA to MS, the transition week may have one AA workout and one MS workout. Or half of each workout in the first week could include AA and the other half MS. Another possibility is to do one or two sets of MS training following one or two sets of AA exercise for a week.

• **Recovery intervals.** In the tables, notice that the time between sets is specified. These recovery periods are important for deriving a benefit from strength work. During this time, your heart rate drops as your short-term energy supply is rebuilt in preparation for the next set. Some phases require longer recovery intervals than others due to the nature of the work. During the recovery time, stretch the muscles just exercised. Later in this chapter, illustrations of stretches are provided.

Stretch during the recovery intervals.

• **Exercise order.** Exercises are listed in the above tables in the order of completion to allow for a progression from big to small muscle groups, and for muscle-group recovery. In the AA and ME phases, you may circuit train by completing the first set of all exercises before starting the second sets. For example, in AA you might do the first set of hip extensions followed by the first set of the next exercise, and then go on to the third station for one set. If the weight room is crowded, of course, this routine won't work. In that case, simply complete all the sets of one exercise before going to the next. In the other phases, all sets of each exercise are done to completion before progressing to the next exercise. If time is tight, two exercises may be done as a "superset" in any phase by alternating sets between the two exercises to completion. Supersetting makes better use of your time in the gym since you spend less time waiting for recovery of a specific neuromuscular group. This does not eliminate the need to stretch following each set, however.

Supersetting makes better use of time.

• **Recovery weeks.** Every third or fourth week is a time of reduced training volume coinciding with your recovery weeks scheduled on the Annual Training Plan. This is accomplished by reducing the number of strength workouts that week, or by reducing the number of sets within workouts.

STRENGTH EXERCISES

If there is any confusion about the following exercises, meet with a certified personal trainer or experienced athlete for clarification.

HIP EXTENSION — SQUAT

(QUADRICEPS, GLUTEUS, HAMSTRINGS)

Improves force delivery to the pedal in cycling. For the novice, the squat is one of the most dangerous exercise options in this routine. Great care is necessary to protect the back and knees.

1. Wear a weight belt during the Max Strength (MS) phase.
2. Stand with the feet pedal-width apart, about 10 inches, center to center, with toes

pointed straight ahead.

3. Head up and back straight.

4. Squat until upper thighs are just short of parallel to floor — about the same knee bend as at the top of the pedal stroke.

5. Knees point straight ahead staying over feet at all times.

6. Return to the start position.

7. Stretches: Stork stand and Triangle.

FIGURE 13.1
Squat

HIP EXTENSION — STEP UP

(QUADRICEPS, GLUTEUS, HAMSTRINGS)

Improves force delivery to the pedal in cycling. The step up mimics the movement of pedaling quite closely, but takes more time since each leg is worked individually. Caution is necessary to assure a stable platform and overhead clearance. The platform should not be higher than the knee as this is likely to cause knee discomfort, and raises the possibility of injury.

1. Place the left foot on a sturdy 13- to 15-inch-high platform with the toes pointing straight ahead.

2. Step up with the right foot touching platform, and immediately return to the start position.

3. Complete all left-leg reps before repeating with the right leg.

4. Stretches: Stork stand and Triangle.

FIGURE 13.2
Step Up

HIP EXTENSION — LEG PRESS

(QUADRICEPS, GLUTEUS, HAMSTRINGS)

Improves force delivery to the pedal in cycling. This is probably the safest of the hip-extension exercises, and generally takes the least time. In the PE phase, be careful not to "throw" the platform since it may damage knee cartilage when it drops back down and lands on legs with locked-out knees.

FIGURE 13.3
Leg Press

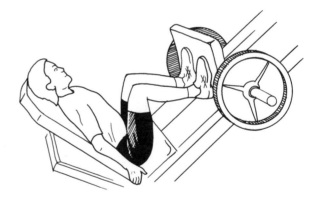

1. Center the feet on middle portion of the platform about 10 inches apart, center to center. Feet are parallel, not angled out. The higher the feet are placed on the platform, the more the gluteus and hamstrings are involved. The lower the foot position, the less the gluteus-hamstring use.

2. Press the platform up until legs are almost straight with the knees short of locking out.

3. Lower the platform until knees are about 8 inches from your chest. No lower.

4. Knees remain in line with feet throughout the movement.

5. Return to the start position.

6. Stretches: Stork stand and Triangle.

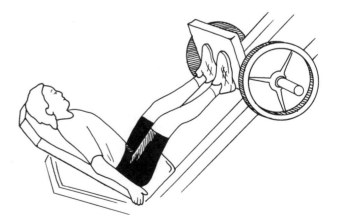

FIGURE 13.4
Seated Row

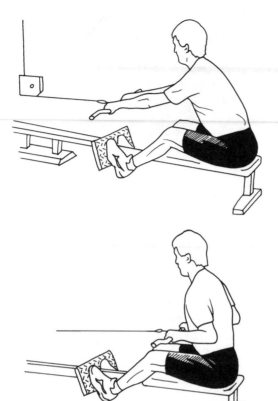

SEATED ROW

(UPPER AND LOWER BACK, LOWER LATS, BICEPS)

Simulates the movement of pulling on the handlebars while climbing a hill in a seated position. Strengthens the core — lower back.

1. Grasp the bar with arms fully extended and hands about 8 to 10 inches apart, inside edge to inside edge.
2. Pull the bar toward lower chest keeping the elbows close to body.
3. Minimize movement at the waist using the back muscles to stabilize position.
4. Return to the start position.
5. Stretch: Pulldown.

FIGURE 13.5
Chest Press

CHEST PRESS

(PECTORALS AND TRICEPS)

Stabilizes the shoulder for swimming and increases force of push phase of stroke. With freeweights, a spotter is necessary in the MS phase.

1. Grasp the bar with hands above shoulders and 10 to 14 inches wide.
2. Lower the bar to chest.
3. Keep the elbows close to body.
4. Return to the start position.
5. Stretch: Pulldown.

PUSH-UP

(PECTORALS AND TRICEPS)

Stabilizes the shoulder for swimming and increases force of push phase of stroke.

1. Hands directly below or slightly wider than the shoulders.
2. Back straight and head up.
3. Keeping body rigid, lower the body until chest touches floor. May be done with knees on floor as strength is developing.
4. Elbows in.
5. Return to the start position.
6. Stretch: Pulldown.

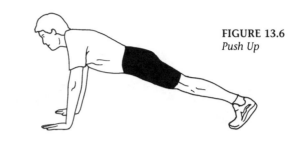

FIGURE 13.6
Push Up

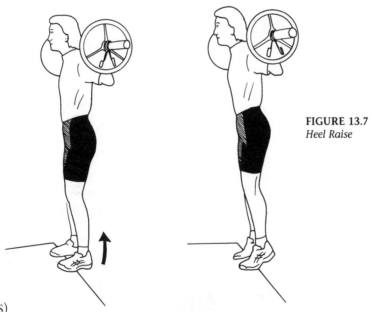

FIGURE 13.7
Heel Raise

HEEL RAISE

(GASTROCNEMIUS)

For athletes who experience calf and Achilles problems, this may reduce susceptibility to such injuries.

1. Stand with the balls of feet on 1- to 2-inch riser, and the heels on floor.
2. Feet are parallel and 6-8 inches apart, inside edge to inside edge.
3. Raise up onto the toes.
4. Return to the start position.
5. Stretch: Wall lean.

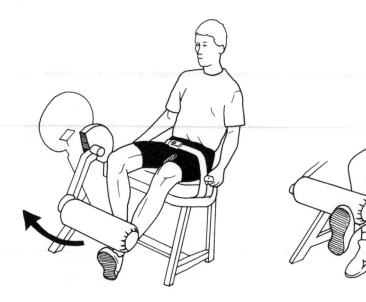

FIGURE 13.8
Knee Extension

KNEE EXTENSION

(MEDIAL QUADRICEPS)

If plagued by kneecap tracking injuries, this exercise may help by improving balance between the lateral and medial quadriceps.

1. Start with the knees fully extended and the toes pointing slightly to outside.
2. Lower the weight only about 8 inches (do not go all the way down).
3. Return to the start position.
4. Stretch: Stork stand.

FIGURE 13.9
Leg Curl

LEG CURL

(QUADRICEPS AND HAMSTRINGS)

By strengthening the hamstrings, the strength ratio between these two major movers is improved. Leg curls are done on either prone or standing machines.

1. Curl leg to about a right angle at the knee.
2. Return to the start position.
3. Stretch: Triangle.

FIGURE 13.10
Abdominal with twist

ABDOMINAL WITH TWIST

(RECTUS ABDOMINUS, EXTERNAL OBLIQUE)

A core exercise to improve transfer of energy from upper to lower body. Also important for maintaining body position in rough, open-water swims.

1. Sit on decline board with the knees bent at about 90 degrees.

2. Arms are crossed over the chest. Holding a weight plate is optional.

3. Lower the upper body to about a 45-degree angle from parallel with the floor.

4. Return to the start position with a twist. With each repetition, alternate looking over the right and left shoulders as the torso twists to the right and left.

5. Stretch: Arch back and extend arms and legs.

LAT PULL DOWN

(LATISSIMUS DORSI, BICEPS)

Stabilizes shoulder.

1. Grasp the bar with the arms fully extended and hands 10 to 14 inches apart, inside edge to inside edge.

2. Pull the bar toward the upper chest keeping the elbows close to body.

3. Minimize movement at the waist and rocking, using the back muscles to stabilize position.

4. Return to the start position.

5. Stretch: Pulldown.

FIGURE 13.11
Lat Pull Down

FIGURE 13.12
*Standing, Bent-arm
Lat Pull Down*

STANDING, BENT-ARM LAT PULL DOWN

(LATISSIMUS DORSI, ROTATORS)

Mimics the movement of the swim pull. Stabilizes shoulder.

1. Standing (or on knees) at the lat pull down station, position the bar so it is a few inches above the head.

2. Place the hands on top of bar, hands 10 to 14 inches apart, inside edge to inside edge, with the arms slightly bent at the elbow.

3. While maintaining a high-elbow position, push the bar down by rotating the shoulder until the bar is a few inches below the head.

4. Return to the starting position.

5. Stretch.

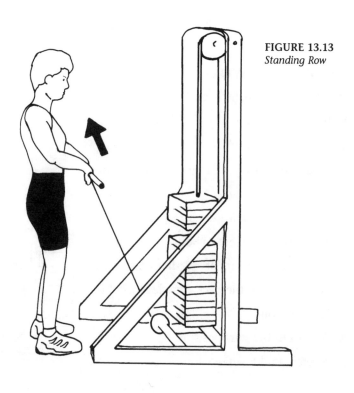

FIGURE 13.13
Standing Row

STANDING ROW

(DELTOIDS, BICEPS)

Stabilizes shoulder.

1. At the low-pulley station (or with free weight), grasp the bar at thigh height and hands 8 to 10 inches apart, inside edge to inside edge.

2. Pull the bar to the chest.

3. Return to starting position.

4. Stretch.

STRETCHING

When it comes to the muscles, swimming, cycling and running are not perfect. No sport is. One of the "problems" resulting from vigorous exercise is a shortening and tightening of connective tissue. Arm and leg muscles lose elasticity since they are trained to contract repeatedly, and seldom go through a full range of motion. On every stroke or stride, they stop short of full extension and complete flexion.

Of the three sports, swimming requires the greatest flexibility, especially in the shoulders and ankles. A flexible shoulder allows the hand to recover close to the body thus permitting a full roll and a long stroke. An ankle capable of completely flattening out (plantar flexion) produces little drag. Try swimming with your ankles at a 90-degree angle sometime and see how much it slows you down.

Increased flexibility may improve performance.

During cycling, banjo-tight hamstrings limit your performance. Rigid hamstrings restrain the leg during the down stroke. They try to prevent the leg from straightening, and in so doing reduce the force produced in hip and knee extension. In an attempt to alleviate the tension felt in the back of the leg, the athlete will often lower his or her saddle. A saddle that is set too low further reduces force generation dropping the power output even more.

Tight hamstrings can also contribute to a tight lower back, which haunts some athletes regardless of the sport, and can result in a race "DNF" (did not finish). When not training, this low-back tightness may become low-back pain requiring medical attention. A consistent and effective program of stretching may prevent such problems from occurring. Prevention is always more comfortable, less time consuming and cheaper that treatment.

Low-back tightness can be a "pain."

STRETCHING BENEFITS

We have already seen how swimming performance benefits from pliable shoulders and ankles, as cycling benefits from supple hamstrings. In the same manner, flexible quadriceps and hip flexors aid running by allowing the recovery leg to swing through a wider arc. Tightness in these muscle groups reduces the range of motion in the hip giving the athlete a constricted look, while possibly increasing the energy cost of running.

Besides improving performance, stretching following workouts also appears to aid the recovery process by improving muscle cells' uptake of amino acids, by promoting protein synthesis within muscle cells and by maintaining the integrity of muscle cells.

According to research, stretching hastens recovery.

In addition, stretching's injury-reducing reputation among multisport athletes is well established, and has garnered some support in the scientific literature, although it's not universally acclaimed by research. For example, a study of 1543 runners in the Honolulu Marathon found that those who stretched regularly following workouts had fewer injuries than those who didn't. It's interesting to note that in this same study, those who stretched only *before* workouts had the highest rate of injuries.

Stretching may reduce injury risk.

Another study conducted by the New Jersey Medical School also reveals that flexibility may play a role in reducing injury risk, especially for men. More than 200 college athletes, at their preseason physical examinations, were graded on a 10-point scale for flexibility of the hip and leg muscles and ligaments. They were then followed over the courses of their seasons. For men, as their muscle tightness increased by one point on the 10-point flexibility scale, their risk of injury increased by 23 percent. There was no relationship between the women's grade on the flexibility scale and their risk of injury.

Don't get the idea, however, that stretching is a panacea for injury. Muscle and tendon trauma in endurance sports are seldom the result of failure to stretch enough, as some athletes believe. At best, stretching may play a minor role in injury prevention, and at worst may actually contribute to injury by making tendons and ligaments overly slack. Moderation in stretching, as in most other aspects of life, is best.

Stretching after a workout takes less than 15 minutes and can be done while downing a recovery drink and chatting with your training partners. This is the best time to work on flexibility as the muscles are warm and supple.

Another important time to stretch is during strength workouts. The act of forcefully contracting muscles against resistance creates extreme tightness. As was described in the previous section, following each strength set, you should stretch the exercised muscles. In fact, correctly doing a strength workout means spending more time in the gym stretching than lifting weights.

Stretching a little bit throughout the day may also benefit long-term flexibility and performance. While sitting at a desk, working or reading, you can gently stretch major muscle groups such as the low back, hamstrings and calves. Stretch gently while watching television, standing in line, talking with friends, and first thing in the morning while still in bed.

STRETCHING GUIDELINES

Stretching didn't become an accepted aspect of fitness training until after World War II. In the last 40 years four major stretching methods have been popular.

Popular stretching methods.

• **Ballistic.** In the 1960s, ballistic stretching was common. Bouncing movements were thought to be the best way to make muscles limber. Later we learned that this technique had just the opposite effect: Muscles resisted lengthening and could even be damaged by overly motivated stretchers. Today almost no one stretches this way.

• **Static**. In the 1970s, a Californian named Bob Anderson developed a stretching method and in 1980 released a book called *Stretching*. Anderson's approach involved static stretching with little or no movement at all. The muscle is stretched to a level of slight discomfort, and then held in that position for several seconds. Static stretching probably remains the most popular style today.

• **PNF**. Another method also surfaced about the same time as static stretching, but never received much exposure or support until recently. Several university studies going back to the early 1970s found it is 10 to 15 percent more effective than static stretching. This method, called proprioceptive neuromuscular facilitation, or PNF, has started to catch on in the last few years.

There are many variations on PNF stretching. Some are quite complex. Here are the steps in one easy-to-follow version:

1. Static stretch the muscle for about 8 seconds.
2. Contract the same muscle for about 8 seconds.
3. Static stretch the muscle again for about 8 seconds.
4. Continue alternating contractions with stretches until you have done four to eight static stretches. Always finish with a static stretch.

You should find that the static stretches become deeper with each repeat as the muscles seem to loosen up. Using this PNF method, a stretch would take one to two minutes.

• **Active isolated**. A relatively new arrival on the fitness scene, active-isolated stretching involves brief, assisted stretches that are repeated several times. Here is a typical routine:

1. Contract the opposing muscle group as you move into position.
2. Use your hands, a rope or a towel to enhance the stretch.
3. Stretch to the point of light tension.
4. Hold for two seconds and then release.
5. Return to the starting position and relax for two seconds.
6. Do one or two sets of eight to 12 repetitions of each stretch.

STRETCHING EXERCISES

The following are selected stretches for each sport. You may find that some are more important for you than others, or that you need to include stretches not illustrated here.

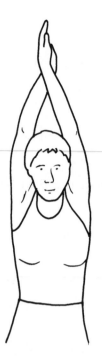

FIGURE 13.14
Shoulder Reach

SHOULDER REACH

(LATISSIMUS DORSI)

Swimming. Weights: Standing, bent-arm, lat pull down.

1. Extend arms overhead and cross one wrist over the other while interlocking hands.
2. With elbows behind ears, straighten arms and reach up.

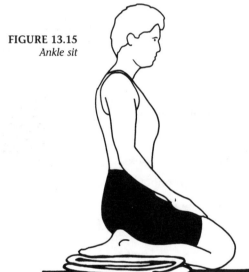

FIGURE 13.15
Ankle sit

ANKLE SIT

(TIBIALIS)

Swimming. Don't do this stretch if you have knee problems.

1. Sit on your shins on a padded surface or towel with toes pointed (not flailed to the sides).
2. Do not sit with your butt between your heels.
3. With your butt on your heels, lean backwards slightly until you feel an easy stretch.

FIGURE 13.16
Twister

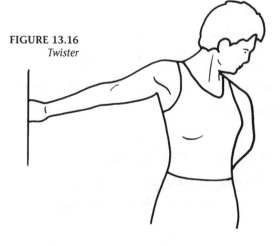

TWISTER

(PECTORALIS)

Swimming. Weights: chest press.

1. With your back facing a wall, grasp a stationary object at shoulder height.
2. Look away from the arm being stretched and twist your body away from it, also.

FIGURE 13.17
Stork Stand

STORK STAND

(QUADRICEPS)

Cycling and running. Weights: hip extension and seated knee extension.

1. While balancing against your bike or a wall, grasp your right foot behind your back with your left hand.

2. Gently pull up and away from your butt with your hand.

3. Keep your head up and stand erect — do not bend over at the waist.

TRIANGLE

(HAMSTRING)

Cycling and running. Weights: hip extension and leg curl

1. Bend over at the waist while leaning on your bike or a wall.

2. Place the leg to be stretched forward with the foot about 18 inches from the support.

3. The other leg is directly behind the first. The farther back this leg is placed, the greater the stretch.

4. With your weight on the front foot, sag your upper body toward the floor. You should feel the stretch in the hamstring of your forward leg.

FIGURE 13.18
Triangle

PULL DOWN

(LATISSIMUS DORSI, TRAPEZIUS, PECTORALIS, TRICEPS)

Swimming and cycling. Weights: standing, bent-arm lat pull downs, chest press and seated rows.

1. Hold onto your bike or a railing for balance with your weight resting on your arms.

2. Allow your head to sag deeply between outstretched arms to create a stretch in your lats.

FIGURE 13.19
Pull Down

SQUAT

FIGURE 13.20
Squat

(LOW BACK, SOLEUS, QUADRICEPS, GLUTEUS).

Cycling and running. Weights: seated row.

1. Holding onto something for balance, squat down keeping your heels on the floor (this is easier with cycling shoes off).

2. Allow your butt to sag close to your heels as you rock forward. Hold this position for about 30 seconds.

WALL LEAN

(GASTROCNEMIUS, SOLEUS)

Running. Weights: heel raise.

1. Lean against a wall with the leg to be stretched straight behind you, and the other forward holding most of your weight.

2. Keep the heel of the rear foot on the floor with the toe pointed forward.

3. The farther forward your hips move, the greater the stretch in the calf.

4. To stretch the gastrocnemius, straighten rear knee. Stretch the soleus by bending the rear knee.

FIGURE 13.21
Wall Lean

REFERENCES

Alter, M.J. 1998. *Sport Stretch*. Champaign, IL: Human Kinetics.

Anderson, B. 1980. *Stretching*. Bolinas, CA: Shelter Publications.

Bompa, T. 1993. *Periodization of Strength*. Toronto: Veritas Publishing.

Bompa, T. 1994. *Theory and Methodology of Training*. Dubuque, IA: Kendall/Hunt.

Brzycki, M. 1993. Strength testing — Predicting a one-rep max from reps to fatigue. *Journal of Physical Education, Recreation and Dance* 64: 88-90.

Goldspink, D.F. 1977. The influence of immobilization and stretch on protein turnover of rat skeletal muscle. *Journal of Physiology* 264: 267-282.

Hamilton, N., et al. 1993. Changes in sprint stride kinematics with age in masters athletes. *Journal of Applied Biomechanics* 9: 15-26.

Hickson, R.C., et al. 1988. Potential for strength and endurance training to amplify endurance performance. *Journal of Applied Physiology* 65: 2285-2290.

Hickson, R.C., et al. 1980. Strength training effects on aerobic power and short-term endurance. *Medicine and Science in Sports and Exercise* 12: 336-339.

Holly, R.G., et al. 1980. Stretch-induced growth in chicken wing muscles: A new model of stretch hypertrophy. *American Journal of Physiology* 7: C62-C71.

Hortobagyi, T., et al. 1991. Effects of simultaneous training for strength and endurance on upper- and lower-body strength and running performance. *The Journal of Sports Medicine and Physical Fitness* 31: 20-30.

Johnston, R.E., et al. 1995. Strength training for female distance runners: Impact on economy. *Medicine and Science in Sports and Exercise* 27 (5): S47.

Kokkonen, J. and S. Lauritzen. 1995. Isotonic strength and endurance gains through PNF stretching. *Medicine and Science in Sports and Exercise* 27 (5): S127.

Kraemer, W.J., et al. 1995. Compatibility of high-intensity strength and endurance training on hormonal and skeletal muscle adaptations. *Journal of Applied Physiology* 78 (3): 976-989.

Marcinik, E.J., et al. 1991. Effects of strength training on lactate threshold and endurance performance. *Medicine and Science in Sports and Exercise* 23 (6): 739-743.

McCarthy, J.P., et al. 1995. Compatibility of adaptive responses with combining strength and endurance training. *Medicine and Science in Sports and Exercise* 27 (3): 429-436.

Nelson, A.G., et al. 1990. Consequences of combining strength and endurance training regimens, *Physical Therapy* 70: 287-294.

Sale, D.G. and D. MacDougall. 1981. Specificity in strength training: A review for the coach and athlete. *Canadian Journal of Applied Sport Sciences* 6: 87-92.

Sale, D.G., et al. 1990. Comparison of two regimens of concurrent strength and endurance training. *Medicine and Science in Sports and Exercise* 22 (3): 348-356.

Schatz, M.P. 1994. Easy hamstring stretches. *Physician and Sports Medicine* 22 (2): 115-116.

Stone, M.H., et al. 1991. Health- and performance-related potential of resistance training. *Sports Medicine* 11 (4): 210-231.

Vanderburgh, H. and S. Kaufman. 1983. Stretch and skeletal myotube growth: What is the physical to biochemical linkage? *Frontiers of Exercise Biology*, K. Borer, D. Edington, and T. White (Editors). Champaign, IL: Human Kinetics.

Wallin, D., et al. 1985. Improvement of muscle flexibility, a comparison between two techniques. *The American Journal of Sports Medicine*: 13 (4): 263-268.

Zatsiorsky, V.M. 1995. *Science and Practice of Strength Training*. Champaign, IL: Human Kinetics.

UNIQUE NEEDS

*"If you want to be competitive with the best as a pro or even
in the hotly-contested age divisions, every minute counts,
and you had better be prepared to race the entire day."*

— BRAD KEARNS, PROFESSIONAL TRIATHLETE

C an everyone train in the same manner using the guidelines presented so far in this
book? Most certainly not. As discussed in Chapter 3, the principle of individualization demands that in order to achieve athletic success, the various training components
(volume, work load, density, mode) must match the unique needs and capabilities of the
athlete. While it is not possible to provide detailed specifics for each individual in a book
such as this, general direction can be provided for rather homogeneous groups. Five clus-
ters of athletes are examined in this chapter — women, masters, juniors, novices and elite.

There is limited scientific information relating to these groups since they are relatively small, and therefore difficult for researchers to recruit in great enough numbers to
draw significant conclusions. University studies are usually based on young, male college
students since they are willing to participate and obviously handy for university-based
research. In addition, due to its relative newness, studies using multisport athletes as subjects are also rare. Consequently "how-to" questions concerning females, old and young
athletes, and those at either end of the multisport experience curve are largely left open
to conjecture. Nevertheless, this chapter attempts to answer some of those questions
using science wherever possible, but also the observations of athletes and coaches.

**Research is rare on
sub-groups of
multisport athletes.**

WOMEN

Throughout much of this century, the only sports considered ladylike, and in which competition was on a nearly equal level with men's, were tennis, golf, gymnastics and figure skating. But despite a lot of male bias and foot-dragging, especially in terms of endurance events, women have made great progress toward full acceptance in this century. For example, in the 1928 Olympic Games in Amsterdam, the longest race in which women were allowed to compete was the 800-meter run. In that Olympiad three runners broke the world record for the distance, but finished in "such a distressed condition," that horrified officials dropped the event from future competition. "Women just weren't meant to run that far," was the position of many men, including scientists. It wasn't until the 1964 Tokyo Games that the women's 800m was resurrected.

Women were excluded from Olympic endurance sports throughout most of this century.

The 1984 Los Angeles Olympics finally included the women's marathon in competition — nearly two decades after women began competing at the distance. To this day, some endurance sports, such as road cycling, continue to discriminate by restricting competitive distances for women.

Multisport reflects the more recent attitudes of our society about women in sport. Race distances are the same regardless of gender. Men and women duathletes and triathletes train and compete together as equals, a situation unheard of in most sports just 20 years ago. Many, but not all races, have equal prize money for females and males.

UNIQUE CONSIDERATIONS

The changes in attitudes toward women over the years reflect the now-dominant view that there is really little difference between male and female athletes. There are, of course, a few obvious female, physical distinctions, such as a greater hip width, a shorter torso relative to leg length, a lower center of gravity and a more "knock-kneed" stance. All of these differences affect the bicycling equipment selected by women, and to some extent, the techniques used in swimming and running. In terms of significant, performance-specific differences between the sexes, women, on average, have a smaller aerobic capacity resulting from a smaller heart and lower oxygen-carrying capacity of the blood relative to men. Also in comparison with men, women have a higher percentage of body weight as fat, and can generate less absolute muscular force due to their smaller muscle mass. These differences contribute to about a 10-percent variance in the world records of males and females in events ranging from weightlifting to sprinting to endurance sports.

Given these basic differences, men and women athletes are really more alike than they are dissimilar. Women can and do train at the same volumes and intensities as their male counterparts. They are fully capable of doing the same workouts as men. And they respond to a relative training load in the same way. There are no reasons why women athletes shouldn't train just as men do, with a few exceptions.

Women can train in much the same manner as men.

Of course, in multisport, women don't train to compete with men — they train to compete with other women. So making training comparisons to men is of little value to the female athlete. The question she ponders is how to improve relative to female competition. Generally, there are three areas a woman should consider concentrating on in order to train better and race more competitively: strength, psychology and diet.

• **Strength.** Most women duathletes and triathletes are relatively stronger in their legs than in their upper bodies. Especially in need of strength are the abdominal muscles and arms. This weakness impacts climbing. While standing on the pedal, the force generated by the leg in powering the bike uphill must be counterbalanced by the arm pulling against the handlebars on the same side, with stability provided by the abdominal and back. If that arm is a wimpy noodle, and the midsection is like an accordion, the unbalanced force will tip the bike over. Upper-body strength, therefore, is required for powerful climbing.

Strength benefits climbing.

In like manner, those female triathletes who develop greater upper-body strength have a definite advantage in rough, open-water swims. Maintaining an effective body position when the chop is great enough to otherwise disrupt the stroke is crucial to success.

Strength means better open-water swimming.

Upper body strength work to improve this relative weakness involves doing pushing and pulling exercises that use all of the arm joints, plus the back and the abdominal. Whenever possible, work the arms in conjunction with the abdominal and back, rather than in isolation. The seated-row exercise described in the previous chapter is a good example of a multijoint exercise that benefits cycling. This station builds the arms and back in a way similar to climbing on a bike. Another exercise to emphasize is the standing, bent-arm lat pull down for swimming. The chest press will also provide muscular balance. In addition, abdominal strength needs emphasizing due to the size and shape of the female pelvis.

• **Psychology.** Women are usually better at dealing with defeat than are men. But when it comes to poor performance, a woman is likely to blame it on a lack of ability. In contrast, men are more inclined to chalk up a poor race to lack of effort. This self-doubt is not unusual for women in which sports performance is concerned, for after all, society has taught them in subtle ways that they are not good at athletics. If you don't agree, just compare the size of crowds at boy's and girl's high school basketball games.

Women tend to lack confidence for sport.

Confidence is as important for success in sport as physical ability. No matter how talented, if you don't believe you can, you won't. A good example of this is a young woman pro who is one of the best in the country, yet always offers reasons to her coach why she can't achieve her high goals. She frequently raises the issue of her limitations and failures in conversations with her coach. And so the coach put her on a confidence-building program. Every night she would use those few minutes in bed between turning the lights off and falling asleep to review and relive the major success of her day, no matter how small it seemed. It could simply be that she finished a tough workout feeling strong, or that she climbed one hill particularly well, or that one interval felt especially good. She would recapture that experience in her mind, and go to sleep feeling good about her ability. That year she had her best season ever, winning a national championship and finishing fifth at the world championship.

Reliving successes builds confidence.

Other ideas for improving confidence include keeping a "success log" in which the day's achievements are recorded. Others are unbeatable when they learn to "act as if" they are confident, no matter how insignificant and unsure they may feel. It may even help to take an acting class to develop this skill. You have got to believe in yourself if you are to succeed.

• **Diet.** Many women triathletes and duathletes overly restrict their food intake. It is not unusual for women athletes to eat less than 2000 calories per day, when they may need up to 3000. With an average of 5 milligrams of iron per 1000 calories in the standard American diet, the woman triathlete and duathlete consumes about 10 mg of iron a day, with a possible need of about 15 mg.

Iron deficiency may result from restricting calories.

To make matters worse, vegetarian diets that are favored by many women athletes are even lower in absorbable iron than the standard diet. Exercise and menstruation further decrease iron levels. Iron deficiency or anemia are a definite possibility under such circumstances. Owen Anderson, Ph.D., the publisher of *Running Research News*, estimates that 30 percent of women athletes have an iron deficiency. Such a condition results in early fatigue and low endurance. One study even linked low iron with an increase in running injuries of high school girls. Such problems are easily corrected by including red meat in the diet three or four times a week. If you are not a meat eater, add vitamin-C rich foods to your meals to improve iron absorption, and eat lots of beans and spinach. Should you become anemic, such a diet may still prove inadequate for correcting the situation, requiring iron supplementation. Do not take iron supplements without the approval of your health-care provider as there are many possible complications.

Also frequently restricted in the female diet are foods high in fat. Dietary fat is necessary for peak performance. A body deprived of essential fats is in danger of being run down and susceptible to illness due to a weakened immune system. If sick, injured or tired, you can't perform at your best. Include fat in the diet every day from good sources such as nuts, nut spreads, avocados and olive oil. Continue to avoid saturated fat and trans fat, a type found in foods that have been "hydrogenated," such as snack foods and pre-packaged meals. Chapter 16 provides more details on the athlete's diet.

Dietary fat is necessary for peak performance.

OTHER FACTORS RELATED TO PERFORMANCE

A recent study at the University of Illinois showed that women who use oral contraceptives may have an advantage in endurance sports. During a period of long endurance sessions at low intensity, women taking the pill showed an increase in growth hormone. They used significantly less carbohydrate and more fat for fuel than those women not on the pill. This suggests that using oral contraceptives may improve a woman's capacity for burning fat, may allow her to get into shape faster, and may extend her endurance range in races. No other studies are known to have confirmed this finding, so the results should be applied with some caution. If you are not currently using an oral contraceptive, but are considering it, talk with your health-care provider before starting. Don't take the pill only for race-performance reasons.

Oral contraceptives may benefit endurance.

Women must be cautious not to overtrain as that is likely to cause menstrual dysfunction and associated medical problems such as osteoporosis and stress fractures. Bone density is known to peak, and then decrease, at about age 35. Excessive training may hasten the process. It is imperative that the female athlete determine the appropriate work load by building up to it rather than shooting high and working down. If a mistake is made in selecting a training load, err on the side of doing too little.

MASTERS

The world has changed a lot in the last 30 to 40 years. And old "coots" have changed the most. In the 1960s, age 40 meant one foot in the grave. The medical community once advised anyone beyond that ancient age to slow down so as not to damage their hearts. Now "old timers" in their 40s accomplish feats once considered practically impossible.

Master athletes are now doing the "impossible."

Take, for example, the Irish runner Eamann Coghlan who at age 41 became the first person over 40 to run a mile in less than four minutes. Then there is Kent Bostick. In 1996, at age 42, Bostick qualified for the U.S. Olympic cycling team by beating 28-year-old Mike McCarthy by nearly a second in the 4000-meter pursuit on the track. In 1992, another old "codger," Mark Spitz, took a serious shot at making the U.S. Olympic team 20 years after winning seven gold medals in swimming at the Olympic Games, in

Munich, Germany. And, a little closer to home, Dave Scott took second in the Hawaii Ironman at age 40.

These athletes are just the tip of the iceberg. There are hundreds more aging athletes in the world of endurance sports who are within seconds of their best performances of all time. Now that the baby boomers are well into their 40s, we can expect to see the number of master athletes swell to record proportion, and the times keep dropping.

FORTY PHYSIOLOGY

Just because there are many fast masters out there, however, doesn't mean that you can stop aging. There's no denying that with increasing age there is an inevitable performance decline. In fact, world records for running events seem to confirm this as records slow by about 1 percent per year after age 30. For a 10km run, that translates into about a 14-second slowdown every year.

Since the 1930s, scientists have studied the link between aging and physiological function. One inescapable conclusion has come from this research: Getting older means reduced function. Aerobic capacity (VO$_2$ max) decline is a good example of what the studies show. You probably recall from an earlier chapter that aerobic capacity is a measure of how much oxygen the body uses to produce energy at a maximal work load. The higher one's aerobic capacity, the greater is the potential for performance in an event like triathlon or duathlon. Studies show that starting at about age 20, on average, aerobic capacity begins dropping, partly because maximum heart rate decreases. A lowered max heart rate means less oxygen delivery to the muscles, and therefore a lowered aerobic capacity. The usual rate of decline measured in the research is in the range of six to 10 beats per decade.

Similar results have come from aging studies on the pulmonary, nervous, muscular, thermal regulatory, immune and anaerobic systems: Sometime in the third and fourth decades of life, functional decreases begin with the average losses in the range of 6 to 10 percent per decade. Compounding the problem is what appears to be a normal increase in body fat after the early 20s, obviously made worse by a sedentary lifestyle.

THE AGING MYTH

A little skepticism is a healthy thing when it comes to research. Most studies of aging are based on "cross-sectional" analysis. That means, for example, that a group of 30-year-olds and a similar group of 40-year-olds are tested for some parameter of fitness, and the difference is assumed as the normal loss.

Attitudes about aging are changing.

Research shows a steady decline with aging.

How aging research is done.

The alternative is "longitudinal" research, which involves following a group of subjects for several years and regular testing to see how they change. This method has many benefits, but time is an obvious downside, so there are few longitudinal studies of athletes.

Cross-sectional studies raise the question of who the subjects were. In research on fitness, many such studies define the subjects as "trained endurance athletes." This vague description is usually based on measures of training volume, such as years of activity, or hours trained in a week. Of course, one study's trained endurance athlete may be another study's novice. Seldom is the intensity of training used to define the groups studied as it is hard to quantify. But since it appears that intensity is the key to maintaining race fitness, this is a crucial issue.

The few longitudinal studies that have been done show that when the intensity of training is maintained, aerobic capacity and other selected measures of fitness decline as little as 2 percent per decade — roughly a third to a fifth of what is usually discovered in sedentary subjects, or even those who maintain health and exercise at low intensities.

Intensity is the key to improvement as a master.

The "normal" decline in performance of 6 to 10 percent per decade is probably more a result of self-imposed training and lifestyle limitations than it is of human physiology. Aging may actually only account for a fourth of the losses while disuse takes the bigger bite.

TRAINING IMPLICATIONS

The bottom line is that intense training keeps the heart, nerves, muscles, lungs and other systems all working to their genetic potential. If you never rev your engine up to high speed, you will lose horsepower more rapidly than is necessary.

Masters' training guidelines.

For masters, the following training guidelines will help to keep your fitness high, and even improving:

• **Train intensely**. Build and maintain endurance, but give a higher priority to intense workouts. This doesn't mean training anaerobically all of the time, but rather planning the most intense sessions meticulously. Know exactly what it is you intend to achieve, and then run or ride with that purpose in mind. "Intense" doesn't mean "killer" efforts, intervals until you throw up or even necessarily redlining. Intense workouts are those incorporating the 4 and 5 zones (see Chapter 4). The most used intense workouts should put you in the 4 zone for extended periods. Such training at near lactate threshold is quite effective. Intense workouts should stress you without leaving you wasted. Always stop before reaching failure. Save the maximum efforts for races.

• **Use intensity sparingly**. Do no more than three intense workouts in a week. That means something such as one intense swim, one bike and one intense run weekly. Some masters should only do two. How quickly you recover is the key to knowing how many is best. You should go into each intense workout feeling ready and eager. The other days are devoted to recovery and the development of skills, such as swimming, cycling and running technique, as discussed in Chapter 12..

• **Plan frequent rest.** Train hard for two or three weeks, and then take a week to recover and rest. Some masters can use Table 7.2 to schedule this rest. For those who need more frequent recovery, Table 14.1 is a better guide. Frequent R & R is the best way for the serious master to improve steadily. Frequent rest time means not only breaks from training every two or three weeks, but also taking one, two or even three days of easy training between intense sessions. Masters may also find greater improvement by allowing more recovery time between intervals within a workout.

• **Strength train year round.** This could be weights or hills. Masters who live in the flatlands will improve their hill strength by lifting weights year round. Aerobic training on flat terrain is insufficient to prevent the loss of muscle mass, especially after the age of 50. The advantage of weight training is that you can also work the upper body, which slows the loss of muscle mass above the waist.

• **Maintain leg speed.** Concentrate on leg turnover until cadences of about 90 rpm, whether running or cycling, are comfortable and come naturally. Count one leg for a minute to check your cadence. You may find this makes you more efficient and reduces your risk of injury while also stimulating nervous system maintenance. Include workouts such as strides, spin-ups and isolated leg training throughout the year (see Appendixes C and D).

Successful racing as a master means refusing to accept loss of physical function as normal, always setting challenging goals and never slowing down. It also means redefining "over the hill" to describe a workout, rather than an age.

JUNIORS

If you are a teenager who has taken up the sport of triathlon or duathlon, you probably already participate in swimming or running programs at your school, and see multisport as a challenging way to combine those sports with cycling. It's because of young athletes like you that the sport is experiencing such rapid change, especially in terms of race performances. For example, in the "old days" of triathlon back in the early 1980s, if a man went under two hours in an international-distance race, he was almost certain to win. Today such a time may not even crack the top 10 in a local event. Times are dropping rapidly as

TABLE 14.1

Weekly training hours by period for select masters

aPeriod	Week	Annual Hours										
		200	250	300	350	400	450	500	550	600	650	700
Prep	All	4.0	4.0	5.0	6.0	7.0	7.5	8.5	9.0	10.0	11.0	12.0
Base 1	1	4.0	5.0	6.0	7.0	8.0	9.0	10.0	11.0	12.0	12.5	14.0
	2	5.0	6.0	7.0	8.5	9.5	10.5	12.0	13.0	14.5	15.5	16.5
	3	5.5	6.5	8.0	9.5	10.5	12.0	13.5	14.5	16.0	17.5	18.5
	4	4.0	4.0	4.0	5.0	5.5	6.5	7.0	8.0	8.5	9.0	10.0
Base 2	1	4.0	5.5	6.5	7.5	8.5	9.5	10.5	12.5	12.5	13.0	14.5
	2	5.0	6.5	7.5	9.0	10.0	11.5	12.5	14.0	15.0	16.5	17.5
	3	5.5	7.0	8.5	10.0	11.0	12.5	14.0	15.5	17.0	18.0	19.5
	4	4.0	4.0	4.5	5.0	5.5	6.5	7.0	8.0	8.5	9.0	10.0
Base 3	1	4.5	5.5	7.0	8.0	9.0	10.0	11.0	12.5	13.5	14.5	15.5
	2	5.0	6.5	8.0	9.5	10.5	12.0	13.5	14.5	16.0	17.0	18.5
	3	6.0	7.5	9.0	10.5	11.5	13.0	15.0	16.5	18.0	19.0	20.5
	4	4.0	4.0	4.5	5.0	5.5	6.5	7.0	8.0	8.5	9.0	10.0
Build 1	1	5.0	6.5	8.0	9.0	10.0	11.5	12.5	14.0	15.5	16.0	17.5
	2	5.0	6.5	8.0	9.0	10.0	11.5	12.5	14.0	15.5	16.0	17.5
	3	4.0	4.0	4.5	5.0	5.5	6.5	7.0	8.0	8.5	9.0	10.0
Build 2	1	5.0	6.0	7.0	8.5	9.5	10.5	12.0	13.0	14.5	15.5	16.5
	2	5.0	6.0	7.0	8.5	9.5	10.5	12.0	13.0	14.5	15.5	16.5
	3	4.0	4.0	4.5	5.0	5.5	6.5	7.0	8.0	8.5	9.0	10.0
Build 3	1	5.0	6.0	7.0	8.5	9.5	10.5	12.0	13.0	14.5	15.5	16.5
	2	5.0	6.0	7.0	8.5	9.5	10.5	12.0	13.0	14.5	15.5	16.5
	3	4.0	4.0	4.5	5.0	5.5	6.5	7.0	8.0	8.0	8.5	10.0
Peak	1	5.0	5.5	6.5	7.5	8.5	9.5	10.5	11.5	13.0	13.5	14.5
	2	4.0	5.0	5.0	6.0	6.5	7.5	8.5	9.5	10.0	11.0	11.5
Race	All	4.0	4.0	4.5	5.0	5.5	6.5	7.0	8.0	8.5	9.0	10.0
Tran	All	4.0	4.0	4.5	5.0	5.5	6.5	7.0	8.0	8.5	9.0	10.0

former junior athletes move up to the senior ranks. Multisport is more competitive now than ever before, due in part to the development of young athletes. It will soon change even faster, if the 2000 Sydney Olympics has the effect on the youth of the world that the sport's leaders anticipate. Expect more competitors and even faster times.

Triathlon and duathlon are not easy sports. They require hours of difficult training in different disciplines. The races aren't over in a few seconds, and there are no "time outs." When the gun goes off starting a multisport race, you know you are in for a long effort. It takes serious commitment to training to be among the best in this sport.

You are undoubtedly serious about multisport since you have gone so far as to buy and read this book. That, in itself, is quite an accomplishment. You' ae probably wondering if everything you have read so far applies to you. With some exceptions, it does. Let's examine the details of training for juniors.

HOW TO IMPROVE QUICKLY

The best way to advance in multisport, just as with your school sports, is by working with a coach, especially one who lives close by. A good coach will help you progress by offering tips on technique, nutrition, race strategy and sports psychology. These are all things you would undoubtedly figure out for yourself, but a coach will speed up the learning process. He or she will also design a training program that fits your personal needs. This is important since triathlon and duathlon are individual sports. With a coach you will also develop more quickly because there will be fewer setbacks due to injury, burnout or overtraining.

Working with a coach is a wise decision.

Another way to speed up your progress is by attending a multisport camp for juniors. USA Triathlon (USAT), the governing body of the sport in the U.S., sponsors junior camps in different parts of the country with camp staff made up of top-level coaches and athletes. You will learn a lot about training, nutrition, technique and racing by attending one of them during your school's summer vacation. If you are concerned about the expense of attending such a camp, there are scholarships available through USAT. For more information on the camps and scholarships, contact USAT at 719/597-9090 (in 1999 USAT will move from Colorado Springs to Clermont, Florida).

Junior camps are great for growth as an athlete.

Triathlon clubs are also good for providing support, expertise, racing experience and the camaraderie of other juniors. Join a club if there is one in your region. Then ask the club to provide events for juniors at their sponsored races, if they don't already do so. They could add an extra wave with little difficulty. Sprint-distance races are best for older juniors (17-19), with shortened distances for younger juniors. USAT can provide guidance for your club in setting up such events.

A local club can provide support and experience.

On a slightly different note, you and your parents have probably come to realize that multisport is an expensive sport, with bike equipment leading the list of costly items. Don't be concerned with having the latest and greatest frame, wheels and pedal system. Instead, concentrate on becoming the best motor, and the most skilled rider in your group. When it's time to replace a bike you have outgrown, talk with other juniors about purchasing a bike for which they have also gotten too big. In the same way, see if younger athletes can use your old bike. Regardless of what you may read in the magazines and what others say, the key to improvement is not equipment, but fitness.

Focus on fitness, not equipment.

TRAINING GUIDELINES

In 1996, Dr. Randy Wilber and his associates at the Olympic Training Center in Colorado Springs, Colorado, studied the physiologies of the U.S. junior triathlon team members. What Dr. Wilber found is that these athletes were relatively weaker on the bike than in the swim or run. Especially noteworthy was that, on average, they became anaerobic on the bike at a relatively low 76 percent of their VO_2 max for cycling, while in swimming they went anaerobic at 83 percent, and in running at an outstanding 89 (girls) to 91 (boys) percent of VO_2 max. This is probably the result of participation in organized swim and run programs at their schools. What this means is that you get good at what you work on. Fitness for one or even two sports, does not "rub off" on another. No matter how good you are, there is always room for improvement somewhere. Your weakest sport is what you need to focus on when it's time to begin specializing in multisport.

Work on weaknesses.

Specialization in triathlon or duathlon probably shouldn't start for juniors until about age 15. The best training still involves participating in your school's swimming and running programs, and riding your bike in the summer. At about age 15, triathlon-specific workouts, such as bricks (see Appendix E), and increased frequency of racing may begin. Until then, play a variety of sports, including swimming, biking and running, but also such team sports as soccer and volleyball. Develop your sports skills and have fun.

A broad base of sport experience will eventually make you a better multisport athlete.

Even when serious multisport training starts, it's still a good idea to keep things in perspective. Remember that you are not an accomplished athlete yet; there is a lot of room for improvement, and steady progression is necessary if you are to eventually achieve your potential. Professional triathlete, and USAT junior coach Cyle Sage, offers the following tips to juniors and their coaches for maintaining a healthy perspective and steady growth.

• **Skills before fitness.** Develop good technique before increasing mileage. Efficient and effective form ultimately means faster race times, and less training time lost to

Be wary of high volume.

injuries. Exercise caution with volume increases as high mileage is more likely to cause breakdowns from injury and burnout than occasional high-intensity workouts.

• **Be patient.** The most important aspect of racing is participation and learning race strategy, especially pacing. Think of races as hard workouts at which you get to observe and learn from other, more experienced athletes. The best adult athletes were seldom the best as juniors, and, in fact, were often not even close. For example, did you know that Michael Jordan was cut from his junior high school basketball team?

• **Think long term.** Rather than simply trying to beat other athletes in every workout and race, develop long-term, personal-improvement goals that focus on advancing to the next level of racing. Such a goal might be to run 10km in less than 40 minutes by the time you turn 17 in two years. Similar, realistic goals are then made for each sport, and you begin steadily working toward them. This takes the pressure off of you to always be the best at the next race, and allows you to focus on what is really important — steady progress.

• **Speed before endurance.** Develop speed with drills and short, race-paced efforts such as running strides (see Appendix D). These will train your nervous system and muscles to develop more efficient and effective patterns of movement. Short, fast efforts done frequently are better for you now than are long, slow endurance workouts.

• **Form before weight.** Improve total-body, and especially hip-extension (leg press, squat, step up), strength by doing body-weight and light weight workouts in the gym. Stay with the Anatomical Adaptation (AA) weight phase (see Chapter 13) until you are 17. Concentrate more on perfecting form than on the amount of weight lifted. Even if you don't start weights until age 17, spend the first year only doing AA workouts. Always stretch following each set.

• **Get a physical.** Before the start of each season, get a complete physical examination done by your doctor. This is something even the pros do, and will allow you and your coach, if you have one, to feel good about starting the year with a clean "bill of health." If your school requires a physical to participate in sports, you can check this off.

• **Have fun.** Always remember why you race. It certainly isn't for money or to get dates. You are probably doing multisport for personal challenges, for the enjoyment of having exceptional fitness, and, most of all, for fun. Keep that perspective. Learn to laugh at yourself, to accept your successes with humility, and to learn from mistakes without complaining or offering excuses.

NOVICES

In the 1980s, multisport drew nearly all of its participants from injured runners, bored swimmers and cyclists looking to expand their horizons. Today people often come into the sport with no background at all in swimming, biking or running. This new breed of triathletes and duathletes is attracted by the challenge of combining two or three sports into one event, by the obvious fitness benefits of cross training, or simply because they saw a race, such as the Hawaiian Ironman, on television.

Whatever your reason for accepting the challenge of multisport, it's important to know the ingredients for success, especially those that are central to the sport. As with all sports, success in duathlon and triathlon, no matter how it's measured, is only as great as your preparation. Training must steel you to the specific demands of the goal event. For example, a hilly course requires training in the hills, and long races demand great aerobic endurance. In fact, endurance is the single most important requirement of the sport regardless of the race. If you can't go the distance, nothing else matters.

Endurance training is the key to multisport fitness.

TRAINING TO GO THE DISTANCE

If pressed, most multisport athletes will admit that they like training more than racing. Races are merely the carrot on the stick that gets them out of bed at 5 a.m. for a swim, and on the road as soon as they get home from work. Without races there would be no feeling of necessity or sense of importance about workouts. Races give a focus and direction to training. Workouts, however, are the fun part. That's when you can drop all of the cares of the day and concerns for tomorrow, while living strictly in the present. Swimming, cycling and running reduce life to its most basic elements — breathing and movement.

Workouts are also times when you may get together with training partners who share common interests. Having groups with whom to train makes the effort seem easier, and boosts motivation. And there will certainly be times when motivation wanes. Even the best in the sport find their desire to workout has highs and lows. This is not a sign of weakness, and may even have self-protection benefits, such as ensuring recovery. But too many workouts missed due to low enthusiasm means erosion of fitness and poor race performance. It is at such times that a training group is most beneficial. Find one for each sport, and schedule your week to regularly join with them.

Occasionally train with groups.

It is also possible to have too much motivation when you are new to the sport as compulsive training is likely to prevent you from achieving goals. Working out excessively leads only to injury, illness and overtraining — not to superior fitness. Chapter 1 presented an argument for training with moderation in a sport that appears, at least on the surface, as one of extremes. At no time in your multisport career is a conservative approach to training more critical than in the early stages of your fitness development.

Avoid excessive training to ensure rapid progress.

Training with excessive volume and intensity at this time is counter productive.

So how do you determine what is appropriate? Here are some tips that may provide guidance in your first year of multisport training.

• **Volume.** Are there externally-imposed limits on the amount of time you have available to train? For example, if you realistically examine your work day and all other daily commitments, you may find that it is possible to fit in only one hour for swimming, biking or running. Perhaps even less is possible. The weekends may then offer the most time for training. You will need to determine how much. Remember that winter brings fewer daylight hours and foul weather, further reducing training time.

> **Time available often determines volume.**

Add up your available weekly hours using a conservative estimate, and multiply by 50 to find your projected annual training volume. This assumes that two weeks will be lost during the year to unavoidable illness, travel or other commitments. The number you come up with includes all training time in addition to swimming, cycling and running, such as weightlifting, cross-country skiing and any other cross training. Round your annual hours off to the closest 50 hours.

Then go to Table 7.2 to find a suggested periodization plan for your volume. You may find that it is necessary to slightly increase the lighter training weeks or decrease the high-volume weeks on this table if your restrictions are imposed more by available time rather than your physical capacity for training and recovery. Remember that this table is merely a suggested guideline, not a requirement.

• **Periodization.** In your first year of multisport, it's best to train primarily in the Transition and Base periods as described in Chapters 3 and 7. This means you will focus on the development of aerobic endurance, strength, technique (speed) and muscular endurance. These are the most important and basic components of triathlon and duathlon fitness, and will take a year, possibly more, to hone. There is no reason to build power and anaerobic endurance, the other fitness components, before the basics are well established. The exception to this is any of the three sports in which you have prior and recent experience. For example, if you have run for several years before coming to multisport, you may include high-intensity power and anaerobic-endurance workouts along with a complete periodization program for running, but limit swimming and cycling to the Transition- and Base-period guidelines.

> **Train in the Transition and Base periods.**

• **Weekly routines.** There are endless possibilities for organizing your training week depending on time available; work schedule; experience in one or more of the sports; ability to recover; established group workouts, such as when your masters swim team meets; the times when a pool or weight room is open; and numerous individual lifestyle issues. There is no standard way to arrange the week's workouts. Most new triathletes and duathletes find, however, that doing one workout a day and alternating the sports every three days, plus a weekly day off, produces good results. Such a pattern is illustrated in Figure 14.1a. This pattern provides adequate weekly time in each sport to create enough fitness to complete a sprint-distance or even an international-distance race.

Weekly training routines depend on many individual variables.

A little more time devoted to training each week, as suggested in Figure 14.1b, may produce a bit more fitness. When doing two workouts in a day, you probably need at least 30 minutes in each workout to get a physiological benefit. Two very short workouts, unless they are put together into a combined workout (see Appendix E), have limited fitness value. Always remember that more workouts or training time is not always better, and may even result in setbacks due to injury.

Occasional two-a-day workouts are appropriate for some.

• **Weights.** If you have only a few hours to train each week and it is difficult to fit everything in, weight workouts are the first ones to omit so that you may concentrate available time on swimming, biking and running. Your greatest need at this stage of training is aerobic fitness. If you have time for the gym, and weight training doesn't compromise your sport-specific training, use only the Anatomical Adaptation (AA) phase as discussed in Chapter 13. Concentrate on perfecting your technique with light weights. You will probably be surprised at how strong you become by doing just this. In the second full year of weight training, you can introduce the other strength-building phases.

Use the AA weights phase, if you lift.

FIGURE 14.1A
Suggested training patterns for novice triathletes and duathletes with time available for one workout per day.

FIGURE 14.1B
Suggested training patterns for novice triathletes and duathletes with time available for occasional two-a-day workouts.

FIGURE 14.1A	MON	TUE	WED	THU	FRI	SAT	SUN
TRIATHLON	SWIM	BIKE	RUN	OFF	SWIM	BIKE	RUN
DUATHLON	RUN	BIKE	RUN	BIKE	OFF	RUN	BIKE

FIGURE 14.1B	MON	TUE	WED	THU	FRI	SAT	SUN
TRIATHLON	SWIM / BIKE	RUN	SWIM / BIKE	OFF	SWIM / RUN	BIKE	RUN
DUATHLON	BIKE	RUN / BIKE	RUN / BIKE	RUN / BIKE	OFF	RUN	BIKE

YOUR FIRST RACE

Several weeks or months prior to your first race, you began building fitness with short, slow workouts and gradually progressed to longer sessions at low effort mixed with shorter workouts at somewhat higher effort. In the first year, you will probably find that there isn't much speed variance between these effort levels. Your purpose in this early stage of training is to develop enough fitness to comfortably go the distance in each sport. In the last two to three weeks before your first race, workouts should become increasingly specific to the demands of the event. This is the time to include combined workouts to prepare you for the exact demands of the race. These might include swim-bike, bike-run and swim-bike-run workouts for a triathlon, and run-bike, bike-run and run-bike-run workouts for a duathlon. Also in the last two or three weeks, you may reduce the training volume by 20 to 30 percent weekly to allow for the slightly higher efforts and stresses of these combined workouts.

Combine sports in the last two to three weeks before a race.

It's wise to have an estimate of how long you will take to finish the race, including each part of it. This provides guidance in determining how long your longest single-sport workouts are. You do not, however, need a goal time for your first race. The objective of this one is to merely finish comfortably with a smile on your face. Once you accomplish that challenge, and know what your capabilities are, realistic time goals can then be determined for the next race. Every time you race, something is learned that makes you a wiser, and ultimately more fit, athlete.

As with any sport, it's important to know the rules of multisport before competing. The essential rules of the sport are obvious: Proceed in order through the three legs of the event from start to finish. Along the course, however, there are a number of issues that may arise to cause a penalty, or even disqualification. The three most common occur in the cycling leg. These are almost always discussed at the pre-race meeting. Let's quickly examine them.

Know and heed the rules of the sport.

When on the bike, including in the transition area, if you are allowed to ride there, your helmet must be on *and buckled at all times*. In the excitement of the race, athletes will sometimes forget to buckle the helmet before mounting the bike, or will unbuckle it just before getting off. You may be penalized for this safety violation. Get into the habit of putting your helmet on first, and taking it off last in the transition area.

Another commonly violated rule has to do with drafting on the bike. For an amateur triathlete it is illegal to ride behind or to the side of another rider in order to gain an advantage. The way to avoid this is to picture each bike rider within a box that extends seven meters behind the leading edge of the front wheel, and one meter to either side. Once you enter that space you have only a few seconds to pass or fall back. Lingering in that box may result in a penalty. Related to this rule is another called "blocking." When being overtaken by another rider, if you position your bike so as to impede their progress, you are blocking. The way to avoid this is to stay to the right side of the road at all times, and to pass on the left.

• **Race week.** In the final four to five days before the race, greatly reduce your training and rest more. The tendency of new triathletes and duathletes is to "test" themselves in the last few days to make sure they are capable of going the distance. This is a sure way to ruin your first race. Trust your training and rest.

Train less and rest more.

Eat normally throughout this week, including the night before, by including foods that are known to suit you. Don't experiment with unusual foods or supplements of any type. The time to experiment is in training several weeks before the race. When it comes to what we put in our stomachs, there is a lot of individual variation in tolerance and benefits. Use only what is known to work for you.

Do not experiment with food or supplements.

The day before the race, pick up your packet that includes your numbers and other information, and attend the pre-race meeting. If possible, also drive the bike and run courses to become familiar with the hills, road surfaces and turns. While it is unlikely that you will get off course, it has happened. The responsibility for knowing where to go is yours, not the officials'.

• **Race morning.** The morning of the race, eat a light breakfast at least two hours before you are supposed to start. Easily digested, low-glycemic index carbohydrate is probably best for this meal (see Chapter 16). Whatever you eat, it should be something you have previously tried with good results before a morning workout. Again, don't experiment on race morning.

Eat a breakfast of what you know works for you.

Time your travel to arrive an hour or so before the start to allow ample time for having your number marked on your body, pumping up tires, arranging the transition area, using the toilet several times and warming up.

• **Race site.** Look around to see how others have arranged their transition stalls. Also notice exactly where your transition stall is in relation to the finish of the swim (triathlon) or first run leg (duathlon). If you are unsure where the first leg finishes, ask an official. Pick out easily identifiable landmarks to help guide you to your bike and equipment.

Be able to quickly find your transition stall.

Keep the warm-up short. Ride just enough to make sure the bike is working well. Then, for a triathlon, swim a few minutes, unless the water is cold. In that case, a short run and some upper body exercises, such as a few push ups and stretches, will have to do. You don't want to become hypothermic before starting. For a duathlon, run for a few minutes before the start.

Keep the warm up short.

For a triathlon, start near the back.

• **Race start.** When your age-group wave is called to the starting line for an open-water-swim triathlon, line up to the side or at the back of the group. Staying away from the front and middle of the pack will help you avoid most of the turmoil at the start. In the middle of the group, it's not unusual to have goggles knocked off and athletes swimming over you. This is best avoided in your first race.

For a run-start duathlon, line up within your group based on the pace you expect to run. The fastest runners, those who will run in about the six-minute range, are in the front rows. The back rows are the slowest runners anticipating a nine-minute-or-so pace. Position yourself accordingly.

Start slowly.

Your pace for the first few minutes of the race is critical to achieving your goal of finishing comfortably with a smile on your face. The tendency is to go out considerably faster than you can maintain, and in the process build up a lot of lactic acid in your muscles and blood. This will come back to "haunt" you later in the race, severely slowing your pace. Continually remind yourself to start slowly regardless of what the others are doing.

Besides finishing the race, you also want to learn as much as you can about your new sport. The way to do this is to watch and listen throughout the day. Observe what the other racers do to warm up, how they start, what they do in the transition area, how they mount their bikes, what happens at the aid stations, how the course marshals direct you and what you are instructed to do at the finish. Talk with other athletes and ask questions after the race. The more you learn in this first race, the faster you will progress in the sport.

Most of all, have fun! Don't take yourself or your results too seriously. Keep in mind why you are racing. You are not a pro who is attempting to make a living from the sport; you are doing this for enjoyment, health and fitness, to challenge yourself physically and mentally, or some other personal reason.

In the days after the race, evaluate how you did and where you can improve your performance. Perhaps you started too fast, or your transitions were slow, or you didn't drink enough on the bike. You now have a good understanding of what it takes to do a triathlon or duathlon, and can begin preparing for the next one with higher goals in mind.

ELITE

Elite endurance athletes are unique and gifted individuals. They have an amazing capacity for physical work, and are blessed with an ability to improve fitness quickly as a result of this capacity. Most have an extreme work ethic which borders on obsession. In addition, they are highly motivated and dedicated to training and their goals, which causes them to persevere through the most demanding workouts and extraordinary environmental conditions. It is because of such qualities, combined with genetic luck, that they have risen to the top one-tenth of 1 percent in sport.

These same physical and psychological talents, however, are also their worst enemies. It is not uncommon for elite athletes, especially those relatively new to the elite ranks, to drive themselves into an overtrained state with frequent regularity. Many never realize their full potential, and soon leave the sport disheartened due to their overzealous and unbridled training methods. This section explores ways in which the elite multisport athlete may avoid such calamity, and steadily progress toward his or her innate fitness summit.

A propensity for training is a double-edged sword.

COACHING

For many, perhaps most, elite triathletes and duathletes, the best way to ensure steady growth accompanied by racing success is to train under the guidance of a knowledgeable and experienced coach. A coach with a good understanding of the scientific aspects of the sport interprets and applies the latest concepts and methods to meet the unique needs of the elite competitor. And by planning and managing training from a more objective point of view than the athlete is capable, the wise coach counsels and directs the athlete's racing career toward the achievement of personal goals and dreams.

A good coach can steer the elite athlete toward success.

A good coach offers many skills and services above and beyond training design and implementation. He or she also helps the athlete clearly define goals and objectives, maintain the vision of the future and cope with unusual psychological stress. The coach provides a sympathetic ear for concerns ranging from financial woes to interpersonal relationship problems. A coach with an extensive network of contacts may recruit others whose unique skills and services assist with the athlete's development, such as doctors and other health-care providers, exercise physiologists, physical therapists, nutritionists, bike mechanics and sports psychologists.

Two (or more) heads are better than one. When new challenges arise, as they often do, an experienced coach may offer fresh views for dealing with them. He or she often has a gut-level solution based on years of experience that might never have occurred to you. In addition, a good coach may even anticipate problems before they appear, and correct your course to avoid them altogether.

Having a coach in your corner lightens the burden of training, and transforms your career from an often frustrating and solitary pursuit into a team effort. All of this means that you are able to put your entire energy and time into what you are already good at — training.

TRAINING

It's obvious to the emerging elite athlete that in order to compete in multisport, he or she must work hard. The typical elite athlete's approach is to do more — more volume, more intensity or both, with the latter being the usual choice. Coupling this decision with inadequate rest is an inevitable path to breakdown from illness, injury, or most likely, overtraining. While at this level limited training is problematic, elite athletes must avoid overtraining at all costs.

Don't overtrain!

The leading cause of overtraining is inadequate recovery time. The smart athlete knows how to balance the stresses of training with growth-producing rest. The second most common factor in overtraining among elite competitors is excessive volume. Constantly placing demands on the body for greater frequency and duration of training is a more probable cause of overtraining than excessive intensity in the absence of high volume. Periodization, as discussed in several previous chapters, is the best way to avoid overtraining since rest, volume increases, and gradual step ups of intensity are all planned in relation to the highest-priority races.

Inadequate recovery and excessive volume cause overtraining.

Other lifestyle factors also contribute to overtraining in the elite athlete. These include diet, social, occupational, academic, travel and financial stresses. Notable on this list, and easily controlled, is diet, especially one low in protein and high in sugar (see Chapter 16). A less well-understood, psychological cause may be monotony of training from doing the same workouts day after day, week after week. The mix of these stresses that produces overtraining is a highly individual matter. Just because a training partner easily handles a certain mix of physical and psychological stress doesn't mean that you can. Find what works for you.

Lifestyle also contributes to overtraining.

When overtraining is suspected, disease and inadequate diet must be eliminated as causes before deciding how to rectify the situation. This is why a close working relationship with a health-care provider or full-service testing facility is recommended, as is a baseline blood test during the winter months when health and training status are known to be normal.

On the positive side, there are several other training considerations that lead to competitive racing form. The following are those that pertain strictly to the elite, multisport athlete.

• **Multiple daily training sessions.** The athlete who wins the race is not always the one who trains with the most volume, yet many elite multisport competitors seem to approach training with such a belief. Peak race performance, however, *always* results from finding the optimal balance between workout stress and rest. At this level, training volume is not determined merely by how much time you have available, but rather by what it is you hope to achieve and how quickly recovery occurs. More is not always better. The athlete who is hungry to win and physically fresh as a result of being slightly undertrained will almost always beat another who is mentally and physically fatigued from chronically overreaching.

Doing less often means attaining more.

That said, it is also obvious that the best endurance athletes in the world typically employ a relatively high volume of training made up of multiple daily workouts. Training three or even four times a day is common among elite multisport athletes, although not universal. It's difficult to compete at the highest levels with a regimen limited to three or four swims, rides and runs in a week for extended periods. This is even less adequate for the aspect of the sport that is your limiter. It may easily take five or six weekly sessions in your weakest sport to ensure achieving a level of performance on par with the competition. If weight training is a part of your training mix, this means 17 to 20 sessions a week, averaging three to four a day, are usually necessary to be competitive at the highest level of the sport.

Multiple daily sessions are necessary at the elite level.

How the duration and intensity of those multiple daily sessions is rationed is critical to steady improvement, and the avoidance of overtraining. The following are general guidelines for providing balance in a week of training in which optimal stress is emphasized. These do not apply to recovery, Peak-, Race- or Transition-period weeks in which optimal recovery is emphasized.

Plan only one or two high-stress, breakthrough (BT) sessions (force, muscular endurance, anaerobic endurance and power) per week, per sport. Include two in the sport that is your limiter. This results in four to six BT sessions each week.

You may find that grouping the BT sessions into two consecutive days followed by at least one day of low-intensity training before the next two-day grouping allows adequate stress and recovery. For example, the four to six high-stress workouts may be planned in a Wednesday-Thursday-Saturday-Sunday pattern, thus providing recovery on Friday, Monday and Tuesday.

Include one or two aerobic-endurance workouts in each sport weekly as this is the most basic and necessary component of multisport competition. These workouts are best completed at a low-intensity level (1 and 2 zones) in order to gain the desired benefits, while allowing for recovery prior to the next BT sessions.

Continue to refine technique with weekly speed sessions in each sport, such as swim or bike drills, or running strides.

Two ability-related workouts may be combined into a single session for the best use

Ability areas may be combined within one sport and session.

of time. For example, in the Base periods, bike force and endurance may be joined by doing a long ride on a hilly course. Or, as another example, combine running anaerobic-endurance and muscular-endurance workouts into one session by doing anaerobic intervals followed by a threshold run. When combining abilities within a single training session, the higher-intensity workout comes first followed by the more-endurance-based workout.

All other sessions are intended for active recovery, such as going for an easy spin on the bike, or a relaxing swim. Active recovery is probably a better way for the elite athlete to recuperate than complete rest as the increased inflow of blood containing amino acids, glucose, hormones and other components encourages restoration. Some, however, may find that a regular day off is necessary for psychological recovery. Days when you are training at a low intensity must be seen as days when you are getting stronger, not as "wasted" workouts.

Active recovery may be better for rejuvenation than total rest.

Figure 14.2 provides an example of a week that follows the above guidelines for an elite triathlete in the Base 3 period. The sessions are numbered each day to suggest an order that places stress earlier in the day followed by easier sessions that encourage recovery. When there are two or more BT sessions on a given day, a meal and rest separating them will bring the best results. A between-workout nap will further enhance the adaptive process. Realize that Figure 14.2 offers just one way in which these sessions could be arranged. There are many other options which are equally as effective.

Supercompensation results from crash training.

• **"Crash" training.** Chapter 3 explained that after a training stress is applied, and the body is allowed to recover, fitness soon develops to a level somewhat higher than originally enjoyed. This process is known as overcompensation. Recent studies show that when the training stresses are closely spaced for an extended period, followed by a long rejuvenation phase, the level of overcompensation is enhanced. This is known as "supercompensation." Such a risky flirtation with overtraining is sometimes called "crashing" — a descriptive, if somewhat ominous name.

FIGURE 14.2
Example of an elite triathlete's Base 3 week. See appendixes B,C and D for workout options for these session categories. Numbers indicate suggested workout order for a given day.

Two studies in the early 1990s explored supercompensation resulting from crash

	MON	TUE	WED	THU	FRI	SAT	SUN
SWIM		2-SPEED DRILLS	2-MUSCULAR ENDURANCE	3-ACTIVE RECOVERY	2-SPEED DRILLS	2-ENDURANCE	2-ACTIVE RECOVERY
BIKE	3-ENDURANCE	3-ACTIVE RECOVERY	3-SPEED DRILLS	1-ENDURANCE & FORCE		3-SPEED DRILLS	1-MUSCULAR ENDURANCE
RUN	1-SPEED DRILLS	1-ENDURANCE	1-MUSCULAR ENDURANCE	2-ACTIVE RECOVERY	1-SPEED DRILLS	1-ENDURANCE & FORCE	
WEIGHTS	2-ME PHASE						

		MON	TUE	WED	THU	FRI	SAT	SUN
"CRASH" WEEK	**SWIM**		2-SPEED	1-ANAEROBIC ENDURANCE	3-ACTIVE RECOVERY	2-MUSCULAR ENDURANCE	1-ANAEROBIC ENDURANCE	OFF
	BIKE	2-ACTIVE RECOVERY	1-ENDURANCE	2-MUSCULAR ENDURANCE	1-ANAEROBIC ENDURANCE	3-ACTIVE RECOVERY	2-MUSCULAR ENDURANCE	OFF
	RUN	1-ENDURANCE		3-ACTIVE RECOVERY	2-MUSCULAR ENDURANCE	1-ANAEROBIC ENDURANCE		OFF
RECOVERY WEEK	**SWIM**	OFF	2-ACTIVE RECOVERY		2-ACTIVE RECOVERY		2-ENDURANCE	2-ACTIVE RECOVERY
	BIKE	OFF	1-ACTIVE RECOVERY	2-ACTIVE RECOVERY		2-ACTIVE RECOVERY	1-ENDURANCE	
	RUN	OFF		1-ACTIVE RECOVERY	1-ACTIVE RECOVERY	1-ACTIVE RECOVERY		1-ENDURANCE

FIGURE 14.3
Example of a 5-day "Crash" cycle for an elite triathlete. See Appendixes B,C,D and E for workout options for these session categories. Numbers indicate suggested workout order for a given day.

cycles. In 1992 a group of seven Dutch cyclists crashed for two weeks by increasing their training volume from a normal 12.5 hours per week to 17.5. At the same time, their intense training went from 24 to 63 percent of total training time. The immediate effect was a drop in all aspects of their fitness. But after two weeks of recovering, they realized a 6-percent improvement in power, their time trials improved by an average of four percent, and they produced less blood lactate at top speed compared with pre-crash levels. Not bad for two weeks of hard training.

A similar study in Dallas put runners through a two-week crash cycle with results similar to the Dutch study, and there was also an increase in aerobic capacities. Again, it took two weeks following the crash cycle to realize the gains. Further research suggests an increase in blood volume, greater levels of hormones that cause muscle growth, and an improved ability to metabolize fat result from a high-stress crash period and the ensuing supercompensation.

These and other studies have revealed three generalizations that guide the elite multisport athlete when designing a crash cycle. The first is that it takes about three weeks to produce overtraining in young, well-trained athletes, so crash cycles must not go that long, and should probably be far shorter. In a study of elite rowers preparing for the world championship, three hours of daily training for three weeks were necessary to produce overtraining. Second, large volume increases are not nearly as effective at producing supercompensation as dramatic increases in intensity. Researchers doubled the weekly mileage of a group of well-trained runners for three weeks, and at another time, doubled the number of miles that they ran at high intensity for three weeks. Following the high-volume phase, endurance and running performance plateaued, but it improved following the increased-intensity period. Finally, studies report that it takes one-half to a full day of active recovery for every day spent crashing. Short crash cycles of, for example, five to seven days are best followed by an equal number of recovery days. Longer

Guidelines for designing a crash cycle.

crash cycles, in the neighborhood of 14 to 21 days, may be matched with fewer recovery days, about one-half day for every day of crashing.

With these guidelines in kind, Figure 14.3 provides an example of a crash cycle for a triathlete. Bear in mind that this is only one way in which a crash cycle may be organized.

Crash training must be approached with caution.

Be careful with crashing. The risk of overtraining rises dramatically during such a build-up. It's important that your fitness base (aerobic endurance, force, speed and muscular endurance) is well established before attempting a crash cycle. If the typical signs of overtraining appear, such as a greatly changed resting heart rate or feelings of depression, cut back on the workload immediately. It is probably best not to attempt a crash cycle more frequently than once for each racing peak in the season. In addition, the last crash workout should probably be no closer to the goal race than two weeks.

• **Draft-legal training.** The advent of draft-legal races is changing the way elite multisport athletes train. Preparation for these events differs from that used for non-drafting races in several ways. The obvious difference is the increased importance of the swim and run legs in the drafting format. If you are not among the leaders out of the water in such an event, the race may well be over. In the same way, running performance is even more important since several athletes will enter the second transition at the same time.

This doesn't mean, however, that the bike leg is unimportant. It merely changes the emphasis of the total training volume slightly more in favor of swimming and running, and the manner in which the bike training is done. Also changed is the bike design and set up. Instead of large seat-tube angles and long top tubes, criterium-style, draft-legal races favor bikes that are shorter, with small seat-tube angles. Such frames are rigid and responsive, which matches the demands of the faster pace and quick speed changes of these events. The bike is adjusted in a way that is similar to how bicycle road racers set theirs up, with the saddle aft so that a plumb line dropped from the *front* of the knee (instead of the side of the knee as for time trialing) intersects the pedal spindle. This allows the application of force to the pedal earlier in the downstroke than in a typical saddle-forward time-trial set up, in effect increasing the time per pedal stroke in which force is applied. It also improves the ability to pedal at a high cadence, which is beneficial when speed changes abruptly.

Bike design and set up is similar to that of bike road racers for draft-legal races.

Ride frequently in packs with USCF racers.

As for training, draft-legal racing requires frequent training with groups, especially in the Build and Peak periods, in order to gain confidence when riding in a pack, and to improve handling skills. An effective way to accomplish these objectives is to ride with United States Cycling Federation (USCF) road racers on their weekly club rides. Many USCF clubs also hold weekly training races in the spring that they may allow you to enter without a USCF license. Be careful, however, of criterium-style races held on courses with tight turns and large fields. The chances of a crash in such a race are high.

Another training change that draft-legal races require is an increased emphasis on anaerobic endurance and power. When in a small group chasing down a break away, or trying to stay away in a break, going deeply anaerobic and staying there for several minutes is necessary. The ability to tolerate high levels of lactate makes this possible. Also required is the ability to quickly produce power, especially on courses with many turns or short hills.

Develop anaerobic endurance and power.

EXTENDING YOUR CAREER

Motivation is necessary for success at the highest level of sport, and may determine who will place in the money on a given day. If you aren't mentally driven and absolutely in love with training and racing, there is little chance of a long and successful career in multisport. But high motivation is also a double-edged sword. Because of it, the elite athlete will push through any formidable training session deemed important for producing faster races. This can lead to burnout, recurring injuries and frequent overtraining. Such interruptions break patterns of training consistency, and force a return to previous levels. Consistency is the single most important component for producing peak race fitness. Inconsistent training results in poor race performances, and even eventual abandonment of multisport. Promising careers sometimes end early due to motivation getting in the way of clear thinking.

Motivation needs to be bridled.

Treat your body with respect — it's a fine instrument, not a blunt object. Avoid anything that has high risk and the potential to interfere with training stability. Close attention to recovery in order to balance stress is the starting point for optimal training and a long, successful career. When rest is adequate, the problems of inconsistency diminish, and you feel positive, confident and eager to race.

Other than the timely inclusion of rest, the best way to prevent breakdowns is by increasing the work load of training incrementally over a period of several weeks by using a program of periodization as discussed in Chapters 3, 7 and 9. Sudden and unusually large increases in volume or intensity, such as the crash training described above, must have pre-determined time limits while the body's response is carefully monitored. At the first sign that something is not right, such as unusual joint discomfort or inability to recover, work load is decreased despite the training goal not being achieved. To continue is to risk set back.

Gradual increases in work load reduce the risk of breakdown.

Also important to extending your career in multisport is thinking and planning long term. It's easy to get caught up in preparing only for the next race, regardless of how insignificant that event may be to your stated, long-term goals. The athlete with training myopia sees every race as having equal importance, and tries to attain peak fitness levels for each. This is physiologically, and perhaps even psychologically, impossible. Know what is important for your career not only for this season, but for the next three or four years, such as a berth on the Olympic team or Ironman placement. Keep such long-term goals uppermost in your thinking when determining your annual training plan design and weekly workout patterns. As discussed earlier, this is where a wise and experienced coach is of great value.

Never lose sight of where you are going.

REFERENCES

Atwater, A.E. 1990. Gender differences in distance running. In P.R. Cavanagh (ed.), *Biomechanics of Distance Running*. Champaign, IL: Human Kinetics.

Balaban, E.P., et al. 1989. The frequency of anemia and iron deficiency in the runner. *Medicine and Science in Sport and Exercise* 21: 643-648.

Bemben, D.A., et al. 1992. Effects of oral contraceptives on hormonal and metabolic responses during exercise. *Medicine and Science in Sport and Exercise* 24 (4): 434-441.

Bompa, T. 1995. *From Childhood to Champion Athlete*. Toronto, ONT: Veritas Publishing.

Brown, C. and J. Wilmore. 1974. The effects of maximal resistance training on the strength and body composition of women athletes. *Medicine and Science in Sports and Exercise* 6: 174-177.

Budgett, R. 1990. Overtraining syndrome. *British Journal of Sports Medicine* 24: 231-236.

Child, J.S., et al. 1984. Cardiac hypertrophy and function in masters endurance runners and sprinters. *Journal of Applied Physiology* 57: 170-181.

Clark. 1993. Red meat: To eat or not to eat. *National Strength and Conditioning Association Journal* 15: 71-72.

Cohen, J. and C.V. Gisolfi. 1982. Effects of interval training in work-heat tolerance in young women. *Medicine and Science in Sport and Exercise* 14: 46-52.

Costill, D.L., et al. 1988. Effects of repeated days of intensified training on muscle glycogen and swimming performance. *Medicine and Science in Sport and Exercise* 20: 249-254.

Cunningham, D.A., et al. 1979. Cardiovascular response to intervals and continuous training in women. *European Journal of Applied Physiology* 41: 187-197.

Deuster, P.A., et al. 1986. Nutritional survey of highly trained women runners. *American Journal of Clinical Nutrition* 45: 954-962.

Dill, D., et al. 1967. A longitudinal study of 16 champion runners. *Journal of Sports Medicine* 7: 4-32.

Drinkwater, B.L., et al. 1984. Bone mineral content of amenorrheic and eumenorrheic athletes. *New England Journal of Medicine* 311: 277-281.

Drinkwater, B.L. 1984. Women and exercise: Physiological aspects. *Exercise and Sports Sciences Reviews* 12: 21-51.

Drinkwater, B.L. (ed.). 1986. *Female Endurance Athletes.* Champaign, IL: Human Kinetics.

Dufaux, B., et al. 1981. Serum ferritin, transferrin, haptoglobin, and iron in middle- and long-distance runners, elite rowers, and professional racing cyclists. *International Journal of Sports Medicine* 2:43-46.

Dutto, D.J. and J.M. Cappaert. 1994. Biomechanical and physiological differences between males and females during freestyle swimming. *Medicine and Science in Sports and Exercise* 26 (5): S1098.

Ekblom, B. 1969. Effect of physical training in adolescent boys. *Journal of Applied Physiology* 27: 350-353.

Fry, R.W., et al. 1991. Overtraining in athletes: An update. *Sports Medicine* 12: 32-65.

Fry, R.W., et al. 1992. Biological responses to overload training in endurance sports. *European Journal of Applied Physiology* 64 (4): 335-344.

Fry, R.W., et al. 1992. Periodization and the prevention of overtraining. *Canadian Journal of Sports Science* 17: 241-248.

Gibbons, T.P., et al. 1996. Physiological responses in elite junior triathletes during field testing. *Medicine and Science in Sports and Exercise* 28 (5): SA756.

Hamilton, N. et al. 1993. Changes in sprint stride kinematics with age in masters athletes. *Journal of Applied Biomechanics* 9: 15-26.

Heath, G. A. 1981. Physiological comparison of young and older endurance athletes. *Journal of Applied Physiology* 51 (3): 634-640.

Hooper, S.L., et al. 1993. Hormonal responses of elite swimmers to overtraining. *Medicine and Science in Sports and Exercise* 25: 741-747.

Jeukendrup, A.E., et al. 1992. Physiological changes in male competitive cyclists after two weeks of intensified training. *International Journal of Sports Medicine* 13 (7): 534-541.

Kirwan, J.P., et al. 1988. Physiological responses to successive days of intense training in competitive swimmers. *Medicine and Science in Sport and Exercise* 20: 255-259.

Koltyn, K.F., P.J. O'Connor and W.P. Morgan. 1991. Perception of effort in female and male competitive swimmers. *International Journal of Sports Medicine* 12: 427-429.

Koutedakis, Y., R. Budgett, and L. Faulmann. 1990. Rest in underperforming elite competitors. *British Journal of Sports Medicine* 24: 248-252.

Koutedakis, Y. 1995. Seasonal variation in fitness parameters in competitive athletes. *Sports Medicine* 19: 373-392.

Leake, C.N. and J.E. Carter. 1991. Comparison of body composition and somatotype of trained female triathletes. *Journal of Sports Science* 9 (2): 125-135.

Legwold, G. 1982. Masters competitors age little in ten years. *The Physician and Sports Medicine* 10 (10): 27.

Lehmann, M.P., et al. 1992. Training-overtraining: Influence of a defined increase in training volume vs. training intensity on performance, catecholamines and some metabolic parameters in experienced middle- and long-distance runners. *European Journal of Applied Physiology* 64: 169-177.

Lehmann, M.P., et al. 1997. Training-overtraining: An overview and experimental results in endurance sports. *Journal of Sports Medicine and Physical Fitness* 37 (1): 7-17.

Malarkey, W.B., J.C. Hall, R.R. Rice, et al. 1993. The influence of age on endocrine responses to ultraendurance stress. *Journal of Gerontology* 48 (4): M134-139.

Malwa, R.M. 1989. Growth and maturation: Normal variation and effect of training. In C.V. Gisolfi and D.R. Lamb (eds.), *Perspectives in Exercise Science and Sports Medicine: Youth, Exercise and Sport.* Carmel, IN: Benchmark Press.

Mayhew, J. and P. Gross. 1974. Body composition changes in young women and high resistance weight training. *Research Quarterly* 45: 433-440.

Nelson. 1986. Diet and bone status in amenorrheic runners. *American Journal of Clinical Nutrition* 43: 910-916.

Newby-Fraser, P. 1995. *Peak Fitness for Women.* Champaign, IL: Human Kinetics.

Newby-Fraser, P. 1998. Personal communication with author.

Pate, R.R., et al. 1987. Cardiorespiratory and metabolic responses to submaximal and maximal exercise in elite women distance runners. *International Journal of Sports Medicine* 8 (S2): 91-95.

Parizkova, J. 1974. Body composition and exercise during growth and development. *Physical Activity: Human Growth and Development.*

Pollock, M., et al. 1987. Effect of age and training on aerobic capacity and body composition of master athletes. *Journal of Applied Physiology* 62 (2): 725-731.

Pollock, M., et al. 1975. Frequency of training as a determinant for improvement in cardiovascular function and body composition of middle-aged men. *Archives of Physical Medicine and Rehabilitation* 56: 141-145.

Richardson, A.B. and J.W. Miller. Swimming and the older athlete. *Clinical Sports Medicine* 10 (2): 301-318.

Rogers, et al. 1990. Decline in VO$_2$max with aging in masters athletes and sedentary men. *Journal of Applied Physiology* 68 (5): 2195-2199.

Rushall, B.S. 1994. Some psychological considerations for US National Swimming Teams. *American Swimming*, Feb-Mar: 8-12.

Seals, D.R., et al. 1984. Endurance training in older men and women. *Journal of Applied Physiology* 57: 1024-1029.

Shangold, M.M. and G. Mirkin (eds.). 1988. *Women and exercise: Physiology and sports medicine.* Davis Publishing.

Shasby, G.B. and F.C. Hagerman. 1975. The effects of conditioning on cardiorespiratory function in adolescent boys. *Journal of Sports Medicine* 3: 97-107.

Speechly, D.P., S.R. Taylor and G.G. Rogers. 1996. Differences in ultra-endurance exercise in performance-matched male and female runners. *Medicine and Science in Sports and Exercise* 28: 359-365.

Thorland, W.G., et al. 1987. Strength and anaerobic responses of elite young female sprint and distance runners. *Medicine and Science in Sports and Exercise* 19: 56-61.

Wells, C.L. 1991. *Women, Sport, and Performance: A Physiological Perspective.* Champaign, IL: Human Kinetics.

Weltman, A., et al. 1986. The effects of hydraulic resistance strength training in pre-pubertal males. *Medicine and Science in Sports and Exercise* 18: 629-638.

Wilmore, J., et al. 1992. Is there energy conservation in amenorrheic compared with eumenorrheic distance runners? *Journal of Applied Physiology* 72: 15-22.

Wilmore, J. and D. Costill. 1994. *Physiology of Sport and Exercise.* Champaign, IL: Human Kinetics.

THE TRAINING DIARY

"A well-kept training log and journal will serve as a window into the vaults of information and experiences you've accumulated through training and racing."

— RAY BROWNING

This book emphasizes planning and managing your race preparation instead of training by impulse, which is all too common among endurance athletes. This methodical approach to training requires a constant feedback of information for effective decision making. A well-kept training diary meets that need. Without a record of your workouts and racing experiences, you must rely on memory, which all too often is spotty or recalls exaggerated versions of what you did a year ago, last month or even yesterday.

A diary is especially helpful to the self-coached, time-constrained triathlete or duathlete who must make every hour of training count. It's also a source of information about what has or hasn't worked in the past, the progress you are making, the need for recovery, how your body responds to a given workout, and how much recovery is necessary following breakthrough workouts and races. The training diary motivates as it builds confidence whenever you review obstacles overcome, such as foul weather that didn't stop you, difficult workouts completed, high work load weeks survived, and days you worked out even though you didn't feel up to it. Confidence grows when successes are written down and remembered later on. These successes may also include successful workouts, personal racing bests and goals accomplished.

In its simplest form, the diary is a log of workouts, races, goals, objectives and distances covered, but it can also provide an early warning system for illness and injury that generally give advance notification, if you are paying attention. Tracing the origins of

The benefits of keeping a training diary.

these setbacks to the circumstances that caused them will educate you so these same problems are avoided in the future. A diary is also a planning tool. Use it to schedule your training week based on the Annual Training Plan you developed in Chapters 7 and 8.

A diary is not an end in itself. If all you do is write down workouts, but never use the data, its full potential to help you achieve peak racing fitness is not realized. A well-kept and used diary is a vehicle that leads you on a journey of personal discovery. It may show you why things aren't going well, or why they are. By paying attention to it, you learn how long it takes to get into race shape following a certain routine. The possibilities are endless. Used wisely, the diary allows you to remember, analyze and modify, motivate and build confidence, plan and hold accountable, all of which sounds surprisingly similar to what a good coach does.

But be aware that there are also downsides to the training diary. It's possible to record too much data, and then spend more time analyzing the data than you did creating it in workouts. The other common shortcoming of some diary keepers is the compulsion to use it as a "score card." Athletes have been known to realize on the last day of the week that they are a few minutes or miles short of their diary-planned, weekly volume, and so head out the door to accumulate the missing numbers. Avoid the compulsion to use your diary this way.

There are several types of diaries.

Where should you record all of the data? The mode you choose is likely to determine how diligent you are with record keeping. If you get a charge out of high technology, and enjoy detailed analysis, one of the new computer-based, software diaries may be just what you need. But if you don't think you will boot up the computer immediately following a workout, then an electronic diary is not for you. Choose a standard, paper format instead.

Most elite athletes prefer to use a simple notebook in which they may record anything they want without being forced into a mold by a standard layout. Others design their own by laying out basic pages, and then making copies, which are kept in a loose-leaf notebook.

Appendix F offers a format, which follows that suggested in this chapter. You may copy it for your own use. Or you can purchase the *Inside Triathlon*, spiral-bound diary based on this format from Velo (800/234-8356).

WHAT TO RECORD

How should you train? There is unlimited information available to help answer this question from such popular sources as training partners, magazine stories, books, television programs, videotapes and even advertising. Given that you are an individual with unique needs, how do you know which to keep and which to discard? The best way is to do what any good scientist does with something suspected of having promise — experiment and observe. In this study, however, you are the only subject. What works, or doesn't work, for you is all that matters when it comes to deciding what workout to do, when to rest, what to eat and the many other details that define training. Think of your diary as the place where the on-going experiment is recorded and observed. The more systematic you are in collecting the data, the greater the chance that you will learn the answers to your questions.

Multisport training is an experiment with one subject.

Although data is required to train scientifically, writing down too much is just as bad as not recording enough. If you have to wade through every minute detail of every workout, you will have a difficult time drawing conclusions. Record only what is important and that you are likely to study. Your diary should be simple and succinct, or you won't use it very long.

The following five categories provide a general framework for collecting information that may help you make daily decisions and analyze what is needed to improve. Don't feel you have to record all of this. Only keep track of those items that you can quickly write down after a workout, and that you are likely to use later on.

BASIC LOG ENTRIES

This is the information that is brief and easiest to record and analyze. It includes the workout date, course or venue, distance and time, weather conditions, time of day, equipment used and training partners. Also make note of the quality indicators of the workout, such as interval times, pace or vertical feet gained. Note anything unusual. This might be a knee that felt "funny," or a slight headache.

MORNING WARNINGS

Following the collapse of the Berlin Wall, one of the administrators of the East German Olympic sports program came to the U.S. and spoke about the accomplishments of the Eastern Bloc athletes. While banned drugs apparently played a role in their success, he explained how individual attention was given to each athlete, and how this contributed to the medal count. He described how each athlete's day began with a visit by a staff of professionals and a quick evaluation of readiness to train. This included medical and psychological evaluation that guided the coaches in refining the day's training plan. The purpose was to have the athlete do only what was appropriate that day — nothing more or less.

Wouldn't it be nice if you had such personal guidance every day? Since it's unlikely to happen, the next best option is to learn to make these decisions for yourself. One

Learning to listen to your body improves training.

way to do that is to start each day with a self-evaluation of your physical and mental readiness. Every morning when you wake up, clues indicate if you are up to the workouts that day. The problem is, most don't listen.

According to an Australian study, there are daily log entries that may help you pay close attention to the clues. The researchers found that rating sleep quality, fatigue, psychological stress and muscle soreness on a scale of one to seven, with one representing the best condition and seven the worst, was highly predictive of readiness to train. All are subjective, but if you are honest, a rating of five, six or seven for any of these warning signs means that something is wrong, and the workload should be reconsidered that day. Three or more such warning signs is probably a good sign that a day off is needed.

Other fairly reliable indicators are waking pulse and body weight. Find your average waking pulse for a week in which you are healthy and rested. Any time your heart rate is five or more beats above this number, take that as a warning. Another warning is your body weight dropping two pounds in 24 hours. This is usually the result of dehydration, but could also signal a diet that does not match your caloric needs or excessive training. Be sure to weigh under the same conditions each day, such as just after waking and using the toilet.

Forces other than training may effect your warning signs. These could include, for example, travel, work stress, relationship issues, financial problems, heat, humidity and home responsibilities. It makes no difference what causes the warning signs, the bottom line is the same: You must reduce the training work load that day.

PHYSICAL NOTES

Note how you felt in the workout.

During workouts, pay close attention to how you feel, and later, translate that into a number on a scale of one to 10 with one meaning you felt great, and 10 that you felt terrible (in which case, you probably won't have finished the workout). Just as with the warning signs, such a rating keeps you in tune with your body.

Also record heart rate data from your monitor. This may be how many minutes you were in each training zone. As the season progresses from the Prep, to the Base and Build periods, the higher 3, 4 and 5 zones should make up increasingly greater percentages of your total weekly volume. Exactly what those percentages are varies a great deal between athletes, and also varies according to the type of event for which you are training. This is one piece of personal data that is ripe for analysis.

You may also want to include other intensity-related workout data such as peak heart rate achieved, average heart rate and how much heart rate dropped in one minute at the end of the workout. If you are using power measurements on the bike, record those.

Another simple way of measuring training intensity, especially in the Build period, is to set the upper range of your heart rate monitor for your lactate threshold (bottom of 5a zone) for each sport, and the lower end for the top of the 1 zone. Then record each day how much time was spent above lactate threshold and how much time at low effort. At the end of the week, add them up by sport and you'll have a good idea of how much quality training you are doing, and how much active recovery you are allowing. Again, there are no established standards for these categories, so you may want to discover what works best for you by experimenting.

An alternative method of using the heart-rate monitor.

MENTAL NOTES

Most athletes think of training as a strictly physical activity and ignore what's happening with the mind and emotions. But sometimes feelings are the most telling aspect of training. For example, low motivation as evidenced by diary comments such as, "I didn't feel like working out today," may signal overreaching, an early stage of overtraining. Again, noting and paying attention to these sometimes hormonally-dependent emotions keeps you in tune with the inner workings of the body.

Emotions are all too often ignored by athletes.

In addition to physical development, workouts should also provide training for mental skills that are necessary for successful racing. For example, how good are you at staying focused during a race? Do you find pace dropping as your mind wanders? If so, work on concentration in certain key workouts. Ones that simulate race effort, such as intervals and threshold workouts, are a great time to practice staying in tune with what your body is doing. Other mental skills that may need development are confidence, relaxation, attitude and visualization. Record daily accomplishments in these areas in your diary.

MISCELLANEOUS NOTES

Other training and racing elements you may include in your diary from time to time are travel, environmental factors such as altitude and humidity, work hours or other work-related stresses, weight-training records and family activities that impact training. You could also add comments on gears used in climbing a local, challenging hill; race information including strategy, results, field size and conditions; or the effects of different types of pre-race meals. The possibilities are endless, and limited only by what you find possibly important to your "experiment."

Record for later comparison any other information you believe may be important.

PLANNING WITH A DIARY

Another way to use your training diary that is quite effective, but seldom done, is as a planning tool. At the end of each week, decide what you need to accomplish in the next week to attain your goals, based on the objectives on your annual training plan, and write them down as weekly goals in your diary. For example, you may set a goal of improving your cycling hill strength by climbing 10 more minutes this week than you did last week. Or perhaps one of your annual objectives is to take a minute off of your 10km run time by a certain point in the season. To accomplish that you will need to improve the quality of certain workouts, so a weekly goal may be to complete a certain number mile repeats at lactate threshold pace. The idea is that your weekly goals should continue to bring you closer to the training objectives necessary to accomplish your season, race-related goals.

Weekly goals lead to the accomplishment of season objectives.

Once you know what it is that needs accomplishing this week, decide on the supporting workouts, and the days on which you will do them. Chapter 8 provides guidance in making these decisions so that recovery is adequate. These planning notes could use a shorthand system of your own making, or the workout codes suggested in Appendixes B, C, D and E. For example, a planned workout might be jotted down with a shorthand such as, "Run, 45, F3." This means run 45 minutes doing workout F3 (hill repeats, as described in Appendix D). Then, on each day before starting the training session, flip to the scheduled workout in the proper appendix to review the details. Always keep in mind that it may be necessary to change the workout once you start if you discover that you just don't feel right for whatever reason. Overtraining and injury starts with the inability to pay attention to the body, and a willful disregard for the future.

Plan workouts based on weekly goals.

At first, this planning may take you 20 to 30 minutes. But as you get onto the routine, it will only take 10 minutes or so. As far as your progress goes, this is the most important 10 minutes you will spend each week. Such weekly planning will do more to improve your racing than anything else you do other than working out, eating and sleeping.

USING A DIARY FOR ANALYSIS

Now that you have recorded all of this information, what do you do with it? The answer depends on what situation you are experiencing. It could be problem-related, such as seeking the cause of an injury, determining why you are chronically tired, or finding out the cause of a poor race. The situation needing analysis might be planning-oriented, for example, deciding what has and hasn't worked in the past in order to peak at the right time for an important race. There are an endless array of situations that you may need to delve into using a diary as you pursue multisport excellence. Hopefully, you have kept your entries brief so that analysis doesn't require sifting through excess verbiage.

TRAINING ANALYSIS

When obstacles appear, as they invariably do, lessening their impact on training and returning to normal workouts is imperative. Injuries, illnesses and overtraining are the most common obstacles for the multisport athlete. The roots of these problems are often found in some combination of excesses in training and lifestyle. Knowing the mistakes you made that caused the setback helps you prevent the same pattern from developing again.

Tracing setback causes makes you wiser.

For some multisport athletes, managing injuries is a way of life. Running is usually the sport that is most likely to produce recurring problems. Training excess isn't always the culprit. Injuries are sometimes related to training in shoes that are breaking down, or from running in shoes that just aren't right for you. Modern running shoes are quite technical and designed to prevent certain foot movements or encourage others. If you don't have the biomechanical or structural need for which the shoes was designed, it may cause injury. Keeping a record of shoes used by workout may help you make such determinations. Knowing how many miles or hours a pair of running shoes have accumulated is also valuable when it comes to deciding when to replace them in order to prevent injury.

Injuries may result from equipment.

In the same way, recording changes made in bike set up, especially saddle position, may prove valuable if a few weeks later a knee flares up. Perhaps the cause is the changes you made, but how much did you move the saddle up-down and fore-aft? Have you ever had it in that position before and experienced anything like this with your knee? Are you able to put it back in the exact same position it was before? Or did something change with your training, such as more hills in a high gear, that might lead to a cause?

Sometimes there are simply nagging questions that beg for answers. Have you done enough training of certain abilities, such as force development? Are you allowing adequate recovery between workouts? What workout sequences produce the best results for you? What taper procedure seems to work? Looking back through your diaries for recent years often provides answers and new directions in training.

Careful analysis may lead to better training.

RACE ANALYSIS

Competitions are ripe for analysis. Why did your race not meet expectations? Was there any particular aspect of it that was especially strong or weak? How about pacing, hills, transitions, endurance, refueling, strategy, tactics, focus and confidence? The answers to such questions often come from race results which indicate splits and group rankings, and by comparing current results with previous performances on the same course. Then again, this

Assessing race performances provides insight for training.

FIGURE 15.1

Race evaluation form

Race name:

Date and start time:

Location:

Type/distance:

Key competitors:

Weather:

Course conditions:

Race goal:

Race strategy:

Warm-up description:

Start-line arousal level: Very low Low   Moderate   High   Very high

Results (place, time, splits, etc.):

What I did well:

What I need to improve:

Aches/pains afterwards:

Other comments:

may not provide enough information. In that case, you need to take a closer look at each race, and write down your observations while it's still fresh in your mind. The Race Evaluation form suggested in Figure 15.1 may help you do that.

Days on which you felt great, especially if they were race days, deserve special analysis. Examine the preceding days to determine what may have led to this high point. Perhaps it was a certain pattern of workouts, or a period of rest, or the elimination of some lifestyle stress, or a dietary change. In the same way, consider what was going on leading up to a particularly bad day. What may have caused this? If trends are identified, you are one step closer to knowing the secret of what does and doesn't work for you. Reproducing the positive forces while minimizing the negative is valuable for race peaking.

Look for trends, both good and bad.

A diary helps you see the big picture while keeping all of the details in focus. When used effectively, it serves as an excellent tool for planning, motivating and diagnosing. It also provides a personal history of training and racing accomplishments. A well-kept diary ranks right up there with training, rest and nutrition when it comes to developing a competitive edge.

REFERENCES

Friel, J. 1996. *The Cyclist's Training Bible.* Boulder, CO: Velo Press.

Hooper, S.L., et al. 1995. Markers for monitoring overtraining and recovery. *Medicine and Science in Sports and Exercise* 27: 106-112.

Rushall, B.S. 1990. A tool for measuring stress tolerance in elite athletes. *Applied Sport Psychology* 2: 51-66.

FUEL

"Some days you want broccoli, other days Hostess Ding Dongs.
Don't ask me why."

— SCOTT TINLEY

How and what should you eat to maximize performance now, and for many healthy years to come? There are many solutions offered: the Zone diet, the Pritikin diet, the Atkins diet, the American Heart Association diet, the vegetarian diet … the list goes on and on. The possibilities are nearly endless — and endlessly confusing. In fact, it seems that whenever you open the daily newspaper, you find that more pieces of the nutrition puzzle have been answered by recent research. The problem is, the answers are often contradictory.

Loren Cordain, Ph.D., professor of exercise and sport science at Colorado State University, in Fort Collins, Colorado, believes that the answers are to be found in the distant past when Mother Nature shaped our ancestors with the hard facts of evolution. He points out that modern-day endurance athletes already have a lifestyle that closely replicates that of Stone Age men and women of 25,000 years ago. His studies reveal that these prehistoric "athletes" probably burned more than 3000 calories a day as they went about the many tasks of staying alive in a demanding environment. The men would often spend the day tracking and hunting animals at a steady clip, and then carry the carcass back to camp. Cordain estimates that they may have run and jogged 10 miles in a day, much of it with about a 25-pound load. The women were also active as they carried children while finding and hauling vegetables and other food stuffs. Life was hard, but they evolved to meet the challenge.

Dr. Cordain points out that the genetic changes evolution brought still shape our dietary needs today, 2 million years after humans first appeared as a separate genus in the anthropological record. He believes that since evolution is a slow and steady process

Modern and prehistoric athletes have much in common.

requiring tens, if not hundreds of thousands of years to produce significant change, our space-age bodies are still best adapted to the diet of our Stone Age ancestors. The foods our predecessors ate for millennia are still the optimal fuels since we long ago developed the mechanics, chemistry and gut to process them. So what did Paleolithic people eat?

Evolution shaped our dietary needs.

By comparison with today, Paleolithic people ate a simple diet consisting primarily of lean meats and organs from wild game, fruits and vegetables. Nuts, seeds, berries and eggs were also eaten. There were no grains or dairy. Saturated fats were low. Products from very lean animals accounted for most of the calories, perhaps 40 to 50 percent, Dr. Cordain estimates. But these animals were not fattened on corn in feedlots or growth enhanced with drugs, so the meat was far different from what we find in our local supermarket. Today, for example, a cut of USDA prime beef contains 560 percent more saturated fat than the same amount of meat from wild game such as elk, which is similar to what our ancestors once ate.

Stone Age people ate far less carbohydrate than is commonly recommended now, and what carbohydrate they *did* eat released its energy slowly. With the rare exception of infrequent honey finds, they ate no foods that were calorically dense and nutritionally empty. Their foods were fresh and high in fiber, vitamins and minerals. Their only fluid was water.

Despite the absence of food pyramids and recommended daily allowances, our Paleolithic ancestors did not suffer from the diet- and lifestyle-induced diseases we now experience: heart disease, hypertension, diabetes and some types of cancers. It appears that they most likely died in their 30s or 40s, usually from accidents or illnesses for which there were no cures. While we don't know exactly what the long-term effects of their diet might have been, we do know that many people still following a Stone Age existence in remote areas today live into their 60s, 70s and even 80s. These modern-day hunter-gatherers are not plagued by the lifestyle diseases listed above. Apparently, they are doing something right.

The Stone Age diet may prevent today's common lifestyle diseases.

Nor were they runts. Research reveals that Stone Age men and women of 25,000 years ago were about the same size as us. The men averaged 5-feet 11-inches, and the women were about 5-feet 6-inches. Over 2 million years, stature gradually increased to these dimensions. In fact, it wasn't until the advent of agriculture about 10,000 years ago that humans lost stature not to be regained until the past 100 years. It appears that something about the dietary change, which accompanied farming, produced smaller people.

With the coming of an agrarian lifestyle also came higher infant mortality, a reduced life span, iron deficiency, and bone disorders such as osteoporosis and dental cavities. Modern people are still afflicted with many of these same disorders.

In only 10,000 years — fewer in most parts of the world — agriculture reshaped our diets and our health. While a hundred centuries may seem like a long time, it's really not in the context of nearly 2 million years of man's time as a genus on earth. If human existence was represented by 24 hours, farming would have been around for only the last eight minutes, far too little time for the body to have adapted to our currently popular diet. Modern men and women have bodies meant for a diet different from what most eat now.

So what should you eat? The short answer is to eat mostly from those foods that our ancestors have eaten throughout most of the last 2 million years: lean meats, preferably from wild game or range-free animals; fish; poultry; shellfish; fresh vegetables and fruits in season, and close to their natural state; and nuts, seeds and dried fruit in small amounts. Those foods that are newest, and especially those that are highly processed, should be eaten in the smallest amounts. Now let's take a look at the details of Mother Nature's training table.

The human body's optimal fuels.

FOOD AS FUEL

Times change. Fifty years ago, endurance athletes were advised to avoid starchy foods such as bread and potatoes, and to eat more vegetables and meats instead. In the 1970s, a dietary shift away from protein with an increase in carbohydrates, especially starches, began. The 1980s brought concerns for fat in the diet, and low-fat and fat-free foods boomed. Now, the pendulum seems to be swinging the other direction with the realization that certain fats are beneficial, and some carbohydrates are deleterious in large quantities.

Sports nutrition is an evolving science.

The crux of your daily dietary decisions is the relative mix of the four macronutrients you consume. Those nutrients are protein, fat, carbohydrate and water. How much of each you include in your diet has a great deal to do with how well you train and race.

PROTEIN

The word protein is derived from the Greek word proteios, meaning "first" or "of primary importance." That's fitting because determining macronutrient balance begins with protein intake.

Protein has a checkered history in the world of athletics. Greek and Roman competitors believed that the strength, speed and endurance qualities of animals could be gained by merely eating their meat. Lion meat was in great demand. In the 1800s, protein was considered the major fuel of exercise, so athletes also ate prodigious quantities of meat. In the early part of the 20th century, scientists came to understand that fat and carbohydrate provide most of our energy for movement. By the 1960s, athletic diets began to change reflecting this shift in knowledge. In fact, little interest was paid to the role of protein in sports fuel throughout most of the 1970s and 1980s. That changed in the last 10 years as more research was done on this almost forgotten macronutrient.

Protein has many functions in the athlete's body.

Protein plays a key role in health and athletic performance. It is necessary to repair muscle damage, maintain the immune system, manufacture hormones and enzymes, replace red blood cells that carry oxygen to the muscles, and produce perhaps 10 percent of the energy needed for long or intense workouts and races. It also stimulates the secretion of glucagon, a hormone that allows the body to use fat for fuel more efficiently.

Protein is so important to the athlete that it may determine the outcome of races. For example, a recent study of Olympians by the International Center for Sports Nutrition in Omaha, Nebraska, compared the diets of medalists and non-medalists. The only significant difference found was that the winners ate more protein than those who did not medal.

Performance is so dependent on dietary protein because the body is unable to produce all it needs from scratch. And, unlike carbohydrate and fat, protein is not stored in the body at fuel depot sites for later use. It is used to meet immediate needs, such as those listed above, with any excesses converted to carbohydrate or fat.

Dietary protein is made up of 20 amino acids useable by the human body as building blocks for replacing damaged cells. Most of these amino acids are readily produced when a need arises, but there are nine that the body cannot manufacture. These "essential" amino acids must come from the diet for all of the protein-related functions to continue normally. If your diet is lacking in protein, the body is likely to break down muscle tissues to satisfy the areas of greater need, thus resulting in muscle wasting. This is evidenced in a 1988 study of the 7-Eleven cycling team. During the Tour de France that year it was discovered that the circumferences of the riders' thighs decreased during three weeks of racing. After studying their diets, the team doctor determined that they were protein deficient.

If essential amino acids are missing from the diet, the body cannibalizes tissue.

The body's demand for protein is quite high as there is a lot of turnover. Approximately 20 percent of your body weight is protein. About two-thirds of a pound of this protein is replaced every day. At least a fourth of this daily requirement must come from your diet with the remainder produced by recycling.

The recommendations for protein intake vary widely.

Unfortunately, there is not a general agreement within the nutritional field regarding the recommended protein intake for endurance athletes. The U.S. recommended daily allowance for protein is 0.013 ounces per pound of body weight (0.8 grams per kilogram) daily, but that is likely far too low for an athlete. Peter Lemon, a noted protein researcher at Kent State University, in Ohio, suggests about 0.020 to 0.022 ounces of protein per pound of body weight each day (1.2-1.4 g/kg). During a period of heavy weightlifting, such as in the MS phase described in Chapter 13, Lemon recommends a high of 0.028 ounces per pound (1.8 g/kg). The American Dietetic Association suggests a high-end protein intake of 0.032 ounces per pound (2.0 g/kg) each day. A 1997 non-scientific survey of sports scientists from around the world found a rather broad range of 0.020 to 0.040 ounces per pound (1.2-2.5 g/kg) suggested for endurance athletes daily. Applying these recommendations for a 150-pound multisport athlete, the possible range, excluding the U.S. RDA, would be three to six ounces of protein each day. Table 16.1 shows how much protein there is in common foods.

So much for numbers and generalizations. How much do *you* need? Are *you* getting enough? One way to determine this is to evaluate your physical and mental well-being. For example, indicators that you may need more protein in your diet are:

- Frequent colds or sore throats.
- Slow recovery following workouts.
- An irritable demeanor.
- Poor response to training (slow to get in shape).
- Slow fingernail growth and easily broken nails.
- Thin hair or unusual hair loss.
- Chronic fatigue.
- Poor mental focus.
- Sugar cravings.
- Pallid complexion.
- Cessation of menstrual periods.

Note that none of these indicators is sure-fire proof of the need for more protein,

TABLE 16.1

Protein content of common foods per 3.5 ounce serving (100 grams)

FOOD	PROTEIN OUNCES (GRAMS)
Animal sources	
Sirloin steak, broiled	1.05 (30)
Chicken breast	1.05 (30)
Swiss cheese	1.01 (29)
Pork loin	0.92 (26)
Hamburger	0.92 (26)
Cheddar cheese	0.85 (24.5)
Tuna	0.82 (23)
Haddock	0.82 (24)
Venison	0.73 (21)
Cottage cheese, low-fat	0.43 (12)
Whole egg	0.42 (12)
Egg white	0.36 (10)
Milk, skim	0.12 (3)
Plant sources	
Almonds, dried, 12	0.71 (20)
Tofu, extra firm	0.39 (11)
Bagel	0.38 (11)
Kidney beans	0.30 (9)
Rye bread	0.29 (8)
Cereal, corn flakes	0.28 (8)
Refried beans	0.22 (6)
Baked beans	0.17 (5)
Hummus	0.17 (5)
Soy milk	0.10 (3)
Brown rice, cooked	0.09 (2.5)
Tomato, red	0.03 (1)

Do you need more protein?

as each may have other causes. A dietary analysis by a registered dietitian, or by the use of a computer software program such as *Diet Balancer*, may help make the determination if you have concerns. Increasing your protein intake to see how it effects you is another, simple option. It's unlikely that you will eat too much protein. Even at 30 percent of daily calories that is often recommended in diets such as the Zone, the excess, if any, will be converted to glycogen or fat and stored. Such high-protein diets pose no health risk for otherwise healthy individuals so long as plenty of water is consumed each day to help with the removal of nitrogen, a by-product of protein metabolism.

If you eat a vegetarian diet and restrict calories, you are probably protein deficient.

Animal foods are the most efficient and effective way to get the nine essential proteins as ounce for ounce they are richer in protein than plant sources and provide all of the amino acids in the proper ratios. Animal sources also provide B vitamins and minerals such as highly absorbable iron and zinc, which are lacking in plant foods. Vegetable protein is of lower quality because it's not as digestible, and lacks one or more of the essential amino acids. It takes large quantities of plant food and smart combining of foods to meet protein needs on a vegetarian diet.

Eat protein at every meal.

Many people think of hamburger, bacon, sausage, luncheon meats and hot dogs when they decide to eat more protein. These foods and certain other protein sources, such as cheese and whole milk, are high in saturated fat, which is closely linked to heart disease in research. Such foods are best eaten infrequently and in small amounts. Better animal sources of protein are lean meats from wild game or free-ranging cattle, seafood, poultry and egg whites. Such foods and others high in protein should be eaten throughout the day and not simply consumed in one meal.

FAT

In the 1980s, Western society created such a terrifying specter of dietary fat that many multisport athletes now see all types of fat as the "enemy" and try to entirely eliminate it from their diet. Indeed, there are some types of fat that should be kept at low levels. These are saturated fats, which are found in prodigious quantities in feedlot cattle, and trans fatty acids, which are the human-made fats found in many highly processed foods and called "hydrogenated" on the label. Hydrogenated fats lead to artery clogging, the same as the saturated variety.

The health benefits of fat.

Don't confuse these "bad" fats with all types of fat. There are, in fact, many health benefits associated with eating fat, such as preventing dry, scaly skin and dull, brittle hair. More importantly, fat helps to maintain a regular menstrual cycle in women and prevent colds and other infections common to serious athletes. It also assists with the manufac-

Are you really overtrained?

Low dietary intake of the mineral iron may be the most common nutritional deficiency for serious multisport athletes, especially women. Unfortunately, it goes undetected in most.

A 1988 university study of female high school cross-country runners found 45 percent had low iron stores. In the same study, 17 percent of the boys were low. Other research conducted on female college athletes showed that 31 percent were iron deficient. Up to 80 percent of women runners were below normal iron stores in a 1983 study.

Commonly accepted, although still debated, causes of iron depletion include high-volume running, especially on hard surfaces; too much anaerobic training; chronic intake of aspirin; travel to high altitude; excessive menstrual flow; and a diet low in animal-food products. Athletes most at risk for iron deficiency, in the order of their risk, are runners, women, endurance athletes, vegetarians, those who sweat heavily, dieters and those who have recently donated blood.

The symptoms of iron deficiency include loss of endurance, chronic fatigue, high exercise heart rate, low power, frequent injury, recurring illness and an attitude problem. Since many of these symptoms are the same as in overtraining, the athlete may correctly cut back on exercise, begin feeling better, and return to training only to find an almost immediate relapse. In the early stages of iron depletion, performance may show only slight decrements, but additional training volume and intensity cause further declines. Many unknowingly flirt with this level of "tired blood" frequently.

If a deficiency is suspected, what should you do? Once a year have a blood test to determine your healthy baseline levels of serum ferritin, hemoglobin, reticulocytes and haptoglobin. This should be done during the Transition, Prep or Base training period when training volume and intensity are low. This blood test should be done in a fasted state with no exercise for 15 hours prior. Your health-care provider will help you understand the results. Then, if the symptoms of low iron appear, a follow-up test may support or rule this out as the culprit. Your blood indicators of iron status may be "normal" based on the reference range, but low in relation to your baseline. Many exercise scientists believe that even this obvious dip may adversely effect performance.

Should the blood test indicate an abnormally low iron status, an increased dietary intake of iron is necessary. You may want to have a registered dietitian analyze your eating habits for adequate iron consumption. The RDA for women and teenagers is 15mg per day. Men should consume 10mg. Endurance athletes may need more. The normal North American diet contains about 6mg of iron for every 1000 calories eaten, so a female athlete restricting food intake to 2000 calories a day while exercising strenuously can easily create a low-iron condition in a few weeks.

Dietary iron comes in two forms — heme and non-heme. Heme iron is found in animal meat. Plant foods are the source of non-heme iron. Very little of the iron you eat is absorbed by the body regardless of source, but heme iron has the best absorption rate at about 15 percent. Up to 5 percent of non-heme iron is taken up by the body. So the most effective way to increase iron status is by eating meat, especially red meat. Humans probably developed this capacity to absorb iron from red meat as a result of our omnivorous, hunter-gatherer origins. Plant sources of iron, although not very available to the human body due to their accompanying phytates, are raisins, leafy green vegetables, dates, dried fruits, lima beans, baked beans, broccoli, baked potatoes, soybeans and brussel sprouts. Other sources are listed in Table 16.1.

Iron absorption from any of these foods, whether plant or animal, is decreased if they are accompanied at meals by egg yolk, coffee, tea, wheat or cereal grains. Calcium and zinc also reduce the ability of the body to take up iron. Including fruits, especially citrus fruit, in meals enhances iron absorption.

Don't use iron supplements unless under the supervision of your health-care provider. Some people are susceptible to iron overload, a condition called hemochromatosis marked by toxic deposits in the skin, joints and liver. Other symptoms, including fatigue and malaise, may mimic iron deficiency and overtraining. Also note that ingesting iron supplements is the second leading cause of poisoning in children. Aspirin is first. ❖

TABLE 16.2

Iron content of common foods per 3.5 ounces (100 grams)

FOOD	IRON (MG)
Heme (up to 15% absorption)	
Canned clams	27.9
Beef liver, braised	6.77
Sirloin steak, broiled	3.36
Canned tuna	3.19
Hamburger, broiled	2.44
Boston Blade, roasted	1.60
Chicken breast, roasted without skin	1.03
Pork loin, broiled	0.81
Manhattan clam chowder	0.77
Turkey breast, roasted without skin	0.46
Non-heme (up to 5% absorption)	
Dried sulfured peaches	4.06
Oatmeal, instant	3.57
Spinach, raw	2.71
Swiss chard, raw	2.26
Dried figs	2.23
Lentils, cooked	1.11
Green pea soup	0.78

ture of hormones, such as testosterone and estrogen, and nerve and brain cells, and is important for carrying and absorbing the vitamins A, D, E and K. Fat is also the body's most efficient source of energy: Every gram of fat provides nine calories, compared with four each for protein and carbohydrate. You may find that eating more fat improves your long-term recovery and capacity to train at a high level, if you previously have been low in fat intake.

After three decades of believing that high-carbohydrate eating is best for performance, there is now compelling evidence, albeit in the early stages, that eating more fat may be good for endurance athletes, especially in very long events such as an Ironman-distance race. Several studies reveal that eating a diet high in fat causes the body to preferentially use fat for fuel, and that eating a high-carbohydrate diet results in the body relying more heavily on limited stores of muscle glycogen for fuel. Theoretically, even the skinniest triathlete has enough fat stored to last for 40 hours or more at a low intensity without refueling, but only enough carbohydrate for about three hours at most.

A study at State University of New York illustrates the benefits of fat. Researchers had a group of runners eat a higher-than-usual fat diet consisting of 38-percent fat and 50-percent carbohydrate calories for one week. The second week they ate a more typical high-carbohydrate diet with 73 percent of calories coming from carbos and 15 percent from fat. At the end of each week the subjects were tested for maximum aerobic capacities and ran to exhaustion on a treadmill. On the higher-fat diet their VO$_2$max was 11 percent greater than when they were on the high-carbohydrate diet. On the higher-fat diet they also lasted 9 percent longer on the run to exhaustion.

A 1994 study conducted by Tim Noakes, M.D., Ph.D., and author of *The Lore of Running* (1991, Leisure Press), along with colleagues at the University of Cape Town in South Africa found that after cyclists ate a diet of 70-percent fat for two weeks, their endurance at a low intensity improved significantly compared with cycling after a diet

New evidence supports eating more fat for improved endurance performance.

high in carbohydrates for two weeks. At high intensities, there was no difference in the performances. Fat did just as well as carbohydrate.

Other research has shown that our greatest fears associated with dietary fat — risk for heart disease and weight gain — do not occur when eating a diet high in what might be called "good" fats. The good fats are "monounsaturated" and "omega-3" and were plentiful in our Stone Age ancestors' diets. These fats include the oils and spreads of almonds, avocado, hazelnut, macadamia nut, pecan, cashew and olive. Other good sources are the oils of coldwater fish, such as tuna, salmon and mackerel. The red meat of wild game also provides significant amounts of monounsaturated and omega-3 fats.

The bottom line on fat is to select the leanest cuts of meat (wild game, if possible), trim all the visible fat from the meat; include seafood and poultry; eat low- or non-fat dairy; avoid hydrogenated, trans fatty acids in packaged foods; and regularly include monounsaturated fat in your diet. Eating 20 to 30 percent of your calories from fat, with an emphasis on the good fats, is not harmful, and may actually be helpful for training and racing.

Dietary-fat recommendations.

CARBOHYDRATE

The overly zealous athlete who learns that carbohydrate is important for performance often overeats carbohydrate at the expense of protein and fat — and his or her health. A day in the life of such a person may find that breakfast is cereal, toast and orange juice; a bagel is eaten as a mid-morning snack; lunch is a baked potato with vegetables; sports bars or pretzels are eaten in the afternoon; and supper is pasta with bread. Not only is such a diet excessively high in starch with an overemphasis on wheat, it is likely to produce dangerously low protein and fat levels. Such a dietary plan could be improved by replacing the cereal with an egg-white omelet and including fresh fruit, topping the potato with tuna, snacking on mixed nuts and dried fruit, by adding shrimp to the pasta and by dipping the bread in olive oil as Italians do.

Look for ways to add protein and good fat to your carbohydrate-rich diet.

When you eat a high-carbohydrate meal or snack, the pancreas releases insulin to regulate the level of blood sugar. That insulin stays in the blood for up to two hours, just in time for another high-carbohydrate snack, during which time it has other effects, such as preventing the body from utilizing stored fat, converting carbohydrate and protein to body fat and moving fat in the blood to storage sites. This may explain why, despite serious training and eating a "healthy" diet, some athletes are unable to lose body fat.

High-carbohydrate meals cause the pancreas to release insulin.

Some carbohydrates enter the blood stream sooner than others producing an exaggerated blood-sugar response and quickly bringing about all of the negative aspects of high insulin described above. These rapidly digested carbohydrates are high on the glycemic index — a relatively new food rating system developed for diabetics. Foods low on the glycemic index produce a less dramatic rise in blood sugar, and help avoid the craving for more sugary food that comes with eating high-glycemic carbohydrates. Table 16.3 lists some common high, moderate, low and very low glycemic foods.

How a carbohydrate food is prepared and the other foods it is eaten with affects its glycemic index. Adding fat to a sugary food lowers its glycemic index. An example of this is ice cream that has a moderate glycemic despite the presence of high sugar. In the same way, adding fat protein or fiber to a meal that includes a high or moderate glycemic-index carbohydrate reduces the meal's effect on your blood sugar levels and turns it into a "timed-release food capsule."

Notice in Table 16.3 that many of the foods that are moderate to high glycemic are

				TABLE 16.3

Glycemic index of common foods

High Glycemic Index (80% or higher)

Bread, French	Molasses	Potatoes, baked	Rice Chex	Rice, white
Corn flakes	Parsnips	Potatoes, instant	Rice, instant	Tapioca
Grapenuts flakes	Pasta, rice	Rice cakes	Rice Krispies	Tofu frozen dessert

Moderate Glycemic Index (50-80%)

All-Bran cereal	Bread, rye	Doughnuts	Pea soup	Pumpkin
Apricots	Bread, wheat	Ice cream	Pineapple	Raisins
Bagels	Bread, white	Mango	Popcorn	Rice, brown
Bananas	Corn chips	Muesli	Potato chips	Rye crisps
Barley	Cornmeal	Muffins	Potatoes, boiled	Soft drinks
Beets	Corn, sweet	Oat bran	Potatoes, mashed	Taco shells
Black bean soup	Couscous	Oatmeal	Potatoes, sweet	Watermelon
Bread, pita	Crackers	Orange juice	PowerBar	Yams

Low Glycemic Index (30-50%)

Apple	Beans, black	Grapefruit juice	Pasta	Rye
Apple juice	Beans, lima	Grapes	Pears	Tomato soup
Apple sauce	Beans, pinto	Kiwifruit	Peas, black-eyed	Yogurt, fruit
Beans, baked	Chocolate	Oranges	Peas, split	

Very Low Glycemic Index (less than 30%)

Barley	Beans, soy	Grapefruit	Milk	Peanuts
Beans, kidney	Cherries	Lentils	Peaches	Plums

the ones we have typically thought of as "healthy" and therefore eaten in the largest amounts. These include the starchy foods — cereal, bread, rice, pasta, potatoes, crackers, bagels, pancakes and bananas. No wonder so many endurance athletes are always hungry and have a have a hard time losing excess body fat. Their blood sugar levels are routinely kept at high levels causing regular cascades of insulin. Not only does high insulin negatively impact food cravings and body weight, it is also associated with such widespread health problems as high blood pressure, heart disease and diabetes. When you feel a craving for sweets and starches between meals, eat some protein. That usually cures it.

It is necessary to replenish carbohydrate stores in the muscles and liver during long and intense training sessions and races. That's why sports drinks and gels are used during exercise. In the 30 minutes immediately following such a breakthrough session is when high-glycemic carbohydrates and insulin are again beneficial. This is the time to use a commercial recovery drink or food. Combining protein with a high-glycemic food has been shown to effectively boost recovery. Otherwise sports drinks, gels and soft drinks should be avoided. Other high and moderate glycemic-index foods should be consumed in moderation.

There are appropriate times to eat high-glycemic foods.

Eating a diet extremely high in carbohydrate is not unanimously supported by the scientific literature, and when compared with a moderate- to low-carbohydrate diet, may cause your body to rely more heavily on glycogen, with an associated increase in blood lactate levels, and reduce your use of fat as a fuel for exercise.

WATER

Many multisport athletes don't drink enough fluids, leaving them perpetually on the edge of dehydration. In this state, recovery is compromised and the risk of illness rises. Drinking throughout the day is one of the simplest, and yet most effective means of boosting performance for such athletes. Since sports drinks and most fruit juices are high to moderate on the glycemic index, the best fluid replacement between workouts is water.

Dehydration results in a reduction of plasma making the blood into a thick sludge, and forcing the heart and body to work harder moving it. Even with slight dehydration, exercise intensity and duration are negatively affected. For example, a runner who normally covers 10,000 meters in 35 minutes, but loses 2 percent of body weight as fluids, will slow by about 84 seconds. Pace decreases by about 2 percent for each 1 percent of body weight lost in dehydration.

Slight dehydration hurts performance.

A 150-pound adult loses a little more than one-half gallon a day just in living, not including swimming, cycling and running. Up to half of this loss is through urine at the

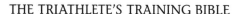

rate of about one-and-a-half to two ounces per hour. Heavy training, or a hot and humid environment can increase the loss to two gallons daily through heavy sweating.

Unfortunately, the human thirst mechanism is not very effective. By the time we sense thirst, dehydration is already well under way. Following prolonged and intense training or racing, it may take 24 to 48 hours to rehydrate if thirst is the controlling factor. In contrast, a dog will drink up to 10 percent of its body weight immediately following exercise, replacing all lost water. It's important to drink water steadily throughout the day when you are training whether you are thirsty or not.

Get in eight to 12 cups of water per day, based on your body size and training load. For every pound lost during exercise, an additional two cups of water is needed. You can also use your rate of urination and urine color as a guide. You should need to visit the toilet at least once every two hours during the day and your urine should be clear to straw colored. If you aren't achieving these standards, drink more.

Thirst is not a good indicator of the need for water.

DIET AND PERFORMANCE

How the macronutrients protein, fat, carbohydrate and water are mixed in your diet has a lot to do with how well you train and race, and certainly no less important, how healthy you are.

In recent human and animal studies examining the effects of diet on performance, several have found that increased dietary fat enhances endurance and aerobic capacity. The benefit seems to increase as the duration of the exercise lengthens. During short, high-intensity efforts there appears to be no significant difference, although most studies find a slight advantage for high-carbohydrate ingestion in such events.

Moderate levels of dietary fat may enhance endurance in long events.

One of the downsides resulting from eating a high-carbohydrate, low-fat diet is a greater production of lactic acid by the muscles during exercise, and even at rest. This is probably the result of the body using carbohydrate preferentially for fuel when it is abundantly available, while not burning as much fat. Carbohydrate seems to "turn off" the body's fat-utilization processes.

Additionally, several studies have found the rather surprising result that coronary heart disease risk factors are made worse on a high-carbohydrate, low-fat diet when compared with a more moderate intake of both nutrients that emphasizes monounsaturated and polyunsaturated fats. These worsening risk-factor shifts include lowered HDL ("good") cholesterol, increased LDL ("bad") cholesterol and elevated triglyceride levels. There is much to be learned about the interaction of diet and health.

A low-fat diet may prolong recovery.

A diet exceptionally low in fat has also recently been shown to depress testosterone levels. Testosterone is an important hormone that assists with rebuilding tissues broken down by exercise. When fat was increased in research subjects' diets, testosterone production increased.

Eating fat in its natural state — for example, in lean meats, plants, nuts, seeds and natural oils — appears to have no deleterious effect on health. Many cultures live quite well on high-fat diets based on such foods. The problem with the standard American diet is that much, if not most, of the dietary fat is saturated, hydrogenated, altered, processed or artificial. Eating fat is not a problem unless its chemical structure is changed by food producers.

Just as with health, the foods you choose to eat immediately before a race has a direct effect on how well you do on any given day. It seems a waste to train for weeks for a certain race and then to blow it by eating inappropriate foods as the race approaches. When making final preparations for a high-intensity event, such as a sprint- or international-distance race, performance may improve if you are eating a moderate-fat diet in the neighborhood of 30 percent of total calories by carbohydrate loading for two or three days prior. On the morning of the race, a suggested pre-race meal includes up to 200 calories eaten for every hour until race time, depending on body size and what you can tolerate. So if you eat three hours before starting your warm up, 600 calories is about the top end. Most of these calories, for events that take on the order of two hours or less to complete, should come mostly from low- to moderate-glycemic index carbohydrates. Small amounts of protein may be included. Longer events may benefit from including more fat in this meal.

Carbohydrate loading may improve performance in two-hour or shorter events.

PERIODIZATION OF DIET

The optimal diet for peak performance must vary with the athlete just as the optimal training protocol must vary from person to person. We can't all eat the same things in the same relative amounts and reap the same benefits. Where your ancestors originated on the planet, and what they ate for the last 100,000 years or so, is the most important determinant of what you should eat now.

So the bottom line is that you must discover what mix of foods works best for you. If you have never experimented with this, don't automatically assume you have found it already. You may be surprised at what happens when changes are made at the training table. A word of caution: Make changes gradually and allow at least three weeks for your body to adapt to a new diet before passing judgment based on how you feel and your performance in training. It usually takes two weeks to adapt to changes before seeing any results. During the adaptation period you may feel lethargic and train poorly. For this reason, changes in diet are best done in the Transition and Prep periodization cycles early

Find the diet that's right for you.

in the season. Also, be aware that as you age, changes may occur in your body chemistry requiring further shifts in diet.

That said, an optimal diet to enhance training, racing and recovery involves not only eating moderate amounts of the macronutrients, but also varying the mix of these foods throughout the year. In other words, diet should cycle just as training cycles within a periodization plan. Protein serves as the anchor for the diet and stays relatively constant throughout the year as fat and carbohydrate rise and fall alternately. Figure 16.1 illustrates this "see-saw" effect of the periodized diet. Note that the numbers used in this figure are merely an example, and the dietary mix right for you may vary considerably.

FUELING THE IRONMAN

There are seven situations that may lead to a poor Ironman performance, or even a failure to finish the race:

- Inadequate training.
- Overtraining with an inadequate taper.
- An overly aggressive pacing strategy, especially on the bike.
- Heat intolerance.
- Dehydration.

FIGURE 16.1
The dietary periodization "seesaw." The percentages are illustration only and will vary between athletes.

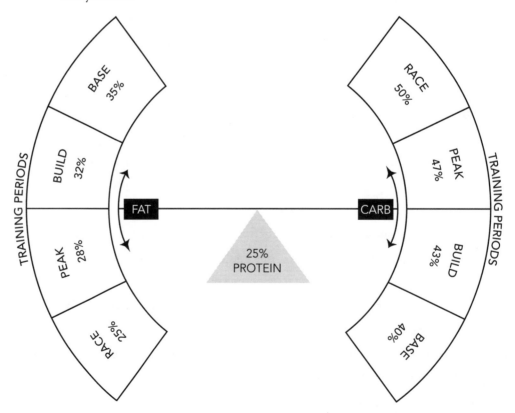

• Glycogen depletion.

• Excessive loss of sodium.

The first four should be addressed by your training program by matching your workouts to the demands of the event and your specific needs, by following a periodization plan that allows for periodic rest, by cutting back on training far enough in advance of the race to recover, by learning to hold back early on the bike, and by training in the heat. The last three are fueling issues. Let's examine them.

Your pre-race fueling strategy must ensure that you will have plenty of water, carbohydrate and sodium throughout the event. If any one of them is slighted, just finishing is a problem. They are closely related.

Fluid, carbs and sodium intake are interrelated.

The sports drink you use on the bike and run is the starting point for your fueling plan. This, of course, is largely decided by the race organizers who will provide fluids at the aid stations, so you must adapt to this product in your training. Plan to drink a lot, perhaps up to 48 ounces per hour. That's two large water bottles full, which will provide you with most of your water and much of your carbohydrate and sodium. You may also want to start the bike leg with enough sports drinks of your own choosing already on the bike for the first hour or so. This might be a MCT-spiked drink (see "Ergogenic Aids" on the following pages) with greater caloric density than a sports drink, such as Gatorlode or Metabolol Endurance. Whatever you decide to use, practice with it on your longest workouts to make sure it agrees with you.

Practice using the race's sports drink.

Maintenance of your body's glycogen stores actually starts months in advance of the race when you "teach" your body to spare glycogen and use more fat for fuel. This is done by eating a diet during your Ironman-extended Base training period that favors fat intake and limits carbohydrate, especially from high-glycemic index sources. In the last three days before the race, it still may be wise to carbohydrate load by increasing your intake of complex carbs while cutting back on fat and fiber. Liquid carbohydrate-replacement or loading drinks may work well the day before. Try it first for a lower-priority race. Such a long-term diet and pre-race shift will ensure you use glycogen sparingly, but have plenty of it on board.

Conserve and load glycogen.

The morning of the race, eat breakfast two to three hours before the start, include about 200 calories for each hour. Eat mostly from low-glycemic carbohydrates, but include some fat and protein. It's best that your fiber intake is low on race morning. In a 1984 Ironman-distance race, Japanese researchers found that those who ate the most calories at breakfast, ran the fastest marathons.

During the bike and run portions of the race, you will need to take in as many calories as you can — up to 400 calories per hour, depending on what you found works best for you in training. Assuming that there are about 100 calories in a 24-ounce bottle of sports drink, and you drink per hour, you'll need up to 200 more calories from other sources. Possibilities are gels, especially for the run; sports bars; and other solid foods. Check the labels on any of these fuels you select to make sure you are getting adequate calories. Then practice using them on a predetermined eating schedule. You may even want to set your wristwatch to beep every 15 minutes or so as a reminder to take in fuel.

Take in up to 400 calories per hour.

Low levels of sodium, called *hyponatremia*, is one of the biggest challenges you face. It's estimated that 30 percent of the Hawaii Ironman finishers have dangerously low levels of sodium in their blood. When sweating profusely, as in Kona, in October, it's possible to lose up to a liter of body fluids an hour. And since a liter of sweat contains about 2 to 3.5 grams of sodium, 24 to 42 grams could be lost in a 12-hour race. If that sodium is not replaced, hyponatremia results.

Early signs of hyponatremia include nausea, vomiting, headache, muscle cramps, weakness, slurred speech or disorientation. In extreme cases there may be seizures or coma. Athletes have died of hyponatremia.

The best way to avoid such problems is to get in plenty of sodium, both before and during the race. While carbohydrate loading, also increase your salt intake. During the race, you probably need to take in about one gram of sodium per hour. Assuming you drink two large bottles per hour on the bike and run, you will be getting about a half gram per hour, or slightly more, depending on the drink used.

Take in about one gram of sodium per hour.

The additional sodium may come from food or salt tablets. Food is preferable, especially carbohydrate-based foods, since energy intake is also necessary. Examples of common foods you may choose from are listed in Table 16.4. Notice that some are low in sodium, and therefore require excessive amounts to meet your needs. Check the labels of other foods for their sodium content. There is one gram of sodium in every 2.5 grams of salt.

The use of aspirin, ibuprofen, acetaminophen (for example, Tylenol) or other anti-inflammatories may magnify hyponatremia, so it's best not to use these products during the race. It's probably also wise to avoid such medications in the last 48 hours before racing.

TABLE 16.4

Examples of foods that may be eaten during an Ironman-distance race to provide sodium.

Food	Eat/hour
Sunshine Bavarian Sourdough Pretzels	2 pretzels
Baked Rold Gold Hard Sourdough Pretzels	2-3 pretzels
Snackwell Wheat Crackers	15 crackers
Premium Fat-Free Saltine Crackers	20 crackers
Protein 21 Bar	2 bars
Balance Bars	4 bars
PowerBar	5-6 bars
PowerGel	10 packets

ANTIOXIDANT SUPPLEMENTS

Generally it's a good idea to meet your nutritional needs with real foods and use food supplements sparingly. Scientists and supplement designers just aren't as smart as nature when it comes to deciding what to include and what to leave out of foods. Real food provides everything needed for health and fitness. Adding lots of pills and potions to your diet is usually a waste of money. The exception is antioxidant supplements. Here's why.

During the process of metabolizing food and oxygen for exercise, free radicals are released which cause damage to healthy cells. This can be compared with the rusting of metal — a breakdown caused by oxidation. Hard training produces large numbers of free radicals that threaten your health and ability to recover following workouts.

Free radicals hinder recovery.

For example, one study measured by-products of free radical damage in highly trained athletes, moderately trained athletes and a sedentary group. The researchers found that the highly trained athletes had the highest levels of damage, while the moderately trained subjects had the least. The sedentary group was in the middle. A little exercise appears to be a healthy thing when it comes to free radicals, but extensive exercise or none at all causes problems.

In recent years, studies have shown that vitamins C and E reduce this damage and prevent upper respiratory infections associated with extreme physical exertion by combining with the free radicals to stop the oxidative process. The research typically uses large doses of each of these micronutrients, usually hundreds of times the RDA. The exact amounts needed have not been determined yet as variables such as age, sex, diet, body composition, size and training load are involved. Recommended daily intakes based on these studies generally fall into the ranges of 400 to 800 IU (international units) of vitamin E and 300 to 1000 mg of vitamin C.

Recommended dosages.

The problem is that in order to get even the lowest of these dosages you would have to eat *all* of these foods *daily*:

Asparagus	15 spears
Avocado	31
Broccoli	4 cups
Peaches	33
Prunes	30
Tomato juice	12 ounces
Spinach	17 cups
Wheat germ	1/4 cup

While it's true that serious athletes tend to eat more than average citizens, they seldom eat enough of the right foods. A 1989 study of triathletes who competed in the national championship, the Hawaii Ironman, or the Alabama Double Ironman found that as a group they had inadequate caloric intakes due to unusual eating habits. They also demonstrated poor food selection resulting from rigorous training schedules and limited time for eating. All of this means that getting in adequate levels of vitamin C and E is unlikely among multisport athletes.

One-a-day multiple vitamins are commonly used, but seldom provide vitamins C and E in large enough quantities, so you may need to supplement your diet with individual dosages, especially vitamin E. It appears that these supplements should be taken with meals twice a day for best results.

Possible problems of taking vitamin E.

Vitamin C has a low level of risk at levels of 300 to 1000mg, but high dosages of vitamin E can cause problems for those who are deficient in vitamin K. Those on blood-thinning medications or high doses of pain relievers should also be cautious with vitamin E. Check with your health-care provider before starting supplementation with either vitamin C or E.

ERGOGENIC AIDS

Several years ago university researchers asked a group of elite athletes, "If you could take a pill that would ensure a gold medal in the next Olympics, but you would die within five years, would you take it?" The overwhelming answer was "Yes!"

Such attitudes have led athletes to experiment with anabolic steroids, erythropoietin (EPO), amphetamines and other dangerous and banned ergogenic aids. Some have consequently died in their quest for athletic excellence. Others have simply wasted their money on products that have no benefit beyond a placebo effect, and have not withstood scientific investigation.

There is no magic pill that will guarantee an Olympic medal, or even a better-than-average performance. Training and habitual diet are still the most important components of athletic excellence. There are, however, a few products that go beyond a normal diet and that science has generally found effective. Realize, however, that in the scientific study of almost anything, there are often contradictory results. Also, not all ergogenic aids have the same benefits for everyone. Individualization applies here just as it does in training.

Ergogenic aids may produce side effects.

Here is a summary of some found to work most of the time for athletes in swimming, cycling and running. Before trying these, or any other dietary supplement, it's a good idea to talk with your health-care provider. Diabetes, hypertension, or any number of other medical conditions may present reasons you shouldn't use one or more of these supplements. They are not free of side effects. It's also a good idea to try out a product in training before using it in a race.

CAFFEINE

No ergogenic aid is more commonly used by athletes than caffeine. While a cup of coffee doesn't sound too sinister, the International Olympic Committee (IOC) has determined that in sufficient quantities caffeine unfairly aids performance, and is illegal.

Numerous scientific studies of caffeine's effects over the past 20 years have produced many contradictions. Most have shown benefits for long-distance endurance athletes. A British study, however, found no benefits for marathoner runners, but significant aid for milers. The majority of studies have suggested that caffeine only helps in events lasting longer than 90 minutes, but others have shown improvement in 60- and even 45-minute competitions.

The reported benefits of caffeine are contradictory.

While the author of a recent study concluded that caffeine causes a complex chemical change in the muscles that stimulates more forceful contractions during a longer period of time than without it, most have found that caffeine simply spares muscle glycogen during endurance exercise. Glycogen is an energy source stored in the muscles. When glycogen runs low, the athlete is forced to slow down or stop. Anything that causes the body to conserve this precious fuel, as caffeine appears to do, allows an athlete to maintain a fast pace for a longer time. For example, a study of cyclists reported a 20-percent improvement in time to exhaustion following two cups of coffee one hour before testing. The beneficial effects peak at about one hour after consumption and seem to last three to five hours.

The IOC's banned limit requires about six to eight five-ounce cups of coffee in an hour, depending on the athlete's size. While that's quite a bit to drink, it's certainly possible. It's interesting to note that some recent research suggests that caffeine at the illegal level actually has a negative effect on performance.

Legal and beneficial levels of caffeine.

Most studies find that 1.4 to 2.8mg of caffeine per pound of body weight taken an hour before exercise benefits most subjects

TABLE 16.5	
Caffeine content in 6 ounces (180 ml) of common products.	
Drip coffee	180 mg
Instant coffee	165 mg
Percolated coffee	149 mg
Brewed tea	60 mg
Mountain Dew	28 mg
Chocolate syrup	24 mg
Coca-Cola	23 mg
Pepsi Cola	19 mg

engaged in endurance exercise. That's about two or three cups of coffee for a 154-pound person. Athletes have also been known to use other products high in caffeine before and during competition. Table 16.5 lists the caffeine content of common products.

Possible side effects are numerous. While caffeine may seem a safe and effective aid, be aware that there are possible complications. Most studies have shown it to have a diuretic effect on non-exercisers, although one using athletes found little increased fluid loss during exercise. In people not familiar with caffeine, it may bring on anxiety, muscle tremors, gastrointestinal cramps, diarrhea, upset stomach and nausea. These are not good things to experience before a race. Caffeine also inhibits the absorption of thiamin, a vitamin needed for carbohydrate metabolism, and several minerals including calcium and iron.

If you normally have a cup or two of coffee in the morning, you will probably have no side effects if it's taken before a race. It appears that the benefits are no different for non-coffee drinkers or for regular users. If you don't drink coffee, but are considering using it before a competition, try it several times before workouts to see how it effects you.

BRANCHED CHAIN AMINO ACIDS

During intense workouts and those lasting longer than about three hours, the body turns to protein to provide fuel. As much as 10 percent of the energy requirement may be met this way. Three essential amino acids, ones that must be present in the diet since the body can't synthesize them, make up about a third of the muscle's protein. These are leucine, isoleucine and valine. Collectively they are called branched chain amino acids (BCAA).

Benefits of BCAA Several studies have shown that supplementing the diet with BCAA enhances endurance performance in several ways:

• BCAA help to maintain the immune system following exhaustive workouts and races reducing the likelihood of overtraining. Thus they have the potential to aid recovery.

• BCAA have been shown to maintain muscle mass, power and endurance during exhaustive, multiday endurance events such as bicycle stage races or crash training (see Chapter 14).

• BCAA may help to reduce central nervous system fatigue thus maintaining speed late in a race.

• BCAA promote the use of fat for fuel while conserving glycogen.

BCAA may be purchased in health food stores and drug stores that sell food supplements. They should come in a dark bottle to protect the capsules from light, and the label should list each of the individual amino acids preceded by an "L" as in "L-valine." This ensures adequate absorption.

There are four times in your season to use BCAA — during the maximum strength (MS) phase, in the Build and Peak training periods, for long and intense races and while training intensely at high altitudes. Here are guidelines for supplementing with BCAA:

How to use BCAA.

• Take about 35 mg of BCAA daily for each pound of body weight, but only at the times indicated above. A 150-pound athlete would take 5250mg, or about 5 grams daily. A 120 pounder could consume 4200mg, or about 4 grams a day.

• One to two hours before an MS strength workout, a high-intensity workout in the Build or Peak periods, or an A-priority race take one-half of your daily dose. Then again one to two hours before bed time the same day take the other half.

The only potential side effect of taking BCAA has to do with imbalances in dietary intakes of amino acids. When eating meat, all of the amino acids are present in the proper ratios, but excessive supplementation with BCAA may upset the balance between them. Some scientists and nutritionists are concerned that this may have long-term health implications.

A possible downside of BCAA use.

MEDIUM CHAIN TRIGLYCERIDES

Medium chain triglycerides (MCT) are processed fats that are metabolically different from other fats in that they are quickly absorbed by the digestive system and aren't readily stored as body fat. Studies have shown that use of MCT can improve endurance and late-race speed in long races such as a half Ironman or Ironman.

MCT is best for long races.

In a recent study at the University of Capetown in South Africa, six experienced cyclists rode two hours at about 73 percent of maximum heart rate. Immediately after this steady, low-intensity ride, they time-trialed 40 kilometers at maximum effort. They did this three times on different days using a different drink for each attempt. One drink was a normal carbohydrate sports drink. Another was an MCT-only beverage. A third ride used a sports drink spiked with MCT.

With the MCT-only drink their average 40km time was 1:12:08. The carbohydrate sports drink produced a 1:06:45. With the mixed MCT-carbohydrate beverage their time was 1:05:00 — a significant improvement. The study's authors believe that the MCT spared glycogen during the two-hour steady ride allowing the riders to better utilize carbohydrate during the more intense time trial.

MCT spares muscle glycogen.

An MCT-sports drink mix may benefit your performance late in races that last three hours or longer. Champion Nutrition (1-800-225-4831) makes a powdered sports drink product called Metabolol Endurance' which contains MCT along with carbohydrate, fat and protein. You can create a long-race drink for yourself by mixing 16 ounces of your favorite sports drink with four tablespoons of MCT. You can purchase liquid MCT at a local health foods store. There are no known side effects for MCT used in this manner.

CREATINE MONOHYDRATE

Creatine monohydrate is one of the most recent additions to the ergogenics field, having its first known usage in athletics in 1993. Since then, the number of creatine studies have steadily increased, but a lot of questions still remain unanswered.

Creatine is a substance found in dietary meat and fish, but can also be created in the liver, kidneys and pancreas. It is stored in muscle tissue in the form of creatine phosphate, a fuel used mostly during maximum efforts of up to about 15 seconds and, to a lesser extent, in intense efforts lasting a few minutes.

Creatine benefits brief, powerful movement.

The amount of creatine formed by the human body is not enough to boost performance, but scientists have found that by supplementing the diet for a few days, certain types of performance are enhanced. In order to get an adequate amount of creatine from the diet, an athlete would have to eat up to five pounds of rare meat or fish daily. Supplementing appears to be quite effective in increasing stored creatine for most people.

A few years ago, scientists from Sweden, Britain and Estonia tried creatine supplements on a group of runners. Following a creatine-loading period, the runners ran a 4 x 1000-meter interval workout at maximum effort. Compared with the pre-test results, the creatine-supplemented subjects improved their total 4000-meter times by an average of 17 seconds while the placebo-control group slowed by one second. The relative advantage the creatine users experienced increased as the workout progressed. In other words, they experienced less fatigue and were faster at the end.

There is still not a lot known about creatine supplementation, but the benefits are probably greatest for maximizing the gains from brief exercise bouts, such as interval and hill repeat workouts. Some users believe that it decreases body fat, but it may only appear that way since body weight increases due to water retention as fat stays the same. Also, creatine does not directly build muscle tissue. Instead it provides the fuel so more power training is possible within a given workout, thus stimulating fast-twitch muscle fiber growth.

Creatine may help in the MS phase and Build period.

The use of creatine by endurance athletes is equivocal. The best times to supplement with creatine for the multisport athlete, if it is used at all, is during the Maximum Strength weight-training phase and the higher-intensity Build period of training. Athletes who are low in force and power qualities stand to benefit the most at these times. About 20 to 30 percent of those who take creatine experience no measurable physiological changes. Vegetarians may stand to realize the greatest gains from creatine since they typically have low levels due to their meat-free diet.

Most studies have used amounts such as 20 to 30 grams a day taken in four to five doses during a four- to five-day loading phase. One found the same muscle levels, however, on as little as three grams daily for 30 days prior to an important. After loading, muscle creatine levels can be maintained at high levels for four to five weeks with two or three grams taken daily. Dissolving the creatine in water and drinking it with grape or orange juice seems to improve absorption.

According to scientists who have studied creatine, there is little health risk since it is passively filtered from the blood and puts no extra work load on the kidneys, but the longest study is only 10 weeks. Scientists do know that once you stop short-term use, natural production of creatine is regained. The only well-established side effect is the addition of two or three pounds of extra body weight during the loading phase, probably from water retention, which quickly disappears. A greater concern is that creatine may give you a false positive in a urine test for kidney problems. There have also been anecdotal accounts of muscle spasm and cramping in power athletes using creatine on a long-term basis, perhaps due to a lowered concentration of magnesium in the muscles. Talk with your health-care provider before using creatine monohydrate.

Side effects are not fully understood.

SODIUM PHOSPHATE

The German Army used sodium phosphate in World War I, and even in the 1930s German athletes knew of it's worth. It has not been widely publicized in recent years, although some athletes have known about it, but kept the secret.

Sodium phosphate has the potential to improve race performance by allowing you to maintain a high pace longer, and make high-intensity efforts feel much easier.

In 1983, researchers working with elite runners found that sodium phosphate increased aerobic capacity by 9 percent and improved ventilatory threshold (like lactate threshold) by 12 percent. A more recent study of cyclists in Florida showed that using phosphate improved low-level endurance time significantly, lowered 40km time trial times by 8 percent, and raised lactate threshold by 10 percent while lowering perceived effort.

Sodium phosphate has great potential for improving endurance performance.

It appears to bring these changes by causing the hemoglobin in the red blood cells to more completely unload their stores of oxygen at the muscle. A greater supply of oxygen allows the muscles to operate aerobically at higher speeds and power outputs that would normally cause an anaerobic state.

Supplementation is similar to creatine loading. Take four grams of sodium phosphate for three days before an A-priority race. To prepare your gut for the change, take one or two grams for one or two days before starting the loading procedure. Spread out

the daily dosage by taking one-third of it with each meal. Don't take it on an empty stomach. It's best not to continue using it more than three or four times each season as continued supplementation reduces the benefits. In studies, the gains from sodium phosphate were still apparent one week after the loading stopped, meaning that races over two weeks can reap the benefits.

How to supplement.

A side effect many athletes experience while sodium phosphate loading is an upset stomach. This may not appear until several days into the routine. Feeling sick right before a race is not good for your confidence, so it's best to try the loading procedure the first time before an early season C-priority race or workout. If you find it upsets your stomach, try the following loading procedure:

Days before "A" race	Daily dosage
16-19	1-1.5g
14-15	none
9-13	1-1.5g
7-8	none
6-race day	1-1.5g

Twin Labs makes a product called Phos Fuel that is available in some health food and specialty stores such as GNC.

Long-term use may affect calcium levels.

If you have a low dietary intake of calcium or have an excessive amount of salt in your diet, sodium phosphate can cause a calcium deficiency. In this case, you would be advised not to use it. Better yet, increase your intake of dietary calcium and decrease your salt intake. Do not use calcium phosphate as no performance benefits have been linked with it.

GLYCEROL

Do you wither in the heat? In long, hot races do you cramp up in the last few miles? Do you dread riding or running on days when the temperature reaches the 90s? If so, glycerol may be just what you need.

Dehydration prevention maintains performance.

As your body loses fluid there is a corresponding drop in performance. As pointed out earlier, even a 1-percent drop in body weight due to dehydration reduces maximum work output by about 2 percent. This reduction is a result of decreased blood volume since the plasma in blood supplies sweat. A 5-percent loss of body weight is common in hot, long races. Losing 7 percent of body weight due to fluid depletion is dangerous to health and may even require hospitalization. Some athletes suffer the effects of heat more than others.

Other than just the heat, other factors may cause you to dehydrate. Sometimes all it takes is a missed aid station, or a dropped bottle on the bike. Beyond these problems, there are also physiological limits on how much fluid the human digestive tract can absorb during high-intensity racing. All of this can lead to disaster in what might have otherwise been an exceptional race.

Glycerol, a syrupy, sweet-tasting liquid, turns your body into a water-hoarding sponge. Used prior to a race, it causes the body to hold onto 50 percent more fluid than when using water alone. Because of this, fluid losses through urination are decreased and there is more water available for sweat.

Glycerol causes the body to retain water.

In one study using cyclists, body temperatures increased 40 percent less when using glycerol as compared with water only. Also, heart rate increased 5 percent less with glycerol and there was a 32-percent improvement in endurance. These are tremendous advantages that could take you from the DNF listing to the top 10. Who wouldn't want these benefits?

In recent years, glycerol products for endurance athletes have become widely available in running stores, bike shops, health-food and specialty stores, and through catalog sales. Simply mix and drink the product according to the instructions on the label. Using more will not help you, and may even cause problems.

As with anything new, you should experiment with glycerol before a workout — not a race. It has been known to cause headaches and nausea in some athletes. Better to find that out in training rather than in the most important race of the season.

There have been no long-term studies on the effect of large doses of glycerol, but it is generally considered safe as it is found naturally in dietary fats.

No side effects are known.

FINAL THOUGHTS

The supplement industry in the U.S. is not closely regulated by the government, so product purity may be an issue if any of the above products are purchased from unscrupulous manufacturers. For example, a recent analysis of a widely advertised category of dietary supplements found unidentifiable impurities in most of the products. Buy only from reputable companies whose products are well-established in the marketplace.

Also, no studies have been done on how any of the ergogenic aids described here may interact if all or most of them are used together, with other supplements, or even with many of the medications commonly used by athletes such as ibuprofen or aspirin. It's always a good idea to talk with your health-care provider before taking any supplement, all the more so if you are on any medications.

Bottom line: Use ergogenic aids cautiously and conservatively.

When using an ergogenic aid it's important that you assess the benefits, if any, for your performance. Not only does using several concurrently increase your risk, it also clouds the issue of which one provided the most the performance gain. In addition, you should always be skeptical of faster race times as a result of supplementation. Was it really the pill, or was it the placebo effect? While many athletes probably don't care, coming to understand what helps you and what doesn't will ultimately lead to your best races.

In the final analysis, training and diet provide 99.9 percent of the impetus for performance improvements. Supplements offer only a small benefit. If your training and diet are less than desirable, there is no reason to add any ergogenic supplement to the mix.

REFERENCES

American College of Sports Medicine. Antioxidants and the elite athlete. Proceedings of panel discussion, May 27, 1992, Dallas, TX.

American Dietetic Association. 1987. Nutrition and physical fitness and athletic performance. *Journal of the American Dietetics Association* 87: 933-939.

Anderson, O. 1996. Carbs, creatine & phosphate: If the King had used these uppers, he'd still be around today. *Running Research News* 12 (3): 1-4.

Appell, H.J., et al. 1997. Supplementation of vitamin E may attenuate skeletal muscle immobilization atrophy. *International Journal of Sports Medicine* 18: 157-160.

Armsey, T.D. and G.A. Green. 1997. Nutrition supplementation: Science vs hype. *The Physician and Sports Medicine* 25 (6): 77-92.

Blomstrand, E., et al. 1991. Administration of branched chain amino acids during sustained exercise — Effects on performance and on plasma concentrations of some amino acids. *European Journal of Applied Physiology* 63 (2): 83-88.

Burke, L.M. and R.S.D. Read. 1993. Dietary supplements in sport. *Sports Medicine* 15: 43-65.

Cade, R., et al. 1984. Effects of phosphate loading on 2,3-diphosphoglycerate and maximal oxygen uptake. *Medicine and Science in Sports and Exercise* 16 (3): 263-268.

Cerra, F.B., et al. 1984. Branched-chain amino acid supplementation during trekking at high altitude. *European Journal of Applied Physiology* 65: 394-398.

Clement, D.B., et al. 1984. Branched-chain metabolic support: A prospective, randomized double-blind trial in surgical stress. *Annals of Surgery* 199 (3): 286-291.

Cordain, L., R.W. Gotshall, and S.B. Eaton. 1997. Evolutionary aspects of exercise. *World Review of Nutrition and Dietetics* 81: 49-60.

Cordain, L. Department of Exercise and Sport Science, Colorado State University, Fort Collins, Colorado 80523. 1998. Personal communication with author.

Davis, J.M. 1995. Carbohydrates, branched-chain amino acids, and performance — the central fatigue hypothesis. *International Journal of Sport Nutrition* 5: S29-S38.

Dufaux, B., et al. 1981. Serum ferritin, transferrin, haptoglobin, and iron in middle- and long-distance runners, elite rowers, and professional racing cyclists. *International Journal of Sports Medicine* 2 (1): 43-46.

Eades, M.R. and M.D. Eades. 1996. *Protein Power.* New York: Bantam Books.

Eaton, S.B. and M. Konner. 1985. Paleolithic nutrition: A consideration of its nature and current implications, *The New England Journal of Medicine* 312 (5): 283-289.

Eaton, S.B., M. Shostak, and M. Konner. 1989. *The Paleolithic Prescription.* New York: Harper & Row.

Eaton, S.B. and D.A. Nelson. 1991. Calcium in evolutionary perspective. *American Journal of Clinical Nutrition* 54: 281S-287S.

Eaton, S.B. 1992. Humans, lipids and evolution. *Lipids* 27 (1): 814-820.

Evans, W., et al. 1983. Protein metabolism and endurance exercise. *The Physician and Sports Medicine* 11 (7): 63-72.

Graham, T.E. and L.L. Spriet. 1996. Caffeine and exercise performance. *Sports Science Exchange* 9 (1): 1-6.

Grandjean, A.C. 1997. Diets of elite athletes: Has the discipline of sports nutrition made an impact? *Journal of Nutrition* 127 (5 Supplement): 874S-877S.

Green, D.R., et al. 1989. An evaluation of dietary intakes of triathletes: Are RDAs being met? *Brief Communications* 89 (11): 1653-1654.

Guilland, J.C., et al. 1989. Vitamin status of young athletes including the effects of supplementation. *Medicine and Science in Sport and Exercise* 21: 441-449.

Harris, R.C., et al. 1992. Elevation of creatine in resting and exercised muscle of normal subjects by creatine supplementation. *Clinical Science* 83 (3): 367-374.

Hawley, J.A. and W.G. Hopkins. 1995. Aerobic glycolytic and aerobic lipolytic power systems: A new paradigm with implications for endurance and ultra-endurance events. *Sports Medicine* 20: 321-327.

Hawley, J.A., et al. 1996. Effects of ingesting varying concentrations of sodium on fluid balance during exercise. *Medicine and Science in Sport and Exercise* 28 (5): S350.

Hopkins, W.G. 1996. Advances in training for endurance athletes. *New Zealand Journal of Sports Medicine* 24 (3): 29-31.

Hu, F.B., et al. 1997. Dietary fat intake and the risk of coronary heart disease in women. *New England Journal of Medicine* 337 (21): 1491-1499.

International Dance and Exercise Association. 1994. Antioxidants: Clearing the confusion.

IDEA Today Sept.: 67-73.

Kanter, M.M. 1994. Free radicals, exercise, and antioxidant supplementation. *International Journal of Sport Nutrition* 4: 205-220.

Lambert, E.V., et al. 1994. Enhanced endurance in trained cyclists during moderate-intensity exercise following two weeks adaptation to a high-fat diet. *European Journal of Applied Physiology* 69: 287-293.

Lapachet, R.A., et al. 1996. Body fat and exercise endurance in trained rats adapted to a high-fat and/or high-carbohydrate diet. *Journal of Applied Physiology* 80 (4): 1173-1179.

Lemon, P.W.R. 1991. Protein and amino acid needs of the strength athlete. *International Journal of Sports Nutrition* 1: 127-145.

Lemon, P.W.R. 1996. Is increased dietary protein necessary or beneficial for individuals with a physically active lifestyle? *Nutrition Reviews* 54 (4): S169-S175.

Lyons, T.P., et al. 1990. Effects of glycerol-induced hyperhydration prior to exercise on sweating and core temperature. *Medicine and Science in Sport and Exercise* 22 (4): 477-483.

Maughan, R.J. 1995. Creatine supplementation and exercise performance. *International Journal of Sports Nutrition* 5: 94-101.

McMurtrey, J.J. and R. Sherwin. 1987. History, pharmacology and toxicology of caffeine and caffeine-containing beverages. *Clinical Nutrition* 6: 249-254.

Muoio, D.M., et al. 1994. Effect of dietary fat on metabolic adjustments to maximal VO_2 and endurance in runners. *Medicine and Science in Sports and Exercise* 26: 81-88.

Nagao, N., et al. 1991. Energy intake in the triathlon competition by means of cluster analysis. *Journal of Sports Medicine and Physical Fitness* 31 (1): 62-66.

Nemoto, I. et al. 1996. Branched-chain amino acid (BCAA) supplementation improves endurance capacities and RPE. *Medicine and Science in Sports and Exercise* 28 (5): S219.

Noakes, T., et al. 1994. Effects of a low-carbohydrate, high-fat diet prior to carbohydrate loading on endurance cycling performance. 1994. *Clinical Science* 87: S32-S33.

O'Toole, M.L. et al. 1995. Fluid and electrolyte status in athletes receiving medical care at an ultradistance triathlon. *Clinical Journal of Sports Medicine* 5 (2): 116-122.

Peters, E.M., et al. Anti-oxidant nutrient supplementation and symptoms of upper respiratory tract infections in endurance athletes. *Medicine and Science in Sports and Exercise* 26 (5): S218.

Phinney, S.D., et al. 1983. The human metabolic response to chronic ketosis with caloric restriction and preservation of submaximal exercise capabilities with reduced carbohydrate oxidation. *Metabolism* 32: 769-776.

Robergs, R.A. 1998. Glycerol hyperhydration to beat the heat? Sportscience web page: http://www.sportsci.org/traintech/glycerol/rar.htm.

Schena, F. 1992. Branched-chain amino acid supplementation during trekking at high altitude. *European Journal of Applied Physiology* 65: 394-398.

Simonson, J.C., et al. 1991. Dietary carbohydrate, muscle glycogen, and power output during rowing training. *Journal of Applied Physiology* 70: 1500-1505.

Somer, E. 1992. *The Essential Guide to Vitamins and Minerals.* New York: Harper Collins.

Stahl, A.B. 1984. Hominid dietary selection before fire. *Current Anthropology* 25 (2): 151-168.

Taimura, A. and M. Sugahara. 1996. Effect of fluid intake on performance, body temperature, and body weight loss during swimming training. *Medicine and Science in Sport and Exercise* 28 (5): S940.

Thompson, P.D., et al. 1984. The effects of high-carbohydrate and high-fat diets on the serum lipid and lipoprotein concentrations of endurance athletes. *Metabolism* 33: 1003-1010.

Venkatraman, J.T., et al. 1997. Influence of the level of dietary lipid intake and maximal exercise on the immune status in runners. *Medicine and Science in Sport and Exercise* 29 (3): 333-344.

Walsh, R.M., et al. 1994. Impaired high-intensity cycling performance time at low levels of dehydration. *International Journal of Sports Medicine* 15: 392-398.

Weltman, A., et al. 1992. Endurance training amplifies the pulsatile release of growth hormone: Effects of training intensity. *Journal of Applied Physiology* 72 (6): 2188-2196.

Wilmore, J.H. and D.L. Costill. 1994. *Physiology of Sport and Exercise.* Champaign, IL: Human Kinetics.

Wemple, R.D., et al. 1997. Caffeine vs. caffeine-free sports drinks: Effects on urine production at rest and during prolonged exercise. *International Journal of Sports Medicine* 18: 40-46.

EPILOGUE

This book was a great challenge. It was not my first, but certainly the most difficult to write owing to the complexity of multisport. Although it's rather long for a training book, there is still much that was omitted. The most glaring void is perhaps in the area of mental skills. Initially, a chapter was planned for this topic, but was eliminated along with a chapter of frequently asked questions in favor of holding down the book's size. If you want to fully develop your ability as a triathlete or duathlete, I highly recommend learning more about the psychology of training and racing. Such mental skills as motivation, confidence, focus, visualization and positive thought habits are every bit as important as swim, bike and run workouts for the athlete who is approaching his or her peak potential. See the "Recommended Reading" list for books on mental training.

The trouble with writing a book is that it is a snapshot of what is believed to be true at one point in time. Even though I've been coaching multisport athletes for 15 years, there has never been a season in which I didn't change something based on new information or experience. I expect that at some point down the road I may well disagree with some point strongly supported on these pages. To do otherwise means never growing.

In fact, during the nine months it took to write this book, I refined methods and concepts related to my training system. That was due primarily to the difficulty of trying to put on paper what you think you understand. Writing a book teaches you how much you don't know. For me that meant constantly returning to the scientific literature to check facts and conclusions. Gale Bernhardt, one of my coaching associates who edited the book from a technical viewpoint, frequently and correctly suggested that I support or clarify some point that seemed obvious to me. Such challenges were often difficult to answer, but the ensuing thought-provoking discussions and research review gave many of the thoughts expressed here much firmer foundations. For this I am indebted to her persistence.

Several hundred pages ago, I explained that the book's purpose is to take the guesswork out of training by giving the serious multisport athlete a scientifically-based system and set of tools for implementing purposeful training. I hope that this goal has been realized, and that your race performance and enjoyment of the sport are better for having read *The Triathlete's Training Bible*.

RECOMMENDED READING

Bompa, T. 1993. *Periodization of Strength.* Toronto: Veritas Publishing Inc.

Bompa, T. 1994. *Theory and Methodology of Training.* Dubuque, IA: Kendall Hunt Publishing.

Burke, E. 1996. *High-Tech Cycling.* Champaign, IL: Human Kinetics.

Cedaro, R. (Ed.). 1993. *Triathlon: Achieving Your Personal Best.* New York: Facts on File.

Evans, M. 1997. *Endurance Athlete's Edge.* Champaign, IL: Human Kinetics.

Elliott, R. 1991. *The Competitive Edge.* Mountain View, CA: TAFNEWS.

Freeman, W. 1991. *Peak When It Counts.* Mountain View, CA: TAFNEWS.

Friel, J. 1996. *The Cyclist's Training Bible.* Boulder, CO: VeloPress.

Janssen, P.G.J.M. 1987. *Training, Lactate, Pulse Rate.* Oulu, Finland: Polar Electro Oy.

Laughlin, T. and J. Delves. 1996. *Total Immersion.* New York: Fireside.

Lynch, J. and C.A. Huang. 1998. *Working Out, Working Within.* New York: Tarcher/Putnam.

Maglischo, E. 1982. *Swimming Faster.* Mountain View, CA: Mayfield Publishing Company.

Martin, D.E. and P.N. Coe. 1997. *Better Training for Distance Runners.* Champaign, IL: Leisure Press.

Niles, R. 1997. *Time-Saving Training for Multisport Athletes.* Champaign, IL: Human Kinetics.

Noakes, T. 1991. *Lore of Running.* Champaign, IL: Leisure Press.

Sleamaker, R. and R. Browning. 1996. *Serious Training for Endurance Athletes.* Champaign, IL: Leisure Press.

Town, G. and T. Kearney. 1994. *Swim, Bike, Run.* Champaign, IL: Human Kinetics.

Williams, M. 1998. *Ergogenics Edge.* Champaign, IL: Human Kinetics.

Wilmore, J.H. and D.L. Costill. 1994. *Physiology of Sport and Exercise.* Champaign, IL: Human Kinetics.

Ungerleider, S. 1996. *Mental Training for Peak Performance.* Emmaus, PA: Rodale Sports.

APPENDIX A

Athlete _____

Annual Hours _____

Season Goals

1. _____
2. _____
3. _____

Training Objectives

1. _____
2. _____
3. _____
4. _____

1999 Training Plan (Nov '98 - Oct '99)

		SWIM							BIKE							RUN					
WEIGHTS	ENDURANCE	FORCE	SPEED	MUSCULAR ENDURANCE	ANAEROBIC ENDURANCE	POWER	TESTING	ENDURANCE	FORCE	SPEED	MUSCULAR ENDURANCE	ANAEROBIC ENDURANCE	POWER	TESTING	ENDURANCE	FORCE	SPEED	MUSCULAR ENDURANCE	ANAEROBIC ENDURANCE	POWER	TESTING

WK# MON	RACES	PRI	PERIOD	HOURS
1-Nov-02				
2-Nov-09				
3-Nov-16				
4-Nov-23				
5-Nov-30				
6-Dec-07				
7-Dec-14				
8-Dec-21				
9-Dec-28				
10-Jan-04				
11-Jan-11				
12-Jan-18				
13-Jan-25				
14-Feb-01				
15-Feb-08				
16-Feb-15				
17-Feb-22				
18-Mar-01				
19-Mar-08				
20-Mar-15				
21-Mar-22				
22-Mar-29				
23-Apr-05				
24-Apr-12				
25-Apr-19				
26-Apr-26				
27-May-03				
28-May-10				
29-May-17				
30-May-24				
31-May-31				
32-Jun-07				
33-Jun-14				
34-Jun-21				
35-Jun-28				
36-Jul-05				
37-Jul-12				
38-Jul-19				
39-Jul-26				
40-Aug-02				
41-Aug-09				
42-Aug-16				
43-Aug-23				
44-Aug-30				
45-Sep-06				
46-Sep-13				
47-Sep-20				
48-Sep-27				
49-Oct-04				
50-Oct-11				
51-Oct-18				
52-Oct-25				

Athlete _____

Annual Hours_____

Season Goals

1._____

2._____

3._____

Training Objectives

1._____

2._____

3._____

4._____

WK# MON	RACES	PRI	PERIOD	HOURS	WEIGHTS	SWIM ENDURANCE	SWIM FORCE	SWIM SPEED	SWIM MUSCULAR ENDURANCE	SWIM ANAEROBIC ENDURANCE	SWIM POWER	SWIM TESTING	BIKE ENDURANCE	BIKE FORCE	BIKE SPEED	BIKE MUSCULAR ENDURANCE	BIKE ANAEROBIC ENDURANCE	BIKE POWER	BIKE TESTING	RUN ENDURANCE	RUN FORCE	RUN SPEED	RUN MUSCULAR ENDURANCE	RUN ANAEROBIC ENDURANCE	RUN POWER	RUN TESTING
1-Dec-07																										
2-Dec-14																										
3-Dec-21																										
4-Dec-28																										
5-Jan-04																										
6-Jan-11																										
7-Jan-18																										
8-Jan-25																										
9-Feb-01																										
10-Feb-08																										
11-Feb-15																										
12-Feb-22																										
13-Mar-01																										
14-Mar-08																										
15-Mar-15																										
16-Mar-22																										
17-Mar-29																										
18-Apr-05																										
19-Apr-12																										
20-Apr-19																										
21-Apr-26																										
22-May-03																										
23-May-10																										
24-May-17																										
25-May-24																										
26-May-31																										
27-Jun-07																										
28-Jun-14																										
29-Jun-21																										
30-Jun-28																										
31-Jul-05																										
32-Jul-12																										
33-Jul-19																										
34-Jul-26																										
35-Aug-02																										
36-Aug-09																										
37-Aug-16																										
38-Aug-23																										
39-Aug-30																										
40-Sep-06																										
41-Sep-13																										
42-Sep-20																										
43-Sep-27																										
44-Oct-04																										
45-Oct-11																										
46-Oct-18																										
47-Oct-25																										
48-Nov-01																										
49-Nov-08																										
50-Nov-15																										
51-Nov-22																										
52-Nov-29																										

Athlete _____

Annual Hours_____

Season Goals

1._____

2._____

3._____

Training Objectives

1._____

2._____

3._____

4._____

1999 Training Plan (Jan '99 - Dec '99)

WK# MON	RACES	PRI	PERIOD	HOURS	WEIGHTS	SWIM							BIKE							RUN						
						ENDURANCE	FORCE	SPEED	MUSCULAR ENDURANCE	ANAEROBIC ENDURANCE	POWER	TESTING	ENDURANCE	FORCE	SPEED	MUSCULAR ENDURANCE	ANAEROBIC ENDURANCE	POWER	TESTING	ENDURANCE	FORCE	SPEED	MUSCULAR ENDURANCE	ANAEROBIC ENDURANCE	POWER	TESTING
1-Jan-04																										
2-Jan-11																										
3-Jan-18																										
4-Jan-25																										
5-Feb-01																										
6-Feb-08																										
7-Feb-15																										
8-Feb-22																										
9-Mar-01																										
10-Mar-08																										
11-Mar-15																										
12-Mar-22																										
13-Mar-29																										
14-Apr-05																										
15-Apr-12																										
16-Apr-19																										
17-Apr-26																										
18-May-03																										
19-May-10																										
20-May-17																										
21-May-24																										
22-May-31																										
23-Jun-07																										
24-Jun-14																										
25-Jun-21																										
26-Jun-28																										
27-Jul-05																										
28-Jul-12																										
29-Jul-19																										
30-Jul-26																										
31-Aug-02																										
32-Aug-09																										
33-Aug-16																										
34-Aug-23																										
35-Aug-30																										
36-Sep-06																										
37-Sep-13																										
38-Sep-20																										
39-Sep-27																										
40-Oct-04																										
41-Oct-11																										
42-Oct-18																										
43-Oct-25																										
44-Nov-01																										
45-Nov-08																										
46-Nov-15																										
47-Nov-22																										
48-Nov-29																										
49-Dec-06																										
50-Dec-13																										
51-Dec-20																										
52-Dec-27																										

Athlete _____

Annual Hours _____

Season Goals

1. _____
2. _____
3. _____

Training Objectives

1. _____
2. _____
3. _____
4. _____

2000 Training Plan (Nov '99 - Oct '00)

WK# MON	RACES	PRI	PERIOD	HOURS	WEIGHTS	SWIM							BIKE							RUN						
						ENDURANCE	FORCE	SPEED	MUSCULAR ENDURANCE	ANAEROBIC ENDURANCE	POWER	TESTING	ENDURANCE	FORCE	SPEED	MUSCULAR ENDURANCE	ANAEROBIC ENDURANCE	POWER	TESTING	ENDURANCE	FORCE	SPEED	MUSCULAR ENDURANCE	ANAEROBIC ENDURANCE	POWER	TESTING
1-Nov-01																										
2-Nov-08																										
3-Nov-15																										
4-Nov-22																										
5-Nov-29																										
6-Dec-06																										
7-Dec-13																										
8-Dec-20																										
9-Dec-27																										
10-Jan-03																										
11-Jan-10																										
12-Jan-17																										
13-Jan-24																										
14-Jan-31																										
15-Feb-07																										
16-Feb-14																										
17-Feb-21																										
18-Feb-28																										
19-Mar-06																										
20-Mar-13																										
21-Mar-20																										
22-Mar-27																										
23-Apr-03																										
24-Apr-10																										
25-Apr-17																										
26-Apr-24																										
27-May-01																										
28-May-08																										
29-May-15																										
30-May-22																										
31-May-29																										
32-Jun-05																										
33-Jun-12																										
34-Jun-19																										
35-Jun-26																										
36-Jul-03																										
37-Jul-10																										
38-Jul-17																										
39-Jul-24																										
40-Jul-31																										
41-Aug-07																										
42-Aug-14																										
43-Aug-21																										
44-Aug-28																										
45-Sep-04																										
46-Sep-11																										
47-Sep-18																										
48-Sep-25																										
49-Oct-02																										
50-Oct-09																										
51-Oct-16																										
52-Oct-23																										
53-Oct-30																										

Athlete _____

Annual Hours _____

Season Goals

1. _____

2. _____

3. _____

Training Objectives

1. _____

2. _____

3. _____

4. _____

2000 Training Plan (Dec '99-Nov '00)

		SWIM							BIKE							RUN						
WK# MON	RACES	PRI	PERIOD	HOURS	WEIGHTS	ENDURANCE	FORCE	SPEED	MUSCULAR ENDURANCE	ANAEROBIC ENDURANCE	POWER	TESTING	ENDURANCE	FORCE	SPEED	MUSCULAR ENDURANCE	ANAEROBIC ENDURANCE	POWER	TESTING	ENDURANCE	FORCE	SPEED	MUSCULAR ENDURANCE	ANAEROBIC ENDURANCE	POWER	TESTING
1-Dec-06																										
2-Dec-13																										
3-Dec-20																										
4-Dec-27																										
5-Jan-03																										
6-Jan-10																										
7-Jan-17																										
8-Jan-24																										
9-Jan-31																										
10-Feb-07																										
11-Feb-14																										
12-Feb-21																										
13-Feb-28																										
14-Mar-07																										
15-Mar-14																										
16-Mar-21																										
17-Mar-28																										
18-Apr-04																										
19-Apr-11																										
20-Apr-18																										
21-Apr-25																										
22-May-02																										
23-May-09																										
24-May-16																										
25-May-23																										
26-May-30																										
27-Jun-06																										
28-Jun-13																										
29-Jun-20																										
30-Jun-27																										
31-Jul-04																										
32-Jul-11																										
33-Jul-18																										
34-Jul-25																										
35-Aug-01																										
36-Aug-08																										
37-Aug-15																										
38-Aug-22																										
39-Aug-29																										
40-Sep-05																										
41-Sep-12																										
42-Sep-19																										
43-Sep-26																										
44-Oct-03																										
45-Oct-10																										
46-Oct-17																										
47-Oct-24																										
48-Oct-31																										
49-Nov-07																										
50-Nov-14																										
51-Nov-21																										
52-Nov-28																										

Athlete _____

Annual Hours _____

Season Goals

1. _____
2. _____
3. _____

Training Objectives

1. _____
2. _____
3. _____
4. _____

2000 Training Plan (Jan '00 - Dec '00)

WK# MON	RACES	PRI	PERIOD	HOURS	WEIGHTS	SWIM							BIKE							RUN						
						ENDURANCE	FORCE	SPEED	MUSCULAR ENDURANCE	ANAEROBIC ENDURANCE	POWER	TESTING	ENDURANCE	FORCE	SPEED	MUSCULAR ENDURANCE	ANAEROBIC ENDURANCE	POWER	TESTING	ENDURANCE	FORCE	SPEED	MUSCULAR ENDURANCE	ANAEROBIC ENDURANCE	POWER	TESTING
1-Jan-03																										
2-Jan-10																										
3-Jan-17																										
4-Jan-24																										
5-Jan-31																										
6-Feb-07																										
7-Feb-14																										
8-Feb-21																										
9-Feb-28																										
10-Mar-06																										
11-Mar-13																										
12-Mar-20																										
13-Mar-27																										
14-Apr-03																										
15-Apr-10																										
16-Apr-17																										
17-Apr-24																										
18-May-01																										
19-May-08																										
20-May-15																										
21-May-22																										
22-May-29																										
23-Jun-05																										
24-Jun-12																										
25-Jun-19																										
26-Jun-26																										
27-Jul-03																										
28-Jul-10																										
29-Jul-17																										
30-Jul-24																										
31-Jul-31																										
32-Aug-07																										
33-Aug-14																										
34-Aug-21																										
35-Aug-28																										
36-Sep-04																										
37-Sep-11																										
38-Sep-18																										
39-Sep-25																										
40-Oct-02																										
41-Oct-09																										
42-Oct-16																										
43-Oct-23																										
44-Oct-30																										
45-Nov-06																										
46-Nov-13																										
47-Nov-20																										
48-Nov-27																										
49-Dec-04																										
50-Dec-11																										
51-Dec-18																										
52-Dec-25																										

Athlete _____

Annual Hours_____

Season Goals

1._____

2._____

3._____

Training Objectives

1._____

2._____

3._____

4._____

2001 Training Plan (Nov '00 - Oct '01)

		SWIM						BIKE						RUN					
WK# MON	RACES	PRI	PERIOD	HOURS	WEIGHTS	ENDURANCE	FORCE	SPEED	MUSCULAR ENDURANCE	ANAEROBIC ENDURANCE	POWER	TESTING	ENDURANCE	FORCE	SPEED	MUSCULAR ENDURANCE	ANAEROBIC ENDURANCE	POWER	TESTING	ENDURANCE	FORCE	SPEED	MUSCULAR ENDURANCE	ANAEROBIC ENDURANCE	POWER	TESTING
1-Nov-06																										
2-Nov-13																										
3-Nov-20																										
4-Nov-27																										
5-Dec-04																										
6-Dec-11																										
7-Dec-18																										
8-Dec-25																										
9-Jan-01																										
10-Jan-08																										
11-Jan-15																										
12-Jan-22																										
13-Jan-29																										
14-Feb-05																										
15-Feb-12																										
16-Feb-19																										
17-Feb-26																										
18-Mar-05																										
19-Mar-12																										
20-Mar-19																										
21-Mar-26																										
22-Apr-02																										
23-Apr-09																										
24-Apr-16																										
25-Apr-23																										
26-Apr-30																										
27-May-07																										
28-May-14																										
29-May-21																										
30-May-28																										
31-Jun-04																										
32-Jun-11																										
33-Jun-18																										
34-Jun-25																										
35-Jul-02																										
36-Jul-09																										
37-Jul-16																										
38-Jul-23																										
39-Jul-30																										
40-Aug-06																										
41-Aug-13																										
42-Aug-20																										
43-Aug-27																										
44-Sep-03																										
45-Sep-10																										
46-Sep-17																										
47-Sep-24																										
48-Oct-01																										
49-Oct-08																										
50-Oct-15																										
51-Oct-22																										
52-Oct-29																										

Athlete _____

Annual Hours _____

Season Goals

1. _____
2. _____
3. _____

Training Objectives

1. _____
2. _____
3. _____
4. _____

2001 Training Plan (Dec '00-Nov '01)

WK# MON	RACES	PRI	PERIOD	HOURS	WEIGHTS	SWIM ENDURANCE	SWIM FORCE	SWIM SPEED	SWIM MUSCULAR ENDURANCE	SWIM ANAEROBIC ENDURANCE	SWIM POWER	SWIM TESTING	BIKE ENDURANCE	BIKE FORCE	BIKE SPEED	BIKE MUSCULAR ENDURANCE	BIKE ANAEROBIC ENDURANCE	BIKE POWER	BIKE TESTING	RUN ENDURANCE	RUN FORCE	RUN SPEED	RUN MUSCULAR ENDURANCE	RUN ANAEROBIC ENDURANCE	RUN POWER	RUN TESTING
1-Dec-04																										
2-Dec-11																										
3-Dec-18																										
4-Dec-25																										
5-Jan-01																										
6-Jan-08																										
7-Jan-15																										
8-Jan-22																										
9-Jan-29																										
10-Feb-05																										
11-Feb-12																										
12-Feb-19																										
13-Feb-26																										
14-Mar-05																										
15-Mar-12																										
16-Mar-19																										
17-Mar-26																										
18-Apr-02																										
19-Apr-09																										
20-Apr-16																										
21-Apr-23																										
22-Apr-30																										
23-May-07																										
24-May-14																										
25-May-21																										
26-May-28																										
27-Jun-04																										
28-Jun-11																										
29-Jun-18																										
30-Jun-25																										
31-Jul-02																										
32-Jul-09																										
33-Jul-16																										
34-Jul-23																										
35-Jul-30																										
36-Aug-06																										
37-Aug-13																										
38-Aug-20																										
39-Aug-27																										
40-Sep-03																										
41-Sep-10																										
42-Sep-17																										
43-Sep-24																										
44-Oct-01																										
45-Oct-08																										
46-Oct-15																										
47-Oct-22																										
48-Oct-29																										
49-Nov-05																										
50-Nov-12																										
51-Nov-19																										
52-Nov-26																										

Athlete _____

Annual Hours _____

Season Goals

1. _____
2. _____
3. _____

Training Objectives

1. _____
2. _____
3. _____
4. _____

2001 Training Plan (Jan '01 - Dec '01)

WK# MON	RACES	PRI	PERIOD	HOURS	WEIGHTS	SWIM ENDURANCE	FORCE	SPEED	MUSCULAR ENDURANCE	ANAEROBIC ENDURANCE	POWER	TESTING	BIKE ENDURANCE	FORCE	SPEED	MUSCULAR ENDURANCE	ANAEROBIC ENDURANCE	POWER	TESTING	RUN ENDURANCE	FORCE	SPEED	MUSCULAR ENDURANCE	ANAEROBIC ENDURANCE	POWER	TESTING
1-Jan-01																										
2-Jan-08																										
3-Jan-15																										
4-Jan-22																										
5-Jan-29																										
6-Feb-05																										
7-Feb-12																										
8-Feb-19																										
9-Feb-26																										
10-Mar-05																										
11-Mar-12																										
12-Mar-19																										
13-Mar-26																										
14-Apr-02																										
15-Apr-09																										
16-Apr-16																										
17-Apr-23																										
18-Apr-30																										
19-May-07																										
20-May-14																										
21-May-21																										
22-May-28																										
23-Jun-04																										
24-Jun-11																										
25-Jun-18																										
26-Jun-25																										
27-Jul-02																										
28-Jul-09																										
29-Jul-16																										
30-Jul-23																										
31-Jul-30																										
32-Aug-06																										
33-Aug-13																										
34-Aug-20																										
35-Aug-27																										
36-Sep-03																										
37-Sep-10																										
38-Sep-17																										
39-Sep-24																										
40-Oct-01																										
41-Oct-08																										
42-Oct-15																										
43-Oct-22																										
44-Oct-29																										
45-Nov-05																										
46-Nov-12																										
47-Nov-19																										
48-Nov-26																										
49-Dec-03																										
50-Dec-10																										
51-Dec-17																										
52-Dec-24																										
53-Dec-31																										

Athlete _____

Annual Hours _____

Season Goals

1. _____
2. _____
3. _____

Training Objectives

1. _____
2. _____
3. _____
4. _____

2002 Training Plan (Nov '01 - Oct '02)

					WEIGHTS	SWIM							BIKE							RUN						
WK# MON	RACES	PRI	PERIOD	HOURS		ENDURANCE	FORCE	SPEED	MUSCULAR ENDURANCE	ANAEROBIC ENDURANCE	POWER	TESTING	ENDURANCE	FORCE	SPEED	MUSCULAR ENDURANCE	ANAEROBIC ENDURANCE	POWER	TESTING	ENDURANCE	FORCE	SPEED	MUSCULAR ENDURANCE	ANAEROBIC ENDURANCE	POWER	TESTING
1-Nov-05																										
2-Nov-12																										
3-Nov-19																										
4-Nov-26																										
5-Dec-03																										
6-Dec-10																										
7-Dec-17																										
8-Dec-24																										
9-Dec-31																										
10-Jan-07																										
11-Jan-14																										
12-Jan-21																										
13-Jan-28																										
14-Feb-04																										
15-Feb-11																										
16-Feb-18																										
17-Feb-25																										
18-Mar-04																										
19-Mar-11																										
20-Mar-18																										
21-Mar-25																										
22-Apr-01																										
23-Apr-08																										
24-Apr-15																										
25-Apr-22																										
26-Apr-29																										
27-May-06																										
28-May-13																										
29-May-20																										
30-May-27																										
31-Jun-03																										
32-Jun-10																										
33-Jun-17																										
34-Jun-24																										
35-Jul-01																										
36-Jul-08																										
37-Jul-15																										
38-Jul-22																										
39-Jul-29																										
40-Aug-05																										
41-Aug-12																										
42-Aug-19																										
43-Aug-26																										
44-Sep-02																										
45-Sep-09																										
46-Sep-16																										
47-Sep-23																										
48-Sep-30																										
49-Oct-07																										
50-Oct-14																										
51-Oct-21																										
52-Oct-28																										

Athlete _____

Annual Hours _____

Season Goals

1. _____
2. _____
3. _____

Training Objectives

1. _____
2. _____
3. _____
4. _____

2002 Training Plan (Dec '01-Nov '02)

					SWIM							BIKE							RUN						
WK# MON	RACES	PRI	PERIOD	HOURS	WEIGHTS	ENDURANCE	FORCE	SPEED	MUSCULAR ENDURANCE	ANAEROBIC ENDURANCE	POWER	TESTING	ENDURANCE	FORCE	SPEED	MUSCULAR ENDURANCE	ANAEROBIC ENDURANCE	POWER	TESTING	ENDURANCE	FORCE	SPEED	MUSCULAR ENDURANCE	ANAEROBIC ENDURANCE	POWER	TESTING
1-Dec-03																										
2-Dec-10																										
3-Dec-17																										
4-Dec-24																										
5-Dec-31																										
6-Jan-07																										
7-Jan-14																										
8-Jan-21																										
9-Jan-28																										
10-Feb-04																										
11-Feb-11																										
12-Feb-18																										
13-Feb-25																										
14-Mar-04																										
15-Mar-11																										
16-Mar-18																										
17-Mar-25																										
18-Apr-01																										
19-Apr-08																										
20-Apr-15																										
21-Apr-22																										
22-Apr-29																										
23-May-06																										
24-May-13																										
25-May-20																										
26-May-27																										
27-Jun-03																										
28-Jun-10																										
29-Jun-17																										
30-Jun-24																										
31-Jul-01																										
32-Jul-08																										
33-Jul-15																										
34-Jul-22																										
35-Jul-29																										
36-Aug-05																										
37-Aug-12																										
38-Aug-19																										
39-Aug-26																										
40-Sep-02																										
41-Sep-09																										
42-Sep-16																										
43-Sep-23																										
44-Sep-30																										
45-Oct-07																										
46-Oct-14																										
47-Oct-21																										
48-Oct-28																										
49-Nov-04																										
50-Nov-11																										
51-Nov-18																										
52-Nov-25																										

Athlete _____

Annual Hours _____

Season Goals

1. _____
2. _____
3. _____

Training Objectives

1. _____
2. _____
3. _____
4. _____

2002 Training Plan (Jan '02 - Dec '02)

WK# MON	RACES	PRI	PERIOD	HOURS	WEIGHTS	SWIM ENDURANCE	SWIM FORCE	SWIM SPEED	SWIM MUSCULAR ENDURANCE	SWIM ANAEROBIC ENDURANCE	SWIM POWER	SWIM TESTING	BIKE ENDURANCE	BIKE FORCE	BIKE SPEED	BIKE MUSCULAR ENDURANCE	BIKE ANAEROBIC ENDURANCE	BIKE POWER	BIKE TESTING	RUN ENDURANCE	RUN FORCE	RUN SPEED	RUN MUSCULAR ENDURANCE	RUN ANAEROBIC ENDURANCE	RUN POWER	RUN TESTING
1-Jan-07																										
2-Jan-14																										
3-Jan-21																										
4-Jan-28																										
5-Feb-04																										
6-Feb-11																										
7-Feb-18																										
8-Feb-25																										
9-Mar-04																										
10-Mar-11																										
11-Mar-18																										
12-Mar-25																										
13-Apr-01																										
14-Apr-08																										
15-Apr-15																										
16-Apr-22																										
17-Apr-29																										
18-May-06																										
19-May-13																										
20-May-20																										
21-May-27																										
22-Jun-03																										
23-Jun-10																										
24-Jun-17																										
25-Jun-24																										
26-Jul-01																										
27-Jul-08																										
28-Jul-15																										
29-Jul-22																										
30-Jul-29																										
31-Aug-05																										
32-Aug-12																										
33-Aug-19																										
34-Aug-26																										
35-Sep-02																										
36-Sep-09																										
37-Sep-16																										
38-Sep-23																										
39-Sep-30																										
40-Oct-07																										
41-Oct-14																										
42-Oct-21																										
43-Oct-28																										
44-Nov-04																										
45-Nov-11																										
46-Nov-18																										
47-Nov-25																										
48-Dec-02																										
49-Dec-09																										
50-Dec-16																										
51-Dec-23																										
52-Dec-30																										

Athlete _____

Annual Hours _____

Season Goals

1. _____

2. _____

3. _____

Training Objectives

1. _____

2. _____

3. _____

4. _____

2003 Training Plan (Nov '02 - Oct '03)

WK# MON	RACES	PRI	PERIOD	HOURS	WEIGHTS	SWIM ENDURANCE	SWIM FORCE	SWIM SPEED	SWIM MUSCULAR ENDURANCE	SWIM ANAEROBIC ENDURANCE	SWIM POWER	SWIM TESTING	BIKE ENDURANCE	BIKE FORCE	BIKE SPEED	BIKE MUSCULAR ENDURANCE	BIKE ANAEROBIC ENDURANCE	BIKE POWER	BIKE TESTING	RUN ENDURANCE	RUN FORCE	RUN SPEED	RUN MUSCULAR ENDURANCE	RUN ANAEROBIC ENDURANCE	RUN POWER	RUN TESTING
1-Nov-04																										
2-Nov-11																										
3-Nov-18																										
4-Nov-25																										
5-Dec-02																										
6-Dec-09																										
7-Dec-16																										
8-Dec-23																										
9-Dec-30																										
10-Jan-06																										
11-Jan-13																										
12-Jan-20																										
13-Jan-27																										
14-Feb-03																										
15-Feb-10																										
16-Feb-17																										
17-Feb-24																										
18-Mar-03																										
19-Mar-10																										
20-Mar-17																										
21-Mar-24																										
22-Mar-31																										
23-Apr-07																										
24-Apr-14																										
25-Apr-21																										
26-Apr-28																										
27-May-05																										
28-May-12																										
29-May-19																										
30-May-26																										
31-Jun-02																										
32-Jun-09																										
33-Jun-16																										
34-Jun-23																										
35-Jun-30																										
36-Jul-07																										
37-Jul-14																										
38-Jul-21																										
39-Jul-28																										
40-Aug-04																										
41-Aug-11																										
42-Aug-18																										
43-Aug-25																										
44-Sep-01																										
45-Sep-08																										
46-Sep-15																										
47-Sep-22																										
48-Sep-29																										
49-Oct-06																										
50-Oct-13																										
51-Oct-20																										
52-Oct-27																										

Athlete _____

Annual Hours _____

Season Goals

1. _____
2. _____
3. _____

Training Objectives

1. _____
2. _____
3. _____
4. _____

WK# MON	RACES	PRI	PERIOD	HOURS	WEIGHTS	SWIM ENDURANCE	SWIM FORCE	SWIM SPEED	SWIM MUSCULAR ENDURANCE	SWIM ANAEROBIC ENDURANCE	SWIM POWER	SWIM TESTING	BIKE ENDURANCE	BIKE FORCE	BIKE SPEED	BIKE MUSCULAR ENDURANCE	BIKE ANAEROBIC ENDURANCE	BIKE POWER	BIKE TESTING	RUN ENDURANCE	RUN FORCE	RUN SPEED	RUN MUSCULAR ENDURANCE	RUN ANAEROBIC ENDURANCE	RUN POWER	RUN TESTING
1-Dec-02																										
2-Dec-09																										
3-Dec-16																										
4-Dec-23																										
5-Dec-30																										
6-Jan-06																										
7-Jan-13																										
8-Jan-20																										
9-Jan-27																										
10-Feb-03																										
11-Feb-10																										
12-Feb-17																										
13-Feb-24																										
14-Mar-03																										
15-Mar-10																										
16-Mar-17																										
17-Mar-24																										
18-Mar-31																										
19-Apr-07																										
20-Apr-14																										
21-Apr-21																										
22-Apr-28																										
23-May-05																										
24-May-12																										
25-May-19																										
26-May-26																										
27-Jun-02																										
28-Jun-09																										
29-Jun-16																										
30-Jun-23																										
31-Jun-30																										
32-Jul-07																										
33-Jul-14																										
34-Jul-21																										
35-Jul-28																										
36-Aug-04																										
37-Aug-11																										
38-Aug-18																										
39-Aug-25																										
40-Sep-01																										
41-Sep-08																										
42-Sep-15																										
43-Sep-22																										
44-Sep-29																										
45-Oct-06																										
46-Oct-13																										
47-Oct-20																										
48-Oct-27																										
49-Nov-03																										
50-Nov-10																										
51-Nov-17																										
52-Nov-24																										

Athlete _____

Annual Hours_____

Season Goals

1._____

2._____

3._____

Training Objectives

1._____

2._____

3._____

4._____

2003 Training Plan (Jan '03 - Dec '03)

WK# MON	RACES	PRI	PERIOD	HOURS	WEIGHTS	SWIM						BIKE						RUN					
						ENDURANCE	FORCE	SPEED	MUSCULAR ENDURANCE	ANAEROBIC ENDURANCE	POWER / TESTING	ENDURANCE	FORCE	SPEED	MUSCULAR ENDURANCE	ANAEROBIC ENDURANCE	POWER / TESTING	ENDURANCE	FORCE	SPEED	MUSCULAR ENDURANCE	ANAEROBIC ENDURANCE	POWER / TESTING
1-Jan-06																							
2-Jan-13																							
3-Jan-20																							
4-Jan-27																							
5-Feb-03																							
6-Feb-10																							
7-Feb-17																							
8-Feb-24																							
9-Mar-03																							
10-Mar-10																							
11-Mar-17																							
12-Mar-24																							
13-Mar-31																							
14-Apr-07																							
15-Apr-14																							
16-Apr-21																							
17-Apr-28																							
18-May-05																							
19-May-12																							
20-May-19																							
21-May-26																							
22-Jun-02																							
23-Jun-09																							
24-Jun-16																							
25-Jun-23																							
26-Jun-30																							
27-Jul-07																							
28-Jul-14																							
29-Jul-21																							
30-Jul-28																							
31-Aug-04																							
32-Aug-11																							
33-Aug-18																							
34-Aug-25																							
35-Sep-01																							
36-Sep-08																							
37-Sep-15																							
38-Sep-22																							
39-Sep-29																							
40-Oct-06																							
41-Oct-13																							
42-Oct-20																							
43-Oct-27																							
44-Nov-03																							
45-Nov-10																							
46-Nov-17																							
47-Nov-24																							
48-Dec-01																							
49-Dec-08																							
50-Dec-15																							
51-Dec-22																							
52-Dec-29																							

APPENDIX B

The following are basic swim sets that may be combined in various ways into one swim session. For example, following the warm up, you may start the session with a Speed set, followed by an Anaerobic-Endurance set, and then an Endurance set before cooling down.

ENDURANCE SETS

E1. **Recovery.** Swim 10 to 20 minutes or more in the 1 zone concentrating on technique. Do this as a workout following a BT-bike or -run workout to speed recovery, or as a swim session cool down. (Periods: All)

E2. **Extensive Endurance Intervals.** Swim intervals of a distance that take six to 12 minutes in the 2 to 3 zones. Recover after each for 10 to 15 percent of the work-interval time. Total work-interval distance may match the distance of the swim portion of your next A- or B-priority race. A variation on this set is to recover with a 25- to 50-meter/yard drill or kick. Example: 4 x 500 meters/yards in 7 minutes, 30 seconds, leaving every 8 minutes, 15 seconds. Or swim long and steady in the 2 zone, especially in open water. (Periods: All)

E3. Intensive Endurance Intervals. Swim intervals that take three to five minutes to complete. Intensity is mostly 3 zone. Recover after each for about 5 to 10 percent of the preceding work-interval time. Total interval time may match the distance of the swim portion of your next A- or B-priority race. Example: 5 x 400 meters in 3:00, leaving every 3:20. (Periods: Prep, Base 1, Base 2, Base 3)

FORCE SETS

F1. Open Water. Swim in a river, lake or the ocean with alternating sets against and with the current. Swim each set against the current at near maximal effort without breaking form, taking 20 to 30 strokes (each arm) in each set. Recover by swimming with the current for 60 to 90 seconds. Complete three to eight of these sets. Do this only with a partner or group. Example: 5 x 30 strokes with one-minute recovery intervals. (Periods: Base 2, Base 3, Build 1, Build 2)

F2. Paddles. Swim any set other than warm up or cool down using paddles. When first beginning to use paddles, start with small ones, use them only on Endurance sets and do no more than 15 percent of the total workout distance with them. Over the course of several weeks, increase the size of the paddles used. Don't do more than 50 percent of a workout with them, and never increase both paddle size and total distance using them within a workout at the same time. (Periods: Base 2, Base 3, Build 1)

F3. Drag Sets. Do any set other than warm up and cool down wearing a drag suit, T-shirt or carpenter's apron with pockets. Initially, limit these to Endurance sets adding drag to higher intensity sets gradually. (Periods: Base 2, Base 3, Build 1)

SPEED SETS

(Remember that "speed" as used here doesn't mean fast velocity, but rather the ability to move effectively.)

S1. Drill Sets. Within a workout, usually near the beginning, include drills that help correct technique flaws (see Chapter 12 for drill descriptions). Practice the drills in repeats each made up of less than 30 strokes (each arm) before stopping to rest and evaluate your technique for 10 to 20 seconds. This is about 50 to 100 meters/yards per repeat. Repeat one drill for no more than 150 strokes (each arm), about 250 to 500 meters/yards, before going to a new drill or set. (Periods: All)

S2. Fin Sets. Do any set, other than warm up and cool down, wearing fins. Fins are especially helpful when doing some drills in order to maintain body position on top of the water. (Periods: All)

S3. Speed Reps. Early in a workout, do fast repeats with each about 30 strokes or less (each arm). The pace should be zone 5b or 5c, but don't sacrifice form for speed. Focus on technique on each repeat. Recover for 30 to 60 seconds between repeats. You must be well recovered to train the nervous system and muscles to work efficiently. Doing speed reps in a fatigued state will only drill in poor technique. Limit a set of speed reps to 150 strokes (each arm). Example: 6 x 50 meters/yards in 40 seconds leaving every 90 seconds. (Periods: All)

MUSCULAR-ENDURANCE SETS

M1. Long Cruise Intervals. Swim work intervals of a distance that takes six minutes or more with recovery intervals approximately one-fourth as long. Intensity is 4 to 5a zone. The total work-interval distance for a set may equal the swim distance of the next A- or B-priority race. Example: 4 x 400 meters/yards in 6:00 leaving every 7:30. (Periods: Base 2, Base 3, Build 1, Build 2, Peak)

M2. Short Cruise Intervals. Swim intervals that take three to five minutes to complete. Intensity is 4 to 5a zones. Recover after each for about 15 percent of the preceding work-interval time. Total work-interval time may match the distance of the swim portion of your next A- or B-priority race. Example: 8 x 200 meters in 3:00 leaving every 3:30. (Periods: Base 2, Base 3, Build 1, Build 2, Peak)

M3. Threshold. Swim 12 to 20 minutes in the 4 and 5a zones without stopping. Example: 1200 meters/yards in 18:00. (Periods: Base 3, Build 1, Build 2, Peak)

ANAEROBIC-ENDURANCE SETS

A1. AE Intervals. Complete work intervals of three- to five-minutes duration with recoveries that are about half of the work-interval time. Intensity is 5b. The combined work-interval duration may equal the anticipated time of your next sprint- or international-distance race. Recovery intervals may be gradually reduced to 25 percent of the work interval during the Build period as fitness improves. Example: 5 x 300 meters/yards in 4:30 leaving every 6:45. (Periods: Build 1, Build 2, Peak)

A2. Lactate Tolerance Reps. Swim repeats of 30-seconds to two-minutes duration at 5c zone effort with recoveries that are one minute up to twice as long in order to clear lactate before the next repeat. Greatest improvement comes from gradually lengthening the repeats while holding effort/pace constant. Total volume of lactate tolerance reps for one swim session is three to 12 minutes. Example: 5 x 100 meters/yards in 1:20 leaving every 2:30. (Periods: Build 2, Peak)

POWER SETS

P1. Sprints. Swim a distance that takes 10 to 30 seconds at maximal (zone 5c) effort. Recover after each for two to three times as long as the work interval. Be careful with sprints as the tendency is to allow form to break down as the effort escalates. Power sprints should be done early in the workout in order to maintain optimal swim technique. One variation of this workout is to do the sprints with paddles, but only if there is no tendency to shoulder injury. Use small paddles initially. The total combined time of sprint work intervals within a set may be one to six minutes. Example: 12 x 25 meters/yards in 15 seconds leaving every 45 seconds. (Periods: Build 1, Build 2, Peak, Race)

TEST WORKOUTS

T1. Broken Kilometer. After a standard warm up, swim 10 x 100 meters/yards at maximal effort with 10-second recovery intervals. Time the entire set, including recovery intervals, with a running clock from the start of the first 100 to the end of the tenth. Subtract 90 seconds (for recovery intervals) to produce a test "score." This test may be done at the end of each four-week period to gauge progress. (Periods: Base 1, Base 2, Base 3, Build 1, Build 2, Peak)

T2. Time Trial. Following a standard warm up, swim 1000 meters/yards at race effort, as described in Chapter 5. Record the time of the swim and your finishing heart rate in your log. This test may be done at the end of each four-week training period as a measure of progress. (Periods: Base 1, Base 2, Base 3, Build 1, Build 2, Peak)

APPENDIX C

ENDURANCE WORKOUTS

E1. Recovery. Done in the 1 zone using the small chainring on a flat course. Do these in the Prep period as the primary aerobic workout and the day after a BT workout in all other periods. An indoor trainer or rollers may be used for these at any time of the year, especially if flat courses are not available. Cross-training is also beneficial for recovery in the Preparation, Base 1 and Base 2 periods. An excellent time to do a recovery ride is in the evening on a day when you have done intervals, weights, a hard group workout, hills or a race. Spinning for 15-30 minutes on rollers or a trainer hastens recovery for most experienced riders. Novices benefit more by taking the time off. These workouts are not scheduled on the Annual Training Plan, but are an integral part of training throughout the season. (Periods: All)

E2. Extensive Endurance. Used for aerobic maintenance and endurance training. Stay primarily in the 1 and 2 zones on a rolling course with small grades up to 4 percent. Remain seated on the uphill portions to build greater strength while maintaining a comfortably high cadence. Can be done with a disciplined group or on an indoor trainer by shifting through the gears to simulate rolling hills. In the Base periods, riding steadily in the 2 zone for 20 to 90 minutes or more is quite effective for developing aerobic endurance. Cross-training is an option during Preparation and Base 1. (Periods: All)

E3. Intensive Endurance. Develops aerobic endurance while stressing muscular endurance. Ride a rolling course with small hills and gear selections that take you into the 3 zone frequently for a few minutes at a time. Remain seated on the hills. Accumulate 10 to 30 minutes or more of 3-zone time in this manner within a ride. A variation on this workout is to run 15 to 20 minutes immediately after the ride, especially when in the early stages of training for an Ironman or half Ironman. Intensive endurance is an excellent workout during the Base period, but should seldom, if ever, be included in the other periods. (Periods: Base 1, Base 2, Base 3)

FORCE WORKOUTS

F1. Moderate Hills. Select a course that includes several moderately steep hills of up to about 6-percent grade that take two to five minutes to climb. Stay seated on all hills pedaling from the hips with little or no rocking of the upper body. Cadence at 60 rpm or higher. Stay in the 1-5a zones on this ride. On a trainer, hills are simulated by placing a 5- to 7-inch riser under the front wheel and selecting resistances and gears that force a slowing of cadence. (Periods: Base 2, Base 3)

F2. Long Hills. Ride a course including several long grades of up to 8 percent that take six or more minutes to climb. Stay seated on most hills, standing only to rest muscles and get up short, steep rises. Cadence at 50 rpm or higher on climbs. Go no higher than 5a zone. Concentrate on bike position and smooth pedaling with minimal movement of the upper body. Simulate this workout on an indoor trainer with an 8- to 10-inch block under the front wheel and higher resistances and gears. (Periods: Base 3, Build 1)

F3. Hills Repeats. Warm up thoroughly. Then on a steep hill of 6- to 8-percent grade that takes 30 to 60 seconds to climb, do three to eight repeats with two to four minutes of recovery between them. Intensity may climb to 5b several times. Recover into the 1 zone with easy spinning while descending and at the bottom. Climb in the saddle holding the handlebar tops with minimal upper body movement. Maintain a cadence of 50 to 60 rpm. Stop the workout if you cannot maintain at least 50 rpm in your easiest gear, or if your knees hurt. Do this workout no more than twice per week with at least 48 hours between them. Do not do this workout if you have knee problems. (Periods: Build 1, Build 2, Peak)

SPEED WORKOUTS

S1. **Spin-ups.** On a downhill or on an indoor trainer set to light resistance, for one minute gradually increase cadence to maximum. Maximum is the cadence you can maintain without bouncing. As the cadence increases, allow your lower legs and feet to relax — especially the toes. Hold your maximum for as long as possible. Recover for at least a minute, and repeat several times. These are best done with a handlebar computer that displays cadence. Heart rate and power ratings have no significance for this workout. (Periods: Prep, Base 1, Base 2, Base 3)

S2. **Isolated Leg.** With a light resistance on trainer or downhill, do 90 percent of work with one leg while the other is "along for the ride." Spin with a higher than normal cadence. Change legs when fatigue begins to set in. You can also do this on a trainer with one foot out of the pedal and resting on a stool, while the other works. Focus on eliminating "dead" spots at top and bottom of the stroke. Heart rate and power ratings have no significance for this workout. (Periods: Base 1, Base 2, Base 3)

S3. **Jumps.** Within an Endurance ride include several eight- to 12-second, maximum-effort sprints with a high cadence rather than a high gear. Alternate in and out of saddle. These can be done with another rider or with a group. Power/RPE should be 5c zone. Heart rate is not a good indicator. Allow at least two minutes recovery between jumps. (Periods: Build 1, Build 2, Peak, Race)

MUSCULAR-ENDURANCE WORKOUTS

M1. **Tempo.** After warm up, on a mostly flat course, or on an indoor trainer, ride in the 3 zone for an extended time without recovery. Avoid roads with heavy traffic and stop signs. Stay in an aerodynamic position throughout. Start with 10 to 20 minutes of 3-zone work and build to 50 to 60 minutes or more by adding 10 minutes or so each week. This workout may be done two or three times weekly. (Periods: Base 2, Base 3)

M2. **Cruise Intervals.** On a relatively flat course, or an indoor trainer, complete three to five work intervals that are six- to 12-minutes duration. Build to the 4 and 5a zones on each work interval. If training with a heart-rate monitor, the work interval starts as soon as you begin pedaling hard — not when the 4 zone is achieved. Recover for two or three minutes after each. Recovery should be into the 1 or 2 zone. The first workout should total about 20 minutes of work intervals. Stay relaxed, aerodynamic and closely listen to your breathing. A variation that develops greater strength is shifting every 30 seconds between your "normal" gear and a higher gear. (Periods: Base 3, Build 1, Build 2, Peak)

M3. Hill Cruise Intervals. Same as M2 cruise intervals, except done on a long, low grade such as 2 to 4 percent, or into a strong head wind. Stay in the aero' position and work on a smooth stroke with minimal upper body motion. A variation on this workout is to shift between a "normal" and a higher gear every 30 seconds to build even greater strength. These are good if muscular endurance and force are both limiters. (Periods: Build 1, Build 2, Peak)

M4. Criss-Cross Threshold. On a mostly flat course with little traffic and no stops, ride 20 to 40 minutes in the 4 and 5a zones. Once the 4 zone is attained, gradually build effort to the top of the 5a zone taking about two minutes to do so. Then gradually back off and slowly drop back to the bottom of the 4 zone taking about two minutes again. Continue this pattern throughout the ride. Complete two or three cruise interval workouts before doing this workout. (Periods: Build 1, Build 2, Peak)

M5. Threshold. On a mostly flat course with little traffic and no stops, ride 20 to 40 minutes non-stop in the 4 and 5a zones. Stay relaxed, aerodynamic and closely listen to your breathing throughout. A variation involves shifting between a "normal" gear and a higher gear every minute or so to develop strength. Don't attempt a threshold ride until you've completed at least four cruise interval workouts. This workout should definitely be included in your training. (Periods: Build 2, Peak)

ANAEROBIC-ENDURANCE WORKOUTS

A1. Group Ride. Ride how you feel. If tired, sit in or break off and ride by yourself. If fresh, ride hard going into the 5b zone several times. (Periods: Build 1, Build 2, Peak)

A2. AE Intervals. After a good warm-up, on a mostly flat course with no stop signs and light traffic, do five work intervals of three- to six-minutes duration each. Build to the 5b zone on each. Recover to the 1 zone for the same time as the preceding work interval. (Periods: Build 1, Build 2, Peak)

A3. Pyramid Intervals. The same as AE intervals, except the work intervals are 1-, 2-, 3-, 4-, 4-, 3-, 2-, 1-minutes building to the 5b zone. The recovery after each is equal to the preceding work interval. Complete one or two of these sets. (Periods: Build 1, Build 2, Peak)

A4. Hill Intervals. Following a thorough warm-up, go to a 6-8 percent hill that takes three to four minutes to go up and do five climbs. Stay seated with cadence at 60 or higher rpm. Build to the 5b zone on each. Recover to the 1 zone by spinning down the hill and at the bottom for a total of three to four minutes depending on how long the climb is. (Periods: Build 2, Peak)

A5. Lactate Tolerance Reps. Done on a flat or slightly uphill course or into the wind. After a long warm-up and several jumps, perform four to eight repetitions of 90 seconds to two minutes each. Intensity is 5c zone. The total of all work intervals should not exceed 12 minutes. Recovery intervals are 2.5 times as long as the preceding work interval. For example, after a two-minute rep, recover for five minutes. Build to this workout conservatively starting with six minutes total and adding two minutes weekly. Do this workout no more than once a week and recover for at least 48 hours after. Do not do this workout if you are in the first two years of training for triathlon. (Periods: Build 2, Peak)

A6. Hill Reps. After a good warm-up go to a 6-8 percent hill and do four to eight reps of 90 seconds each. The first 60 seconds are seated building to the 5b zone just as in AE intervals. With about 30 seconds remaining on the climb, shift to a higher gear, stand and drive the bike to the top attaining the 5c zone. Recover completely for four minutes after each rep. Do not do this workout if you are in the first two years of training for cycling. (Periods: Build 2, Peak)

A7. AE Intervals + Threshold. Combine A2 and M5 into one workout by completing the AE intervals and then riding 20 minutes of threshold. This is an excellent workout for simulating the stresses of racing. (Periods: Build 2, Peak)

POWER WORKOUTS

P1. Sprints. Following a warm up, do six to nine, 30-second sprints in a big gear. Stand for the first 10 seconds while increasing the cadence to 90 rpm or higher. Then sit for 20 seconds and maintain the cadence in the same gear. Recover for three to five minutes after each sprint. (Periods: Build 1, Build 2, Peak, Race)

P2. Hill Sprints. Early in the workout, after a good warm-up, go to a hill with a 4-6 grade grade. Do six to nine sprints of 20 seconds each. Use a flying start for each sprint taking 10 seconds to build speed on the flat approach. Climb the hill in the saddle for 10 seconds applying maximal force to the pedals with a high cadence. Recover for three minutes after each sprint. Power/RPE should be zone 5c. Heart rate is not a good indicator of exertion for this workout. (Periods: Build 2, Peak)

TEST WORKOUTS

T1. Aerobic Time Trial. This is best on an indoor trainer with a rear-wheel computer pick-up, or on a CompuTrainer or Electronic Trainer. May also be done on a flat section of road, but weather conditions will have an effect. After a warm-up, ride five miles with heart rate nine to 11 beats below lactate threshold heart rate. Use a standard gear without shifting. Record time. The conditions of this workout must remain constant from one test to the next. This includes the amount of rest since the last BT workout, the length and intensity of the warm-up, the weather if on the road and the gear used during the test. As aerobic fitness improves, the time should decrease. (Periods: Base 1, Base 2, Base 3)

T2. Time Trial. After a 15- to 30-minute warm-up, complete a 10km time trial on a flat course. Go 5km out, turn around and return to the start line. Mark your start and turn for later reference. Look for faster times as your anaerobic-endurance and muscular-endurance improve. In addition to time, record average power/heart rate and peak power/heart rate. Keep the conditions the same from one time trial to the next as in the aerobic time trial. Any gear may be used and you may shift during the test. (Periods: Build 1, Build 2, Peak)

APPENDIX D

ENDURANCE WORKOUTS

E1. Recovery. Done in the 1 zone on a flat, soft course such as a park or golf course. Check cadence several times by counting right-foot strikes for 20 seconds and attempting to achieve about 30. Do this run in the Prep period as the primary aerobic workout, and the day after a BT workout in all other periods. A treadmill may be used for these at any time of the year, especially if flat courses are not available. Cross-training is also beneficial for recovery in the Preparation, Base 1 and Base 2 periods. Novices recover faster by taking the time off. These workouts are not scheduled on the Annual Training Plan, but are an integral part of training throughout the season. (Periods: All)

E2. Extensive Endurance. Used for aerobic maintenance and endurance training. Stay primarily in the 1 and 2 zones on a rolling course with small grades up to 4 percent. Can be done with a disciplined group or on a treadmill with gradient control to simulate rolling hills. Check cadence aiming for about 30 right-foot strikes in 20 seconds. In the Base periods, running steadily in the 2 zone for 20 to 90 minutes or more is quite effective for developing aerobic endurance. Cross-training is an option during Preparation and Base 1. (Periods: All)

E3. Intensive Endurance. Develops aerobic endurance while stressing muscular endurance. Run a rolling course with small hills that take you into the 3 zone frequently for a few minutes at a time. Check cadence aiming for about 30 right-foot strikes in 20 seconds. Accumulate 10 to 30 minutes or more of 3-zone time in this manner within a run. This is an excellent workout during the Base period, but should seldom, if ever, be included in the other periods. (Periods: Base 1, Base 2, Base 3)

FORCE WORKOUTS

F1. Moderate Hills. Select a course that includes several moderately steep hills of up to about six-percent grade that take two to five minutes to run up. Maintain a "proud" posture — head up and back straight — while going up the hills. Stay in the 1-5a zones. Can also do these on a treadmill. (Periods: Base 2, Base 3)

F2. Long Hills. Run a course including several long grades of up to eight percent that take six or more minutes to ascend. Maintain a proud posture. Go no higher than 5a zone. Concentrate on proud posture while getting a full extension on the drive leg on each stride. Simulate this workout on a treadmill. (Periods: Base 3, Build 1)

F3. Hills Repeats. Warm up thoroughly. Then on a steep hill of 6- to 8-percent grade that takes 30 to 60 seconds to run up, do three to eight repeats with two to four minutes of recovery between them. Intensity may climb to 5b several times. Recover into the 1 zone while jogging and walking to the bottom. Maintain a proud posture. Stop the workout if your knees hurt. Do this workout no more than twice per week with at least 48 hours between them. Do not do this workout if you have knee problems. (Periods: Build 1, Build 2, Peak)

SPEED WORKOUTS

S1. Strides. On a very slight, soft downhill such as in a park, run 20 seconds at 95-percent effort (RPE 5c), four to eight times. Relax face and fingers while running with proud posture and a quick cadence. A variation on this workout is to count your right-foot strikes for 20 seconds with a goal of about 30. Another variation is to run these barefoot, but only if the grass is free of sharp objects and there are no breaks in the skin on your feet. Heart rate and power ratings have no significance for this workout. (Periods: All)

S2. Pick ups. Within an endurance run, insert several 20-second accelerations to the 5c zone. Heart rate is not a good indicator of intensity for these. Maintain a proud posture and quick cadence. Recover for several minutes between these pick ups. (Periods: Base 1, Base 2, Base 3, Build 1, Build 2, Peak, Race)

MUSCULAR-ENDURANCE WORKOUTS

M1. Tempo. Warm up first. Then on a mostly flat course, or on a treadmill, run in the 3 zone for an extended time without recovery. Maintain a proud posture and quick cadence. Start with 10 to 15 minutes and build to 30 to 45 minutes or more by adding five minutes each week. This workout may be done two or three times weekly. (Periods: Base 2, Base 3)

M2. Cruise Intervals. On a relatively flat course or treadmill, complete three to five work intervals that are six- to 12-minutes duration. Build to the 4 and 5a zones on each work interval. If training with a heart rate monitor, the work interval starts as soon as you begin running with high effort — not when the 4 zone is achieved. Recover for two or three minutes after each. Recovery should be into the 1 or 2 zone. A variation is to run cruise intervals on the track with one- to two-mile work intervals. Stay relaxed and proud with a quick cadence while closely monitoring your breathing. (Periods: Base 3, Build 1, Build 2, Peak)

M3. Hill Cruise Intervals. Same as M2 cruise intervals, except done on a long, low grade such as two to four percent, or into a strong head wind. Maintain a proud posture and quick cadence. These are good if muscular endurance and force are both limiters. (Periods: Build 1, Build 2, Peak)

M4. Criss-Cross Threshold. On a mostly flat course, run 15 to 30 minutes in the 4 and 5a zones. Once the 4 zone is attained, gradually build effort to the top of the 5a zone taking about two minutes to do so. Then gradually back off and slowly drop back to the bottom of the 4 zone taking about two minutes again. Continue this pattern throughout the run. Complete two or three cruise interval workouts before doing this workout. (Periods: Build 1, Build 2, Peak)

M5. Threshold. On a mostly flat course, run 15 to 30 minutes non-stop in the 4 and 5a zones. Keep a proud posture and quick cadence while listening to your breathing throughout. Don't attempt a threshold run until you've completed at least four cruise interval workouts. (Periods: Build 2, Peak)

ANAEROBIC-ENDURANCE WORKOUTS

A1. Group Run. Run with others of similar ability. Treat this like a "controlled" race. Gradually increase the tempo until you are running in the 4 and 5a zones. Throw in periodic surges that take you into 5b. (Periods: Build 1, Build 2, Peak)

A2. AE Intervals. On the track, run three to five work intervals that take three to six minutes to complete, achieving the 5b zone on each. Jog (don't walk) for half the distance of the preceding work interval for recovery. For example, run 4 x 800 meters with 400-meter recoveries. These may also be run on the road using time, instead of distance, for duration. Recoveries in this case are equal to the time of the work intervals. Run these on soft surfaces, not on concrete. (Periods: Build 1, Build 2, Peak)

A3. Surge Intervals. Warm up well. Then on a fixed-distance course, such as 10km, run two minutes to the 5b zone and recover for one minute, one minute to 5b and recover for 30 seconds, and 30 seconds to 5b and recover for 30 seconds. Repeat this pattern for the entire distance before cooling down. (Periods: Build 1, Build 2, Peak)

A4. Hill Intervals. Following a thorough warm-up, go to a 6-8 percent hill that takes three to four minutes to go up and do three to five climbs. Run with a proud posture and powerful toe off. Build to the 5b zone on each. Recover to the 1 zone by jogging and walking down the hill and at the bottom for a total of three to four minutes. Complete at least two or three A1 and F2 workouts before doing this one. (Periods: Build 2, Peak)

A5. Lactate Tolerance Reps. After a long warm up, on the track or other soft surface, run a distance that takes 30 seconds to two minutes at maximum speed. The total of all work intervals should not exceed 12 minutes. Recovery intervals are 2.5 times as long as the preceding work interval. For example, after a two-minute rep, recover for five minutes. Build to this workout conservatively starting with six minutes total and adding two minutes weekly. Do this workout no more than once a week and recover for at least 48 hours after. Do not do this workout if you are in the first two years of training for triathlon. (Periods: Build 2, Peak)

A6. Hill Reps. After a good warm-up go to a 6-8 percent hill and do three to six reps of 90 seconds each. In the first 60 seconds build to the 5b zone just as in AE intervals. With about 30 seconds remaining on the hill, increase the effort attaining the 5c zone by the top. Recover completely for at least four minutes after each rep. Do not do this workout if you are in the first two years of training for running. Recover for at least 48 hours following this run. (Periods: Build 2, Peak)

A7. AE Intervals + Threshold. Combine A2 and M5 into one workout by completing the AE intervals and then running a fixed distance, such as two miles, or a fixed time, such as 20 minutes, in the 4 and 5a zones. This is an excellent workout for simulating the effort required in the run portion of a triathlon. (Periods: Build 2, Peak)

POWER WORKOUTS

P1. Sprints. On a track or other soft surface, following a thorough warm up, do four to eight, 20- to 30-second sprints at maximum effort — RPE 5c zone. Emphasize proud posture and quick cadence. Don't try to "muscle" it. Recover by walking and jogging for three to five minutes after each sprint. (Periods: Build 1, Build 2, Peak, Race)

P2. Hill Sprints. Early in the workout, after a good warm-up, go to a hill with a 4-6 percent grade. Do four to eight sprints of 20 seconds each. Use a flying start for each sprint taking 10 seconds to build speed on the flat approach. Run up the hill for 10 seconds emphasizing good technique. Recover by walking and jogging for three to five minutes after each sprint. Power/RPE should be zone 5c. Heart rate is not a good indicator of exertion for this workout. (Periods: Build 2, Peak)

P3. Plyometrics. After a good warm up include several bounding, jumping and skipping exercises on grass, track or another soft surface. Do only 30 to 50 landings broken into three to five sets within the first workout, depending on your ability to tolerate lower-leg stress. Over the next six to eight weeks, build to 80 to 100 landings within three to five sets. There are several possibilities. For example, on a hill amplify knee lift and vertical bounce. Or, on a flat surface run strides exaggerating float time with each step. Other exercises include single-leg and double-leg hops, skipping for distance rather than height and squat jumps. (Periods: Base 2, Base 3)

TEST WORKOUTS

T1. Aerobic Time Trial. This is best on a track. May also be done on a flat section of road. Extreme weather conditions will skew the results, so seek out days when the temperatures are moderate and there is little wind. After a warm up, run one mile with heart rate nine to 11 beats below lactate threshold heart rate. Record time. The conditions of this workout must remain constant from one test to the next. This includes the amount of rest since the last BT workout, the length and intensity of the warm-up, the weather and the shoes (racing or training) used during the test. As aerobic fitness improves, the time should decrease. (Periods: Base 1, Base 2, Base 3)

T2. Time Trial. After a 10- to 20-minute warm-up, complete a 1.5-mile, maximum effort time trial on a track or road course. Look for faster times as your race fitness improves. In addition to time, record average heart rate and peak heart rate. Keep the conditions the same from one time trial to the next as in the aerobic time trial. (Periods: Build 1, Build 2, Peak)

APPENDIX E

ENDURANCE WORKOUTS

E1. Extensive-Endurance Brick. Complete a long ride on a rolling course staying in the 1 and 2 zones. Then transition to a long run on a mostly flat course also staying in the 1 and 2 zones. The total time for this brick may vary from two to six hours. One week the run portion may be longer, and the next the bike is emphasized. Duathletes may run first as a warm up. (Periods: Base 2, Base 3, Build 1, Build 2)

E2. Intensive-Endurance Brick. Ride long on a rolling course with more than half of the time in the 2 and 3 zones accumulating as much 3 zone as possible. Then transition to a long run also primarily in the 2 and 3 zones. The emphasized portion of this workout may vary from week to week by alternately lengthening the bike or the run. This is an especially good workout when preparing for a half-Ironman- or Ironman-distance race. Duathletes may run first slowly building intensity to the 3 zone by the end of the first run. (Periods: Base 3, Build 1, Build 2)

FORCE WORKOUTS

F1. Hill Brick. Ride and/or run on a hilly course at intensities ranging from the 1 to 5a zones. On the bike, stay in the saddle on most climbs to build hip-extension force.

This can be a relatively short brick broken into bike and run portions that are 30 to 60 minutes long, or in preparation for a hilly half-Ironman or Ironman race, treat it more as an intensive-endurance brick done on a hilly course with higher intensities due to the hills. Duathletes may run first. (Periods: Base 3, Build 1, Build 2)

SPEED WORKOUTS

S1. Pre-Race Brick. The day before an A- or B-priority race, complete a combined workout including a 30-minute bike and a 15-minute run. During each leg of the workout include three to five accelerations to slightly faster than race pace with long recoveries. The start-finish area of the race is a good venue for this workout. Tighten all bolts on your bike following this workout. (Periods: Build 1, Build 2, Peak, Race)

MUSCULAR-ENDURANCE WORKOUTS

M1. Tempo Brick. Bike 60 to 90 minutes including a 10km to 20km time trial on a course similar to that of your next A- or B-priority race. Ride the time trial at an intensity similar to or slightly greater than that planned for your next important race. Then transition to a 15- to 45-minute run at goal race pace. Duathletes may run first for 20 to 30 minutes building to planned race intensity by the end. (Periods: Build 2, Peak)

ANAEROBIC-ENDURANCE WORKOUTS

A1. Bike-Intervals Brick. Ride a flat to rolling course. After warming up, do three to five work intervals each of about 2km to 5km so that the shortest is at least two minutes and the longest takes no more than six minutes. Intensity is the same or slightly greater than that anticipated for the next A- or B-priority race. Recover for a time equal to half of the preceding work interval time. For example, after a six-minute work interval, recover for three minutes. Transition to a run of about half the duration of the bike portion (for example, if you rode for 60 minutes, run for 30). Include 10 to 20 minutes of steady state in the 4 to 5a zones. Duathletes may run first primarily as a warm up. (Periods: Build 2, Peak)

A2. Run-Intervals Brick. Take your indoor bike trainer to a track. Run for 10 to 20 minutes in the 1 to 3 zones to warm up. Then, on the bike trainer, ride for five to 10 minutes achieving the 4 or 5a zones the last minute or so. Change into running shoes and complete two to four work intervals that last two to four minutes with intensity rising into the 5b zone on each. Recovery intervals are half the duration of the previous work interval. Return to the bike and again ride five minutes or so building to the 4 or 5a zones. Repeat this pattern one to three more times before cooling down for 10 minutes or so on the bike. Aim for about 20 minutes or three miles of total work-interval time for running. (Periods: Build 2, Peak)

APPENDIX F

Week's Goals (Check off as achieved)

◯ 1._____

◯ 2._____

◯ 3._____

MONDAY / /

◯ SLEEP   ◯ FATIGUE

◯ STRESS   ◯ SORENESS

◯ PULSE   WEIGHT

WORKOUT #1:   S   B   R   O _____

WEATHER   ROUTE

DISTANCE   TIME

TIME BY ZONE [ ]1 [ ]2 [ ]3 [ ]4 [ ]5

WORKOUT RATING

1   2   3   4   5   6   7   8   9   10

NOTES _____

_____

_____

_____

WORKOUT #1:   S   B   R   O _____

WEATHER   ROUTE

DISTANCE   TIME

TIME BY ZONE [ ]1 [ ]2 [ ]3 [ ]4 [ ]5

WORKOUT RATING

1   2   3   4   5   6   7   8   9   10

NOTES _____

_____

_____

_____

TUESDAY / /

◯ SLEEP   ◯ FATIGUE

◯ STRESS   ◯ SORENESS

◯ PULSE   WEIGHT

WORKOUT #1:   S   B   R   O _____

WEATHER   ROUTE

DISTANCE   TIME

TIME BY ZONE [ ]1 [ ]2 [ ]3 [ ]4 [ ]5

WORKOUT RATING

1   2   3   4   5   6   7   8   9   10

NOTES _____

_____

_____

_____

WORKOUT #1:   S   B   R   O _____

WEATHER   ROUTE

DISTANCE   TIME

TIME BY ZONE [ ]1 [ ]2 [ ]3 [ ]4 [ ]5

WORKOUT RATING

1   2   3   4   5   6   7   8   9   10

NOTES _____

_____

_____

_____

WEDNESDAY / /

◯ SLEEP   ◯ FATIGUE

◯ STRESS   ◯ SORENESS

◯ PULSE   WEIGHT

WORKOUT #1: S   B   R   O _____

WEATHER   ROUTE

DISTANCE   TIME

TIME BY ZONE [ ] 1 [ ] 2 [ ] 3 [ ] 4 [ ] 5

WORKOUT RATING

1   2   3   4   5   6   7   8   9   10

NOTES _____
_____
_____
_____

WORKOUT #1: S   B   R   O _____

WEATHER   ROUTE

DISTANCE   TIME

TIME BY ZONE [ ] 1 [ ] 2 [ ] 3 [ ] 4 [ ] 5

WORKOUT RATING

1   2   3   4   5   6   7   8   9   10

NOTES _____
_____
_____
_____
_____
_____
_____

THURSDAY / /

◯ SLEEP   ◯ FATIGUE

◯ STRESS   ◯ SORENESS

◯ PULSE   WEIGHT

WORKOUT #1: S   B   R   O _____

WEATHER   ROUTE

DISTANCE   TIME

TIME BY ZONE [ ] 1 [ ] 2 [ ] 3 [ ] 4 [ ] 5

WORKOUT RATING

1   2   3   4   5   6   7   8   9   10

NOTES _____
_____
_____
_____

WORKOUT #1: S   B   R   O _____

WEATHER   ROUTE

DISTANCE   TIME

TIME BY ZONE [ ] 1 [ ] 2 [ ] 3 [ ] 4 [ ] 5

WORKOUT RATING

1   2   3   4   5   6   7   8   9   10

NOTES _____
_____
_____
_____
_____
_____
_____

FRIDAY / /

○ SLEEP ○ FATIGUE
○ STRESS ○ SORENESS
○ PULSE WEIGHT

WORKOUT #1: S B R O _____

WEATHER ROUTE

DISTANCE TIME

TIME BY ZONE ☐ 1 ☐ 2 ☐ 3 ☐ 4 ☐ 5

WORKOUT RATING

1 2 3 4 5 6 7 8 9 10

NOTES _____
_____
_____
_____

WORKOUT #1: S B R O _____

WEATHER ROUTE

DISTANCE TIME

TIME BY ZONE ☐ 1 ☐ 2 ☐ 3 ☐ 4 ☐ 5

WORKOUT RATING

1 2 3 4 5 6 7 8 9 10

NOTES _____
_____
_____
_____
_____
_____
_____

SATURDAY / /

○ SLEEP ○ FATIGUE
○ STRESS ○ SORENESS
○ PULSE WEIGHT

WORKOUT #1: S B R O _____

WEATHER ROUTE

DISTANCE TIME

TIME BY ZONE ☐ 1 ☐ 2 ☐ 3 ☐ 4 ☐ 5

WORKOUT RATING

1 2 3 4 5 6 7 8 9 10

NOTES _____
_____
_____
_____

WORKOUT #1: S B R O _____

WEATHER ROUTE

DISTANCE TIME

TIME BY ZONE ☐ 1 ☐ 2 ☐ 3 ☐ 4 ☐ 5

WORKOUT RATING

1 2 3 4 5 6 7 8 9 10

NOTES _____
_____
_____
_____
_____
_____
_____

SUNDAY   /   /

◯ SLEEP   ◯ FATIGUE
◯ STRESS   ◯ SORENESS
◯ PULSE   WEIGHT

WORKOUT #1:   S   B   R   O _____

WEATHER   ROUTE

DISTANCE   TIME

TIME BY ZONE [   ] 1 [   ] 2 [   ] 3 [   ] 4 [   ] 5

WORKOUT RATING

1   2   3   4   5   6   7   8   9   10

NOTES

WORKOUT #1:   S   B   R   O _____

WEATHER   ROUTE

DISTANCE   TIME

TIME BY ZONE [   ] 1 [   ] 2 [   ] 3 [   ] 4 [   ] 5

WORKOUT RATING

1   2   3   4   5   6   7   8   9   10

NOTES

RACING

RACE

	DISTANCE	TIME	PLACE OVERALL/DIVISION
SWIM	SWIM	/	
	TRAN 1	/	
BIKE	BIKE	/	
	TRAN 2	/	
RUN	RUN	/	
	FINISH	/	

NOTES

WEEKLY SUMMARY

SWIM	TIME/DIST.	YEAR TO DATE
BIKE	TIME/DIST.	YEAR TO DATE
RUN	TIME/DIST.	YEAR TO DATE
STRENGTH	TIME/DIST.	YEAR TO DATE
_____	TIME/DIST.	YEAR TO DATE
TOTAL	WEEKLY TIME	YEAR TO DATE

SORENESS

NOTES

GLOSSARY

Adaptation. Refers to the body's ability to adjust to various demands placed on it over a period of time.

Aerobic capacity. The body's maximal capacity for using oxygen to produce energy during maximal exertion. Also known as VO_2 max.

Aerobic. In the presence of oxygen; aerobic metabolism utilizes oxygen. Below the anaerobic-intensity level.

Agonistic muscles. Muscles directly engaged in a muscular contraction.

Anaerobic threshold (AT). When aerobic metabolism no longer supplies all the need for energy, energy is produced anaerobically; indicated by an increase in lactic acid. Also known as lactate threshold.

Anaerobic-endurance. The ability resulting from the combination of speed and endurance allowing the athlete to maintain a high speed for an extended period of time while anaerobic.

Anaerobic. Literally, "without oxygen." Exercise that demands more oxygen than the heart and lungs can supply. The intensity of exercise performed above the lactate threshold.

Antagonistic muscles. Muscles that have an opposite effect on movers, or work against other muscles, by opposing their contraction. For example, the triceps is an antagonistic muscle for the biceps.

Base period. The period during which the basic abilities of endurance, speed and force are emphasized.

Bonk. A state of extreme exhaustion mainly caused by the depletion of glycogen in the muscles.

Breakthrough (BT). A workout intended to cause a significant, positive, adaptive response.

Build period. The specific preparation mesocycle during which high-intensity training in the form of muscular-endurance, speed-endurance and power are emphasized, and endurance, force and speed are maintained.

Cadence. Revolutions or cycles per minute of the swim stroke, pedal stroke or running stride.

Capillary. A small vessel located between arteries and veins in which exchanges between tissue and blood occur.

Carbohydrate loading (glycogen loading). A dietary procedure that elevates muscle glycogen stores by emphasizing carbohydrate consumption.

Cardiorespiratory system. Cardiovascular system and lungs.

Cardiovascular system. Heart, blood and blood vessels.

Central nervous system. The spinal cord and brain.

Circuit training. Selected exercises or activities performed rapidly in sequence; used in weight training.

Concentric contraction. The shortening of a muscle during contraction.

Cool down. Low-intensity exercise at the end of a training session.

Criterium. A multilap race held on a short course.

Cross-training. Training for more than one sport during the same period of time.

Drafting. Swimming, biking or running behind others in order to reduce effort.

Drops. The lower portion of turned-down handlebars.

Duration. The length of time of a given workout.

Eccentric contraction. The lengthening of a muscle during contraction. For example, slowly setting down a heavy, hand-held weight.

Endurance. The ability to persist, to resist fatigue.

Ergogenic aid. A substance, device or phenomenon that can improve athletic performance.

Fartlek. Swedish for "speed play," or an unstructured, interval-type workout.

Fast-twitch fiber (FT). A muscle fiber characterized by fast contraction time, high anaerobic capacity, and low aerobic capacity, all making the fiber suited for high-power activities.

Force. The strength evident in a muscle or muscle group while exerting against a resistance.

Free weights. Weights not part of an exercise machine (i.e., barbells and dumbbells).

Frequency. The number of times per week that one trains.

Glucose. A simple sugar.

Glycemic index. A system of ranking carbohydrate foods based on how quickly they raise the blood's glucose level.

Glycogen. The form in which glucose (sugar) is stored in the muscles and the liver.

Growth hormone. A hormone secreted by the anterior lobe of the pituitary gland that stimulates growth and development.

Hammer. A fast, sustained effort.

Hamstring. Muscle on the back of the thigh that flexes the knee and extends the hip.

Hoods. On drop handlebars, the covers of the brake handles.

Individuality, principle of. The theory that any training program must consider the specific needs and abilities of the individual for whom it is designed.

Intensity. The qualitative element of training referring to effort, velocity, maximum strength and power.

Interval training. A system of high-intensity work marked by short, but regularly repeated periods of hard exercise interspersed with periods of recovery.

Isolated leg training (ILT). Pedaling with one leg to improve technique.

Lactate threshold (LT). The point during exercise of increasing intensity at which blood lactate begins to accumulate above resting levels. Also known as anaerobic threshold.

Lactate. Formed when lactic acid from the muscles enters the blood stream.

Lactic acid. A by-product of the lactic acid system resulting from the incomplete breakdown of glucose (sugar) in the production of energy.

Long, slow distance (LSD) training. A form of continuous training in which the athlete performs at a relatively low intensity for a long duration.

Macrocycle. A period of training including several mesocycles; usually an entire season.

Mash. To push a big gear.

Mesocycle. A period of training generally two to six weeks long.

Microcycle. A period of training of approximately one week.

Muscular endurance. The ability of a muscle or muscle group to perform repeated contractions for a long period of time while bearing a load.

Overload, principle of. A training load that challenges the body's current level of fitness.

Overreaching. Training above the work load that would produce overtraining if continued long enough.

Overtraining. Extreme fatigue, both physical and mental, caused by extensively training at a work load higher than that to which the body can readily adapt.

Peak period. The mesocycle during which volume of training is reduced and intensity is proportionally increased allowing the athlete to reach high levels of fitness.

Periodization. The process of structuring training into periods.

Power. The ability resulting from force and speed.

Preparation (Prep) period. The mesocycle during which the athlete begins to train for the coming season; usually marked by the use of cross-training and low work loads.

Progression, principle of. The theory that the work load must be gradually increased accompanied by intermittent periods of recovery.

Quadriceps. The large muscle in front of the thigh that extends the lower leg and flexes the hip.

Race period. The mesocycle during which the work load is greatly decreased allowing the athlete to compete in high-priority races.

Rating of perceived exertion (RPE). A subjective assessment of how hard one is working.

Recovery interval. The relief period between work intervals within an interval workout.

Recovery. A period of training when rest is emphasized.

Repetition maximum (RM). The maximum load that a muscle group can lift in one attempt. Also called "one-repetition maximum" (1RM).

Repetition. The number of times a task, such as a work interval or lifting of a weight, is repeated.

Session. A single practice period that may include one or more workouts.

Set. A group of repetitions.

Slow-twitch fiber (ST). A muscle fiber characterized by slow contraction time, low anaerobic capacity, and high aerobic capacity, all making the fiber suited for low power, long-duration activities.

Specificity, principle of. The theory that training must stress the systems critical for optimal performance in order to achieve the desired training adaptations.

Speed. Within the context of this book, the ability to move the body in ways that produce optimum performance. For example, the ability to turn the cranks quickly on the bike.

Tapering. A reduction in training volume prior to a major competition.

Tops. The portion of the handlebar closest to the stem.

Training zone. A level of intensity based on a percentage of some measure, such as heart rate or power, of the individual's capacity for work.

Training. A comprehensive program intended to prepare an athlete for competition.

Transition (Tran) period. The mesocycle during which the work load and structure of training are greatly reduced allowing physical and psychological recovery from training and racing.

Ventilatory threshold (VT). The point during increasing exertion at which breathing first becomes labored. Closely corresponds with lactate threshold.

VO$_2$ max. The capacity for oxygen consumption by the body during maximal exertion, also known as aerobic capacity and maximal oxygen consumption. Usually expressed as liters of oxygen consumed per kilogram of body weight per minute (ml/kg/min).

Volume. A quantitative element of training, such as miles or hours of training within a given time. The combination of duration and frequency.

Warm up. The period of gradually increasing intensity of exercise at the start of a training session.

Work interval. High intensity efforts separated by recovery intervals.

Workload. Measured stress applied in training through the combination of frequency, intensity, and duration.

Workout. A portion of a session that is focused on a specific aspect of training, such as power.

INDEX

ABOUT THE AUTHOR

Joe Friel has trained endurance athletes since 1980. His clients include elite amateur and professional road cyclists, mountain bikers, triathletes and duathletes. They are located around the globe from Belgium to the Caribbean, from British Columbia to Florida, and from Boston to San Diego. They include U.S. and foreign national champions, and world championship competitors. Several are Olympics hopefuls.

Friel is also the author of *The Cyclist's Training Bible* (1996, VeloPress), *Cycling Past 50* (1998, Human Kinetics) and *Precision Heart Rate Training* (1998, co-author, Human Kinetics); he holds a masters degree in exercise science.

He is a contributing editor to *Inside Triathlon* and *VeloNews*, and writes feature stories for *Performance Conditioning for Cycling*. He has written a weekly fitness column for the *Fort Collins Coloradoan* newspaper since 1981.

He conducts workshops around the country on training and racing for cyclists and multisport athletes, and provides consulting services for corporations in the fitness industry. He also serves on the USA Triathlon Coaching Committee, and is an advisor to the Royal Society of New Zealand's Sport Science Web site.

Friel is also an age-group competitor. He is a Colorado State Masters Triathlon Champion, a Rocky Mountain region and southwest region duathlon age-group champion, and has been named to several All-American teams. A member of the USA Triathlon Federation's national teams in 1993, 1994 and 1996, he is a contender in world-class events. He also competes in road-running races and U.S. Cycling Federation races.

From his home at the foot of the Rocky Mountains in Fort Collins, Colorado, Friel enjoys mountain biking in the foothills with his wife Joyce, trail running with friends, and hiking and cross-country skiing on mountain trails with his son Dirk, who is a professional bicycle racer.

For more information on seminars and personal coaching, Friel can be reached by fax at 970/204-4221, or by e-mail at jfriel@ultrafit.com.